5. Writing
(60 minutes)

- Genres
  - personal narrative
  - nonfiction
  - letters
  - poetry

- Writing workshop
  - mini-lessons
  - independent writing
  - conferences
  - partner writing
  - illustrating
  - authors' chair
  - publishing

Assessment

- Goals
  - fluency
  - comprehension
  - attitude
  - state and district goals
  - teaching team goals

- Assessment schedule

- Standardized tests
  - state core test
  - SAT, CAT, CTBS, etc.

- Screening and monitoring assessments
  - Dynamic Indicators of Basic Early Literacy Skills (DIBELS) subtests
  - Oral Reading Fluency (ORF; words correct per minute)
  - Phonological Awareness Literacy Screening (PALS)

- Diagnostic assessments
  - informal reading inventories
  - running records
  - word lists

- Other assessments
  - conferences, checklists/rubrics, retellings, reading lists, attitude inventories, interest inventories, and writing drafts

- Feedback to
  - students
  - parents
  - faculty

Parent Involvement

- Communication

- At-home follow-through

- Classroom involvement

Struggling Readers

- Areas of focus
  - fluency
  - comprehension
  - attitude

- Additional instructional support

- One-on-one tutoring
  - classroom teacher
  - paraprofessional
  - classroom volunteer
  - other student

- Focused instruction
  - language development
  - automaticity

- Continuous assessment

- Extensive easy reading

- Classroom and resource coordination

D0025490

Early Literacy Instruction

A Comprehensive Framework for Teaching Reading and Writing, K-3

John A. Smith
Utah State University

Sylvia Read
Utah State University

PEARSON

Merrill
Prentice Hall

Upper Saddle River, New Jersey
Columbus, Ohio

Library of Congress Cataloging-in-Publication Data

Smith, John A.
   Early literacy instruction : a comprehensive framework for teaching reading and writing,
K-3 / John A. Smith, Sylvia Read.
      p. cm.
   Includes bibliographical references and index.
   ISBN 0-13-098960-6
   1. Language arts (Primary) 2. Reading (Primary) 3. English language—Composition and
exercises—Study and teaching (Primary) I. Read, Sylvia– II. Title.
   LB1528.S57 2005
   372.6—dc22

2004055212

Vice President and Executive Publisher: Jeffery W. Johnston
Senior Editor: Linda Ashe Montgomery
Editorial Assistant: Laura J. Weaver
Development Editor: Dawne Brooks
Production Editor: Linda Hillis Bayma
Production Coordination: Ann Mohan, WordCrafters Editorial Services, Inc.
Design Coordinator: Diane C. Lorenzo
Cover Designer: Terry Rohrbach
Cover Image: Getty One
Production Manager: Pamela D. Bennett
Director of Marketing: Ann Castel Davis
Marketing Manager: Darcy Betts Prybella
Marketing Coordinator: Tyra Poole

This book was set in Garamond Book by Carlisle Communications, Ltd. It was printed and
bound by Courier Kendallville, Inc. The cover was printed by Coral Graphic Services, Inc.

Photo Credits: pp. 3, 14, 39, 61, 62, 120, 126 by Steven Von Niederhausern; p. 34 by Brenda
Richards; pp. 68, 73, 81, 82, 141, 143, 144, 145, 147, 148, 153, 154, 155, 206, 207, 209, 212, 217,
218, 219, 221, 228, 234, 238, 242, 249, 253, 258, 261 by Sylvia Read.

Pearson Education Ltd.
Pearson Education Singapore Pte. Ltd.
Pearson Education Canada, Ltd.
Pearson Education—Japan

Pearson Education Australia Pty. Limited
Pearson Education North Asia Ltd.
Pearson Educación de Mexico, S.A. de C.V.
Pearson Education Malaysia Pte. Ltd.

10 9 8 7 6 5 4 3 2 1
ISBN: 0-13-098960-6

About the Authors

John A. Smith is an Associate Professor in the Department of Elementary Education at Utah State University. He holds a bachelor's degree in Elementary Education from Brigham Young University, a master's degree in Elementary Curriculum from the University of Utah, and a doctorate in Curriculum and Instruction from the University of North Carolina at Chapel Hill.

Dr. Smith has 10 years of elementary classroom teaching experience in second and fifth grades and as a Chapter 1 reading teacher, and 16 years of experience teaching at the university level. He also taught at-risk students entering kindergarten and first grade for three summers at the Frank Porter Graham Child Development Center in Chapel Hill, North Carolina. Dr. Smith served 3 years as Reading Coordinator for the Chapel Hill City School District, during which time the district's Chapter 1 program was recognized by the U.S. Department of Education as an Exemplary Program. A highlight of Dr. Smith's teaching was taking a year off from university teaching to return to a first-grade classroom to implement the balanced, comprehensive literacy instruction curriculum described in this book.

Dr. Smith has worked extensively with teachers in elementary school classrooms as a Reading Excellence Act reading coach and currently as a consultant and Reading First technical assistant. His publications and presentation topics include implementing balanced, comprehensive literacy instruction, implementing a variety of reading instruction strategies, and enhancing literacy instruction with children's songs. He is reviewer for *The Reading Teacher* and *Reading Research & Instruction* and currently serves as a member of the Executive Board of the College Reading Association.

Dr. Smith's teaching awards include USU College of Education Teacher of the Year, USU Department of Elementary Education Teacher of the Year, USU Extension Program Teaching Award, and the Mortar Board "Top Prof" award.

Sylvia Read is an Assistant Professor in the Department of Elementary Education at Utah State University. She holds a bachelor's degree in English from the University of Illinois, a master's degree in Education from the University of Illinois, and a doctorate in Curriculum and Instruction from Utah State University. Dr. Read has 13 years of classroom teaching experience in first, second, sixth, and seventh grades and 4 years of experience teaching at the university level.

Dr. Read works extensively with teachers in elementary school classrooms as a writing instruction mentor, as a professional developer for school districts in the area of reading and writing, and as the leader of professional study groups locally. Dr. Read's publications and presentation topics include incorporating nonfiction in the reading and writing curriculum, implementing effective writing instruction strategies, and using children's literature effectively in language arts instruction. She is a reviewer for *The Reading Teacher* and the *International Journal of Learning*.

Preface

Teachers have a huge responsibility to know and use research-proven methods. When they graduate and get their first jobs, teachers often find themselves doing the things their own elementary teachers did or what the teacher across the hall is doing, or simply following the teacher's manual of the basal textbooks that their district has adopted and provided for their use.

This book was written with these new teachers in mind. Both new and experienced teachers need a practical plan to follow that gives them the flexibility to use the effective practices learned in preservice programs and ongoing professional development programs. They also need substantive, evidence-based support so they can use their basal teachers' editions judiciously, and, most of all, ensure that all their students are becoming literate.

We provide new teachers a *framework* for a comprehensive literacy program that includes all of the main elements of the National Reading Panel's report *Teaching Children to Read*. This framework also includes important elements that the report did not specifically address, such as writing, reading aloud, independent reading, and assessment. Within this flexible framework, we describe a variety of strategies, models, research-based practices, and well-established best practices for teaching reading and writing to young children.

 ## HOW THIS BOOK IS ORGANIZED

Early Literacy Instruction: A Comprehensive Framework for Teaching Reading and Writing, K–3 draws heavily on our experience as both classroom teachers and teacher educators, which has given us the background we need to help preservice teachers understand theory and research in the context of real classroom practice. The book ties narrative descriptions directly to established theory and proven practices, making them understandable and immediately useful. The content covers the most important aspects of early literacy, K–3.

Chapter 1, "Reading and Writing Instruction Frameworks," begins by explaining the difference between a flexible reading instruction framework and a reading program. The chapter provides descriptions of three nationally known literacy instruction frameworks and shows how essential elements of literacy instruction are common to all three frameworks. Finally, in this chapter we present an overview of our own five-part—comprehensive and practical—literacy instruction framework.

Chapter 2, "What Is Reading?", describes reading as a process of constructing meaning by using both the reader's background knowledge and information from the text. Common word identification processes, such as using sight vocabulary, structural analysis, phonics, context, and syntax, are discussed. The chapter also describes aspects of reading comprehension, including the importance of background knowledge and meaning vocabulary and understanding texts at the literal, inferential, and critical reading levels. All of these components of the reading process are then put into perspective through a discussion of their interactive relationships. The chapter concludes with a few thoughts on the importance of attitude and the teacher's role in teaching students not just *how* to read but also to *want* to read.

Chapter 3, "Foundations of Literacy," describes how some children come to our kindergarten classrooms well prepared for learning as a result of being read to, sung to, taught the alphabet, and included in stimulating conversations by family members for literally thousands of hours (Adams, 1990a). Unfortunately, increasing numbers of children are arriving in our kindergartens unprepared for learning, with virtually none of these family-based literacy experiences. Chapter 3 describes four important foundations for literacy learning: developing oral language, knowing the alphabet letter names and sounds, understanding how speech sounds and printed letters blend together to form spoken and written words, and familiarity with the conventions of print (i.e., left-to-right, top-to-bottom, punctuation).

Chapter 4, "Reading Aloud," provides a multifaceted argument for the importance of reading aloud and has read-aloud strategies embedded throughout. It shows how reading aloud is a valuable context in which to teach comprehension strategies and explicitly model fluency. It also provides a brief overview of the world of children's literature.

Chapter 5, "Word Study," provides an overview of phonics—the common spelling patterns and word parts that comprise most of the words we encounter in print. We are convinced that you must understand the basics of phonics yourself to be effective in teaching them to children. This chapter provides descriptions of effective instructional activities for helping students recognize and apply spelling patterns in their reading. Many of these activities focus on spelling patterns in isolation, as word families. Others teach phonics in context so students will come to understand that phonics is an important contributor to meaningful reading.

Chapter 6, "Independent Reading," explains the importance of independent reading and how to implement a teacher-monitored, independent reading program in the classroom. Year after year, the National Assessment of Educational Progress, the Nation's Report Card, shows that students who read the most, read best. Just as in skiing, playing the piano, or speaking a new language, it takes practice to improve. Independent reading provides students with a critically important opportunity to practice applying their reading skills in the context of real reading.

Chapter 7, "Guiding and Supporting Student Reading," describes five lesson formats and plans for guiding and supporting students as they read. Language experience, shared reading, guided reading, literature circles, and group lessons are important instructional opportunities for reinforcing word study, building reading fluency, and teaching reading comprehension strategies. Chapter 7 concludes with a description of Reading Workshop, a popular approach to orchestrating reading instruction and independent reading.

Chapter 8, "Writing Instruction," explains Writing Workshop and writing as a process and clearly emphasizes the importance of having students write every day, teaching mini-lessons, conferring with students, and asking students to share their writing with the class. It provides a balanced view of writing as both a skill and a meaning-making process.

Chapter 9, "Nonfiction Reading and Writing," discusses the need for and the importance of reading and writing across the curriculum. It explains expository text structures and how to integrate instruction in expository text structures within Writing Workshop.

Chapter 10, "Reading Assessment," begins with an overview of factors commonly associated with reading problems. It includes descriptions of the types, purposes, and uses of formal and informal testing as well as many commonly used classroom assessments. Other assessment topics include locating reading assessments, developing an annual assessment plan, and analyzing and communicating assessment data.

Chapter 11, "Interventions for Struggling Readers," describes classroom-based reading interventions, including increased instructional time, focused small-group instruction, and one-on-one tutoring. Overviews of resource programs, including Title I, special education, speech and language programs, and Reading Recovery, are also provided. Finally, the chapter describes school-level interventions such as before- and after-school programs and reading incentive programs.

Chapter 12, "Putting It All Together," gives an overview of a typical day in both a first-grade and a second-grade classroom. These longer vignettes synthesize and summarize the best practices described in this book by showing them in action in the authors' former classrooms.

SPECIAL FEATURES

This book includes a number of features readers will find especially helpful:

- Vignettes that describe authentic classroom practices, many of them our own
- Instructional procedures with directions for engaging children in specific literacy activities
- A framework that allows you to customize a literacy program and differentiate instruction based on the needs of your students and the resources you have on hand
- Struggling Readers and English Language Learner boxes that provide concrete, specific directives for working with these children
- Connections to the IRA Standards for Reading Professionals
- A developmental time line for monitoring children's growth in reading and writing
- Application activities that fall at the end of each chapter

Acknowledgments

We extend thanks to our many colleagues and friends who have asked about the progress of this book and given us encouragement. Our editors, Linda Montgomery and Dawne Brooks, have provided advice and support along the way. We also appreciate the contributions of the following professionals, who reviewed earlier versions of the manuscript and made excellent suggestions for improvement: Helen R. Abadiano, Central Connecticut State University; Bonnie B. Armbruster, University of Illinois at Urbana-Champaign; Joyce Armstrong, King's College; Margaret S. Carter, James Madison University; Pamela O. Fleege, University of South Florida; Carol J. Fuhler, Iowa State University; Porfirio M. Loeza, California State University, Sacramento; Mona W. Matthews, Georgia State University; Sandra Michelsen, Valparaiso University; Barbara Perry-Sheldon, North Carolina Wesleyan College; Robert J. Rickelman, University of North Carolina, Charlotte; Jill E. Steeley, Oral Roberts University; and Mary Jo Young, Roosevelt University.

I would like to acknowledge and thank my parents, Dr. Ralph B. and Barbara A. Smith, for showing me the value of education. My father, a former Dean of Education at Brigham Young University, provided an example of professionalism and love for teaching that continues to guide and support me. I thank my wife Joanne and our children for their love, encouragement, and patience during my many hours away from them.

John A. Smith

I would like to thank the members of my writing group for reading and responding to some very long chapters. I also want to thank all those former students of mine who gave me the chance to learn and grow as a teacher by teaching them. I hope that some of them will become teachers. Most of all, I'd like to thank my husband, Michael Spooner, who read every word I wrote and gave me encouragement and the response I needed.

Sylvia Read

Discover the Companion Website Accompanying This Book

THE PRENTICE HALL COMPANION WEBSITE:
A VIRTUAL LEARNING ENVIRONMENT

Technology is a constantly growing and changing aspect of our field that is creating a need for content and resources. To address this emerging need, Prentice Hall has developed an online learning environment for students and professors alike—Companion Websites—to support our textbooks.

In creating a Companion Website, our goal is to build on and enhance what the textbook already offers. For this reason, the content for each user-friendly website is organized by topic and provides the professor and student with a variety of meaningful resources. Common features of a Companion Website include:

For the Professor—

Every Companion Website integrates **Syllabus Manager**™, an online syllabus creation and management utility.

- **Syllabus Manager**™ provides you, the instructor, with an easy, step-by-step process to create and revise syllabi, with direct links into Companion Website and other online content without having to learn HTML.
- Students may log on to your syllabus during any study session. All they need to know is the web address for the Companion Website and the password you've assigned to your syllabus.
- After you have created a syllabus using **Syllabus Manager**™, students may enter the syllabus for their course section from any point in the Companion Website.
- Clicking on a date, the student is shown the list of activities for the assignment. The activities for each assignment are linked directly to actual content, saving time for students.
- Adding assignments consists of clicking on the desired due date, then filling in the details of the assignment—name of the assignment, instructions, and whether it is a one-time or repeating assignment.
- In addition, links to other activities can be created easily. If the activity is online, a URL can be entered in the space provided, and it will be linked automatically in the final syllabus.
- Your completed syllabus is hosted on our servers, allowing convenient updates from any computer on the Internet. Changes you make to your syllabus are immediately available to your students at their next logon.

For the Student—

- ❀ **Topic Overviews**—outline key concepts in topic areas
- ❀ **Strategies**—these websites provide suggestions and information on how to implement instructional strategies and activities for each topic
- ❀ **Web Links**—a wide range of websites that allow the students to access current information on everything from rationales for specific types of instruction, to research on related topics, to compilations of useful articles and more
- ❀ **Electronic Bluebook**—send homework or essays directly to your instructor's email with this paperless form
- ❀ **Message Board**—serves as a virtual bulletin board to post—or respond to—questions or comments to/from a national audience

To take advantage of these and other resources, please visit the *Early Literacy Instruction: A Comprehensive Framework for Teaching Reading and Writing, K-3* Companion Website at

www.prenhall.com/smith

EDUCATOR LEARNING CENTER:
AN INVALUABLE ONLINE RESOURCE

Merrill Education and the Association for Supervision and Curriculum Development (ASCD) invite you to take advantage of a new online resource, one that provides access to the top research and proven strategies associated with ASCD and Merrill—the Educator Learning Center. At **www.EducatorLearningCenter.com** you will find resources that will enhance your students' understanding of course topics and of current educational issues, in addition to being invaluable for further research.

How the Educator Learning Center Will Help Your Students Become Better Teachers

With the combined resources of Merrill Education and ASCD, you and your students will find a wealth of tools and materials to better prepare them for the classroom.

Research
- More than 600 articles from the ASCD journal *Educational Leadership* discuss everyday issues faced by practicing teachers.
- A direct link on the site to Research Navigator™ gives students access to many of the leading education journals, as well as extensive content detailing the research process.
- Excerpts from Merrill Education texts give your students insights on important topics of instructional methods, diverse populations, assessment, classroom management, technology, and refining classroom practice.

Classroom Practice
- Hundreds of lesson plans and teaching strategies are categorized by content area and age range.
- Case studies and classroom video footage provide virtual field experience for student reflection.
- Computer simulations and other electronic tools keep your students abreast of today's classrooms and current technologies.

Look into the Value of Educator Learning Center Yourself

A four-month subscription to Educator Learning Center is $25 but is **FREE** when ordered in conjunction with this text. To obtain free passcodes for your students, simply contact your local Merrill/Prentice Hall sales representative, who will give you a special ISBN to give your bookstore when ordering your textbooks. To preview the value of this website to you and your students, please go to **www.EducatorLearningCenter.com** and click on "Demo."

Brief Contents

Contents

Note: Every effort has been made to provide accurate and current Internet information in this book. However, the Internet and information posted on it are constantly changing, and it is inevitable that some of the Internet addresses listed in this textbook will change.

Early Literacy Instruction

Reading and Writing Instruction Frameworks

by John A. Smith

A Beginning Teacher

*T*wo weeks before the beginning of my first year of teaching, I walked into my school district's new-teacher workshop for a half-day presentation on reading instruction. As a new second-grade teacher I was very excited and appreciative because, frankly, I didn't remember a whole lot about reading instruction from my college days, other than something called a diphthong and an hour spent listening to a tape recording of a poor reader while I marked his errors on a scoring sheet.

The new-teacher workshop person gave me a large blue three-ring binder with the school district's logo on the front above the words, GORP: Goal-Oriented Reading Program. *The district had invested hundreds of thousands of dollars in developing its own reading program, which looked to me like a large collection of tests and worksheets.*

I was instructed to give all my students Reading Skill Pretest 1. Students who passed this test with 80% mastery (4 of 5 correct) could be given Reading Skill Pretest 2. Students who didn't pass the first test with 80% mastery would be given instruction and worksheets 1 to 5 and then Reading Skill Posttest 1. Students who passed this posttest could then be given Reading Skill Pretest 2. Students who didn't pass the first posttest would be given more instruction and worksheets 6 to 10. I was also given a list of the 180 GORP reading skills and a punch card with which I was to keep track of each student's progress.

When I got back to my school, I went to see the teacher in the classroom next door, who was my team leader. I showed her my big blue GORP binder and asked her, "How do we teach reading here?" She took me to the supply room and showed me a shelf full of second-grade basal readers and said, "Here are the reading books." She also said, "Make sure to read them a story each day." Actually, my team leader was very helpful and spent a lot of time answering my many questions about how to start and maintain a reading program. My principal came by and gave me some forms so that I could send my struggling readers down the hall to the Resource room.

But the fact remained that my students would arrive in 7 days and I really didn't know how I would teach reading. I was becoming familiar with some of the pieces of a reading program. What I lacked was the big picture, a conceptual framework for reading instruction within which I could fit the individual pieces into a coherent whole.

This chapter provides a framework, or big picture, of reading and writing instruction. The sample instructional frameworks presented should help you make more sense of the many reading and writing pieces described in chapters 2 through 11. This chapter covers the following topics:

✻ Why a reading framework, rather than a reading program
✻ Sample reading and writing instruction frameworks
  ● Cunningham's Four Blocks framework
  ● Fountas and Pinnell's eight-part framework
  ● The National Reading Panel's five essential elements of reading
✻ A five-part reading and writing instruction framework

As we describe the frameworks, notice how the same instructional components keep reappearing. The point is that there is a set of reading instruction components that is common to many reading instruction programs. Effective reading teachers know these components and combine them flexibly to meet their students' instructional needs.

 **WHY A READING FRAMEWORK RATHER THAN A READING PROGRAM**

A reading instruction framework might be thought of as a set of flexible reading instruction components taught every day using instructional materials from a variety of sources. For example, we believe that, every day, teachers should (a) read aloud to students, (b) teach systematic phonics, (c) provide instruction in reading groups, (d) provide time for students to practice reading independently or with a partner, and (e) provide writing instruction. The specifics within each component will vary according to students' instructional needs.

Addresses IRA Standard 1.2

Demonstrate knowledge of reading research and histories of reading.

A reading program is typically thought of as a single published package with a teacher's manual that outlines instructional activities for the teacher. New teachers often rely heavily on a published reading program until they gain the instructional experience and skills to adapt components of multiple programs into a single, more flexible, **comprehensive reading instruction framework** that can meet a broader range of student needs.

Reading researchers (Bond & Dykstra, 1967/1997; National Reading Panel, 2000; Pressley, 2002) and classroom teachers (Baumann et al., 1998) agree that there is no single best approach for teaching all students to read and write. Reliance on a single approach cannot meet all students' diverse instructional needs. Wise teachers know from experience that *the best instructional method is a combination of methods.*

In the 1960s the federal government funded perhaps the largest single reading research project ever, known as the First Grade Studies (Bond & Dykstra, 1967/1997). The purpose of the First Grade Studies was to determine "which of the many approaches to initial reading instruction produces superior reading and spelling achievement" (p. 348). Researchers compared reading test scores of students in more than 700 first-grade classrooms across the country. Specifically, the researchers wanted to see what kind of reading instruction was best: **basal reading programs,** basal reading programs with extra phonics, **decodable texts, language-experience approaches,**

A comprehensive literacy instruction framework can meet learners' varying needs.

or decodable texts plus extra phonics. Among Bond and Dykstra's many conclusions were these:

- ❀ Children learn to read by a variety of materials and methods.
- ❀ No one approach is so distinctly better in all situations and respects that it should be considered the one best method and the one to be used exclusively.
- ❀ Combinations of programs, such as a basal program with supplementary phonics materials, often are superior to single approaches.
- ❀ It is likely that improvement would result from adopting certain elements from each of the approaches used in this study. (pp. 415, 416)

Pressley, Rankin, and Yokoi (1996) surveyed teachers across the country who were identified by their school language arts supervisors as being "exceptional" in promoting literacy achievement (p. 183). Pressley and colleagues' purpose was to identify the instructional practices of effective reading teachers. What they found was that effective reading teachers provided their students with **balanced reading instruction** by "integrating attractive features of whole language with explicit skills instruction" (p. 188). Other characteristics of these effective teachers included a literate classroom environment, writing instruction, additional direct teaching for weaker students, and an emphasis on motivation.

Having a comprehensive framework for reading and writing instruction helps teachers to select and organize **literacy learning** experiences flexibly and knowledgeably, based on student needs. The report of the National Reading Panel (2000, p. 11) affirms that teachers should be provided with "decision-making frameworks" to guide their selection, integration, and implementation of instructional strategies.

A flexible, comprehensive framework is also important because of the strong synergistic relationship among the various framework components. For example, teacher read-alouds support independent reading practice and guided reading by helping to provide the background knowledge and vocabulary necessary for success-ful **word identification. Independent reading** practice supports **decoding** in-struction and writing by allowing students to process common **spelling patterns** and word parts. **Guided reading** supports teacher read-aloud and independent read-ing by providing the strategies needed for making meaning from text.

Another important benefit of using a reading and writing instruction frame-work is the flexibility necessary for a classroom teacher to focus on an individual student's instructional needs. Every student and every class of students present unique instructional strengths and challenges. A flexible framework allows teachers to make instructional adjustments in the amount of time allotted to and the specific activities and materials used with each component while still covering all needed as-pects of the framework. Like a road map, a flexible framework provides an overall route to follow, but it also provides for needed instructional detours. As Duffy (1998) points out,

> In practice, however, there are no panaceas. The best teachers never follow a sin-gle program, theory, model, or philosophy, nor do they play a single role or employ one set of materials to the exclusion of others. Instead the best teachers draw thoughtfully from various sources, play many roles, and use many techniques and materials. (p. 360)

 ## SAMPLE READING AND WRITING INSTRUCTION FRAMEWORKS

CUNNINGHAM'S FOUR BLOCKS FRAMEWORK

The concept of organizational frameworks for reading and writing instruction has be-come increasingly popular in recent years. Perhaps the first well-known example is Cunningham's popular Four Blocks framework (Cunningham & Allington, 2003; Cun-ningham, Hall, & Defee, 1998). The Four Blocks framework is divided fairly evenly among four major emphases in reading instruction: guided reading; self-selected read-ing; writing; and working with words. Each block gets 30 to 40 minutes of instruc-tional time, for a daily total of 2.25 to 2.5 hours.

In the Guided Reading block, students read stories from **leveled books, big books,** basal reading books, and children's literature. The purpose of this block is to expose children to a wide range of children's literature and to teach comprehension skills. Guided reading for younger readers involves much teacher-assisted **shared reading,** in which the teacher first reads the book to the students and then reads it together with them. As readers become more skilled, the instructional emphasis shifts to more guided reading, in which the teacher provides an introduction but the stu-dents do the first reading themselves.

The Self-Selected Reading block includes two components: teacher read-aloud and individual reading time. The teacher begins this block by reading aloud and discussing stories and information books from a wide variety of children's literature to build chil-dren's background knowledge, vocabulary, and love of reading. Individual reading time (sometimes called *sustained silent reading [SSR]*) gives students an opportunity to practice reading skills by reading self-selected books at an easy level. Teachers meet individually with students during this time to confer with them about their reading.

The Writing block begins with a whole-class teacher **mini-lesson** on writing skills. The teacher models aspects of writing, such as using dialogue and revising, as well as more basic writing skills, such as punctuation and spelling. Next, students go to their desks and work on their personal writing projects while the teacher meets with them individually in writing conferences to provide additional instruction. A highlight of the writing block occurs when students publish their completed writing pieces in the form of small class-made books.

The Working with Words block teaches students to recognize the common spelling patterns and sight words that allow them to decode and read many words. This block begins with activities that explore high-frequency words displayed on a classroom word wall. The remaining Working with Words time is spent in activities that teach children to decode and spell, such as *Rounding Up Rhymes* and *Making Words*.

FOUNTAS AND PINNELL'S EIGHT-PART FRAMEWORK

Fountas and Pinnell (1996) suggest an eight-part framework that emphasizes oral language across the curriculum combined with word study. The framework uses much **teacher modeling** and instructional support with beginning readers, which is gradually replaced by increasing the level of student responsibility as students develop reading ability. Here are the eight parts of the Fountas and Pinnell framework:

1. The teacher *reads aloud* for a variety of instructional purposes, including demonstrating reasons for reading, developing vocabulary and sense of story, and making reading enjoyable.
2. The teacher uses *shared reading* lessons with big books to model the reading process by reading the story to students first and then reading together with students to prepare them for independent reading.
3. The teacher uses *guided reading* lessons with better readers to introduce reading selections and then guide the students as they read.
4. Students *read independently* to practice reading skills and build reading fluency and confidence.
5. The teacher provides *shared writing* lessons in which students watch the teacher write simple sentences or stories that they compose together.
6. The teacher also provides *interactive writing* lessons that are similar to shared writing lessons, except the teacher "shares the pen" and supports students as they write as much of the text as they can.
7. *Writing workshop* provides an opportunity for students to write personal stories as the teacher provides writing instruction through mini-lessons and individual writing conferences.
8. *Independent writing* gives students a chance to extend their writing skills across different writing genres and curriculum areas.

Teachers who use Fountas and Pinnell's framework combine these instructional activities with carefully selected reading texts to meet students' instructional needs.

THE NATIONAL READING PANEL'S FIVE ESSENTIAL ELEMENTS OF READING

In 1997, the U.S. Congress commissioned the Department of Education to put together a National Reading Panel (NRP) of leading researchers to determine the most effective ways of teaching reading. The 14 NRP panel members reviewed more than 100,000 reading research studies and combined the data from the best studies to identify the approaches to reading instruction that produced the greatest gains in student reading achievement. The findings of the NRP report (NRP, 2000) are frequently referred to as *scientifically based reading research* (SBRR) and have led to a national focus on five essential elements of reading: phonemic awareness; phonics; **fluency;** vocabulary; and comprehension.

The NRP also provides specific guidelines about how these five elements should be taught. For example, **phonemic awareness** (the awareness of how speech sounds are manipulated and blended to form spoken words) is best taught to kindergarten and first-grade students in small groups. Phonics is best taught explicitly and in a carefully designed instructional sequence. Oral reading fluency is best developed through repeated readings of texts with teacher support and guidance. Vocabulary is best learned through both wide reading and direct teaching of important words. Comprehension instruction is most effective when multiple comprehension strategies (predicting, clarifying, questioning, and summarizing) are taught together in a multiple strategies or transactional strategies comprehension lesson.

The NRP panel members acknowledge the NRP's narrow focus on the five elements and the omission of other important reading instruction topics, including oral language development, writing, and children's literature. Similar large-scale research summaries in the areas of oral language development, writing, and instruction for struggling readers are being developed.

These five essential elements have become an influential instructional framework for many classrooms across the country. NRP enthusiasts call for daily reading instruction in the five essential elements. Funding for large-scale federal reading programs such as *Reading First* is based on adherence to the five essential elements. Many state departments of education are rewriting core curriculum documents based on these elements. Basal reading programs now feature them along with a few additional elements, including oral language development, alphabet learning, and writing instruction.

A FIVE-PART READING AND WRITING INSTRUCTION FRAMEWORK

Addresses IRA Standard 2.2

Use a wide range of instruction practices, approaches, and methods, including technology-based practices, for learners at differing stages of development and from differing linguistic and cultural backgrounds.

An examination of reading and writing instruction frameworks, including the three examples just described, reveals common instructional components that appear over and over across frameworks. Through wide professional reading and classroom teaching experience, we have distilled and combined these common instructional components into a simple, flexible, and comprehensive reading and writing framework to provide a road map for teachers in designing and implementing effective instruction. This five-part framework is composed of the following components:

1. Teacher read-aloud
2. Word study instruction
3. Independent reading practice
4. Guiding reading instruction
5. Writing workshop

Taken together, these components comprise a daily 3-hour literacy block as recommended by members of the National Reading Panel. Teachers who are fully committed to producing students who love to read and write fluently and with comprehension understand that 60 or 90 minutes per day is simply not enough time to accomplish this most fundamental educational goal. Additional aspects of the framework include a language and print-rich classroom environment; a dynamic, well-organized classroom library; ongoing assessment, extra support for struggling readers; and parental involvement in the classroom and at home.

Our framework is conceptually simple, yet it includes each of the basic instructional necessities for a balanced and comprehensive reading and writing program. A brief summary is given here. Chapters 2 through 11 describe the framework in detail.

Teacher read-aloud provides students with much of the vocabulary and background knowledge needed for reading comprehension. It also provides students with an enjoyable positive experience with books and is one of the most powerful ways of building the motivation to read. Teachers should read aloud from a wide variety of genres and information books to give students every opportunity to discover books that they love. An important aspect of teacher read-aloud is the accompanying discussions that maximize student enjoyment and learning. Teachers ask open-ended questions about the read-aloud that lead students to discover important insights about setting, characters, events, themes, and information. Students share their personal responses, connections, questions, and favorite parts as they experience firsthand the joys of good literature.

Word study instruction helps students to recognize the common spelling patterns and sight words that make up so much of our printed language. Chapter 5 presents seven common spelling patterns that will enable beginning readers to read close to 1000 words. Good word study lessons are **explicit and systematic** and begin with the teacher providing examples of spelling patterns in **word families** and explaining how the pattern affects the letter sounds. The teacher then provides follow-up activities that allow students to play with and explore the spelling patterns to deepen their understanding and recognition. Finally, the teacher helps students make the critically important connection between word study lessons and real reading by helping them to recognize and apply the spelling patterns in **meaningful texts.**

Independent reading practice provides an important opportunity for students to practice reading skills in an enjoyable, meaningful context. If students are to become better readers, they need to practice reading, just as beginning piano players, skiers, and drivers need practice in order to improve. To be effective, independent reading practice needs to be carefully structured so that students are choosing and reading books at an appropriate level of difficulty and are using independent reading time productively. Independent reading time is an important classroom organization tool allowing teachers to teach small-group lessons and to confer with individual students.

Guiding reading instruction gives teachers an opportunity to coach and support their students during the actual process of reading stories and information texts. Teachers carefully select texts that are just difficult enough to provide both learning opportunities and successful reading experiences. They provide just enough information to get students off to a good reading start. Teachers then guide students through the texts by providing varying amounts of **instructional support** in the form of questions, explanations of content concepts, and on-the-spot word study mini-lessons. Following the reading, teachers lead students in such follow-up activities as discussions of the reading content, related writing experiences, and other art or research projects designed to extend student learning.

Writing instruction teaches students to express themselves fluently and meaningfully and deepens their understanding of every aspect of the reading process. Teachers begin writing instruction with whole-class mini-lessons: 10-minute lessons in which the teacher demonstrates writing concepts and skills that students will apply in their personal writing. Next, students return to their seats to begin or continue working on writing pieces on self-selected topics. As students write, the teacher goes from student to student, conferring individually with students and providing instruction on both the content and mechanics of their writing. At the end of writing time, a few students are invited to sit in the "authors' chair," share excerpts from their writing with classmates, and receive feedback and ideas. Finally, students' polished writing pieces are published and displayed for classmates and eventually taken home for the family to read.

Chapter 11 provides two descriptions of how this five-part reading and writing instruction framework is implemented in the authors' recent first- and second-grade classrooms. The specifics of implementation may vary from one class to another, but the five major reading and writing framework components are the same.

 *CONCLUSIONS*

Although the terminology and organization may vary from one framework to another, the basic daily components of a reading and writing instruction framework are the same. Teachers need to read aloud to their students. Students must learn to apply knowledge of common spelling patterns and word parts automatically to identify words in print. Students need extensive time to practice reading, both independently and with partners. Teachers need to provide guided reading lessons in small groups in which students learn important reading skills and apply them to meaningful texts. Students must have opportunities to write for real purposes with teacher guidance and support. In addition, there must be an ongoing assessment program, extra instructional support for struggling readers, and active parent involvement both in the classroom and at home.

Most elementary schools have an existing reading program, usually a basal reading program. Basal reading programs can easily and effectively constitute one or more parts of the five-part reading and writing instruction framework. When teachers understand the functions of the five-part framework, they will be able to evaluate where their basal reading programs are strong and where they need supplemental materials and instruction. With this knowledge, they will be able to produce a comprehensive reading and writing instruction program that provides students with the skills and understandings they need to flourish as readers and writers.

Calkins (2001) describes how over time her focus on the parts of reading instruction grew into an understanding of the need for an integrated and flexible instructional framework:

> Once upon a time I believed that the solution to teaching reading lay in the independent reading workshop. . . . Then I came to understand the exquisite intimacy and power of reading aloud. . . . Then I discovered the power of response groups. . . . Next came our researching guided reading groups and strategy lessons. . . . But then we delved deep into word study and found that when we invested our time in helping children puzzle over the patterns in words, we were enabling them as readers in visible, exponential ways. . . . Finally over time, I have learned that each of these (and other) structures for teaching reading has special powers and particular limitations. Each structure is suited to certain jobs in the reading curriculum. (pp. 41, 42)

It is our hope that over time you, too, will develop a deep and practical understanding of the essential components of comprehensive reading and writing instruction. We hope that our experiences in orchestrating the implementation of such instruction will be instructive and useful and that you will share our satisfaction in teaching well and helping students to experience the joy and benefits of learning to read and write.

 SUGGESTED ACTIVITIES TO EXTEND YOUR LEARNING

1. Interview a K–3 classroom teacher and ask what are the most important parts of a reading and writing instruction curriculum. How do the teacher's responses compare with the components described in this chapter? Are there components the teacher added or left out?
2. During the teacher interview, ask follow-up questions about topics such as how the teacher decides what to teach and how much time to allocate to it and how much the teacher may know about the frameworks described in this chapter.
3. Arrange for a group of students using this text to complete Activities 1 and 2 and then meet in class in a discussion group to compare notes.

 *REFERENCES*

Bond, G. L., & Dykstra, R. (1997). The cooperative research program in first-grade reading instruction. *Reading Research Quarterly*, *32*(4), 345–427. (Original work published 1967).

Calkins, L. M. (2001). *The art of teaching reading.* New York: Longman.

Cunningham, P. M., & Allington, R. L. (2003). *Classrooms that work: They can all read and write* (3rd ed.). New York: Longman.

Cunningham, P. M., Hall, D. P., & Defee, M. (1998). Non-ability grouped multilevel instruction: Eight years later. *Reading Teacher*, *51*(8), 652–664.

Duffy, G. G. (1998). Powerful models or powerful teachers? An argument for teacher as entrepreneur. In S. Stahl & D. Hayes (Eds.), *Instructional models in reading*. Mahwah, NJ: Erlbaum.

Fountas, I., & Pinnell, G. S. (1996). *Guided reading: Good first teaching for all children*. Portsmouth, NH: Heinemann.

National Reading Panel. National Institute of Child Health and Human Development. (2000). *Report of the National Reading Panel. Teaching children to read: Reports of the subgroups*. Available online at www.nichd.nih.gov./publications/pubs/readbro.htm

Pressley, M. (2002). *Reading instruction that works: The case for balanced teaching* (2nd ed.). New York: Guilford.

Pressley, M., Rankin, J., & Yokoi, L. (1996). A survey of instructional practices of primary teachers nominated as effective in promoting literacy. *Elementary School Journal*, *96*, 363–384.

What Is Reading?

by John A. Smith

The Importance of Knowing About Reading

"Sound it out, José, /t/ /h/ /i/ /s/, you can do it, /t/ /h/ /i/ /s/," says student teacher Mr. Jones. "Say it the slow way." His student, José, methodically applies the blending process to the letter sounds. He points to the individual letters and pronounces their sounds, "/t/ /h/ /i/ /s/." Then he blends the letter sounds together and comes up with a word that sounds something like /t-hiss/. José is puzzled. Mr. Jones is puzzled as well. The phonics isn't working.

Serendipitously, the school reading specialist, Mrs. Stewart, is visiting the classroom, and, because she knows reading, she instantly recognizes the problem that is perplexing José and his student teacher. "May I give it a try?" she asks politely, recognizing that she'll be teaching both José and Mr. Jones.

"José, when you see a t *and an* h *together in a word, they most often make just one sound, the sound /th/, like in the word /that/. Sometimes they make the /th/ sound you hear in the word /think/. T and* h *together are called a* consonant digraph," *she adds for Mr. Jones's benefit, "like /ch/, /sh/, and /wh/." José makes the /th/ sound and continues blending the* i *and* s *letter sounds so that he now comes up with the correct pronunciation, /this/.*

Well-intentioned Mr. Jones, soon to finish his student teaching, was unable to help his student José because his own knowledge of the components and mechanics of reading was insufficient. Whether it's phonics spelling patterns, comprehension strategies, or ways to motivate reluctant readers, teachers must know how reading works in order to teach it effectively.

To be able to teach reading effectively, you must be familiar with the components of reading and how they work together. The more you understand the reading process, the better you'll be able to recognize what your students are able to do and what they need to learn next. The more you understand the reading process, the better you'll be able to recognize your students' various reading problems and give them the tailored reading instruction they need. Specifically, this chapter will provide information about the following topics:

* Reading is constructing meaning
* Two components of reading
  * Word identification
  * Comprehension
* A current model of reading
* Attitude toward reading

 ## READING IS CONSTRUCTING MEANING

There are many varying and often conflicting definitions of reading. Some people feel that reading means pronouncing words on a page quickly and smoothly. Others claim that reading is getting the meaning from a book, magazine, or other printed text. Still others argue that reading requires an emotional or intellectual response to a text. I believe that a comprehensive view of reading includes elements of all these perspectives.

The 1985 landmark report published by the National Institute of Education titled *Becoming a Nation of Readers* (Anderson, Hiebert, Scott, & Wilkinson, 1985) contains a short sentence that provides a simple, straightforward definition of reading:

> *Reading is a process in which*
> *information from the text and the*
> *reader's background knowledge*
> *act together to produce meaning. (p. 8)*

I have separated this definition into four lines to highlight some important aspects of reading. First, reading is a complex process. Second, two sources of information come into play during reading: information in the text and information in the reader's mind. Third, these two sources of information act together to produce meaning. The key concept in this definition is that reading is about constructing meaning. I will elaborate on each of these three aspects of reading.

First, reading is a very *complex process*, much like a symphony orchestra. In an orchestra, string players, brass players, woodwind players, percussion players, and the conductor are all doing different things simultaneously to produce a magnificent single product: a symphony. In reading, the reader's eyes are tracking across and down each page, fixating on words and clusters of letters. The reader's brain automatically recognizes familiar words and spelling patterns. The recognition of familiar printed words triggers the reader's memory for both the spoken version of these words (print to sound) and their meaning versions (print to meaning). Adams (2001) describes how "recognition of a familiar word will automatically evoke its personal history of usage and interpretation in print and, through that, its previously experienced meanings in general" (p. 70). The reader's mind then carries out interactions and comparisons among the printed, spoken, and meaning aspects of words automatically, simultaneously, and "in mutual coordination" to confirm the identity and meanings of recognized words. When encountering unfamiliar words or spelling patterns, the reader often takes a second look, trying to recall other words with similar spelling patterns or similar words that might make sense. Like a symphony orchestra, all these mental processes work together to produce a magnificent single product: meaning.

Figure 2.1 Traditional Conceptualization of Reading

Figure 2.2 Reading as a Meaning-Constructing Process

Second, the information contained in the text is compared with and screened by the reader's *background knowledge*. This results in adding to and in many cases changing the reader's knowledge in part or altogether. Each person has a unique collection of personal experiences. This background knowledge and these experiences have the effect of emphasizing, disregarding, and connecting to different aspects of texts to create an individual interpretation. Thus, 30 university students in a reading methods course could read a short story or poem and each write a one-page response different from all others.

A *Family Circle* cartoon some years ago illustrated this principle of differing background knowledge. Reading aloud to four young children, Dad read the phrase "standing by the water's edge." This phrase evoked a different response from each child: standing at the beach, standing at a mountain lake, standing by a river, and standing next to a stream behind the house.

Third, the information in the text and the reader's background knowledge act together to *produce meaning*. Many people typically think of reading as getting information from the text. This implies that all the information involved in reading flows in one direction: from the book to the brain, as represented in Figure 2.1. This textbook, however, is based on the definition represented in Figure 2.2, which shows the reader's background knowledge interacting with information from the text to produce a new and unique interpretation or meaning. The meaning of the text is actually created in a transaction somewhere between the text and the reader, as influenced by the context or purpose of the reading situation.

Rosenblatt (1994) states that:

> every reading act is an event, or a transaction involving a particular reader and a particular pattern of signs, a text, and occurring at a particular time in a particular context. Instead of two fixed entities acting on one another, the reader and the text are two aspects of a total dynamic situation. The "meaning" does not reside ready-made "in" the text or "in" the reader but happens or comes into being during the transaction between reader and text. (p. 1063)

Literacy learners need instruction in all aspects of reading and writing.

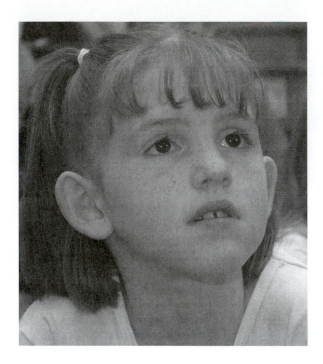

A clear understanding of how reading works is important because it will influence how you teach reading. When you are aware of the critical role of students' background knowledge, you are more likely to spend instructional time activating and developing your students' background knowledge prior to reading and helping your students to "connect the new to the known." If you view reading primarily as fluently blending letter sounds, you may not guide your students to also use sentence structure and contextual information to process print. Conversely, if you are mostly concerned with making meaning and developing reader response, you may overlook the need to help your students to process print fluently and automatically as a necessary contributor to reading comprehension.

Research has shown that effective reading teachers understand the need for helping readers to attend to all aspects of the reading process. They pay instructional attention simultaneously to the decoding skills and strategies of reading in close connection with the meaning-producing aspects of reading in a balanced, comprehensive instructional framework (Pressley, Yokoi, Rankin, Wharton-McDonald, & Mistretta, 1997).

Addresses IRA Standard 1.4

Demonstrate knowledge of the major components of reading (phonemic awareness, word identification and phonics, vocabulary and background knowledge, fluency, comprehension strategies, and motivation) and how they are integrated in fluent reading.

COMPONENTS OF READING

Classroom teachers, reading researchers, and others in the field of education generally agree that there are two major components of the reading process: word identification and comprehension (Hoover & Gough, 1990). These two components are both necessary for reading to occur. In describing them, the *Report of the National Reading Panel* (National Reading Panel, 2000) states the following:

> One process involves learning to convert the letters into recognizable words. The other involves comprehending the meaning of the print. When children attain reading skill, they learn to perform both of these processes so that their attention

and thought are focused on the meaning of the text while word reading processes operate unobtrusively and out of awareness for the most part. (p. 2–106)

Whitehurst and Lonigan (2001, p. 13) describe two "domains of information" involved in the reading process. An *inside-out* domain (word identification) refers to "sources of information within the printed word that support children's ability to translate print into sounds and sounds into print." The *outside-in* domain (comprehension) represents "sources of information outside the printed word that directly support children's understanding of the meaning of print (e.g., vocabulary, conceptual knowledge, and story schemas)." Whitehurst and Lonigan emphasize that these two domains of information are interdependent and that information from each domain influences the processing of information in the other domain. I will describe the word identification and comprehension components of reading and their subcomponents and then present a contemporary model that shows how all these parts work together in the reader's mind to produce meaning.

Word identification refers to recognizing or decoding printed words. This is often associated with phonics, word attack, or "sounding out." But the term *word identification* is more inclusive because it includes both words that are recognized and words that are decoded. *Comprehension* means making sense of what is read. Readers combine their background knowledge with information contained in the text to create meaning. For each of these two major components, there are several subcomponents or "parts" of reading. Your familiarity with these will enable you to better understand what readers need to know and be able to do in reading, what they are doing well, and where they need support and guidance.

An additional component of reading that needs to be acknowledged is *attitude toward reading*. The benefits of learning how to read are greatly diminished if students don't also learn to *want* to read. Students who do not enjoy reading will spend their time on things other than reading and will miss critical opportunities to improve their reading through practice. Readers must read often to become better readers. If students are to read often and by choice, then it is imperative that teachers focus not only on the mechanics of reading, but also on the rewards of reading.

WORD IDENTIFICATION

Readers use several sources of information to identify words: **sight vocabulary, context, syntax, word structure,** and phonics. Good readers use these strategies flexibly, simultaneously, and automatically. Just as nutrition experts stress the importance of a balanced diet, teachers should keep in mind the importance of providing students with a balanced and comprehensive approach to identifying printed words.

The following contributors to word identification are listed in a sequence that somewhat approximates the steps of learning to identify printed words:

1. Beginning readers often start by learning about alphabet letter names and sounds. This includes the *alphabetic principle* that the printed alphabet letters represent speech sounds.

2. Beginning readers must also develop *phonemic awareness*, the understanding that spoken words are composed of discrete speech sounds and that individual speech sounds are manipulated and blended to form all our spoken words (see chapter 3). Knowing the alphabet letters and the speech sounds they represent

and understanding the principle of blending the speech sounds represented by letters in printed words provide students with the conceptual foundation for blending letter sounds to read words.

3. As readers apply the alphabetic principle and phonemic awareness to blend letter sounds in simple beginning words like *sat, bed,* and *top,* they begin to recognize some of these words quickly and effortlessly. These words are referred to as *sight words* or *sight vocabulary*.

4. As readers encounter more complex words such as *stop, chirp,* and *baseball,* they will use the word parts and spelling patterns that they recognize to help identify the more complex words.

5. As good readers use the printed letters to produce approximate pronunciations of words, they compare the pronunciation to words in their oral vocabulary that fit within the patterns of spoken English. For example, is the pronunciation a verb where the sentence structure calls for a verb (She will *hit* the ball)?

6. Similarly, when good readers use printed letters to generate a pronunciation, they will also intuitively check to see that it makes sense in the context of the sentence.

7. When a pronunciation based on printed letters does not fit English speech patterns (She will *hat* the ball) or doesn't make sense in a sentence, good readers will recognize that there is a problem and try another pronunciation until they find one that looks right, sounds right, and makes sense.

8. Readers develop *oral reading fluency* as they are able to combine all the preceding steps to read words easily, quickly, accurately, and with proper expression.

Contributors to Word Identification

Phonics	Blending letter sounds to identify words
Sight vocabulary	Words that are recognized automatically
Structural analysis	Analyzing and combining word parts to identify words
Syntax	Using sentence structure to identify words
Context	Using meaning to identify words

Phonics

The term *phonics* is used interchangeably with other terms, including sounding out, decoding, word attack, and word identification. The word *phonics* refers to *sound* as in tele*phone* or *phono*graph. Phonics simply means combining the sounds of the letters in a word to produce its pronunciation. For example, beginning readers will blend "s–a–t: sat" or "th–i–s: this." With phonetically regular words such as *cat, draft, steam, chip, floor,* and *twine,* phonics works very nicely. With irregularly spelled words such as *does, is, love, said, some,* and *was,* using the sounds of the letters at least gives readers a place to begin trying to produce a pronunciation of the word.

In chapter 5 I describe in detail the aspects of phonics that need to be taught and how to teach them. I will not emphasize students' memorizing a large number of phonics rules; that would be very inefficient. Rather, I will focus on teaching students to recognize common spelling patterns in words. Our minds are wired to find visual and sequential patterns in our world. Cunningham (2000) refers to our minds as pattern detectors. Patterns allow our minds to organize large amounts of data in useful categories so that we can more readily perceive, connect, store, retrieve, and process information. Similarly, recognizing and manipulating spelling patterns is the most efficient way to identify printed words.

There are several important reasons for beginning readers to learn to apply phonics generalizations or patterns. First, as students learn to apply phonics, they will be able to unlock the pronunciations of the many unfamiliar words they encounter in print. Second, as young readers become proficient at blending letters, they will apply the same principle to begin blending parts of words, that is, they will use **structural analysis.** Third, as unfamiliar words are decoded repeatedly in meaningful contexts, they become sight words, thus increasing the reader's fluency.

Research shows that good readers use phonics so efficiently that they rely less on syntax and context because they can come up with the words mostly from looking at the letters. Conversely, struggling readers who are not proficient with phonics make more use of syntax and context, sometimes guessing what an unfamiliar word might be.

FOR STRUGGLING READERS

Readers' Problems

An insufficient understanding of the alphabetic principle and an inability to easily blend letter sounds is at the heart of many struggling readers' problems. When some of my first-grade students began to fall behind their classmates, one-on-one tutoring sessions with decodable texts (Nan can fan Dan) provided the repetition and practice my students needed to catch up.

Sight Vocabulary

Sight vocabulary refers to words that a reader can instantly recognize. Words in a reader's sight vocabulary do not need to be sounded out or decoded. Common words and spelling patterns that appear often in print (e.g., *the, and, for, some*) quickly become sight words through repetition. Other words easily become sight words because of their interest value to young readers (e.g., *love, dinosaur, mother, McDonald's*). At home or at work, we instantly recognize the people we see on a regular basis. On a printed page we can also come to instantly recognize many words that we see often. Being able to recognize and process many printed words easily, quickly, and accurately is often referred to as **automaticity.**

Automaticity has important implications for reading comprehension. Learning theory suggests that each of us has a limited amount of attention capacity to allocate among several items simultaneously. The more attention we shift to one item, the less there is for other items. For example, I can take two routes from my driveway to the parking lot at school. Being a person who likes variety, I often drive a different way each morning. Frequently, I find myself arriving in the parking lot and wondering, "How did I get here?" Does that ever happen to you? The fact is, I have achieved automaticity in driving my car. Driving to work, I listen to the news and think about class, my family, and the weekend. I think about almost everything except driving my car. I am so practiced at pushing the pedals and turning the wheel that I allocate only a very small percentage of my attention to driving. The majority of my attention is allocated to other things I want to think about.

Reading should operate the same way. Readers should be able to identify printed words effortlessly and automatically so they can allocate greater portions of their attention to the more important component of reading: comprehension. Adams (1990) documents the important role of automaticity in reading as follows:

> Laboratory research indicates that the most critical factor beneath fluent word reading is the ability to recognize letters, spelling patterns, and whole words effortlessly, automatically, and visually. The central goal of all reading instruction—comprehension—depends critically on this ability. (p. 54)

An additional reason that building sight vocabulary is necessary is that *many of the words beginning readers see cannot be sounded out.* Try to apply phonics rules to the first word of each pair in the following columns of beginning reading words and see what you come up with. The second word in each pair represents how these words would be spelled if phonics rules were applied consistently in our printed language. These are just a few of the many beginning reading words that must be learned as sight words because the phonics rules don't apply.

above	ubuv	from	frum	said	sed
again	ugen	give	giv	says	sez
because	beekuz	love	luv	school	skule
bought	bot	lose	luze	walk	wok
build	bild	of	uv	was	wuz
come	cum	off	of	what	whut
does	duz				

Because recognizing printed words and spelling patterns is so efficient and because many common words can't be decoded using phonics rules, beginning readers must quickly develop a strong sight vocabulary. This will enable them to read quickly and effortlessly while allocating their attention to the meaning of the text. Sight vocabulary is also important because the words and spelling patterns a reader can recognize instantly become the building blocks for identifying more complex and multisyllabic words.

I do not mean to endorse a return to flashcard drills. Sight vocabulary is best developed by repetition, by seeing words over and over during the course of substantial amounts of meaningful reading. Instructional suggestions for developing sight vocabulary are covered in subsequent chapters.

Structural Analysis

No matter how many words we are able to recognize, we will always come across words that we haven't seen before in print. What do readers do in this situation? The next step for many readers is to look at the word, try to find familiar parts, and then combine this information with the oral speech patterns and passage context to generate a word that makes sense from their spoken vocabulary. For example, a reader may not recognize the printed word *slight,* but may recognize the *ight* part of the word from other, more familiar words, such as *light, might,* and *right.* This is *structural analysis:* recognizing and combining familiar parts of words, including prefixes, root words, suffixes, and common letter combinations such as *ing, ble,* and *tion.* The following example of words from a medical journal should help you recognize just how important structural analysis is in word identification:

neuropharmacology

postganglionic

phylogenetic

Figure 2.3 A Meaningless Passage

> **A Pidder Flaster Chiffel**
>
> Berm kerp a pidder flaster chiffel. Berm foober hep pidder flaster chiffel um vistar. At nogom Berm zonk hep pidder flaster chiffel in hep borm. On Bister Berm foobers hep pidder flaster chiffel to meddar's seppum.
>
> 1. Who kerp a pidder flaster chiffel?
> 2. What did Berm do with help pidder flaster chiffel?
> 3. Where did Berm zonk hep pidder flaster chiffel at nogom?
> 4. Where did Berm foober hep pidder flaster chiffel on Bister?

renocorticotropic

periacquaductal

neospinalthalamic

Study these words for a moment and try to pronounce them aloud. As you do, chances are you will use structural analysis to look for familiar parts of the words, such as *neuro, pharm*, and *ology* or *peri, acqua, duct*, and *al*. You still may not know what any of these words mean, but you should at least be able to pronounce them using structural analysis.

When good readers encounter unfamiliar words, words not in their sight vocabulary, they use structural analysis to look for familiar word parts to produce an approximate pronunciation of the unfamiliar words and then match these pronunciations to words already in their speaking and listening vocabularies. Good readers like you use structural analysis continually, flexibly, and automatically.

Syntax

Readers also use syntax (sentence structure) to identify words. For example, in reading the meaningless passage in Figure 2.3 and trying to answer the questions, phonics won't help because the pronunciations won't approximate real words. Context won't help because the passage has no meaning to rely on. Yet you will be able to "read" this passage and successfully answer the questions because of your familiarity with the structures of the English language.

Fountas and Pinnell (2001) describe how readers "use their knowledge of the rules of syntax (the grammar of a language) as a way to monitor reading" (p. 308). A beginning reader who reads "Sally wents a drink of water" will be alerted by his or her knowledge of syntax that something is wrong, something doesn't sound right. The reader will then use context to adjust the reading to the meaningful sentence "Sally wants a drink of water." Fountas and Pinnell also emphasize that good readers use syntax to recognize the phrase units of printed text and to read in phrases, thus helping to reproduce the author's meaning. Students learn the rules of language structure from listening and speaking, and they then apply these rules to printed language to both support word identification and build comprehension.

FOR ENGLISH LANGUAGE LEARNERS

The Challenge of Syntax

Syntax is a particular challenge for ELL students. For example, the English oral language syntactic structure *big house* is reversed in the Spanish translation *casa grande*. In other words, the oral language patterns that native speakers rely on are of less or little help to ELL students.

Context

How would you pronounce the word *read*? It could be pronounced with a long E sound as in, "I want to read this book" or the short E sound as in "I read this book yesterday." How you pronounce the word *read* depends on the context of the sentence. An important part of identifying words in print is using context to select words that make sense in the sentence or passage. When encountering an unknown printed word, many good readers simply plug in a temporary approximate meaning for the unknown word based on the meaning of the preceding paragraphs, sentences, and words and then continue reading, relying on the meaning in subsequent lines to confirm or change the temporary meaning.

Popular fiction author Tom Clancy used a lot of Russian vocabulary in his book *Red Storm Rising*. In one of the early chapters I encountered the printed Russian word *rodina*. Not knowing the Russian language, I intuitively used the context of the passage to infer that *rodina* had something to do with Russian land and tradition. After two more encounters with the word *rodina,* I felt 100% sure that *rodina* meant motherland. Years later I confirmed in a Russian–English dictionary what I had inferred from context .

The passage in Figure 2.4 provides another example of how context helps readers identify words. The content of the passage is a familiar fairy tale. The words have been changed so that a word-by-word oral reading only gives a vague approximation of the familiar spoken words and will likely make no sense. As you read this passage, notice how you must use the context of each paragraph and sentence to identify the words. For those of you who need a head start, the first three printed words in the fairy tale translate to "Once upon a time."

As you can now plainly see, reading by phonics alone won't help at all with *Ladle Rat Rotten Hut*. You had to look at the letters in the words to generate a pronunciation. But because the pronunciations alone didn't make sense, you used contextual information to modify the pronunciations into words that did make sense. It

Figure 2.4   A Fairy Tale

Ladle Rat Rotten Hut

Wants pawn term, dare worsted ladle gull hoe lift wetter murder inner ladle cordage honor itch offer lodge dock florist. Disk ladle gull orphan worry putty ladle rat cluck wetter ladle rat hut, and fur disk raisin, pimple colder Ladle Rat Rotten Hut.

Wan moaning, Ladle Rat Rotten Hut's murder colder in said, "Ladle Rat Rotten Hut, heresy ladle basking winsome burden barter and shirker cockles. Tick disk ladle basking tutor cordage offer groin-murder how lifts honor udder site offer florist. Shaker lake! Dun stopper laundry wrote! Dun stopper peck floors! Dun daily doily inner florist, and yonder nor sorghum stenches, dun stopper torque wet strainers!"

"Hoe-cake, murder," resplendent Ladle Rat Rotten Hut, and tickle ladle basking and stuttered oft.

Honor wrote tutor cordage offer groin-murder, Ladle Rat Rotten Hut mitten anomalous woof.

"Wail, wail, wail!" set disk wicket woof, "evanescent Ladle Rat Rotten Hut! Wares are putty ladle gull goring wizard ladle basking?"

"Armor goring tumor groin-murder's," reprisal ladle gull. "Grammar's seeking bet. Armor ticking arson burden barter and shirker cockles."

Note. Original version written in 1940 by H. L. Chace.

was context that told you the printed word *ladle* was really the spoken meaningful word *little*. This principle holds true with all our reading: We look at the letters to get a pronunciation and then use context to see whether the pronounciation makes sense. If it makes sense, we continue. If not, we go back and try another pronunciation. Good readers continually combine information from phonics and context as they read.

The Need for Balanced Word Identification

A very important point to be made here is that these word identification strategies are not used individually, sequentially one-at-a-time, or in isolation from each other. Good readers use all these strategies simultaneously, flexibly, and automatically. Take, for example, the following sentence: *Bob sleeps in his house.* Imagine a beginning reader reading this sentence and coming on the word *house*, which is not in his or her sight vocabulary. If we could peek inside that reader's mind, we might see a thought process like this:

> This is easy. I know the first words "Bob sleeps in his." Oh oh, I don't recognize this last word [sight vocabulary]. It's not an action word because of *in his* . . . . It must be someplace Bob sleeps [syntax and context]. It can't be his bed because it does-n't start with *b*. The first two letters are *ho* [phonics]. Maybe it's *home,* that makes sense [phonics and context]. Let's take another look at the word. Oops, it has an *s* toward the end and no *m* [phonics]. It can't be *home*. The middle has *ou* like *out* [structural analysis]. *H/ou/s . . . house*. And the *e* on the end is probably silent [phonics]. That must be it. It makes sense and all the letters fit [syntax, phonics, structural analysis, and context]. Bob sleeps in his house.

This example shows how good readers flexibly and simultaneously use letter sounds, sight vocabulary, structural analysis, syntactic, and contextual information to identify words not in their sight vocabularies, much like fitting together the pieces of a jigsaw puzzle. A basketball team that relies on one star player to score most of its points will be seriously handicapped against a team that has balanced scoring from all its players. Similarly, readers who rely on a single word-identification strategy (i.e., phonics or context) every time they encounter an unfamiliar word will have a much harder time identifying words quickly, accurately, and automatically.

Developing Oral Reading Fluency

Many beginning readers in the process of learning to recognize and process printed words and spelling patterns read slowly, with many errors and little expression. Other beginning readers develop the ability to recognize words fairly accurately but still read slowly and monotonously. Beginning readers can be balanced and still not be fluent. The goal of word identification instruction is for all beginning readers to develop oral reading fluency, defined by the National Reading Panel (2000) as reading quickly, accurately, and with expression. While much of word identification instruction takes place at the word level, studying word families and word parts, fluency instruction takes place at the passage level as students practice reading large sections of text over and over until they can read aloud quickly, accurately, and with expression. Several approaches to fluency instruction are described in chapter 5.

COMPREHENSION

The purpose of reading is to understand what authors have to say, to make meaning from texts, to comprehend (Block & Pressley, 2002). Word identification is important only as it contributes to comprehension. Like word identification, comprehension also has several subcomponents:

Aspects of Comprehension

Vocabulary and background knowledge	Familiarity with words and concepts
Text structure	Knowing how to use the organizational patterns of narrative, expository, and other texts

Levels of Comprehension

Critical reading	Evaluating the quality of the text
Inferential comprehension	Using background knowledge to supplement information provided in the text
Literal comprehension	Knowing the basic facts: who, what, when, where, how, why

Vocabulary and Background Knowldege

To understand the meaning of a text, the reader must know the possible meanings of the individual words and also be reasonably familiar with the concepts discussed in the text. Simply sounding out the phonetically regular word *cheetah* will not be of any use to a young reader who has never heard the word or seen a cheetah on television or at the zoo.

Many years ago, I provided remedial reading instruction to struggling readers whose classroom teachers and low IRI and standardized test scores suggested that they were significantly behind their classmates in reading. One day, I read the book *Island of the Blue Dolphins* with a small group of 5th-grade reading students. When my reading students returned to their homeroom classes, one student lingered in my resource room. Having a few minutes before my next class, I went over to Tyrone and said, "Come with me over to the map on the wall and I'll show you where the island was where Karana lived alone for 17 years." As I pointed to a group of islands off the coast of Southern California, Tyrone ran his hand down the Pacific Ocean on the map and asked, "Mr. Smith, is this blue part the water?" I was amazed that an 11-year-old 5th-grade student wouldn't know this and, seeing a teachable moment at hand, I launched into the following conversation with Tyrone.

John	Yes, the blue part is the water and the colored parts are the different countries. Here's the United States, it's yellow. Here are Canada, Mexico, and South America. These dots in the ocean are islands, and these yellow dots are Hawaii, part of the United States.
Tyrone	Mr. Smith, could you drive to Hawaii?
John	No, you'd have to take a boat or an airplane to get to Hawaii.
Tyrone	Where is Hollywood and where are the Bahamas?
John	(shows these locations on the map)
Tyrone	Is Norfolk in South America?
John	No, Norfolk is right here by North Carolina, it's about 4 hours' drive.
Tyrone	Can you drive to Hollywood?
John	Yes, you can drive to Hollywood from here and it would take about 4 days.

Based on this conversation, you can guess that Tyrone did not have a lot of background knowledge, at least about geography. His life, at the time, consisted of getting up, going to school, baby-sitting his siblings in the afternoon while watching cartoons, eating dinner, and then watching television sitcoms until he went to bed. His family was unable to provide a computer, music lessons, summer educational programs, vacations outside of the county, books and magazine subscriptions, or other opportunities to learn about the world through travel and firsthand experiences, discussions, or wide reading.

Ironically, I could hand Tyrone a 5th-grade reading book, open it to any page, and say to Tyrone, "Read this to me." Tyrone could read the words aloud almost effortlessly. He was bright and learned the decoding aspects of reading very well. But when I asked him to explain to me what he had just "read," Tyrone would stare at me with a blank expression. He could seldom tell me about the ideas contained in the words he read. Tyrone couldn't comprehend what he was reading because he generally lacked the necessary background knowledge and vocabulary.

The following example illustrates the central role of meaning vocabulary in reading comprehension. These 10 words would be considered sight words for competent adult readers. Read them to yourself:

individual	variable
mean	blocks
error	square
effect	random
nuisance	differences

Now read the same words again, this time in a paragraph:

> *A randomized block design permits an experimenter to minimize the effects of individual differences by isolating that portion of the total effect due to blocks. As a result, the error term for testing the treatment mean square is free of the nuisance variable of individual differences.*

Would you care to summarize the meaning of this paragraph? No? Why not? You read all the words! Even though most adult readers can read all the individual words in the paragraph, most would have trouble comprehending the paragraph because they lack the necessary background knowledge of, in this case, inferential statistics. The point is that too many students, like Tyrone, come to our classrooms without the background knowledge needed to make sense of the materials they are expected to read. For such students, much of what they are given to read is as incomprehensible to them as statistics.

Text Structure

Stories (**narrative text**) are structured or organized differently from information texts

---

FOR ENGLISH LANGUAGE LEARNERS

The Challenge of Vocabulary

Vocabulary is also a major challenge for ELL students. An ELL student may be familiar with a background knowledge concept such as *horse*, but not know the specific English words associated with the concept of horse. Simply teaching ELL students the word identification skills needed to pronounce words such as horse will do little good unless we also give them ample instructional opportunities to develop the English vocabulary needed to understand what the pronounced words mean.

(**expository texts**). Stories generally contain the structural elements of setting, characters, events, and theme. For example:

> *One day in the deep dark woods (setting) Little Red Riding Hood's mother asked her to take a basket of cookies to her grandmother (characters, event). Her mother told her not to talk to anyone along the way. On the path Little Red Riding Hood met a wicked wolf (character, event). He hurried to Grandmother's house (event), dressed up like Grandmother (event), and was about to gobble up Little Red Riding Hood when a woodsman saved them (event). The moral of this story is to always obey your mother (theme).*

Conversely, information texts, particularly textbooks, generally follow a sequence of main ideas, each supported by one or more details. For example:

> *Water on our planet goes continuously up into the air and back down to Earth in a process known as the water cycle (main idea). Water comes down from the sky in the form of rain and snow (detail). The water collects in streams and rivers and flows into lakes and oceans (detail). Then the water evaporates back up into the sky (detail). The water molecules in the sky collect together to form clouds (details). When the clouds get full enough with water molecules, they fall back to Earth as rain or snow (detail).*

Teaching students to recognize text structure gives them a way to anticipate, look for, and organize the information they will process. Research has shown that teaching students to recognize the structure of narrative text, sometimes referred to as **story grammar,** improves students' reading comprehension. Personally, I like to begin each new reading selection with my students by inviting them to examine the text for a minute and then tell me if it will be a story or an information text. I often use the text structure elements to help my students to generate a summary at the end of a reading lesson.

Literal-Level Comprehension

Educators generally refer to three levels of comprehension: **literal, inferential,** and **critical.** These levels are generally found in the comprehension questions in basal reading lessons, in informal reading inventories and other assessments, and in many curriculum guides. Literal-level comprehension (also known as explicit comprehension) simply means understanding the literal meaning of the words on the page. We often say about literal comprehension, "It's right there, in black and white." In a story, this would mean understanding where and when the story takes place, who is in the story, and what is going on. At the literal level, the reader doesn't need to make any inferences about *why* characters are doing what they're doing. For example, read the following story.

> *Michael and Dianne were preparing to go for a bicycle ride on Sunday. The night before the bicycle ride, Michael broke Dianne's bicycle.*

Several literal-level questions could be asked about this little story. For example, "Who broke Dianne's bicycle?" or "Whose bicycle did Michael break?" or "When did Michael break Dianne's bicycle?" The point is that the reader doesn't need to know anything about bicycles in order to answer these literal-level questions. As in the example of Berm and the pidder flaster chiffel, familiarity with English syntax allows the reader to answer these questions simply by rearranging the order of the words in the sentences.

Inferential-Level Comprehension

Inferential comprehension (also known as implicit comprehension) is the next higher level of comprehension. The following analogy may clarify the nature of inferential comprehension. A text is much like a fishing net. The structure of a fishing net allows a large catch of fish to be held together by a relatively small amount of string. The knots where the net's strings are tied together are much like the words in a text. A relatively small amount of words can evoke a large amount of meaning because readers use their background knowledge to fill in the gaps among the words. We often call this *reading between the lines*.

For the bicycle story, inferential-level questions might include "Why did Michael break Dianne's bicycle?" or "How do you think Dianne felt when she learned that her bicycle was broken?" The answers to these two questions are not contained in the text. Perhaps Michael was simply trying to tune up Dianne's bicycle before their ride. Perhaps breaking her bicycle was an accident. Maybe Dianne really wanted a new bicycle so she wasn't too upset about it. The reader is expected to use background knowledge to make inferences to answer these questions.

Critical Reading

At the critical level, a reader goes beyond just understanding a text. The reader evaluates the quality and effectiveness of a text, just as critics evaluate the quality of a Hollywood movie or a Broadway play. At this level, a reader should be able to answer questions such as these:

- How well did I like this Michael and Dianne story?
- Would I recommend this story to a friend? Why or why not?
- What was the author's purpose for writing the Michael and Dianne story?
- How well did the author achieve this purpose?

As we teach reading, it is important to teach students to comprehend at all three levels. A majority of the questions in a typical basal reading program teacher's manual tend to be at the literal level. Literal-level questions are important in reading instruction because they help students to understand the basics. For example, when reading a story, literal questions focus on who's in the story, where the story takes place, and what is going on in the story. But students also need plenty of opportunities to consider and respond to higher-level inferential and critical questions. Just as a *balanced and comprehensive approach* is most effective in word identification instruction, students also need balance in their comprehension instruction.

 A CURRENT MODEL OF READING

The preceding pages have described individual components of both word identification and comprehension. It is important to understand that good readers use all these components simultaneously, flexibly, and automatically. Figure 2.5 depicts a model of reading that shows how all the components work together to produce meaning. In this model, the components are organized into three **cueing systems** (or sources of information) that readers use together as they process text and meaning: semantic, syntactic, and **graphophonic.**

The first cueing system is the *graphophonic* system. This refers to the reader using the print information on the page, including letters, spelling patterns, and word

Figure 2.5   Three Cueing Systems for Reading

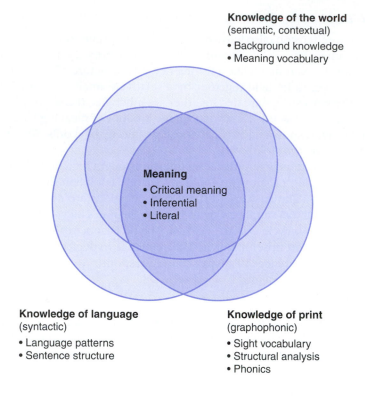

Knowledge of the world
(semantic, contextual)
• Background knowledge
• Meaning vocabulary

Meaning
• Critical meaning
• Inferential
• Literal

Knowledge of language
(syntactic)

• Language patterns
• Sentence structure

Knowledge of print
(graphophonic)

• Sight vocabulary
• Structural analysis
• Phonics

parts, to identify printed words. Readers will convert printed letters to their corresponding sounds and blend the sounds together to form spoken words (phonics). Readers also come to recognize many whole words automatically (sight vocabulary) and recognize and manipulate parts of words (structural analysis). Graphophonic information can also provide clues about what words mean. The prefix on the word *replay* tells readers to adjust the meaning of the word accordingly.

The second cueing system is the *syntactic* system. This refers to the reader using the patterns and structure of spoken language to identify words. Beginning readers already have an intuitive sense, from their years of hearing and using spoken language patterns, of sentences being composed of subjects and predicates and that some words in a sentence modify or describe others. These language patterns help readers to anticipate the kinds of words that follow other words in a sentence. For example, when you read *Ladle Rat Rotten Hut* and figured out the first two words *once upon*, your familiarity with English helped you to identify the next two words, *a time*. During reading, readers compare syntactic and semantic information in their heads with the graphophonic information on the page to predict and confirm the identities and meanings of unfamiliar printed words. If reading doesn't "sound" right syntactically, good readers know something is amiss and go back to fix it.

The third cueing system is the *semantic* system. This system includes the reader's background knowledge, vocabulary, and the context of the reading passage. In other words, this is the "meaning" aspect of reading. Good readers expect reading to make sense, and as they read they use their background knowledge and the context of the passage to monitor the meaningfulness of their reading. When the meaning breaks down, good readers locate the problem and correct it.

As good readers process text, they simultaneously, flexibly, and automatically use all three cueing systems to predict what upcoming words will be. Then they use this same information to confirm these predictions as they read. For example, in the sentence "At the grocery store, Chris bought some red ripe *strawberries*," the contextual information tells you that a person named Chris is in a grocery store buying something red and ripe. Therefore, the italicized word is probably a fruit, probably apples, cherries, or strawberries. The syntactic information tells you that the italicized word is probably a noun because of the verb *bought* and the adjectives *red* and *ripe*. Finally, the graphophonic information tells you that the italicized word cannot be apples or cherries because it begins with *str*.

As readers process these three sources of information during reading, they search their mental vocabularies for words that fit all three criteria. Reading teachers tell their students to make sure that the words they read (1) look right (graphophonic), (2) sound right (syntactic), and (3) make sense (semantic). As long as readers come up with words that meet all three criteria, the selection of words is confirmed and the reading proceeds meaningfully.

Reading teachers refer to students' ongoing monitoring of the three cueing systems during reading as **cross-checking.** When reading doesn't make sense, sound right, or look right, good readers look back and search again for words that meet all three criteria. Good readers have a balanced approach to reading by using all three cueing systems simultaneously, flexibly, and automatically.

Sometimes readers get out of balance. Some readers rely too much on the graphophonic information and do not pay enough attention to the context or meaning of the passage. These readers often pronounce words that look similar to the printed words, but don't make sense with the context of the passage. For example, "Bob slept in his *horse*," instead of the printed word *house*. Other readers may pay attention to the context of the passage, but don't focus enough on the letters. Such readers pronounce words that sound appropriate and make sense, but are not the printed words. For example, "Bob slept in his *home*," instead of the printed word *house*. I was the second kind of reader. I distinctly remember my third-grade teacher telling me repeatedly, "John, read the words on the page." She was trying to nudge me back into balance.

ATTITUDE TOWARD READING

The news media often run stories or documentaries about the personal and national costs of adult illiteracy in this country. Kozol (1985) provides horrifying accounts of large-scale industrial, agricultural, and military accidents and near accidents due to workers' inability to read operators' manuals or safety regulations. Most estimates place the adult illiteracy rate at about 20%, though some estimates go much higher depending on the varying criteria for what it means to be literate.

Another related problem in this country receives very little media attention. This is *aliteracy*, the problem of people who can read but choose not to. It can be argued that our schools have focused almost exclusively on the mechanics of learning to read and have often ignored teaching students to want to read. Trelease (1995) argues that in kindergartens nearly 100% of students enthusiastically want to learn to read, but by 12th grade only 24.4% of students read anything for pleasure.

The National Assessment of Educational Progress (NAEP), also known as The Nation's Report Card, paints a picture of two groups of students, those who choose to read and those who don't, and the increasing achievement gap between them. Over the past

Addresses IRA Standard 4.1

Use student interests, reading abilities, and backgrounds as foundations for the reading and writing program.

decade, the reading scores of students who chose to read every day have increased, while those of students who chose to read less than twice a month have gone down.

Educators must help students to see that reading is a desirable pastime, a valuable means of relaxing and learning, a satisfying way of life. Calkins (2001) argues as follows:

> Teaching reading, then, begins with helping children to want the life of a reader and to envision that life for themselves. It is important for the child just learning to ride a bike to see others riding with vigor, joy, and power. "I want that for myself," the child says. In a reading workshop, children watch each other swapping books, gossiping about characters, reading favorite passages aloud to friends, or searching for information about a hobby, and they say, "I want that for myself." (p. 9)

To help students become genuine readers, teachers must provide opportunities for students to experience both the informational and recreational aspects of reading. Students should be able to cry when Little Ann and Dan die at the end of Wilson Rawl's *Where the Red Fern Grows* and laugh with the characters in *Tales of a Fourth Grade Nothing* by Judy Blume. This emotional response, more than classroom reading incentive charts and rewards, will ultimately let students come to view reading as a valued means of recreation, relaxation, and learning.

 ## CONCLUSIONS

When considering the many interrelated facets of the reading process and their implications for reading instruction, it is important for teachers to keep in mind the need for balanced and comprehensive reading instruction. Successful beginning readers are those who have a balanced approach to reading and can easily and effectively use phonics, sight vocabulary, structural analysis, syntax, and context to identify words. Successful readers also know what words mean and can understand text at varying levels of comprehension. Balanced and comprehensive reading instruction distributes emphasis on the mechanics, meaning, and the pleasure of reading based on students' instructional needs.

In this book I promote the notion of a balanced, comprehensive, and flexible *framework* for organizing reading instruction. Those who study literacy instruction frequently acknowledge that there is no single best method for teaching reading and writing (Adams, 1990; Cunningham, Hall, & Defee, 1998). Duffy (1998) suggests that entrepreneurial teachers should create "coherent combinations" of many instructional models (p. 359). In a study of effective reading teachers, Baumann, Hoffman, Moon, and Duffy-Lester (1998) found that "a majority of teachers embrace a balanced, eclectic approach to elementary reading instruction, blending phonics and holistic principles and practices in compatible ways" (p. 640).

Too often, classroom teachers and administrators refer to "adopting a reading program," thus emphasizing materials rather than teachers and students. Rather than relying on commercially packaged one-size-fits-all reading programs, we must all remember that it is knowledgeable, creative, dedicated teachers that have the greatest impact on students' reading success. Teachers must be familiar with a wide variety of instructional options and their purposes. Then, guided by carefully collected and analyzed ongoing assessment data, teachers must know how to structure instructional experiences for individual students and groups to cover important curricular territory, while adapting these to meet students' needs.

I suggest throughout this textbook that teachers use a flexible, consistent five-part instructional framework each school day. The instructional specifics within the framework should vary from student to student, based on individual needs. Every day, teachers should do all the following:

1. Read aloud and discuss captivating and informative books, poems, and other materials with their students.
2. Provide word study instruction to help students to develop automaticity in recognizing printed words through using common spelling patterns and word parts.
3. Provide time for their students to read carefully selected books and materials independently.
4. Read together with their students, providing needed guidance and support for fluency and comprehension.
5. Help students to write on a variety of topics for meaningful purposes.

By providing all students with these five instructional experiences each day, along with critical additional support for struggling readers, teachers can make huge strides in ensuring that all students learn to enjoy reading fluently and meaningfully.

SUGGESTED ACTIVITIES TO EXTEND YOUR LEARNING

1. Find a beginning reader (kindergarten or 1st grade) in your family or neighborhood. Invite him or her to read aloud a few beginner books with you. As the child reads, try to determine how well he or she uses the various word identification and comprehension strategies described in this chapter. Does the child rely primarily on phonics or context or both? Does the child make inferences about the content? What is the child's attitude toward reading?
2. Think back to how you learned to read. How much did your family read to you? Did your primary-grade teachers use materials that promoted primarily phonics or sight word recognition? Were you ever taught to comprehend what you read? Assemble a group of classmates and share your collective experiences about being taught to read.

REFERENCES

Adams, M. J. (1990). *Beginning to read: Thinking and learning about print*. Cambridge, MA: MIT Press.

Adams, M. J. (2001). Alphabetic anxiety and explicit, systematic phonics instruction: A cognitive science perspective. In S. B. Neuman & D. K. Dickinson (Eds.), *Handbook of early literacy research*. New York: Guilford.

Anderson, R. C., Hiebert, E. F., Scott, J. A., & Wilkinson, I. A. G. (1985). *Becoming a nation of readers: The report of the commission on reading*. Washington, DC: National Institute of Education.

Baumann, J. F., Hoffman, J. V., Moon, J., & Duffy-Lester, A. M. (1998). Where are teachers' voices in the phonics/whole language debate? Results from a survey of U.S. elementary classroom teachers. *Reading Teacher, 51*(8), 636–650.

Block, C. C., & Pressley, M. (2002). *Comprehension instruction: Research-based best practices*. New York: Guilford.

Blume, J. (1972). *Tales of a fourth grade nothing*. New York: Bantam Doubleday Dell.

Calkins, L. M. (2001). *The art of teaching reading*. Portsmouth, NH: Heinemann.

Clancy, T. (1997). *Red storm rising*. New York: Berkley Books.

Cunningham, P. M. (2000). *Phonics they use: Words for reading and writing* (3rd ed.). New York: Longman.

Cunningham, P. M., Hall, D. P., & Defee, M. (1998). Nonability-grouped instruction: Eight years later. *Reading Teacher, 51*(8), 652–664.

Duffy, G. G. (1998). Powerful models or powerful teachers? An argument for teacher as entrepreneur. In S. Stahl and D. Hayes (Eds.), *Instructional models in reading*. Mahwah, NJ: Erlbaum.

Fountas, I. C., and Pinnell, G. S. (2001). *Guiding readers and writers grades 3-6*. Portsmouth, NH: Heinemann.

Hoover, W., & Gough, P. (1990). The simple view of reading. *Reading and Writing, 2,* 127–160.

Kozol, J. (1985). *Illiterate America*. Garden City, NY: Doubleday.

National Reading Panel. National Institute of Child Health and Human Development. (2000). *Report of the National Reading Panel. Teaching children to read: Reports of the subgroups.* Available online at www.nichd.nih.gov/publications/pubs/readbro.htm

O'Dell, S. (1971). *Island of the blue dolphins*. New York: Random House.

Pressley, M., Yokoi, L., Rankin, J., Wharton-McDonald, R., and Mistretta, J. (1997). A survey of instructional practices of grade 5 teachers nominated as effective in promoting literacy. *Scientific Studies of Reading, 1,*(2), 145–160.

Rawls, W. (1984). *Where the red fern grows*. New York: Random House.

Rosenblatt, L. M. (1994). The transactional theory of reading and writing. In R. B. Ruddell, M. R. Ruddell, & H. Singer (Eds.), *Theoretical models and processes of reading* (4th ed.). Newark, DE: International Reading Association.

Trelease, J. (1995). *The read-aloud handbook*. New York: Penguin.

U.S. Department of Education, National Center for Education Statistics. (2001, June). *NAEP 2000 reading report card for the nation and the states.* Available online at nces.ed.Gov/nationsreportcard

Whitehurst, G. J., & Lonigan, C. J. (2001). Emergent literacy: Development from prereaders to readers. In S. B. Neuman & D. K. Dickinson (Eds.), *Handbook of early literacy research*. New York: Guilford.

Foundations of Literacy 3

John A. Smith

Moving on Without Sally

One Wednesday morning I visited a 1st-grade classroom in the school district where I worked as reading coordinator. I recognized Sally, a girl from a summer reading program for at-risk students. I knelt down beside her desk to say a cheerful hello and noticed that she had tears in her eyes. I asked her what was wrong, and she pointed to a pile of 11 worksheets on her desk. The plaintive look in her eyes told me that she didn't understand what to do on the worksheets. Her teacher was in a corner of the classroom with a reading group.

Unfortunately, Sally frequently didn't understand what to do or what was happening during her reading instruction. The problem was that Sally's home environment provided her with very little literacy preparation or support. She seldom observed family members reading and writing. There were virtually no reading or writing materials available to her at home. Nobody read to her. Vacations, dance and music lessons, and other enriching experiences were beyond her family's means.

Sally's lack of literacy preparation put her at a great disadvantage during reading instruction. She didn't know what many of the stories were about. Many of the words she heard and saw were unfamiliar to her. She didn't understand what to do with the letter–sounds that her teacher pronounced. Sally saw many other classmates responding confidently to the teacher and wondered what was wrong with her.

———————   ———————

Beginning reading students who don't have a solid foundation of literacy preparation are at substantial risk for experiencing reading problems. A solid literacy foundation is comprised of four broad areas: (1) facility with **oral language,** including background knowledge and vocabulary, (2) knowledge of letter names and sounds, (3) phonemic awareness, and (4) knowledge of **print conventions.** Although I discuss these four areas one after the other, they should not be considered sequentially or separately. All four areas can be developed very effectively together and will complement and reinforce each other.

Table 3.1 lists the developmental benchmarks for oral language, as well as for reading and writing.

Table 3.1 Oral Language, Reading, and Writing Developmental Benchmarks

Age or Grade	Oral Language	Reading	Writing
Birth to 3 years	Enjoys rhyming and nonsense word play Listens to stories Pretends to read books Comments on characters in books	Recognizes specific books by cover May attend to letters in names and other print	Begins to distinguish between drawing and writing Produces some letterlike forms
3 to 4 years	Pays attention to individual and repeating sounds in spoken words Uses new vocabulary and grammatical constructions in own speech Is aware of some sequences of events in stories Connects story events to personal experiences Questions and comments demonstrate an understanding of the story being told or read	Recognizes that letters are a specific category of graphics that can be individually named Recognizes print in the environment Understands that it is the print that is read in stories Can identify 10 alphabet letters, especially those from own name	Writes or scribbles messages as part of playful activities
Kindergarten	Uses new vocabulary and grammatical constructions in own speech Notices when simple sentences fail to make sense Retells, reenacts, or dramatizes events from stories Can name some favorite titles and authors Demonstrates familiarity with a number of genre types Correctly answers questions about stories read aloud Can identify and blend speech sounds Can produce rhyming words	Begins to track print when being read to Recognizes and can name all upper- and lowercase letters Understands that the sequence of letters in print represents the sequence of sounds in spoken words Learns many one-to-one letter–sound correspondences. Begins to recognize a few common sight words	Independently writes many upper- and lowercase letters Uses phonemic awareness and letter knowledge to attempt to spell words Can spell own name and names of some classmates

Table 3.1 Continued

Age or Grade	Oral Language	Reading	Writing
First Grade	Predicts and justifies what will happen in stories Uses how, why, and what-if questions to discuss stories Discusses prior knowledge of topics in expository text Can count the number of syllables in a word Expands vocabulary and use of formal language	Can read aloud and comprehend text designated for 1st grade Accurately decodes orthographically regular one-syllable words Recognizes common irregularly spelled (is, said, love) words Has a reading vocabulary of 300 to 500 sight words Notices and self-corrects many of own oral reading miscues Can read at least 40 words correctly per minute	Correctly spells three- and four-letter short-vowel words Composes fairly readable first drafts Uses basic punctuation and capitalization
Second Grade	Discusses similarities in characters and events across stories Connects and compares information across nonfiction stories	Reads aloud and comprehends both fiction and nonfiction designated for 2nd grade Accurately decodes orthographically regular multisyllable words Accurately reads many irregularly spelled words and also diphthong and other vowel spelling patterns Rereads sentences when meaning is not clear Interprets information from diagrams, charts, and graphs Can read at least 90 words correctly per minute	Correctly spells previously studied words and spelling patterns in own writing Productively discusses ways to clarify own and others' writing With help, writes well-structured reports Attends to spelling and mechanics for final written products
Third Grade	Summarizes major points from fiction and nonfiction texts Can interpret and discuss themes in stories Uses information and reasoning to examine hypotheses and opinions	Reads aloud and comprehends both fiction and nonfiction designated for 3rd grade Reads longer nonfiction selections and chapter books independently Can clearly identify words or phrases that cause comprehension difficulty Infers word meaning from taught words, prefixes, and suffixes Can read at least 110 words correctly per minute	Correctly spells previously studied words and spelling patterns in own writing Begins to incorporate literacy words and figurative language patterns in own writing With support, uses all aspects of the writing process to produce own compositions and reports Combines information from multiple sources in own writing

ORAL LANGUAGE: A NECESSARY FOUNDATION

Addresses IRA Standard 1.3

Demonstrate knowledge of language development and reading acquisition and the variations related to cultural and linguistic diversity.

Reading instruction begins in infancy as parents speak and read to their children. Facility with oral language and a growing vocabulary are critical foundations upon which young readers must build their understanding of written language. Students who have never heard or don't know the meanings of words that they are being asked to decode are at a severe disadvantage. Adams (1990) points out that many mainstream children experience "thousands of hours of pre-reading activities" (p. 86) at home during their preschool years, but their less fortunate classmates may receive as few as 200 hours of such support. Parents' oral language interactions with their children, including conversations, questions and answers, lullabies, and especially hours engaged with picture books, fairy tales, and Mother Goose, will provide children with the oral language background that serves as the foundation for understanding printed language.

The necessary emphasis on oral language activities at home also applies to classrooms. Unfortunately, research has shown that "many classrooms have a teacher-dominated language environment that does little to promote children's oral language growth" (Christie, Enz, and Vukelich, 1997, p. 89). Such classrooms are characterized by students spending most of their time listening passively to the teacher and responding only to closed-ended questions that have one right answer. Christie et al. suggest that teachers promote "reciprocal discussions and conversations" (p. 91) in which teachers listen carefully to what students have to say and then respond with questions of genuine interest.

The two best ways for classroom teachers to develop students' oral language proficiency are to read aloud to the students frequently and interactively and engage students in frequent language-rich activities. The report of the Commission on Reading, *Becoming a Nation of Readers* (Anderson, Hiebert, Scott, & Wilkinson, 1985) stated that "The single most important activity for building the knowledge required

One literacy learner helps another learn foundations concepts.

for eventual success in reading is reading aloud to children" (p. 23). Oral language activities like sharing time (formerly known as show-and-tell), singing, learning and reciting poetry and nursery rhymes, riddles and jokes, tongue twisters, choral readings, readers' theaters, and classroom discussions give students enjoyable opportunities to listen to and use language. Teachers who read aloud to their students several times each day (see chapter 4) and then follow up immediately with short, genuine discussions of the books' characters, settings,

events, themes, language, and illustrations and, most importantly, the students' personal responses to the books do much to build their students' oral language skills.

FOR ENGLISH LANGUAGE LEARNERS

English Learners Need Oral Language Foundation

ELL students need increased amounts of oral language development activities. Time spent teaching word identification skills will be of little value unless ELL students develop a solid foundation in oral English.

SHARING TIME

When many of us attended elementary school, show-and-tell was a fixture in every primary-grade classroom. Now, as teachers, we hear stories about everything from families taking trips to Disneyland to an account of a dad taking a trip to jail for poaching ducks. We see toys, books, Beanie Babies, science kits, marathon medallions, and many pets, posters, and seashells.

Traditional show-and-tell was often not very effective because one student would make a brief presentation while the others were expected to sit quietly and listen. Discussion was not encouraged. When done properly, sharing time can serve two very important purposes: (1) building students' background knowledge vocabulary and (2) providing students with opportunities to use and develop their oral language skills.

I like to structure sharing time to maximize learning and minimize confusion. I post a sharing time schedule in the classroom on which each student is assigned a day of the week as his or her sharing day throughout the school year. I also send a note home to parents to discourage their children from bringing toys and instead encourage them to bring items or stories of educational value.

The most important aspect of sharing time is the explanation and discussion associated with the items and stories brought to class. I frequently stimulate such sharing time discussion with questions for the sharer such as these:

- Where did you get this?
- How does it work?
- What do you do with it?
- What happened next?
- What did you say (to the people involved)?
- How did you feel about that experience?

I encourage classmates to ask similar questions. When students know they will be invited to ask questions, they are more likely to become active listeners. Seating students in a circle on the carpet or rug during sharing time brings them closer together and enhances opportunities to see an item or hear about an event.

I also encourage parents to participate during sharing time. They often bring pets or items too bulky or fragile for their children to carry to school and provide an excellent opportunity for students to ask questions and learn about the neighborhood and world.

PLAY TIME

Early childhood and literacy educators recognize the vital role of dramatic play in developing young children's oral language skills. The time children spend playing in a classroom shopping center or home-making center is not just for fun and enjoyment. The verbal interactions among children as they engage in imitative and make-believe play provide important opportunities for students to develop their vocabularies and comprehension skills as they hear and use language.

Play experiences support children's ongoing cognitive development. Through play, children learn to understand and respond to the content of oral language, integrate new information into their conceptual understandings, clarify misunderstandings, ask questions, create meaning, and solve problems. These are some of the same thinking processes that children will use as they learn to comprehend written language.

Cooper and Dever (2001) describe a card shop learning center in which students created and exchanged greeting cards. Teacher Jaclyn Cooper showed her 1st-grade students a number of sample greeting cards and then told them that they were going to create a classroom card shop. Together Jaclyn and her students looked through the contents of a prop box that she had assembled, and the students took the responsibility for making signs and additional props that they felt where necessary for their classroom card shop. Jaclyn showed examples of birthday, friendship, holiday, wedding, and thank you cards. She helped the students develop a pricing structure for their cards. The students took on the roles of cashier, clerk, customers, and observers.

The level of student engagement, learning, and motivation was understandably very high as students integrated math, literacy, and art curriculum concepts during their activities in the card shop. Engaging in card shop preparation and activities provided "a meaningful context for the children to practice their developing skills" (Cooper & Dever, 2001, p. 62).

My favorite experiences with play were bringing to class a very large box of my children's older stuffed animals and dolls and letting my students use them to dramatize selected stories that I read during teacher read-aloud. A long piece of plastic PVC sprinkler pipe with a sheet draped over it provided a great stage as the students organized themselves into the roles of narrators, characters, and audiences.

Sylvia Read provides her 2nd-grade students with free time each day when they can play with board games, work puzzles, build with blocks, use the "talking globe," and explore the classroom collection of math **manipulatives.** The students play in twos, threes, and fours, talking about and cooperating on their chosen activity. Like Jaclyn, Sylvia and I find that play activities are invaluable for building not only the social skills of sharing and taking turns, but also the language skills that students will use throughout their lives.

FOR ENGLISH LANGUAGE LEARNERS

Social Interaction

Role-playing games are effective for promoting language acquisition. In role-playing games, students need to interact (and sometimes read) in order to participate. Interactions naturally have comprehensible input, especially when native speakers of English are also participating (Pica, Young, & Doughty, 1987).

NURSERY RHYMES

Nursery rhymes provide wonderful opportunities to build students' vocabulary and oral language skills. The content of the rhymes is delightful and often enchanting to young children. The singsong rhythm and rhyme help to develop phonemic awareness by letting children experience the manipulation of the building block sounds of language.

Unfortunately, many children grow up without opportunities to hear nursery rhymes. Research and the practical experience of many kindergarten teachers have found a direct correlation between children's knowledge of nursery rhymes at the beginning of kindergarten and their reading achievement scores in later years. I remember when teaching **low-SES at-risk students** that many were generally unacquainted with nursery rhymes. One group had such trouble pronouncing the name *Humpty Dumpty* that I eventually gave up and also began calling the unfortunate character Humpy Dumpy.

Students in beginning reading and writing programs should be taught to recite, sing, dramatize, and do many other follow-up activities with nursery rhymes. My students and I enjoy writing nursery rhymes on chart paper (much like language-experience stories), learning to read the nursery rhymes through shared reading, and following up with sentence strip and word card matching activities. Many teachers like to use pocket charts and substitute class members' names into the rhymes or have students generate silly alternative endings to the rhymes. Stuffed animals brought from home also make excellent props for puppet show presentations of nursery rhymes.

Cunningham (2000) suggests dividing the class into two groups and having group 1 say the first two lines of a nursery rhyme, but allowing group 2 to say the rhyming word at the end of the second line. For example:

Group 1 Hickory dickory dock. The mouse ran up the . . .
Group 2 clock.

I need to add a few comments about Dr. Seuss books and other similar rhyming books. Books like *Green Eggs and Ham* offer many opportunities for beginning readers to develop foundation understandings about reading and writing. Texts like *I am Sam. Sam I am . . .* offer experience with word families. The repetition and predictable nature of *Would you, could you in a box? Would you, could you with a fox?* allow young readers to begin participating in the reading process. In fact, the nightly repeated read-alouds of *Green Eggs and Ham* at our home was the key that unlocked the decoding process for our daughter Abbey. The cadence of Bill Martin, Jr., and John Archambault's wonderful books *Chicka Chicka Boom Boom* and *Brown Bear, Brown Bear* helps to support beginning readers' attempts to make sense of print. These and other wonderful books, like Dr. Seuss's *The Foot Book* and *Hop on Pop,* make great read-alouds. The rhyming and repetition support that these books provide to beginning readers make them extremely valuable for independent reading during sustained silent reading.

POETRY

> *My tooth ith loothe! My tooth ith loothe!*
> *I can't go to thchool, that'th my excuthe.*
> *It wath fine latht night when I went to bed,*
> *But today it'th hanging by a thread!*
> *My tooth ith loothe! My tooth ith loothe!*
> *I'm telling you the honetht truth.*
> *It maketh me want to jump and thout!*
> *My tooth ith loothe . . . . oopth! Now ith out!*

"My Tooth Ith Loothe," from *My Tooth Ith Loothe* by George Ulrich, copyright © 1995 by George Ulrich. Used by permission of Random House Children's Books, a division of Random House, Inc.

Like nursery rhymes and rhyming books, poetry also has the power to delight beginning readers and help them to develop insights about the nature of our oral and written language. Poetry should be a regular part of teacher read-alouds, and it also provides a way to make effective use of those occasional spare moments waiting in the lunch line. Our students have benefited from reading, reciting, and illustrating favorite poems. Books of poetry for children by Bruce Lansky, Jack Prelutsky, Shel Silverstein, Michael Spooner, and Michael Strickland provide wonderful read-aloud opportunities for savoring the sounds of language. John Ciardi's delightful book *You Read to Me, I'll Read to You* has poems printed in two colors for reading together with a companion. There are also many wonderfully illustrated poetry anthologies available. One of my personal favorites is *Sing a Song of Popcorn* (de Regniers et al., 1988) in which the poems were illustrated by Caldecott Award winning artists.

One of my favorite classroom poetry activities is to read a poem aloud to my students, discuss it, copy it onto an overhead transparency, and then project it onto the chalkboard for choral reading. I also distribute printed copies of the poems to each of my students to practice reading, illustrate, and take home.

Harwayne (1992) provides many suggestions for using poetry to stimulate students' love for words, language, and literature. She suggests encouraging students to keep favorite poems in their writer's notebooks and to use the poems as a seedbed for writing ideas. First-grade teacher Vicki Olson has her students read and memorize favorite poems that they add to their personal poetry collection and take home at the end of the year. It was not uncommon for Vicki's entire class to march unannounced into my classroom at any time of the school day, recite a newly learned poem in unison, and then smugly march back out.

SINGING

Some of my most enjoyable instructional experiences have been developing students' oral language through singing (Smith, 2000). Fifteen to twenty minutes of singing each day develops a wonderful sense of classroom community and warmth. Singing also provides an opportunity for students to hear and use many words in an enjoyable and meaningful context.

Many classroom teachers are intimidated by music, feeling that a degree from a music conservatory or a Grammy Award is necessary. Not so. It is perfectly acceptable to sing unaccompanied with the students or to strum the simple children's song chords on an autoharp or guitar. I have had many delightful experiences displaying enlarged, printed song lyrics and then having the students sing along with a cassette or CD player.

It is helpful to write and display the song lyrics in large print on chart paper. We attach a coat hanger (with the hanger's hook extending above the top of the chart) to the back of each chart with adhesive tape. This allows for easy display, changing, and storage in a classroom closet. You may also find it handy to hang the song lyric charts on an inexpensive, portable, clothesrack on wheels, available at many department stores.

Each day I designate a student as the "song chooser" and another as the "song pointer." The song chooser gets to select a song for the day from the growing "Songs We Know" list displayed on the wall. I also get to choose a song or two. The song pointer uses a yardstick or other pointing device to point to the words on the chart

Singing can help children develop phonemic awareness.

(usually line by line rather than word by word) as the class and I sing. The pointing process helps beginning readers to match the words they are singing to their printed representations on the chart paper.

Song lyric charts provide wonderful opportunities for spontaneous discussions of background knowledge, vocabulary, and spelling patterns. For example, when singing the ever-popular John Denver song "Grandma's Featherbed," it is important to begin by activating students' background knowledge with a class discussion of what the students see and do during their own occasional visits to their grandparents. It is also important to discuss the meaning of unfamiliar words and expressions from that song such as *bolt of cloth, tick, ballad, cobwebs filled my head,* and of course *featherbed.* I also take an occasional opportunity to use the printed lyrics on the charts to point out that *featherbed* and *homemade* are compound words or that *wake, made, whole,* and *wide* follow the CV_e pattern.

Rosenblatt (1980) cautions against analyzing the print and grammatical features of literary works because this may diminish the quality of students' esthetic experiences with these works. My personal experience with teaching literacy through singing is that singing and enjoying the songs first and then using the printed song lyrics to highlight common spelling patterns and word parts does not diminish students' enthusiasm for learning and singing the songs. Instead, focusing on some print features and word meanings increases students' ability to participate more fully in the enjoyment of the songs.

Singing existing children's and folk songs is an easy way to get started. You can find appropriate songs in your own music collections at home, in the children's sections at libraries and music stores, and especially from friends and the students themselves. Popular children's song singers like Raffi and artists from *Sesame Street* are a great source of delightful children's songs. Public and university libraries generally have anthologies of American folk songs, often including lyrics, chords, melody lines, and background notes (Lomax, 1960).

Echo songs are extremely popular with younger students. The song "Polly Wolly Doodle" lends itself well to dividing the class into two groups and having one group sing the first part of each line and the other sing the echo part (the "Polly Wollys"). The groups trade parts on each verse.

Group 1	*Group 2*
Oh, I went down south to see my Sal,	(Singing Polly Wolly Doodle all the day)
My Sal she is a spunky gal.	(Singing Polly Wolly Doodle all the day)
My Sal she is a maiden fair,	(Singing Polly Wolly Doodle all the day)
With curly eyes and laughing hair.	(Singing Polly Wolly Doodle all the day)

Another song that works the same way is "The Other Day I Met a Bear."

Group 1	*Group 2*
The other day	(The other day)
I met a bear	(I met a bear)
Out in the woods	(Out in the woods)
Away out there	(Away out there)
[Then all together:]	
The other day I met a bear,	
Out in the woods away out there.	

Another option for using music to build students' language facility is to adapt or rewrite existing song lyrics based on their existing patterns (McCracken & Mc-Cracken, 1998). For example, our students enjoyed rewriting the line from the song "Skip to My Lou" that says "Chicken in the breadpan pickin' out dough." I noticed the pattern *animal, place,* and *action* in that line and used it to generate many original lyrics with my students. For example:

	Animal	*Place*	*Action*
1.	monkeys	at McDonald's	eatin' all the fries
2.	bears	in the bathroom	soakin' in the tub
3.	cows	at Disneyland	riding Space Mountain

My students and I sing each line three times followed by "Skip to my Lou my darling." The list in Figure 3.1 contains familiar songs with easy melodies and repetitive patterns that lend themselves to classroom song-writing activities. For example, the melody to "Twinkle Twinkle Little Star" worked well for our short- and long-vowel songs:

> *Short a sounds like bat bat bat,*
> *Long a sounds like bait bait bait.*
>
> *Short e sounds like set set set,*
> *Long e sounds like seat seat seat.*

Figure 3.1   Simple Melodies for Classroom Song Writing

A-Hunting We Will Go

Are You Sleeping

Buffalo Gals

Crawdad Song

Did You Ever See a Lassie

Go Tell Aunt Rhody

Head, Shoulders, Knees, and Toes

Here We Go 'Round the Mulberry Bush

If You're Happy and You Know It

It Ain't Gonna Rain No More

Jimmy Cracked Corn

Lazy Mary, Will You Get Up

London Bridge

She'll be Comin' Round the Mountain

Shortnin' Bread

The Ants Go Marching

The Bear Went over the Mountain

The Wheels on the Bus

Three Blind Mice

Short i sounds like bit bit bit,
Long i sounds like bite bite bite.

Short o sounds like not not not,
Long o sounds like note note note.

Short u sounds like cut cut cut,
Long u sounds like cute cute cute.

The chorus to the song is sung after each verse and goes like this:

Vowels are short, and vowels are long,
Oh, we love to sing this song.

TEACHING THE NAMES AND SOUNDS OF THE ALPHABET LETTERS

Researchers have found "the best predictor of beginning reading achievement to be a child's knowledge of letter names" (Adams, 1990, p. 61) and have given several

FOR ENGLISH LANGUAGE
LEARNERS

CREDE Standards for Effective Pedagogy and Learning

CREDE (Center for Research on Education, Diversity, and Excellence) has five standards for developing all students' language regardless of their culture or ethnicity.

1. Joint productive activity: students and teachers should be engaged together in learning activities.

2. Developing language across the curriculum: throughout the school day during all activities, teachers should be working to develop students' language abilities through purposeful conversation, rather than through drills and the teaching of decontextualized rules.

3. Making meaning (Connecting School to Students' Lives): the abstract concepts of school learning need to be applied to experiences in students' everyday world for maximum learning to take place.

4. Teaching complex thinking: students should be given a challenging curriculum so that they stay engaged in learning.

5. Teaching Through Conversation: during instructional conversation, teachers listen carefully to students, guessing at their meaning and adjusting their responses accordingly so that students' efforts at conversation and learning are supported and extended.

explanations for this finding. First, a child who can already name the letters has an easier time learning about letter–sounds and spelling patterns than a child who is still learning the letters. Second, children who are confident with letters are in a better position to focus on words and recognize that words are composed of patterns of letters. Third, the sounds of many letters closely resemble their names, providing an easy transition from names to sounds. Understanding this connection between the letters and their sounds, called the **alphabetic principle,** is a critical first step toward the ability to decode words.

TEACHING LETTER NAMES

Alphabet Song

Perhaps the most common activity for beginning to teach the names of the alphabet letters is the "ABC Song," sung to the tune of "Twinkle Twinkle Little Star." Many students entering kindergarten already know this song. Kindergarten and first-grade teachers should sing this song frequently at the beginning of the school year and regularly thereafter.

When all students can sing the song proficiently, display a chart like that in Figure 3.2 that corresponds to the song and point to the printed letters as the students sing, much like choral reading with a big book.

Sing through the "ABC Song" several times. Then focus on singing and pointing to the letters in just the first two lines (a, b, c, d; e, f, g). Next, ask students to come to the chart and point to the letters that you name ("Who can come to the chart and point to the letter *e*?" "Who can come to the chart and point to the letter *b*?"). It is heartwarming to watch a beginning student identify a printed letter on the Alphabet Song Chart, silently singing the song while simultaneously counting the letters on the chart to make the connection. When students are ready, you can invite them to do the pointing to the printed letters on the Alphabet Song Chart as the class sings along.

A natural follow-up activity is to distribute printed alphabet letter cards (or plastic magnetic alphabet letters) corresponding to the letters being learned and ask, "Who has the letter _____? Would you bring it to the chart and hold it next to the printed letter _____?" By cumulatively adding a line at a time (h, i, j, k) and reviewing letters already learned this way, you can quickly and easily help students to learn to identify the names of the alphabet letters. (The "l, m, n, o, p" line is often a real eye-opener to many students.)

Figure 3.2 Alphabet Song Chart

Alphabet Concentration

You can also play a classroom version of the game Concentration to reinforce the students' learning the letter names. Introduce the game to the whole class by writing two copies of about six alphabet letters on index cards and displaying them (backward) in a pocket chart or on a tabletop. Have students take turns trying to match the pairs of letters. Small groups can play the game as a follow-up center activity. A variation of this game is to have students match index cards, one with an alphabet letter and the other with a picture of an object that begins with that letter.

Student-Illustrated Alphabet Books

Individual student-illustrated ABC books are popular. Prepare a 26-page "book" for each student with the upper- and lowercase letters printed in the upper-left corner of each page. Don't forget to include an attractive front and back cover. Over a month's time, help students to identify and illustrate objects on the appropriate letter page of the book. Encourage students to review the letters by sharing their books with partners.

Student-illustrated ABC books for more advanced students may include a complete sentence describing a familiar object or concept on each page, along with illustrations. For example:

*Sometimes there is an **a**pple on the teacher's desk.*
*There are **b**ooks all around in our classroom.*
*Our **c**lass really likes to write.*
*We like to **d**ance to fast music.*

Alphabet Flashcards

Perhaps the most time-honored approach to teaching alphabet letters is direct teaching with alphabet flashcards. Using a set of these, begin with the first five letters and review them with small groups of your students. When all students in the group can recognize all five letters instantly, add another letter and review all six letters. Then add one more letter and review until all students can recognize seven letters instantly. For many students, this will be enough for one day.

The next day, reassemble the group, review the seven letters from yesterday, then add an eighth and a ninth letter and review. The number of letters added each day depends on how quickly group members make progress in recognizing them instantly. As you introduce and review alphabet letter flashcards, try to make sure that your students connect the flashcards to the alphabet letters displayed above the chalkboard, on the word wall, and on other classroom print.

FOR STRUGGLING READERS

Recognizing Alphabet Letters

For students who lag behind in recognizing alphabet letters, do the flashcard activity individually, using only the letters from the student's own name. Help the student locate the same letters displayed in classroom print.

Other Alphabet Activities

Many other activities will help students to learn the names of the letters. For example, you can ask four or five students to come to the front of the classroom and give each one an alphabet letter card (c, d, e, f, g) in random order; then ask them to hold up the cards so that all the classmates can see them. Then ask the students to reorder themselves to put the cards in proper alphabetical order.

Another alphabet game is called I Spy. Write an alphabet letter (b) on the chalkboard and ask students to look around the classroom and find objects that begin with this letter (books, baskets, bottles, boxes). Write these words on the board and reinforce the letter's name and sound. A variation of this game is to say to the students, "I'm thinking of a student whose name begins with _____."

Send a note home asking parents to help their children to find and bring to school large printed letters in newspaper and magazine advertisements; then use these letters to construct a class-made alphabet song chart. This will help students to be more aware of printed letters in their environment.

TEACHING LETTER NAMES AND SOUNDS

Many students will learn the sounds of the alphabet letters during the activities already described because many letters have a sound that is similar to their names (b, d, f, j, k, l, m, n, p, r, s, t, v, x, z). Students will also learn that the vowel letters' names are the same as their long sounds.

Using Students' Names

Cunningham (2000) has shown that students' names can provide an effective vehicle to teach the alphabet letter names and sounds. She begins by writing each student's name on a piece of oaktag or index card. Then she prepares a classroom bulletin board where all these name cards will eventually be displayed. Pat selects one name card (for example, Abbey) and attaches it to the board. She points out that this *word* has five *letters* and pronounces the letters to the children. She chants the letters with the children and points out any other peculiarities, such as "Becca's name has two *c*s and contains the first three letters of the alphabet." She reminds the students to watch as she prints the word *Becca* on a second card. She cuts this second card into individual letters, mixes up the order of the letters, and has the students reassemble the letters in the proper order. Finally, Pat has each student write the word *Becca* on one side of a piece of paper and then draw a picture of Becca on the other side.

The next day Pat adds another student's name to the board and repeats the process. Then she draws her students' attention to the letters again as she compares the two names. Which name has more letters? How many more letters does the longer name have? Do the two names have any letters in common?

Pat repeats this procedure each day by adding another name to the bulletin board and going through the examining and comparing process. Other activities include giving each student an alphabet card, pronouncing a student's name, and then having the students with the letters in the name come to the front of the room to physically spell the name with the cards. When all of the name cards are on the bulletin board, the names can be categorized into columns by number of letters.

Alphabet Wall

Wagstaff (1999) describes how to use an ABC Wall to teach the alphabet. Developed as an alternative to the traditional "letter of the week" instruction common in many kindergartens, Janiel wanted a faster and more practical way to introduce the alphabet. An ABC Wall consists of the upper- and lowercase alphabet letters arrayed in three rows (a–i, j–r, s–z) across the wall on a large piece of butcher paper, with room below each row for adding word cards and illustrations. Each week Janiel focuses on two alphabet letters. She and her students select and display a key word on a word card and an illustration of the key word below each selected consonant. There are two key words and illustrations for each vowel, for the short and long sounds.

She begins her ABC Wall activities each week by reading a nursery rhyme, poem, or other chant together with her students to bring attention to the sounds of our words. Then she and her students select (harvest) key words from the rhymes to represent alphabet letters on the ABC Wall. Janiel then prints the key word on a word card and invites a student to make an illustration. These are added to the ABC Wall. She spends the next several days involving her students in a variety of activities using the ABC Wall to strengthen their letter-sound knowledge and phonemic awareness. These include forming, sorting, and hunting for letters and words. Janiel and her students refer to the ABC Wall continually as a resource during most of their reading and writing activities.

Link to Action Words

Cunningham (2000) suggests teaching the letter sounds by linking action words to each alphabet letter. For example, an action words alphabet chart could include the words *bounce, catch, dance, . . . , vacuum, walk, yawn, zip.* With the students standing beside their desks, the teacher displays the chart and calls out a letter name. The students then do the corresponding action. A variation of this activity is to have a student come to the front of the class, choose an alphabet letter, and perform the corresponding action and then have the other students identify which letter was chosen. During these activities, you should frequently remind students of the connection between the beginning sound of the action word and the sound of the first letter in the word.

FOR STRUGGLING READERS

Word Identification Lessons

Some teachers believe that they should not begin formal reading instruction until students have 100% mastery of the alphabet letter names and sounds. Research and experience suggest otherwise. Many students who struggle to learn the alphabet letters may learn them more easily and inductively within the context of beginning word identification lessons.

Alphabet Books

An increasing number of captivating alphabet books are available to teachers and students. A few favorites are listed in Figure 3.3. I enjoy introducing these books as read-alouds and discussing the delightful concepts and vocabulary contained in the illustrations. The students then love to reread the alphabet books individually during **SSR** or together on the couch with a classmate, parent, or other classroom volunteer.

Direct Teaching of Letter Names and Sounds

Some teachers may prefer a more explicit approach to teaching alphabet letter names and sounds. Such instruction makes a nice complement to the activities described previously when students are in need of a more structured approach. You may choose to do **direct instruction** with the whole class or with a group of students using an alphabet chart or with individual students using a personal-sized (8.5 by 11 inches) alphabet chart. Alphabet charts with an illustration for each letter corresponding to its sound are most effective. Direct instruction involves a simple three-step procedure: (1) naming the letter for the students, (2) asking the students to repeat the letter name, and (3) the students give you the letter name. For example:

1. You point to the letter *a* and say, "This is the letter *a.* It makes the sound /*a*/."
2. You ask, "What's this letter?"
3. The students respond "*a.*"

Follow the same procedure for the letter *b* and then go back and review the letter *a* by pointing to the letter and asking, "What's this letter?" If the students can't remember the name of letter *a,* then reteach the letter *a* using the three-step procedure again. As more letter names are learned, you can review the previously learned letter names in random order. Cumulatively go through the letter names teaching, reviewing when necessary, and adding more letters.

The same three-step procedure may also be used to teach letter sounds.

1. You point to the letter *a* and say, "The letter *a* makes the sound /*a*/."
2. You ask, "What sound does the letter *a* make?"
3. The students respond "/*a*/."

Figure 3.3   Some Favorite Alphabet Books

A Is for Asia by Cynthia Chin-Lee. New York: Orchard, 1997.

A Mountain Alphabet by Margriet Ruurs and Andrew Kiss. New York: Tundra Books, 1996.

Alpha Bugs: A Pop-up Alphabet Book by David A. Carter. New York: Little Simon, 1994.

Alphabet Adventure by Audrey Wood. New York: Blue Sky Press, 2001.

The Alphabet Tree by Leo Lionni. New York: Dragonfly Books, 1990.

Alphabet under Construction by Denise Fleming. New York: Henry Holt, 2002.

Anno's Alphabet by Mitsumas Anno. New York: Crowell, 1975.

Antelope, Bison, Cougar: A National Wildlife Alphabet Book by Steven Medley. Boston: Houghton Mifflin, 2002.

Antler, Bear, Canoe: A Northwoods Alphabet Year by Betsy Bowen. New York: Little Brown,1991.

Chicka Chicka Boom Boom by Bill Martin and John Archambault. New York: Simon & Schuster, 1989.

Dr. Seuss's ABC by Dr. Seuss. New York: Random House, 1991.

Eating the Alphabet: Fruits and Vegetables from A–Z by Lois Short. San Diego: Harcourt Brace, 1989.

Eh? to Zed: A Canadian Abecedarium by Kevin Major and Alan Daniel. Red Deer, Alberta: Red Deer College Press, 2003.

The Graphic Alphabet. by David Pelletier. New York: Orchard, 1996.

Kipper's A to Z by Mick Inkpen. San Diego: Harcourt Brace, 2000.

Maisy's ABC by Lucy Cousins. Cambridge, MA: Candlewick Press, 1995.

My Pop-up Surprise ABC by Robert Crowther. New York: Orchard Books, 1997.

Navajo ABC: A Dine Alphabet Book by Luci Tapahonso and Eleanor Schick. New York: Aladdin, 1999.

Parading with Piglets by Biruta Akerbergs-Hansen. Washington, DC: National Geographic Society, 1996.

Prairie Primer A to Z by Caroline Stutson. New York: Dutton, 1999.

Q Is for Duck by Mary Elting and Michael Folsom. New York: Clarion, 1985.

Robert Crowther's Most Amazing Hide-And-Seek Alphabet Book by Robert Crowther. Cambridge. MA: Candlewick Press, 1999.

The Z Was Zapped by Chris Van Allsburg. Boston: Houghton Mifflin, 1987.

My experience is that not all students require this level of explicitness to learn the alphabet letters and sounds. I believe that beginning reading and writing instruction should be relaxed, enjoyable for the students, and gamelike. I recommend using this more structured model of instruction only for those students who need it and who learn effectively from it.

DON'T WAIT

You will notice that some students are having a difficult time learning the names and sounds of the letters. Memorizing alphabet letters' names and sounds is rote learning, much like learning people's names or phone numbers. The important principle here is that it is not necessary to postpone formal decoding instruction until a student has learned all the letter names and sounds perfectly. Decoding instruction includes constant use of the letter names and sounds, and many students will learn these more easily from hearing and seeing them used in the context of decoding lessons. Other students learn the alphabet letter names and sounds most readily by using their personal alphabet charts and books to figure out the sounds that they want to use in their writing.

HELPING STUDENTS DEVELOP PHONEMIC AWARENESS

WHAT IS PHONEMIC AWARENESS?

Phonemic awareness is the understanding that speech is composed of discrete sounds and that these sounds can be joined in varying combinations to form words (Neuman & Dickinson, 2001). Research has found consistently that students' levels of phonemic awareness and letter recognition are the two best predictors of first-grade reading achievement (Adams, 1990).

Phonemes are the smallest individual sounds of speech. The word *cat* has three letters and three phonemes: /c/ /a/ /t/. The word *choose* has six letters, but only three phonemes: /ch/ /oo/ /z/. Three levels of understanding are associated with phonemic awareness: (1) streams of speech can be segmented into discrete words, (2) spoken words can be segmented into syllables, and (3) words and syllables can be segmented into individual speech sounds that can be manipulated and combined to produce other words.

Phonemic awareness instruction might be thought of as prephonics or phonics without printed letters. Children entering kindergarten have 5 years of experience using oral language from listening and speaking. They can intuitively segment and make sense of streams of speech sounds; conversely, they can use the sounds of speech to communicate their thoughts and feelings to others. For example, if we want to know if a student has had lunch, we think the three-word question *Did you eat?*; however, we usually pronounce only one syllable, "*Jeet?*" Our student hears *jeet?,* interprets its meaning and replies, "*Yes, Joo?*" However, these young language users don't yet realize that these streams of speech are composed of individual words and that these words are composed of syllables and phonemes.

WHY IS PHONEMIC AWARENESS SO IMPORTANT?

The understanding that speech is composed of discrete sounds that can be manipulated and blended is the foundation for the understanding that print is composed of letters, with their associated sounds, that by **manipulating** sounds and **blending** them we make printed words. Research (Ehri, 1994a, 1994b; National Reading Panel, 2000) has identified several ways that people read words.

1. When encountering an unfamiliar word, a reader will often blend the sounds of its individual letters. This involves converting each letter in the word to its associated letter–sound (**phoneme**) and then blending the phonemes to produce a pronunciation that hopefully matches a word in the reader's oral vocabulary. Instruction in blending letter–sounds supports this way of reading.

2. When encountering an unfamiliar word, a reader will focus on word parts. This is known as structural analysis or reading by analogy (Cunningham, 2000). The reader compares the parts of an unfamiliar word (v/at) to the parts of familiar

words (b/at, c/at, f/at) and then makes substitutions to produce a pronunciation ("I know *v* and I know *at,* so together they must form the word *vat*"). Generally, readers will break the unfamiliar printed word into its beginning and ending parts, known as **onsets** and **rimes** (s/ing), and then think of other words with the same ending and combine the beginning of the unfamiliar word with the familiar word ending. Reading instruction featuring word families supports this way of reading.

3. Readers will simply recognize and remember many familiar words. These are known as a reader's sight words or sight vocabulary. Many words decoded by ways 1 and 2 become sight words through repetition. Regular independent reading and word wall activities help promote the development of sight vocabulary.

Phonemic awareness instruction provides a foundation for each of these three ways of reading. Phoneme blending activities teach students the concept of blending speech sounds. Once students understand this, it is easier to blend the sounds associated with printed letters. Phoneme segmentation activities teach students to analyze words into their individual spoken parts. This is a necessary skill for reading printed words by analogy. Finally, a student's ability to associate letters and sounds and to blend these sounds helps to develop the mental glue that strengthens the associations that lead to remembering words by sight.

It is important to remember that good readers use all three ways of reading printed words flexibly, simultaneously, and automatically. Good instruction helps beginning readers develop all three ways of reading words.

Adams (1990) concludes that "knowledge of letters and phonemic awareness were found to bear strong and direct relationship to success and ease of reading acquisition, and both seem to do so regardless of the approach through which reading per se is taught" (p. 82). In fact, Juel, Griffith, and Gough (1986) argue that children lacking phonemic awareness are unlikely to benefit fully from phonics instruction. We have observed the frustration and failure felt by beginning readers who have been asked to decode or spell words in reading lessons when they still don't understand the underlying principle of isolating and then blending together the sounds.

GUIDELINES FOR TEACHING PHONEMIC AWARENESS

Phonemic awareness (PA) instruction generally consists of teaching children to identify, segment, manipulate, and blend phonemes. Members of the National Reading Panel (2000) formulated the following guidelines after reviewing 52 phonemic awareness research studies.

1. **Keep it simple and explicit.** The panel concluded that "focusing instruction on one or two skills was significantly more effective for teaching phonemic awareness than focusing on multiple skills" (p. 2–20). Students who are taught three or more phonemic awareness skills may become overloaded or confused as to when to apply the skills.

2. **Teach students to segment and blend phonemes.** The panel found that two types of phonemic awareness skills, segmenting and blending, were "most directly involved in reading and spelling processes (p. 2–21).

3. **Include printed letters.** The panel concluded that "PA training is more effective when children are taught to use letters to manipulate phonemes. This is because knowledge of letters is essential for transfer to reading and writing" (p. 2–41). Some educators argue that the introduction of printed letters

constitutes a move away from phonemic awareness instruction to phonics. I see it instead as a natural and necessary transition from one to the other.

4. **Teach phonemic awareness to students in small groups.** The panel found that instructional effects for teaching small groups were "over twice the size" of effects when teaching individual students or the whole class together (p. 2–22).

5. **Keep it short.** The panel also found that "PA instruction does not need to be lengthy to exert its strongest effect on reading and spelling" (p. 2–22). PA instruction lasting 5 to 18 hours spread out over a number of weeks was more effective than longer and shorter instructional programs. In fact, "the lengthiest training was associated with the smallest effect size" (p. 2–29). Assessment of students' instructional needs is the best indicator of how much phonemic awareness training is necessary.

Remember that phonemic awareness training is a means to an end. It is a beginning step on the long and complex road to reading fluency and comprehension.

Phonemic awareness activities are an important supplement to children's interactions with meaningful print. Adams (1990) reports that phonemic awareness training is most effective when coupled with reading instruction. A few minutes spent in daily phonemic awareness activities provides the necessary foundation that beginning readers need to make the transition from oral language to print language.

Phonemic awareness is best nurtured through exploring and playing with the sounds of language. These activities involve the printed text and also oral language activities. Tongue twisters, jump-rope rhymes, pig Latin, singing, poems, and nursery rhymes all provide enjoyable opportunities for students to explore and play with the sounds of language. For some students, phonemic awareness activities are easy and fun. For others, these activities can compensate for inadequate preparation for literacy learning and help to provide success in beginning reading.

Phonemic awareness instruction usually follows a sequence that develops a student's basic awareness of the speech sounds of language and then shows how these sounds can be manipulated in a variety of ways to form words. Many phonemic awareness programs begin with *rhyming* activities and games. These activities sensitize students to the sounds of language, an often overlooked aspect of language, as people generally attend to the meaning-conveying aspects of language. Activities that follow rhyming generally focus on *segmenting* sentences into words, words into syllables, and syllables into sounds (Adams, Foorman, Lundberg, & Beeler, 1998). These are the building blocks of spoken and written language. The final set of phonemic awareness activities focuses on *blending* and *manipulating* speech sounds (phonemes) into words.

It is important to keep records as to which students have mastered phonemic awareness concepts and which need additional instruction. We suggest doing phonemic awareness instructional activities with the whole class or small groups as needed. Then, as time permits, pull individual students aside and ask them to do the activities individually as an assessment measure. Chapter 10 contains several phonemic awareness assessments that will be helpful in monitoring your students' acquisition of these important foundational concepts.

DEVELOPING PHONEMIC AWARENESS

Recognizing Speech Sounds

The following simple activity is an easy way to get students to listen consciously to the sounds in spoken words:

Teacher   Who can tell me a word that begins with the same sound as the word bed?
Students   bat, breakfast, ball, blue, Benjamin, braids

Rhyming

The most basic of rhyming activities is to ask students for rhyming words. The following example describes a simple playful rhyming activity:

Teacher   Who can tell me a word that rhymes with cat?
Students   bat, mat, fat, hat, sat
Teacher   Who can tell me a word that rhymes with bed?
Students   said, fed, head, red, Ted
Teacher   Who can tell me a word that rhymes with go?
Students   snow, slow, no, toe, show

Adams et al. (1998) suggest a "rhyming phrases" variation of this activity. Pronounce a phrase and invite students to complete it with a rhyming word.

Teacher   I know a *cat* who's wearing a _____.
Students   hat
Teacher   I see a *goat* that is sailing a _____.
Students   boat
Teacher   Airplanes *fly* up in the _____.
Students   sky

You can use songs and poems for a variety of rhyming activities. For example, sing or recite two rhyming lines from a song or poem and ask the students to listen for and identify the rhyming words.

Teacher   Humpty Dumpty sat on a wall,
               Humpty Dumpty had a great fall.
               Which two words rhyme?
Students   wall and fall

Cunningham (2000) suggests a variation of this activity. Have one group of student recite the two rhyming lines of a familiar song or nursery rhyme, but leave the second rhyming word for the other group to pronounce.

Group 1   Little Miss Muffet, sat on a _____.
Group 2   tuffet

Counting Words in Sentences

Students need to understand that spoken sentences are comprised of discrete words. This understanding will help students to segment sounds within individual words. Begin by pronouncing a brief sentence in regular speech tempo. A phrase or line from a familiar nursery rhyme works well. Say the sentence slowly, pausing between the words, and ask the students to count the words in the sentence.

Teacher   I'm going to say part of a nursery rhyme.
               You count the number of words I say: Jack – and – Jill.
Students   three
Teacher   Mary had a little lamb.

Students	five
Teacher	It is time for lunch.
Students	five (or yay)!

Students especially like it when you use short statements about them for this activity.

Teacher	Shanika has new shoes.
Students	four
Teacher	Michael ate three hot dogs.
Students	five

For classes needing more support with this, you can begin by holding up a finger as you pronounce each word. Then gradually fade out using your fingers.

This activity can make a nice complement to LEA activities. Select a few sentences from an LEA chart. Pronounce them slowly as the students listen and count. Then point to the printed words on the chart to further reinforce the concept of individual words comprising a sentence. Shorter sentences from read-alouds also work well. After reading aloud the last sentence from *Where the Wild things Are,* "And it was still hot," ask the students how many words are in the sentence. Then write the sentence on the chalkboard and help the student to count the printed words as you point to them and pronounce them again.

Counting Syllables

This is a natural follow-up when teaching students to segment speech sounds. Begin by pronouncing and clapping a student's name and explaining how many syllables (or *beats*) it contains. Repeat the process with other students' names. Using names of popular television and movie characters, singers, athletes, foods, and animals provides variety.

Next, pronounce some names and have the students clap along and count the beats. Call on students to suggest a name. Other actions, such as stamping feet, snapping fingers, slapping thighs, and tapping pencils, can replace clapping.

A natural follow-up is to categorize the students' names into number-of-syllables columns on the chalkboard. For example:

One	*Two*	*Three*	*Four*
Trent	Stevie	Erika	Alexander
Blake	Miesha	Cassidy	
Mark	Riley	Shanika	
Tim	Kiley	Allison	
Jai	Maggie	Jeremy	
	Missey	Maria	
	Jose	Laticia	
	Taylor		
	Whitney		

These columns provide a nice printed representation of the syllables. You can construct and display around the room syllable charts categorizing other groups of words (foods, famous people, animals, classroom objects).

I've enjoyed counting syllables as an every-pupil-response time-filler activity. For example, while standing in the lunch line, I pronounce a word and count, "One, two, three." At the count of three, each student holds up the number of fingers corresponding to the number of syllables in the word. This method of responding lets me see instantly which students are correct and confident, which are less correct and confident, and which will need additional instruction and practice.

Blending Sounds

Teaching students to blend speech sounds is an important precursor to their blending the sounds represented by letters in print. Pronounce the individual sounds of a simple CVC (consonant–vowel–consonant) word and let the students blend and pronounce the word back to you. For example:

Teacher   I'm thinking of a secret word that has three sounds. Listen to the three sounds and then put the sounds together in your mind and see if you can tell me what the secret word is. Here are the three sounds: /h/ /a/ /t/.

Students   hat

Repeat the process with other CVC words. When the students become proficient with CVC words, challenge them with four-letter words beginning or ending with consonant blends (play, grin, stop, past, hold, jump). This activity is especially motivating if you have a hand puppet that will pronounce sounds. Refer to Appendix A for a list of CVC words and words with consonant blends.

Blending Sounds with Printed Letters

When students demonstrate that they are catching on to the concept of blending, repeat the activity, this time including the printed letters along with the sounds. Select three students to stand in front and hold up cards that spell the word *big.* Have the cards a foot or so apart from each other. Pronounce each sound while pointing to the card, and then ask students to mentally blend the three sounds and then say the word. Have the three students holding the cards move together side by side so that the word is shown unbroken. Repeat the blending process while the students hold the cards together.

Manipulating Sounds

This activity gives students an opportunity to combine the two important phonemic awareness skills of segmenting and blending speech sounds. Begin this activity by saying to the students:

Listen to the sounds in the word cat. *If I took off the first sound /c/ and made the word start with /b/ instead, what new word would it make?*   (bat)

Repeat this process with other *at* family words. When students become proficient at substituting the initial consonants orally, do the game with final consonants:

Listen to the sounds in the word mom. *If I took off the last sound /m/ and made the word end with the sound /p/, what new word would it make?* (mop)

Again, repeat this process until the students become confident in substituting final consonants. You can now make the activity more challenging by alternating the substituting of initial and final consonants or even do both at the same time.

Listen to the sounds in the word pin. *If I took off the first sound /p/ AND the last sound /n/ and made the word begin with the sound /f/ AND end with the sound /t/, what new word would it make?   (fit)*

When students demonstrate proficiency with manipulating sounds, it is fun to string together a series of these sound manipulations, sometimes substituting the vowel letter:

1. *Ok, students, listen to the sounds in the word* sad. *If I take off the first sound /s/ and put on a new first sound /m/, what new word will it make?   (mad)*

2. *Now, if I take that word* mad *and take off the last sound /d/ and put on a new last sound /p/, what new word will it make?   (map)*

3. *Now, if I take the word* map *and take out the middle sound /a/ and put in a new middle sound /o/, what new word will it make?   (mop)*

4. *Now, if I take off the first sound /m/ and put on a new first sound /t/, what new sound will it make?   (top)*

5. *Repeat this process with more words.*

As students become proficient, another variation is to use words that include consonant blends:

Listen to the sounds in the word cat. *If I take off the first sound /c/ and made the word begin with the sounds /f/ AND /l/, what new word will it make?   (flat)*

Manipulating sounds is an easy activity to do during reading instruction time or spontaneously during the occasional few extra minutes during transition times. It is important to keep phonemic awareness instruction playful. Parents can also be encouraged to do this substitution game around the dinner table with their young children. Students who can make these substitutions orally will be well prepared to make them with printed letters during formal reading instruction.

Manipulating Sounds with Printed Letters

A natural follow-up to phonemic awareness instruction is to do the same activities and including printed letters. As you introduce printed letters to associate with their sounds, you are making the transition from phonemic awareness instruction to actual phonics instruction. Using print–sound activities to extend and reinforce phonemic awareness instruction can enhance students' understanding of the connections between spoken and printed language (Adams et al., 1998).

I love to teach sound and letter blending and manipulating by printing each of the alphabet letters on a Post-It note. Then I display the 26 Post-It notes on the chalkboard, use three of the letters to form the word *cat,* and then say to the students:

Look here. I've made the word cat. *Now, watch while I take off the letter* c *and put the letter* b *in its place. Now it makes the word* bat.

Model this process a few more times with other *at* family words. Then invite the students to make the manipulations:

Look here. I've made the word hat. *Now, who can come up here and move the letters to change the word* hat *to* mat?

Again, when students become proficient at physically manipulating the initial consonants, have them manipulate final consonants and then both ("Who can change *cat* to *ran*?"). Also, repeat the process with the other vowel letters. We have found that many students can learn the short-vowel sounds inductively through these activities. This letter manipulation activity can also be done with plastic alphabet letters displayed on an overhead projector.

We have also found it effective to display a word family chart while doing the letter manipulation activities. After the game, lead the students in reading the word family charts. This allows them to apply the letter manipulation skill in a different context. In keeping this instruction playful, we like to read the word family lists with variety. This includes reading the lists in Daddy Bear and Baby Bear voices, from bottom to top, in various student groupings, and in varying volumes.

Writing

As students write (using **invented spellings**), they necessarily go through the processes of listening for, segmenting, and organizing the sounds in the words they want to put on paper. A daily writing journal serves this purpose well. You should model this process at the beginning of the year by drawing a picture on the chalkboard of something interesting or meaningful. When the drawing is complete, label it underneath with a short caption.

Then invite the students to draw a picture in their journals of something important and to write a caption underneath. When students ask for help with spelling the captions early in the year, I am inclined to write the captions for them and discuss the words and letters with the students. Later in the year, I nudge the students to write the captions themselves, instructing them to "Write down the letters that you hear in the words." Also, it is helpful to write each student's caption in standard spelling at the bottom of the page during the early months. In my experience, students are neither offended nor discouraged when the teacher writes the caption at the bottom of the page in "the book way."

Even in 2nd grade, some students still strengthen their phonemic awareness through writing. I often kneel beside a student who has asked me to spell a word. I pronounce the word very slowly over and over, stretching out the sounds so that the student can hear and write them.

Students' written journals make a nice chronological record of their development over time. These journals are especially helpful in discussions with parents at conference time. Writing experiences, coupled with other phonological awareness activities, allow students to develop these understandings from both perspectives: interpreting print and producing print. Writing will be discussed in detail in chapter 8.

 ## TEACHING PRINT CONVENTIONS AND TERMINOLOGY

OVERVIEW

All professions have their own ways of describing what they do. Physicians, attorneys, economists, and other professionals often use vocabulary that seems incomprehensible to many of us. Similarly, many beginning readers and writers, particularly those with meager literacy preparation, often seem baffled by the terminology of reading and writing. After all, many beginners know perfectly well that a letter comes in the mailbox, a sentence is what you do in jail, a title is for champion athletes, and that a capital is where the president lives. Imagine the consternation of beginning readers asked to "point to the diphthong in the third capitalized word of the second sentence in the first paragraph."

For beginning reading and writing instruction to be fully effective, beginners need to be familiar with the conventions and terminology of reading and writing. Students usually learn these concepts best in the context of reading and writing lessons.

Some common *print conventions* that beginning readers and writers must learn are these:

❀ Reading and writing proceed from left to right and from top to bottom.

❀ Words are made up of letters.

❀ Sentences are made up of words.

❀ Sentences begin with capital letters and end with periods, question marks, or exclamation points.

Some common reading and writing *terminology* terms are these:

letter	word	sentence	period	capital
vowel	long/short	blend	edit	publish

LANGUAGE-EXPERIENCE APPROACH

Addresses IRA Standard 4.1

Use student interests, reading abilities, and backgrounds as foundations for the reading and writing program.

My favorite activity for teaching students about print conventions and jargon is called the language-experience approach (LEA) (Nelson & Linek, 1999; Stauffer, 1970). LEA consists of the following basic steps:

1. You and the students experience a stimulating activity together.
2. The students tell you about the activity as they watch you write their spoken sentences on a piece of chart paper.
3. You teach the students to read the LEA chart by reading it *to them*, reading it *with them* in unison, and then having *them read it* back to you.
4. You can engage the students in multiple follow-up activities with their student-generated text to teach them about the conventions of letters, words, and sentences.

Consider the possibilities for teaching print conventions and terminology during one of my previous LEA lessons as described in the following vignette:

Six of my kindergarten and first-grade students, enrolled in a special summer program for rural, impoverished, at-risk students, chattered excitedly after their morning field trip to a nearby sheep ranch. I guided them in a discussion about the trip and then suggested (as if this were a spontaneous idea), "Hey, let's write a story about our trip to the sheep ranch." My students thought this was a great idea.

I then asked them, "How shall we begin?" They eagerly contributed sentences about our field trip as I wrote them on a piece of chart paper.

My students watched and listened as I discussed the letters, words, and sentences as I wrote them. After each of my students had contributed a sentence, I read the LEA chart back to them and then several times together with them together, **choral** *reading fashion. Then I had the students read the chart back to me as I pointed to the words.*

The Sheep Ranch

We went to the sheep ranch.
The sheep like to "Baaaa."
The sheep like to eat.
The sheep like to run.
The sheep like to play.
The sheep like to sleep.

I spent the remainder of the week rereading the chart with my students, counting words and sentences, matching sentence strips and word cards to the original chart, studying spelling patterns in the words, and playing a variety of games with the words from the chart. Each student also illustrated a personal book version of the sheep ranch story. On Friday my students were thrilled to take home a book about their trip to the sheep ranch that they could successfully read to their family.

Most beginning reading programs require students to read existing texts such as **preprimers,** leveled books, or big books written by reading experts or children's authors. Reading a text written by someone else requires readers to perform two tasks simultaneously: (1) decode the printed words and (2) process the vocabulary and background knowledge to make sense of the text. LEA eliminates the second task because the students themselves have generated the text about a familiar topic using their own vocabulary. This allows you and the students to focus entirely on print conventions, word recognition, spelling patterns, and other reading skills, as appropriate.

Language experience can be done with a whole class, but is best done in small groups of students or on an individual basis. Smaller groups give students more opportunity to contribute sentences to the LEA chart and to participate in follow-up word study activities. LEA is especially good for very beginning readers and leads easily into a variety of follow-up activities for teaching reading skills. LEA is also valuable for ESL instruction and is an effective way to integrate beginning reading and writing into the content areas.

We think of LEA as having two parts: (1) generating and learning the LEA chart and (2) using the LEA chart to teach print conventions and other reading skills. We will describe LEA as used in a small-group lesson, though it can be used with modifications for whole-class and individualized lessons.

FOR ENGLISH LANGUAGE LEARNERS

Formal and Informal Language Development

An effective teacher of English language learners will give students plenty of opportunities to develop their language skill through informal means, such as peer discussion, instructional conversations, and small-group cooperative learning activities. But because academic language takes longer to develop and has specialized syntax and vocabulary, formal instruction in the English language is also necessary (Dutro & Moran, 2003).

Generating an LEA Chart

LEA lessons begin with an experience. Group members share an experience, such as listening to a story or looking at a nonfiction picturebook, participating in a science demonstration, going on a field trip, or learning about a group member's pet brought to school for sharing time. The shared experience should be of sufficient interest to generate a lively group discussion.

After the shared experience, lead the students in a discussion of what they saw, did, noticed, thought, or wondered during the experience. The purpose of this discussion is to enhance and extend students' learning through the sharing of concepts and insights and to build students' vocabulary through the words used in the discussion. You may want to conclude the discussion by having the group brainstorm a list of interesting words from the discussion on the chalkboard. This list may help students in generating ideas and sentences for the LEA chart.

As the discussion winds down, you say to the students, "Let's write our own story about _____ (the experience). How should our story start?"

At this point, the students will begin contributing sentences for you to write on the LEA chart. It is important to write the students' sentences on chart paper exactly as they are dictated. Paraphrasing or changing the students' words diminishes their sense of ownership toward the LEA chart and may confuse them during follow-up activities.

This emphasis on using the students' own words brings up an important issue that must be addressed: what to do about nonstandard sentences dictated by students just beginning to learn English or who speak an English dialect. For example, a student may contribute a sentence such as "Sam is boy." Our approach has been to praise a student for the content of such a sentence and then to ask, "Since we are learning to read books, would it be okay if I wrote that sentence on the chart the *book way*?" This response praises the student's thinking, honors his or her speech patterns, and provides the group with a model of standard English for the reading lesson. I am more inclined to write nonstandard sentences in an LEA lesson when doing the lesson with a student on an individual basis. This is a sensitive issue and you should address it in a manner consistent with your own beliefs.

A number of instructional options are available during this dictation portion of the LEA lesson for focusing on print conventions. You can pronounce the letters and words as they are written on the chart paper. You may invite students to read each sentence aloud in choral fashion one or two times as you point to the words. You can also comment on spelling and punctuation patterns and the left-to-right, top-to-bottom convention of writing. You may ask beginning students to count the number of words in each sentence or the number of letters in selected words. You should see that all students in the group are watching closely as the sentences are being written.

For beginning readers, the stories should be only one or two sentences long. You may also want to use a patterned LEA format in which the students' dictated sentences repeat a pattern such as this:

> *I like to eat pizza.*
> *I like to eat apples.*
> *I like to eat spaghetti.*
> *I like to eat peanut butter.*
> *I like to eat grapes.*

The repetition in this patterned format makes it easier for the students to pay attention to the print features of the "important" words that they contributed to the LEA chart.

You may also want to write each contributing student's name in parentheses after his or her sentence:

> *I like to eat pizza.   (Michael)*
> *I like to eat apples.   (Whitney)*

and so on. Adding the students' names after the sentences further contributes to the sense of ownership and may help beginning students to find and read their sentences aloud during follow-up reading activities.

Most LEA charts are between six and eight sentences long. Longer charts may overload students' ability to learn to read the chart quickly, which may diminish the effectiveness of the chart for follow-up reading activities. If it appears that the LEA chart may be getting too long, you can bring it to a conclusion by saying, "What would be a good way to end this chart?"

After the LEA chart is complete, give the students an opportunity to revise it. Read the LEA chart aloud to the students and ask, "Is there anything we need to change or add? Are there words that you would like to substitute? Are there changes in sentence order that might improve the chart?" This is also a good time to choose a title for the LEA chart.

The next step is to teach the students to read the LEA chart using the three-step shared reading procedure (see chapter 7):

1. Read the finished LEA chart *to* the students.
2. Read the LEA chart several times *with* the students in choral fashion, pointing out word features, similarities, and conventions of print (punctuation, directionality, etc.).
3. Ask the students to read the LEA chart back *to you.*

The purpose of the rereadings is to make the students very familiar with the text of the LEA chart so that they can participate knowledgeably in the follow-up activities, which will focus on print conventions and reading skills.

I have included some of my favorite LEA stories here to give you a sense of the language and length generated by beginning readers. This story shows the patterned LEA approach with sentences beginning alike.

Our Walk (kindergarten)

> *On our walk, we saw dandelions.*
> *We saw tulips.*
> *We saw a robin and his home.*
> *We saw violets.*
> *We saw ants.*
> *We saw blossoms.*
> *We saw a prickly bush that scratches.*
> *We saw rocks.*
> *We saw a spider.*

This next story shows the personal nature of many LEA stories.

Soccer (Michael, first grade)

Today I played a game of soccer. It was so much fun. And they were very good. But, I must admit that we won instead of them. During the last part of the game, I was goalie, that was my favorite part. This time we wore blue uniforms. Sometimes we wear yellow. Soccer is my favorite game.

This LEA story was generated in response to Shel Silverstein's book *The Giving Tree*.

Craig's Story (first grade)

Once upon a time, there was an old tree, and he got cut down. He was happy because he didn't want to stand there all the time. He was happy to be a boat and he got to go to Australia. He could float on the water, and the water made him cool.   The End

Marci's LEA story shows integration of content information. It also reflects attention to the introduction, conclusion, and sequence aspects of revision.

The Garden (Marci, first grade)

Planting a garden is hard work.

We tilled the dirt.

We put manure on it.

We made signs.

We planted the seeds.

We gave the seeds water.

It was hard work, but it was fun.

Although Justin's LEA story is an example of a classic piece of very descriptive student work, I'm not sure that I want to see it illustrated.

The Butterfly (Justin)

A butterfly was born in time for summer. It was red and green and purple—really pretty. The butterfly wanted to have babies so it laid eggs. It is sad but the butterfly died on the front of someone's car.

LEA Follow-up Teaching

The second part of an LEA lesson is follow-up teaching in which you use the LEA chart to teach print conventions and selected reading skills. This often begins on the day after the LEA chart is generated, giving you time to prepare follow-up teaching materials.

The first step in follow-up teaching is to review and reread the LEA chart with the students. It is important to refresh the students' memories of the text to prepare them for the activities.

Sentence-strip matching is a popular follow-up activity. Copy each sentence of the LEA chart verbatim onto a sentence strip. Introduce the sentence strips to the group by showing one of the strips, reading it aloud, and then showing the students how it corresponds to one of the sentences on the LEA chart. This is done by physically holding the sentence strip up against the chart directly below the corresponding

A literacy learner matches a sentence strip to a language experience chart.

sentence. The students then take turns matching the sentence strips to the sentences on the chart paper. Ask pairs of students to reconstruct the entire chart using the sentence strips in their spare time. I make a practice of leaving the sentence strips in an accessible location so that pairs of students may practice matching the strips to the LEA chart or reassembling the strips in the correct sequence.

Individual word cards provide opportunities for a number of follow-up activities. Give students a word card and ask them to match the card to the corresponding word on the LEA chart. Place the word cards (along with the appropriate punctuation mark on a separate card) for a sentence on the LEA chart in mixed up order on the chalk tray. Then invite the students to rearrange the word and punctuation cards into the proper sequence.

A variation of this activity is to distribute the word and punctuation cards from a sentence among the same number of students. Have the students stand side by side, in mixed up order, in front of the group, displaying their word cards in front of them. Then instruct the students to rearrange themselves in the proper sequence to reconstruct the sentence. Cunningham (2000) calls this activity "Being the Words."

Another activity is to construct a set of word cards representing all the words on the LEA chart. Then have the students, working in pairs, spread out the word cards on the floor and reconstruct the entire LEA chart, word by word. It is interesting to watch

Students collaborate to reconstruct a sentence from a language experience chart.

students intuitively adopt the roles of chart reader and word card mover as they work together to reconstruct the chart.

Many teachers who use LEA have their students compile an individual **word bank.** Its purpose is to make the words a permanent part of each student's sight vocabulary. Each student selects two favorite words from the LEA chart. You also select two words from the chart. These four words are each written on an index card. The word, in its sentence from the LEA chart, is also written on the back of the card. You and the student read and review these four cards together. Then place the cards in the student's word bank.

A word bank can be a Zip-Lock freezer bag, a diaper wipes box, a recipe box, or a similar container. Review the word bank words frequently as a flashcard activity by matching them to the same words on the LEA charts. Students can also use their word bank cards for personal writing, alphabetizing, word sorting, and other teaching opportunities. You can also instruct students to find their word bank words in other printed materials. Each student's word bank expands as more word bank words are added from each new LEA chart.

The highlight of LEA is having each student make and illustrate a personal book from the text of the LEA chart. Begin this bookmaking process by typing the text of the LEA chart onto a separate piece of paper, making sure the sentences are spaced well apart. Make a copy of the paper for each student. Also make a construction-paper book for each student. Lay three pieces of copy machine paper on top of a piece of colored paper. The four pieces are folded and stapled width-wise, with the colored paper on the outside, forming the front and back covers.

Instruct your students to cut apart the sentences from their copy of the text, paste them into the book, and add illustrations. Have the students read their books to the teacher and to each other as they finish. Many teachers like to hang recent LEA charts on a wall or display them in some other place where they can be reviewed on a regular basis.

Comments on LEA

LEA fits well into a 5-day school week. Generating and learning to read the chart often takes place on the first day of the week. Reviewing the chart, decoding skill mini-lessons, and playing games and matching activities with sentence strips and word cards may take the next 3 days. Making and illustrating individual student LEA books is a great way to finish up the week.

Like all reading approaches, LEA has both distinct advantages and limitations. LEA's greatest strength may be its high level of motivation. The students feel a great deal of involvement and ownership because they have shared the initial experience and generated the text of the LEA chart. LEA is also effective because it uses conversational language and the students' own vocabulary.

FOR ENGLISH LANGUAGE LEARNER

Meaningful Learning

ELL students learn best when they are engaged in activities that have personal meaning and purpose for them. When lessons are related to solving a real problem in their lives, in or out of school, ELL students (and native English users) will be more engaged, try harder, and use language in more sophisticated ways (Freeman & Freeman, 1998).

LEA's flexibility and spontaneity are also strengths. LEA charts can be generated from read-alouds, basal stories, guest speakers, field trips, and other exciting school events. LEA is a wonderful way to integrate and supplement content-area activities.

LEA is limited in that it is primarily a beginning reading approach. Students are naturally eager to do things by themselves, so it is normal that students will soon want to begin writing on their own. Thus, LEA leads easily into writers' workshop activities.

You must also be aware that, although LEA charts and activities are fun and highly engaging, they are not sufficient. Students must be led to recognize words from the LEA charts in other printed materials. Students must be able to transfer what they learn in LEA activities to what they read in other formats.

CONCLUSIONS

Many 1st-grade teachers begin the school year by jumping right into formal reading instruction. Many of their students succeed. Many of them struggle. Some fail. Why do some students have a harder time learning to read and write than others?

Some teachers blame their students' struggles on the students' lack of innate ability or a developmental delay. The fact that many teachers place students in "ability groups" suggests that we tend to think of our students in terms of their IQ.

Adams (1990) has helped many professional educators to change this type of thinking by associating their young students' academic performance with their level of preparedness, rather than with their level of intelligence. Morris (1999) likens learning to read to running a race. Some students, through no fault of their own, begin the race far behind the other racers. Other students begin the reading race well prepared, at a distinct advantage. This focus on preparedness places more responsibility on teachers to ensure that students, especially at-risk students, possess the literacy foundations needed for success in formal reading and writing instruction.

SUGGESTED ACTIVITIES TO EXTEND YOUR LEARNING

1. Begin an oral language activities file. Collect songs, poems, tongue twisters, jokes, riddles, jump-rope rhymes, and stories that will help children to delight in and develop oral language. You and your education classmates could share copies of these to further expand your file.

2. Find a beginning reader in your family or neighborhood and do some phonemic awareness activities together. Try to determine how well the child can hear speech sounds and blend them together to form spoken words.

3. Find a beginning reader in your family or neighborhood and do a language-experience lesson together. Go for a walk, bake cookies, or do some other fun activity; then follow the steps outlined in this chapter to help the child to generate a brief story about the experience. Help the child to learn to read the story and do some follow-up teaching.

 ## REFERENCES

Professional

Adams, M. J. (1990). *Beginning to read: Thinking and learning about print.* Cambridge, MA: MIT Press.

Adams, M. J., Foorman, B. R., Lundberg, I., & Beeler, T. (1998). *Phonemic awareness in young children: A classroom curriculum.* Baltimore, MD: Paul H. Brookes.

Anderson, R. C., Hiebert, E. F., Scott, J. A., & Wilkinson, I. A. G. (1985). *Becoming a nation of readers: The report of the commission on reading.* Washington, DC: National Institute of Education.

Christie, J., Enz, B., & Vukelich, C. (1997). *Teaching language and literacy: Preschool through the elementary grades.* New York: Addison Wesley Longman.

Cooper, J. L., & Dever, M. T. (2001). Sociodramatic play as a vehicle for curriculum integration in first grade. *Young Children, 56*(3), 58–63.

Cunningham, P. M. (2000). *Phonics they use: Words for reading and writing* (3rd ed.). New York: Longman.

Dutro, S., & Moran, C. (2003). Rethinking English language instruction: An architectural approach. In G. G. Garcia (Ed.), *English learners: Reaching the highest level of English literacy* (pp. 227–258). Newark, DE: International Reading Association.

Ehri, L. (1994a). Developing the ability to read words. In R. Barr, M. L. Kamill, P. Mosenthal, & P. D. Pearson (Eds.), *Handbook of reading research* (Vol. 2, pp. 383–417). New York: Longman.

Ehri, L. (1994b). Development of the ability to read words: Update. In R. Ruddell, M. Ruddell, & H. Singer (Eds.), *Theoretical models and processes of reading* (4th ed., pp. 323–358). Newark, DE: International Reading Association.

Freeman, Y. S., & Freeman, D. E. (1998). *ESL/EFL teaching: Principles for success.* Portsmouth, NH: Heinemann.

Harwayne, S. (1992). *Lasting impressions.* Portsmouth, NH: Heinemann.

Juel, C., Griffith, P. L., & Gough, P. B. (1986). Acquisition of literacy: A longitudinal study of children in first and second grade. *Journal of Educational Psychology, 78,* 243–255.

Lomax, A. (1960). Folk songs of North America. Garden City, NY: Doubleday.

McCracken, R., & McCracken, M. (1998). *Stories, songs, and poetry to teach reading & writing.* Winnipeg, Manitoba: Peguis Publishers.

Morris, D. (1999). *The Howard Street tutoring manual: Teaching at-risk readers in the primary grades.* New York: Guilford.

National Reading Panel. National Institute of Child Health and Human Development. (2000). *Report of the national reading panel. Teaching children to read: Reports of the subgroups.* Available online at www.nichd.Nih.Gov/publications/pubs/readbro.htm

Nelson, O. G., & Linek, W. M. (1999). *Practical classroom applications of language experience: Looking back, looking forward.* Boston: Allyn and Bacon.

Neuman, S. B., & Dickinson, D. K. (2001). *Handbook of early literacy research.* New York: Guilford.

Rosenblatt, L. (1980). What facts does this poem teach you? *Language Arts, 57*(4), 386–394.

Smith, J. A. (2000). Singing and songwriting support early literacy instruction. *Reading Teacher, 53*(8), 646–649.

Stauffer, R. (1970). *The language-experience approach to teaching reading.* New York: Harper & Row.

Wagstaff, J. M. (1999). *Teaching reading and writing with word walls: Easy lessons and fresh ideas for creating interactive word walls that build literacy skills.* New York: Scholastic.

Children's Literature

Ciardi, J. (1962). *You read to me, I'll read to you.* New York: Harper Collins.

de Regniers, B. et al. (1988). *Sing a song of popcorn.* New York: Scholastic.

Lansky, B. (1993). *The new adventures of Mother Goose: Gentle rhymes for happy times.* New York: Simon & Schuster.

Martin, B. (1967). *Brown bear, brown bear.* New York: Holt, Rinehart & Winston.

Martin, B., & Archambault, J. (1989). *Chicka chicka boom boom.* New York: Simon & Schuster.

Offen, H. (1989). *Mother Goose nursery rhymes.* London: Octopus Books.

Sendak, M. (1988). *Where the wild things are.* New York: HarperCollins.

Dr. Seuss. (1960). *Green eggs and ham.* New York: Random House.

Dr. Seuss. (1963). *Hop on pop.* New York: Random House.

Dr. Seuss. (1968). *The foot book,* New York: Random House.

Ulrich, G. (1995). *My tooth ith looth.* New York: Bantam Doubleday Dell.

Reading Aloud

Sylvia Read

4

Letters From Yellowstone

When a teacher friend and I traveled to Yellowstone National Park, we carried Letters from Yellowstone *by Diane Smith to read aloud to each other. This novel is written as a set of letters from scientists exploring the park in 1898—about specimens they found, their relationships, and their debates concerning the nature of science and inquiry. My friend and I traveled the same route through the park that the scientists took. We began in Mammoth Hot Springs, where we saw the flowers and travertine terraces that the letters describe so beautifully. On the next day, we stopped at the Yellowstone Hotel, a massive clapboard building with late 19th-century charm situated on the shore of Yellowstone Lake.*

As we relaxed for an hour and read aloud to each other, we could easily imagine the characters passing through the lobby, booking rooms, or camping outdoors near by. Through the large lobby windows, we watched a storm darken and sail toward us across the lake, even as we read about how the scientists dealt with the weather in the book. It was as if we were magically living in two eras at once, with the scene and the reading voice conspiring to bring this novel to life for both of us. My friend later described this as one of the best moments of our trip—two teachers simply reading aloud to each other, watching a storm.

Why did we find this read-aloud experience so satisfying? Why do children respond with such warmth to read-aloud time at both home and school?

Reading is about making meaning, first and foremost. When we read aloud to our students, they can set aside the work of decoding for awhile and focus instead on meaning and enjoyment.

In this chapter, I discuss the various ways to make reading aloud to children a flexible and effective instructional strategy. I also give examples of the following strategies for focusing on meaning:

❀ Teaching children to respond to literature through personal responses, connections, questions, favorite parts, and "Say Something"

❀ Developing children's background knowledge of content, vocabulary, and genres

❀ Strengthening students' comprehension through predicting, clarifying, questioning, summarizing, and evaluating

PURPOSES FOR READING ALOUD

Addresses IRA Standard 4.1

Use students' interests, reading abilities, and backgrounds as foundations for the reading and writing program.

Reading aloud to students has been described as "the single most important activity for building the knowledge required for eventual success in reading" (Anderson et al., 1985, p. 23). Research ties the practice of reading aloud by the teacher with increased student vocabulary and background knowledge, improved reading comprehension, and a better attitude toward reading (Elley, 1992). When we read aloud to students, we relieve them of the decoding work for awhile, allowing them to focus on meaning. Effective teachers set aside at least two times a day for reading aloud, and many find more opportunities throughout the day—in minilessons for writing and reading, in science and social studies inquiries, and even in math.

Addresses IRA Standard 4.4

Motivate learners to be lifelong readers.

ENJOYMENT

Enjoyment is the most immediate purpose for reading aloud. Jim Trelease, author of *The New Read-Aloud Handbook* (2001), feels that a child's desire is the key ingredient for real success in reading. He argues that too often we teach children *how* to read, but forget to teach them to *want* to read. However, when we read aloud to a child, we're sending a "pleasure message" to the child's brain (one we hope will be as strong as what they get from Nintendo and TV). We could even say we're conditioning the child to associate books and print with pleasure (Trelease, 2001, pp. 7, 9). Thus, as we read aloud to students in the classroom, our first purpose is to lead them to enjoy books and enjoy being read to. It's a simple but fundamental point: Hearing a book read aloud is fun for children (and adults), and pleasure is absolutely crucial for fostering lifelong readers.

Although we will often read aloud books that are somewhat beyond what the students can read independently, it is important, especially at the beginning of the school year, to read aloud books that are within their independent reading range. Students will naturally want to read for themselves the books we read aloud to the class, and by encouraging this natural impulse, we can help them to warm up their reading muscles.

Ms. Hsu reads aloud *Click, Clack, Moo* and then asks the students to respond to it.

Creating the Moment

Lucy Calkins (2001) points out that sometimes "children consider the read-aloud as a time to doze, dream, fiddle, and snack" (p. 63). I want my students to take teacher read-alouds seriously, so I prefer to have my students sitting on the floor, gathered together in our meeting area. I invite them to close their eyes, not only to encourage them to ignore the possibly distracting behaviors of other students, but also to give them that movie screen in their minds on which they can play their vision of the book. I make this idea explicit at certain moments: "Are you making a picture of this in your mind? Can you see it? Can you hear it? Can you taste it, smell it, feel it?" Later in the day, when they're reading independently, I remind them that they can be making movies in their heads.

In my classroom, we read aloud novels like DiCamillo's *The Tale of Despereaux,* Blume's *Tales of a Fourth Grade Nothing,* and Cleary's *Ramona the Brave.* We also read and reread favorite picture books. We read poetry, both silly and serious. We read nonfiction books, magazines, newspaper articles and even textbooks, dictionaries, and encyclopedias. We read aloud our own writing, both mine and that of the students.

Lately, I've realized that I need to slow down as I read aloud; depth of reading is more important than breadth. As teachers, we need to read not with the goal of finishing a book, but with our full attention on the moment of the story, wherever it is. Students can better hear and savor the language and rhythm when we slow down a bit. With picture books, we may need to stop reading "sideways" all the time so that students can see the illustrations. With the text in our lap, we should read slowly, dramatically, and with gestures. Then we can turn the book and show the illustrations. We may read fewer books this way, but the experience will be richer, deeper, and more memorable.

PERSONAL RESPONSES

Pleasure is fundamental, but important opportunities would be wasted if reading aloud didn't have instructional value, too. So we also use the read-aloud time to encourage and develop our students' responses to literature. Personal response is an important strategy used by proficient readers to make meaning from what they read. Our students need to talk to us and to each other about books. Their talk might stray a bit as connections are made, but it should find its way back to the text, like Hansel and Gretel following the bread crumbs in the woods.

Students need to understand that reader responses to stories are unique, that their individual interpretation of a passage may differ from that of their classmates. We encourage them to make connections to events in their own lives, to other books they've read or heard, to events of the world, or to things they've learned from watching TV or movies. Why is personal response important? Research is clear that students achieve comprehension more effectively when they connect what they hear to something they know, feel, understand, or believe already. In foundational work many years ago, Anderson and Pearson called this principle **"schema theory"** (1985). Humans learn, these researchers tell us, by building new knowledge onto schema for knowledge that we already have.

Although K–3 students are newcomers to the academic world, they have a wealth of personal experience, and when we encourage their personal response to read-alouds, we help them connect what they hear to their own established schema.

Through read-aloud discussions, we can add to their background knowledge and vocabulary. We can draw, discuss, or explain words and concepts that are new to them. Our students have a network of words and ideas already in their heads; we add to that network every time we read and discuss books.

We want them to experience a wide variety of genres such as historical fiction, biography, and poetry, but we especially need to read aloud information texts. Our students will be reading and writing information texts extensively as they move up through the grades and on into adult life, and information texts predominate in many school and work settings.

Addresses IRA Standard 1.2

Demonstrate knowledge of reading research and histories of reading.

Addresses IRA Standard 1.4

Demonstrate knowledge of the major components of reading (phonemic awareness, word identification and phonics, vocabulary and background knowledge, fluency, comprehension strategies, and motivation) and how they are integrated in fluent reading.

Encouraging Personal Response

Of course, responses can be useful or not so useful. We can teach students to ask key questions of the text, the author, or other listeners.

Why do you think Fudge swallowed Peter's turtle?
What do you think about how Peter's mom reacted?

We can teach them to find the most illuminating connections to their lives by searching their own experience.

When have you experienced adults apologizing to you and admitting they were wrong?
How do you think Fudge is feeling in the hospital? What do you think of Peter worrying about the turtle instead of his brother? How would you react?

Asking students about their favorite parts of stories helps to develop their evaluative skills. My students often finish a book and begin to reread it immediately, although not necessarily the whole book. Usually, they tell me, they're going back to reread the parts they liked best.

The talk can happen as a whole group with everyone listening as one child makes a comment, or it can happen through "say something"; students think about what they just heard, pair up, and share those thoughts with a partner.

INTRODUCING COMPREHENSION STRATEGIES

Finally, we read aloud to develop students' comprehension strategies. The research on proficient readers (Pearson et al., 1992) suggests that we teach comprehension through a focus on making connections, questioning, visualizing and inferring, determining importance, and synthesizing. **Reciprocal teaching** (Oczkus, 2003; Palinscar & Brown, 1984), a proven strategy for building comprehension, focuses on predicting, clarifying, questioning, and summarizing. The National Reading Panel's report (2000) concluded that using graphic organizers in content area reading, providing vocabulary instruction, questioning, and summarizing are effective comprehension strategies. We teach and model all these strategies when we read books aloud and discuss them with our students.

As we read aloud, we need to keep these important purposes—pleasure, response, and comprehension—in mind. We will think about them in more detail in the rest of this chapter. However, although a chapter like this forces us to treat them separately, we need to remember that these purposes are not discrete. In the daily give and take of a classroom, they overlap constantly. We should allow them to blur and co-operate, as we discover ways to apply them flexibly, with the particular needs of our current students in mind.

Keeping Students Engaged During Read-Aloud

We stop to discuss, to ponder, and to reflect. But we must caution against stopping too often or too long. Many times, when a discussion is headed too far off the mark, a student will say, "Can we just read the book?" Students understand, intuitively, that too much discussion ruins the flow of the book. Sometimes it works to read aloud a short work in its entirety without stopping at all; and then reread it the next day so that discussion is less intrusive. Engagement in the reading experience is crucial when reading aloud.

Modeling Response

Before reading aloud Taro Yashima's picture book Crow Boy, *Mrs. Gonzales started four columns on the whiteboard:* Feelings, Connections, Questions, *and* Favorite Parts. *She then explained:*

> Feelings *means how the book makes you feel as you listen to it. "I feel happy because . . . ." "I feel angry because . . . ." "I feel anxious because . . . ."*
>
> Connections, *means what the book reminds you of. Connections can be to your own life, to other books, or to things in the world. "This part reminds me of something that happened to me . . . ." "This part reminds me of something I saw on the news . . . ." "This part reminds me of another book I read . . . ."*
>
> Questions *are about parts of the book that make you curious. "Why did the character do that?" "What is a moat?" "Why did the author make the book end that way?"*
>
> Favorite Parts *could be your favorite events from the book, favorite characters, or your favorite snippets of the author's writing. I sometimes call these power sentences.*

Mrs. Gonzales read Crow Boy *aloud in its entirety and then went back to the whiteboard and modeled her own feelings, connections, questions, and favorite parts. For example, she said, "I felt angry during the first part of the book because of how Crow Boy was treated by his classmates and teachers. I also felt happy at the end when the townspeople recognized and applauded his wonderful talent." She wrote these comments on the board in the Feelings column. Then she asked the students for their responses and wrote these on the board under her own responses.*

Moving to the Connections column, she told the students the true story of Mark, a student in one of her elementary school classes years ago who had poor social skills and, consequently, no friends. She described her repeated attempts to help Mark make friends rather than antagonize his classmates—to no avail. She wrote the words "Mark, no friends" in the Connections column and asked students for their own connections to Crow

Boy. *She repeated this modeling and eliciting process for Questions and Favorite Parts.*

It is important to realize that just one such modeling lesson will not be enough to ensure that students understand how to respond to literature or that they will incorporate this into their own listening. You may need as many as half a dozen such lessons with brief, powerful books. Students respond strongly to books like *Alexander and the Terrible, Horrible, No Good, Very Bad Day,* by Judith Viorst; *Too Many Tamales,* by Gary Soto; *Amazing Grace,* by Mary Hoffman; *My Rotten Redheaded Older Brother,* by Patricia Polacco; *Marianthe's Story,* by Aliki; and *Chester's Way,* by Kevin Henkes.

 ## TEACHING CHILDREN TO RESPOND TO LITERATURE

I enjoy reading the reader reviews of books on Amazon.com. It is amazing to me how varied these responses can be. For example, some readers of *My Heart Is on the Ground: The Diary of Nannie Little Rose, A Sioux Girl* by Ann Rinaldi found that they learned a lot about Indian culture and that it was sad, but beautifully written. Others found it an offensive and inaccurate portrait of an important part of Native American history. These readers read the same book, but they came to it with different background knowledge and attitudes and, ultimately, came away from the book with widely different experiences of it.

Louise Rosenblatt, one of the first literature scholars to study the importance of reader response to literature, discusses reading in terms of a transaction involving the reader, the text, and the reader's experience of the text, which Rosenblatt calls "the poem" (1936/1978). According to **reader-response theory,** we can say in a sense that the literary work ("the poem") doesn't really exist until it's experienced in the mind of the reader. This is how reader-response theory explains why one reader's understanding of a text can be different from every other reader's. Rosenblatt would say that our "poems" are different.

Many of us have experienced the traditional kind of literature teaching in which there is one correct interpretation, right there in the text, if only you read carefully enough. We may have had to face literal, inferential, and even evaluative questions for which there were predetermined answers, and it was our job to figure out these "right" answers. Reader-response theory has, in many ways, liberated the experiencing of literature so that each person's personal response to a text has legitimacy. This doesn't mean we aren't accountable to the text, but it is acceptable to have divergent responses.

RESPONDING WITH FEELINGS

We need to encourage children to respond to texts authentically so that they can understand how their reactions differ from their peers' reactions and how they are similar. When reading a work of fiction, for example, one child might focus on the characters while another might focus on the action, not even remembering the characters' names. Children need to learn that many different responses to the same book are valid.

In addition, we want children to try to understand why they respond to texts the way they do. What is it in their own experience that makes them respond a certain way? What is the source of the feelings that a book may draw from them? We also want them to learn about themselves as they listen to stories. They learn vicariously through events in characters' lives. They will identify with certain characters and not with others. We say to ourselves, "Oh yes, I remember how hard it was for me when I did that" or "I hope I can be more understanding if I ever go through that experience." We want our students to feel free to respond this way too. We stifle their natural responses, however, when we ask questions to which we already know the answers. We need to ask authentic, open-ended questions such as these:

> What do you think of this character?
>
> What would you do if you were that person?
>
> What do you think will happen next?
>
> What were you thinking when . . . ?
>
> How did you feel when . . . ?

Responses may also be as simple as laughter, gasping, groaning ("Oh no . . . "), sitting up straighter and widening your eyes, wondering noises ("Hmmm . . . "), snorting in disbelief or disgust, or applauding. I have often found that when children are talking as I read aloud they're talking about the book. I ask them to share what they're saying without making them feel guilty for talking. These are often the most honest responses because they're spontaneous.

We can ask children to respond in other ways, too, such as through writing, drawing, and dramatizing. For some books and some children, these activities work well. But we must take care not to have an extension activity for every book, for then we foster the idea that a book is always followed by an assignment of some sort. Also, it seems that many extension activities take longer than reading the book. If we fill up our time with puppet making, we steal time from reading. Writing in response to reading takes less time, but because writing can be laborious for primary-grade students, it can kill the love of reading and should be used judiciously.

I recently visited my 95-year-old grandfather, who reads voraciously. He shared with us his stack of index cards on which he records the title, author, and a summary and short critique of each book he reads. He admitted, "Some of them are

Miss Cook asked the students for their personal responses after reading *Owl Moon*.

really short. I'm anxious to get it written so I can start reading the next book." And isn't that the most natural response to reading a good book? We want to read another one!

RESPONDING WITH CONNECTIONS

As we read aloud, our students will make connections between what we're reading to them and their own lives, other books, poems, movies, television shows, and what they already know about the author or the topic. Keene and Zimmerman's book *Mosaic of Thought* (1997) introduces the idea of explicitly teaching our students about text-to-text, text-to-self, and text-to-world connections. Students can use stick-on notes to mark places in a book where they make these sorts of connections by writing T-T, T-S, or T-W on the sticky note and placing it on or near the words or sentences that triggered the connection. This is an efficient and concrete way for children to reinforce the connection-making experience.

On the other hand, Atwell (2001), in a recent conference keynote speech, told of asking her eighth graders to use this technique during reading workshop. She said they gamely went along with her for a month or so but soon began to complain that the sticky notes were preventing them from comprehending; they were distracting. Atwell went on to say that the flow of reading was disrupted not only by having to stop and use the sticky notes, but also by the connections themselves.

In another teacher's classroom during a reading lesson, the teacher had the students use sticky notes to mark the places where they made connections. Later, in class discussion, the book itself was never discussed—only the connections that the students and teacher had made while reading. Did the students understand the book? Probably. Did their marking and discussion of the connections deepen that understanding? Maybe. The point I want to stress is that, although good readers naturally make connections and poor readers may need to be taught this skill, we need to be wary of asking readers to make too many side trips along their reading journey.

Schema theory suggests that these connections are very important. One's schema, simply, is everything we know about the world and how we cluster this knowledge into a network of related ideas. When we read, we rely on this knowledge to make sense of the text.

Rather than make elaborate use of sticky notes and the like, we can model the way we make connections while reading aloud. We can invite students to voice their connections, but we need to make sure they can explain what part of the text they've connected with and why. This is sometimes called *accountable talk:*

> Accountable talk is not empty chatter; it seriously responds to and further develops what others in the group have to say. Students introduce and ask for knowledge that is accurate and relevant to the text under discussion. They use evidence from the text in ways that are appropriate and follow established norms of good reasoning. (New Standards Primary Literacy Committee, 1999, p. 25)

When I read aloud to my students, they often make connections with other books they've read or heard. When we were previewing the cover of Samuels's *Duncan and Dolores,* Regina noticed that Dolores was pushing Duncan around in a stroller and it reminded her of White's *Charlotte's Web,* when Fern pushes Wilber around in a stroller. Also, when I was reading aloud Cherey's *A River Ran Wild,* I emphasized how the white people took over the Indians' land. Brock pointed out, "That's kinda like Stonefox, because Stonefox got kicked off his land in Wyoming."

In the classroom we like to read aloud lots of folktales. We read a few and then begin to make connections. "Hmm . . . . Three wishes. I've noticed that things tend to happen in threes in folktales. Three bears. Three billy goats. Three pigs." The children begin noticing threes in subsequent stories.

The connections that children make with their own lives can be the most powerful for cementing the love of reading, for when we see ourselves in a story, the story is all the more meaningful and memorable. When I read aloud Blume's *Tales of a Fourth Grade Nothing* to my group of second graders, they connected with Peter more than Fudge. When Peter's mother gets angry at him after Fudge swallows Peter's turtle, she later apologizes. I stopped to ask the students whether an adult had ever apologized to them before. Many had stories; some had never had that experience. Much later in the year, at the end of a rough day during which I had been crabby with the students, I apologized to them for my behavior. We remembered together our discussion of adults saying they were sorry. They were quick to forgive me, just as Peter forgave his mother. *Tales of a Fourth Grade Nothing* also allowed the students to reminisce about their own hospital experiences, bad accidents, and difficulties with siblings.

RESPONDING WITH QUESTIONS

Teaching our students to generate questions during reading is an effective means of raising their level of comprehension. Curiosity about a story or topic propels us forward as we read; voicing this curiosity in questions during a read-aloud lets students explore the possibilities of meaning. However, framing a meaningful question about what they have read is something that primary-grade students have to learn. Effective teachers find moments to model questioning for their students.

Young students may not feel that having a question is appropriate. Teachers often seem to have all the answers, and we often ask students inauthentic questions to which we already know the answer. There may sometimes be good reasons for this, but when we model questioning as a response to literature for students, we must ask real questions that we truly wonder about. Some may be factual; for example, they may have concrete answers in the text. But others may remain in the realm of speculation. We want our students to ask both kinds of questions, but most of all we want them to know that having questions about a text is a good thing; it means that we're interested in what we're reading and we're learning.

With younger students, I have to teach the difference between a question and a statement or comment. Sometimes I find myself saying, "You're telling us something; you're not quite asking a question. Sometimes questions begin with 'Who,' 'What,' 'Where,' 'Why,' or 'When.' Sometimes they begin with 'I wonder. . . . '"

Inevitably, students will try to begin a statement with "When" and think that they've created a question. For example, Ryan said, "When baby chicks are born, they stay in the nest and tweet." He was sure this was a question because it began with "When"! I explained by saying, "You are telling us something. If you say, 'When do we go to lunch?' that's a question. If you say, 'When we go to lunch, we always wash our hands,' that is not a question, even though it starts with the word *when*. With questions, you need to be asking something, not telling."

I try to model for my students the kinds of questions that clarify meaning. I want them to wonder about the puzzling parts of books. For example, when we recently read McClosky's *Make Way for Ducklings,* I wondered aloud about duck behavior.

"How do baby ducks know about staying in line? And how do they know what to do when they dive for food?" This made Dallin wonder how Mrs. Mallard would know when to meet Mr. Mallard in the park. In the example that follows I describe some instances of how these kinds of questions arise.

Students Ask Authentic Questions

When reading Hirschland's How Animals Care for Their Babies, *I invited the students to focus on questions that came up in their minds. I read, "Some animals, like these monkeys, live together in large groups. Grownups and older brothers and sisters often share the job of protecting the babies."*

Shannon asked, "Why do the brothers and sisters have to guard the babies and not the mom and dad?" Shannon's question is particularly good because it develops directly from the text. "Many creatures make nests for their babies," I continued. "Are those rabbits?" asked Jaren, genuinely curious and anticipating what comes next. I read on:

"[T]here are many nests you can't see. . . . A European rabbit collects grass for her underground nest. The grass makes a soft bed for her babies."

Students' questions also often refer to the illustrations. "The Northern Flicker, a woodpecker, makes its nest inside a tree," I read. Brock wondered, "Is that a male or a female woodpecker [in the picture]?" This is fine, but when reading and writing are our instructional purposes, we want them to focus primarily on the ideas and words. Sometimes I deliberately don't show the pictures when I read aloud so that the students have to think about the words they hear.

My students and I discuss the possible answers to their questions and, whenever possible, I help them to look back to the text for the answer. I will say, "Sometimes we can figure out the answer by reading it again. Sometimes we can figure out the answer by looking at the pictures. And sometimes we can't figure out the answers, and that's okay." I try not to set myself up as the keeper of all knowledge, and I often say, "I don't know. Where could we find the answer?" Sometimes another student is the expert, such as when Bethany was able to explain to Evan why male birds are often more colorful than females. When we can't find the answer, I suggest that we just don't have enough information, but I invite the students to speculate. Most of all, it's important to have the students think of themselves as flexible meaning makers.

Students' questions will generate more questions. When they hear each other's thoughts, new questions often arise in their minds. This is the beauty of using the read-aloud to teach questioning—everyone gets to hear everyone else's questions.

RESPONDING WITH FAVORITE PARTS

When we ask students to tell us after a read-aloud what their favorite parts were, we are fostering their critical or evaluative levels of thinking. First, we're asking them to have a favorite part—that is, to evaluate the story—and, second, we want them to be able to explain why it was their favorite. Younger children often say they "liked it all" and explain their favorite part by saying "It was funny." This is a great reason, of course, especially if they can explain why it was funny, but through modeling we can show them how to go beyond that. These second-grade children responded to *Ox-Cart Man* by Donald Hall by telling about their favorite parts:

❀ "I like the part where it tells the details about what he bought."

❀ "I like the part when he sold the cow and all the things because he was making more money for his family and how he gave the presents to his kids."

❀ "I like the maple tree part—how they made the maple honey."

❀ "I like the part where he sells his cow because I think that would be hard."

❀ "I like the part where it told how long it took him to get there."

❀ "I like the part where he kisses his ox on the nose because it reminds me of how my brother and sister sometimes kiss my dog and cats on the nose."

When they responded to *Rumpelstiltskin,* Emma said, "I like the last page where it says, 'The devil told you that. The devil told you that,' "but the maid actually spied on him and he looks all grumpy on that page and he's like, oh you know my name! How could you find that out?" Dakota liked it when "she teased him because then he wouldn't be exactly sure that she knew it and because if she said it first then he would know that someone told her."

Since I also want my students to be able to discuss the book's use of language, I sometimes combine purposes and ask my students to find their favorite sentence or a powerful sentence. This encourages them to begin thinking about writing in terms of its style or craft.

RESPONDING WITH "SAY SOMETHING"

Usually, responding with personal feelings, making connections, asking questions, and identifying favorite parts are practiced in whole-class discussions. But, not every student gets a turn to talk in a whole-class discussion, which is why I also use other techniques to encourage student response to texts we read aloud. One of my favorites is called "Say Something."

Say Something is a technique described by Short, Harste, and Burke (1996). When reading aloud, we use this engagement to encourage all students to participate in thinking about the reading. Say Something capitalizes on the social nature of language and learning as students interact with each other and enhance each other's meaning-making process. The "Say Something" box explains how it works.

Say Something

Before we begin the read-aloud, students choose a partner, which usually increases their motivation and decreases the anxiety of speaking to the whole group. When the reader stops (whether we're reading in a large group or just in twos), partners face each other, knees to knees, and say something to each other about the reading. It can be something they've noticed, what they're reminded of, what they think will happen next, how they feel while hearing the text, or what questions they have. When all students have a partner to talk to, instead of only one student talking at a time to the whole group, much more discussion is possible. Everyone gets to say something, instead of just a few students.

The students should be encouraged to think of Say Something as an activity in which there are no right or wrong answers. But when they make a comment, you should ask them, "Why do you think that?" or "What makes you feel that way?" It is important to keep the pace going quickly with this type of engagement so that the majority of time is spent reading and the talk doesn't become too irrelevant.

Depending on the text you are reading, read a page or two or a paragraph or two and stop. After the pairs of students make several comments, read another section of the text and repeat. Try to catch their comments and thus learn from them what they're thinking and how they're responding to what's being read. This kind of kid watching is crucial to understanding the workings of children's minds. It can help us to support their reading as we both marvel at their amazing ability to comprehend and note the ways in which comprehension breaks down for some children. Say Something should be followed by class-level discussion so that some of the students' thinking can be shared.

 ## READING ALOUD TO DEVELOP BACKGROUND KNOWLEDGE

Even if teachers never stopped to discuss and wonder about what has been read aloud, students would still benefit. Not that I recommend never stopping, but the reading aloud itself will develop students' background knowledge like nothing else can. Think about it. No one alive today has ever seen a live woolly mammoth, but we know about them because we've read about them. We know about many things we will never see—black holes, the Earth's mantle, the passenger pigeon—because we have read about them. We can give this kind of content knowledge to our students, too, by reading aloud to them.

Language learning, too, is enhanced by the daily classroom read-aloud, because children internalize the language patterns they hear even without explicit instruction. In Beatrix Potter's *Tale of Peter Rabbit,* the sparrows "implored him to exert himself." In the poem "Where Go the Boats," Robert Louis Stevenson wrote, "Dark brown is the river, golden is the sand." These are examples of literary language that are generally encountered only in stories and poetry. Exposure to language this highly refined empowers children not only to develop their vocabulary, but also to understand how words can be put together in varying ways to make meaning and to make language beautiful.

Young children naturally mimic the language of books. At age 8, my son reported to his grandmother that, while he was trying to feed a prairie dog, it "crept cautiously forward," imitating language he had heard in *Battle for the Castle,* by Elizabeth Winthrop, in which "the cat crept cautiously forward." While standing in a checkout line, I heard an older woman compliment a young boy on his big, beautiful eyes, to which he replied, "the better to see you with." He obviously had experience with the story *Little Red Riding Hood* and had recognized the woman's comment as similar to the language of that story. He responded with more storybook language. You, of course, have your own favorite examples of amazing things children say. This literary language is not the same as the everyday spoken language students hear in conversation. Developing students' background knowledge of literary language not only helps them when they encounter it in all kinds of literary texts, but it develops their own facility in making meaning through language.

Discussions about texts before, during, and after reading aloud can also increase students' background knowledge in important ways. Students learn from each other as they interact as partners, in small groups, or as a whole class. When reading aloud a book about snakes, for example, one student may be able to explain to the whole class how a snake unhooks its jaws to eat food larger than its head. As adults we can quickly explain the meanings of words such as "reeds" or "rushes," discuss why the author used these words instead of "grass," and thus enlarge our students' background knowledge and vocabulary about swamps or marshes.

SCHEMA THEORY

As we read aloud books, we can often provide students' very first encounter with a concept such as "black hole," but they probably already have a concept of "star" or "stuff in space." As we read aloud to them, they attach this new idea to their existing schema for space and all things associated with space. Rumelhart (1980) calls this **accretion.** Students may have a concept of mammal that includes dogs, cats, and bears, but when we read aloud a book about whales and learn that whales also are mammals because they give birth to live babies and nurse their offspring, students experience what Rumelhart calls *tuning,* as their schema for mammal alters given this new information. Less often, people's schemas are restructured. For children, this happens when they learn that spiders are not insects. Acceptance of this idea requires that learners' schemas be dramatically rearranged.

We don't build students' background knowledge from nothing; they are not blank slates. They come to us knowing a little bit about a lot of things. Our job is to capitalize on the connections they make and build from their background knowledge using these connections.

CONSTRUCTIVIST VIEW OF READING

Readers take their existing knowledge or schema and put it together with new information encountered in a text to construct meaning from the text. The meaning does not reside solely within the text, nor is meaning totally formed by the reader (Pearson & Stephens, 1998). Students may not naturally draw on their prior knowledge, which is why we must teach them to consciously activate their prior knowledge by asking questions such as "What do you already know about how spiders are born?" before reading aloud a book about the life cycle of spiders. Modeling and practicing this through read-aloud sessions give children the opportunity to see how powerful the strategy can be for enhancing their understanding and enjoyment of a text. When a student is actively constructing meaning, he or she is becoming a reader in the truest sense of the word.

FOR ENGLISH LANGUAGE LEARNERS

ESL Learners and Activating Schema

Maria likes to stop frequently while reading to look at the pictures, point to objects and talk about them, or share a story about her sister that relates to the story. These are important side trips for Maria to take on her journey to becoming a proficient reader. Even simple texts with few words give her opportunities to build vocabulary as we stop to talk about the pictures. When we were reading a book about a boy who was scared to climb down a pole on a jungle gym, she encountered the word "ladder," which she was able to decode but didn't understand. The picture that accompanied the text gave her an efficient way to connect her knowledge of playground equipment and the new word "ladder." Often second-language learners have only phonetic clues to use when figuring out words. Their sense of English syntax may not be developed enough to help them figure out what the word could be, and the semantic clues may also be missing. All emergent readers benefit from books in which pictures support the text, but English language learners especially need high-quality texts and illustrations to help them develop not just their decoding skills, but also their sense of natural English syntax, and to build their vocabulary and storehouse of concepts.

BUILDING VOCABULARY WHILE READING ALOUD

Vocabulary is best taught with young children through books that teachers have read aloud, rather than books that students have read independently (Beck et al., 2002). When students are first learning to read, the words they encounter in books read independently can be simple words such as "friend" or "house," words that are already in their oral vocabulary. This makes them ideal words for early reading material, but not very useful for building vocabulary.

Books that teachers read aloud, however, can be a rich source of words for vocabulary instruction. Beck and colleagues (2002) suggest focusing on about three words per book. The covers of the books read aloud can be displayed on a bulletin board along with the chosen vocabulary words. When opportunities occur for the teacher or a student to refer to previously discussed words, the teacher can put a tally mark next to the word. The class then develops a bank of "favorite words," which is how the teacher can keep children thinking about and using these words.

Here are a few guidelines for teaching vocabulary with read-alouds:

1. Initially discuss the target word place with reference to its context in the book.
2. Provide student-friendly definitions.
3. Provide examples of how the word is used beyond the context of the read-aloud.
4. Provide situations in which children can interact with the focus word. Ask questions that use the word, such as "Could you walk down the street *morosely*? What would that look like?"
5. End the vocabulary lesson with a short activity in which all the focus words are used together. If all the words are related, you can ask questions such as "Could you wash the dishes *frenetically* or could you find the *circumference* of an hour? Why?" Or you can find one context in which all the words can be used. "What would it look like to measure the *circumference* of a *sphere frenetically*?"
6. Maintain understanding of the focus words by referring to them frequently. Apply previously learned words to new books, and use the words in other reading and writing contexts throughout the day. "Let's be sure to walk to lunch calmly, not frenetically!"

Addresses IRA Standard 4.2

Use a large supply of books, technology-based information, and nonprint materials representing multiple levels, broad interests, and cultural and linguistic backgrounds.

READING ALOUD TO DEVELOP BACKGROUND KNOWLEDGE OF GENRES

Most students come to school knowing a lot about stories. Probably this is because parents and teachers tend to emphasize narrative texts when they read aloud to young children. Stories are wonderful, of course, but K–3 students also need experience with poetry, nonfiction, folktales, biography, and specific fiction genres, such as historical fiction, realistic fiction, fantasy, and science fiction. Through the read-aloud, we can introduce the structures and conventions of these genres. When students have a schema for and background knowledge about a particular genre, they can recognize it in an unfamiliar text and draw on informed expectations for that genre. For example, when reading fairy tales, a subgenre of folktales, students begin to see the important role of magic elements in this genre. When they approach a new text, knowing it is a fairy tale, they will expect to find magic. Similarly, if they're instructed in other genres, they will learn what to expect when they encounter them in the future. Their informed expectations will strengthen their understanding of the text.

This is only part of one teacher's extensive classroom library.

Each year, as we begin to read aloud a number of folktales and fairy tales, I start a labeled basket with a wide variety of folktales and fairy tales from my own and the school library's collection. When I teach the class about biographies, I add a basket for these. Gradually, as needed, our scheme for organizing our books becomes more refined. Although I begin the year by sorting the books myself and teach the students to put the books back where they were found, throughout the year I teach them how to distinguish genres. Soon, when we check out a new stack of books from the school library, the students themselves decide where the books belong on the shelves.

Not surprisingly, students often find that certain books can be categorized in more than one way. The *Magic School Bus* volumes, for example, are a blend of fiction and nonfiction. Having noticed this uniqueness for themselves, my students often suggest that they deserve their own basket.

FORMAT AND GENRE

We need to distinguish between genre and what we might call *format.* A picture book, for example, may contain fiction, nonfiction, an illustrated poem, or a song; the picture book format spans the genres. *Owl Moon,* for example, is an award-winning picture book, but its genre is poetry. *Make Way for Ducklings* (McClosky, 1941) is also an award-winning picture book, but its genre is fiction. Robert Frost's "Stopping by Woods on a Snowy Evening" is a poem that has been published in a number of formats, including as a picture book. *Genre* refers to the literary structure of the text. Poetry is a genre, as is biography, folktale, novel, and so on (see Figure 4.1). In contrast, *format* is a choice made about the published features in which the text is packaged. The picture book, chapter book, big book, comic book, and CD-ROM are formats, not literary genres.

This is not to say that formats are unimportant; they can be very influential in learning. The picture book format is a unique combination of text and illustration in which the illustrations either balance or dominate the text. In the best picture books, the text and illustrations fit together so seamlessly that one would be diminished without the other. How the illustrations support the text and how the text elaborates on the illustrations can be discussed usefully with students. For example, *The Tale of Peter Rabbit* (Potter, 1902) is the quintessential picture book. In one text and picture spread, Mrs. Rabbit is saying to her three daughters and Peter, who is turned away,

The rest of the classroom library is organized into baskets labeled by author or topic.

Figure 4.1 Some Common Genres and Their Definitions

> *Folktales:* traditional stories that are passed along orally; some eventually become part of printed literature
>
> *Fantasy and science fiction:* imaginative stories that explore an alternative reality
>
> *Realistic fiction:* plausible stories about people and events that could actually happen
>
> *Historical fiction:* imaginative stories grounded in the facts of our past
>
> *Nonfiction:* books of information and fact
>
> *Poetry:* compressed language arranged in an interesting form, often with rhythm and rhyme and other techniques to enhance the sound of the language
>
> *Biography:* the story of a person's life and achievements, embedded in the time and culture of the person

"Now, my dears, you may go into the field or down the lane, but don't go into Mr. McGregor's garden: your Father had an accident there; he was put in a pie by Mrs. McGregor." The text gives us part of the story, but the fact that Peter is turned away and his eyes are looking away from his mother suggests something about his character that the text doesn't tell us. Without the illustrations, we wouldn't know as much about Peter.

Student's background knowledge is developed through exposure to the pictures and text and the talk that surrounds both. Picture books provide a unique opportunity to discuss, on a daily basis, concepts of art such as line, texture, shape, and color. Principles of design combine to create the composition of the art. Balance—the way that lines, shapes, textures, and colors are weighted in a piece of art—and size, placement, color, and line are choices that an artist makes to emphasize certain elements of the composition. The cover, endpapers, typography, text placement, illustrations, and white space all work together to create the total design of a picture book. In *Math Curse,* Jon Scieszka even incorporates the book's subject matter into the price that is printed on the dust jacket of the book. Debra Frasier explains in the front matter of *Vocabulary Disaster* that she used only the art supplies she could find in her daugh-

Figure 4.2 The Sounds of Poetry

> *Alliteration:* the repetition of consonants such as the *s sounds* in "the expense of the spirit"
> *Assonance:* the repetition of vowels such as the *a*'s in "*a waste of shame*"
> *Onomatopoeia:* words whose sound matches their meaning: boom, hiss, flutter, tinkle

ter's school desk to create the illustrations for the book: notebook paper, marker, pencil, and the like. The endpapers of *Vocabulary Disaster* are a word search using the words from the story. Students' knowledge about art can also be enhanced by discussing the medium with which the illustrations are made: acrylics, oils, watercolors, clay, wood, metal, fabric, ink, pencil, charcoal, pastels, photography, or a combination of media. As a follow-up, students can create art projects using the medium of the book whose artwork they have studied.

COMMON GENRES IN CHILDREN'S LITERATURE

Poetry

Poems emphasize imagery and figurative language. Growing used to poetic language can encourage students to write in ways that move beyond the level of casual conversation with their peers, parents, and teachers.

Students most easily identify poetry by how it looks on a page, but there's so much more to teach them about poetry than that. Through exposures to many kinds of poetry, they come to expect poetry to look and sound a variety of ways. Good poetry does not have to rhyme, although poetry for children often does. Poetry can also have rhythm and sound elements such as alliteration, assonance, and onomatopoeia (see Figure 4.2).

These concepts and terms are easily taught to young children; even second graders can learn about onomatopoeia—and they love using the word. Knowledge of the conventions of poetry increases their understanding when they read poetry, and it opens new possibilities to them as they write it.

Children love poetry that is funny or has silly or nonsense words, such as "hickety pickety," "higglety pigglety" or "diffendorfer." But they also need to hear poetry that is (within their ability range) thoughtful, reflective, or serious. They need to hear poetry that is very short and makes its point quickly, but also poetry that is long and tells a story. Children enjoy poetry that has a concrete shape that repeats or supports the ideas in the poem. It is important to expose students to a wide variety of poetic forms. The world is full of wonderful poetry that isn't written by Shel Silverstein or Jack Prelutsky. Students read and hear plenty of these two poets' work; but they also need to get to know poetry by Robert Louis Stevenson, Valerie Worth, Karla Kuskin, Nikki Grimes, Christina Rosetti, Michael Strickland, Robert Frost, Douglas Florian, and many others. See Figure 4.3 for some of my favorites.

Building Fluency with Choral Reading and Read Alouds

Choral reading of poetry can be an effective way to improve students' oral reading fluency. When reading poetry aloud to children, be sure to use the most natural intonation

Figure 4.3   Poetry for Your Classroom

Cullinan, Bernice. *A Jar of Tiny Stars: Poems by NCTE Award-Winning Poets.*
Florian, Douglas. *Bing Bang Boing.*
Frost, Robert. *Poetry for Young People.*
Greenfield, Eloise. *"Honey, I Love" and Other Love Poems.*
Grimes, Nikki. *Meet Denitra Brown.*
Grimes, Nikki. *My Man Blue.*
Hoberman, Mary Ann. *Fathers, Mothers, Sisters, Brothers.*
Hopkins, Lee Bennett. *Side by Side: Poems to Read Together.*
Kuskin, Karla. *Dogs and Dragons, Trees and Dreams.*
Merriam, Eve. *You Be Good and I'll Be Night.*
Nye, Naomi Shihab. *The Space Between Our Footsteps: Poems and Paintings from the Middle East.*
Pomerantz, Charlotte. *If I Had a Paka: Poems in Eleven Languages.*
Pomerantz, Charlotte. *The Tamarindo Puppy and Other Poems.*
Prelutsky, Jack. *The Random House Book of Poetry.*
Spooner, Michael. *A Moon in Your Lunch Box.*
Stevenson, Robert Louis. *A Child's Garden of Verses.*
Worth, Valerie. *All the Small Poems.*

and inflection that you can so that children don't come to expect poetry to sound either monotonic or sing-song. Even poems with a strong rhythm should be read in a way that emphasizes the meaning.

Reading aloud is also a good time to model both fluent and nonfluent reading. When the teacher reads a sentence word by word or in a monotone, students are usually able to describe why that just doesn't sound right and give the teacher "advice" on how to improve her fluency.

Historical Fiction

Historical fiction is uniquely able to build students' background knowledge because historical facts are added carefully to the fictional story, and stories, as we know, are what make history seem real and therefore exciting. Although fictional, the events in high-quality historical fiction are plausible. That is, they really could have occurred, given the real historical circumstances; the characters could have lived at that time and made the choices they make in the story. Often historical fiction includes historical figures, sometimes as the focus of the story, as in *Minty: A Story of Young Harriet Tubman,* by Alan Schroeder, and sometimes as a supporting character, as in Jane Yolen's *Encounter,* a story of the Tainos Indians' first encounter with Christopher Columbus. Examples of historical fiction are given in Figure 4.4.

When students understand the relationship of fact and fiction in historical fiction, it increases their understanding of both. Textbook presentations of facts lack the narrative context that makes historical fiction so memorable. By reading aloud historical fiction, you increase not only your students' historical background knowledge, but also their understanding of this blended genre.

Figure 4.4 Historical Fiction for the Primary Grades

Ackerman, Karen. *When Mama Retires.*
Aliki. *A Medieval Feast.*
Bartone, Elisa. *Peppe the Lamplighter.*
Brett, Jan. *The First Dog.*
Bulla, Clyde Robert. *A Lion to Guard Us.*
Bunting, Eve. *Dandelions.*
Bunting, Eve. *The Wall.*
Coerr, Eleanor. *Buffalo Bill and the Pony Express.*
Coerr, Eleanor. *The Josephina Story Quilt.*
Goodall, John. *The Story of an English Village.*
Haley, Gail. *Jack Jouett's Ride.*
Hall, Donald. *Lucy's Christmas.*
Hall, Donald. *Lucy's Summer.*
Houston, Gloria. *But No Candy.*
Hunt, Jonathan. *Illuminations.*
Johnston, Tony. *The Quilt Story.*
Joose, Barbara M. *The Morning Chair.*
Lasker, Joe. *Merry Ever After: The Story of Two Medieval Weddings.*
Lucas, Barbara M. *Snowed In.*
Lyon, George Ella. *Dreamplace.*
McGel, Alice. *Molly Bannaky.*
McKissack, Patricia. *Mirandy and Brother Wind.*
Mitchell, Margaree King. *Uncle Jed's Barbershop.*
Oppenheim, Sulamith Levey. *The Lily Cupboard.*
Paek, Min. *Aekyung's Dream.*
Rappaport, Doreen. *The Boston Coffee Party.*
Ray, Mary Lyn. *Alvah and Arvilla.*
Say, Allen. *Tea with Milk.*
Schroeder, Alan. *Minty: A Story of Young Harriet Tubman.*
Stevenson, James. *Don't You Know There's a War On?*
Turner, Ann. *Dakota Dugout.*
Turner, Ann. *Dust for Dinner.*
Winter, Jeanette. *Follow the Drinking Gourd.*
Yolen, Jane. *Encounter.*

Fantasy

Children are often taught in the primary grades to distinguish "make-believe" books from factual or realistic works. Although it's obvious that kids know, for example, that horses aren't purple (as they are depicted, say, in Carle's *Brown Bear, Brown Bear*), we can still help students to develop their background knowledge about fantasy as a genre. In doing so, we give them an added reading advantage—a more sophisticated understanding of how books and writing work. As they read, their predictions and inferences will be more reliable, providing a positive loop of feedback to reinforce their progress.

Figure 4.5   Fantasy for the Primary Grades

Conrad, Pam. *The Tub People.*
Dahl, Roald. *The BFG.*
Fleishman, Paul. *Time Train.*
Fleishman, Paul. *Westlandia.*
Freeman, Don. *Corduroy.*
Joyce, William. *George Shrinks.*
Lobel, Anita. *The Dwarf Giant.*
Nickle, John. *The Ant Bully.*
Norton, Mary. *The Borrowers.*
Osborne, Mary Pope. *The Magic Tree House.*
Sendak, Maurice. *Where the Wild Things Are.*
Van Allsburg, Chris. *The Garden of Abdul Gasazi.*
Van Allsburg, Chris. *Jumanji.*
Wiesner, David. *Sector 7.*
Yorinks, Arthur. *Hey, Al.*

Books that more clearly fall within the genre of fantasy include those in which there are miniature worlds, such as *The Borrowers* by Mary Norton or *George Shrinks* by William Joyce. Stories of alternative realities, dream worlds, time travel, and the like are fantasy books. Thus, the *Magic Tree House* books are fantasy, along with works such as *The Polar Express* (Van Allsburg, 1985), *Jumanji* (Van Allsburg, 1995), or *Where the Wild Things Are* (Sendak, 1963). Books in which magic plays an important role, such as *The Garden of Abdul Gasazi* by Chris Van Allsburg, qualify as fantasy. Like folktales, fantasy narratives sometimes make use of myth traditions and legends; thus, the themes of fantasy often echo the themes of folktales. Examples are given in Figure 4.5.

Science Fiction

Science fiction stories create settings, characters, and events based on scientific principles, often asking "What if" and exploring the answer. For example, a science fiction novel that I read aloud to my second graders is *The Green Book* by Jill Paton Walsh, in which the planet Earth is dying and Pattie and her family are among a group who travel to a new planet, Shine, and establish a new settlement there. A blend of science fiction and fantasy works well with younger children. My students particularly enjoy Jane Yolen's *Commander Toad in Space* and Edward Marshall's *Space Case,* which are lighter treatments of science fiction. Children's background knowledge helps them understand that science fiction has elements that are forecast into the future, with scientific principles underlying them. With this in mind, their understanding of science fiction will be stronger. Examples of science fiction books are given in Figure 4.6.

Contemporary Realistic Fiction

This genre is a huge avenue for children's social and emotional growth because they can identify so closely with the characters and settings. Readers see themselves in the

Figure 4.6 Science Fiction for Young Children

Marshall, Edward. *Space Case.*
Marzollo, Jean. *Jed and the Space Bandits.*
Marzollo, Jean. *Ruthie's Rude Friends.*
Standiford, Natalie. *Space Dog the Hero.*
Walsh, Jill Paton. *The Green Book*
Yolen, Jane. *Commander Toad in Space*
Yolen, Jane. *Things That Go Bump in the Night: A Collection of Stories.*

story, feel what the characters feel, experience the events, and live in the setting. Vicariously, readers of realistic fiction learn important lessons about life. As we read aloud to our students, realistic fiction presents many opportunities to discuss the social and emotional realities they are experiencing as they grow up.

The narratives may be humorous or serious, playful or thoughtful, joyful or painful. A book like Eve Bunting's *Fly Away Home,* which depicts a homeless father and son living in an airport, presents a complex problem with no easy answers. In realistic fiction, the characters could exist in the contemporary world and the events are plausible. Without magical creatures or futuristic technology, realistic fiction includes adventure stories, mysteries, animal stories, sports stories, comic or tragic stories, and many other subgenres. Examples are given in Figure 4.7.

Folktales

As a genre separate from fiction, folktales are catalogued under nonfiction by many libraries. Folktales include the stories of Mother Goose and Uncle Remus, fables and legends of all cultures, mythologies, hero tales, religious literature, and folksongs. The genre can be further broken down into fairy tales, talking beast tales, noodlehead tales, trickster tales, cumulative tales, and many others. When we read folktales aloud to children, we not only offer them a pleasant read-aloud experience, but we also build their background knowledge of both the genre and culture. We build cultural literacy by exposing them to themes, narratives, and characters that are known and alluded to by a broad cross-section of people in Western culture. Allusions to folktales exist in many kinds of texts and in common conversation as well. When we hear that something is a "Sisyphean task," we get the picture immediately—if we know about the myth of Sisyphus. When we recite "Slow and steady wins the race," we're likewise alluding to a common Western body of folk literature.

We also build children's multicultural literacy when we read folktales to them. When we expose children to Anansi stories from Africa, Manabozho stories from the Ojibwe, Coyote stories from the Navajo, or folktales of Japan, we are building their knowledge about the cultures from which these tales arise and creating intercultural common bonds. But a word of caution is in order here. When choosing folk literature to read aloud from cultures other than our own, we need to be careful that the works we choose are authentic and are used appropriately. Sadly, many books, due to insufficient research by the author or illustrator, misrepresent the source culture or perpetuate stereotypes. Naturally, this is a more common problem when the author

Figure 4.7   Contemporary Realistic Fiction for Primary Grades

Aliki. *Marianthe's Story: Painted Words.*

Aliki. *The Two of Them.*

Aliki. *We Are Best Friends.*

Blades, Ann. *Mary of Mile 18.*

Bunting, Eve. *Fly Away Home.*

Clifton, Lucille. *My Friend Jacob.*

Cohen, Miriam. *See You in Second Grade.*

Cohen, Miriam. *Will I Have a Friend?*

de Paola, Tomie. *Nana Upstairs, Nana Downstairs.*

de Paola, Tomie. *Now One Foot, Now the Other.*

Fox, Mem. *Wilfrid Gordon McDonald Partridge.*

Havill, Juanita. *Jamaica and the Substitute Teacher.*

Henkes, Kevin. *Chester's Way.*

Henkes, Kevin. *Chrysanthemum.*

Hesse, Karen. *Sable.*

Kellogg, Steven. *Best Friends.*

Lasker, Joe. *He's My Brother.*

Lears, Laurie. *Ian's Walk: A Story of Autism.*

Little, Jean. *Emma's Magic Winter.*

Rosenberry, Vera. *Vera's First Day of School.*

Saenz, Benjamin Alire. *A Gift from Papa Diego/Un Regale de Papa Diego.*

Sharmat, Marjorie W. *Nate the Great.*

Viorst, Judith. *Rosie and Michael.*

Willner-Pardo, Gina. *Jumping into Nothing.*

Zolotow, Charlotte. *The Hating Book.*

Zolotow, Charlotte. *My Grandson Lew.*

Addresses IRS Standard 2.3

Use a wide range of curriculum materials in effective reading instruction for learners at different stages of reading and writing development and from different cultural and linguistic backgrounds.

does not come from the culture of the folktale he or she is retelling. The culture should be accurately portrayed, and the values presented in the book should reflect the authentic values of the culture. If we feel we do not have enough expertise to make this kind of judgment about a given book, we have some homework to do. We can research the culture or the author on our own, consult a member of the culture in question, interview a scholar with expertise in the area, or at least read reviews of the book. Often the reader reviews on Internet sites are very helpful in this regard; comments from readers who are members of the culture may illuminate problems we would never see on our own.

We need to make a special effort to read aloud books about a wide range of cultures because so few books are published for children in North America about non-Euro-American cultures. Sometimes our students can be sources of folktales for us. One teacher I know went into the homes of her Tongan and Samoan students and collected folktales from the family elders. She typed up the stories, had the children from those homes illustrate them, and bound them sturdily for classroom use.

Culturally diverse literature should be read throughout the school year. For example, we should not save books depicting African American characters for reading

Figure 4.8 Folktales from Around the World

Brett, Jan. *The Mitten: A Ukrainian Folktale.*

Bruchac, Joseph. *The Story of the Milky Way: A Cherokee Way.*

Climo, Shirley. *The Egyptian Cinderella.*

Climo, Shirley. *The Korean Cinderella.*

Demi. *The Empty Pot.*

Goble, Paul. *Crow Chief: A Plains Indian Story.*

Grifalconi, Ann. *The Village of Round and Square Houses.*

Hogrogian, Nonny. *The Contest.*

Hutton, Warwick. *The Trojan Horse.*

Jaffe, Nina. *The Golden Flower: A Taino Myth from Puerto Rico.*

Martin, Rafe. *The Rough-Faced Girl.*

McDermott, Gerald. *Raven: A Trickster Tale from the Pacific Northwest.*

Onyefulu, Obi. *Chinye: A West African Folk Tale.*

Oughton, Jerrie. *Magic Weaver of Rugs: A Tale of the Navajo.*

Pitcher, Caroline. *Mariana and the Merchild: A Folk Tale from Chile.*

Rockwell, Anne. *The Boy Who Wouldn't Obey: A Mayan Legend.*

San Souci, Robert D. *The Talking Eggs.*

Sierra, Judy. *The Beautiful Butterfly: A Folktale from Spain.*

Young, Ed. *Seven Blind Mice.*

only during Black History Month. Children in areas of the country where the population is still predominately White need to hear and read culturally diverse literature as much as, if not more than, children who are part of a culturally diverse population. Examples of folktale titles are given in Figure 4.8.

NONFICTION

It is important to read nonfiction aloud. The conventions of nonfiction are unique and need to be taught specifically. Background knowledge about the conventions of nonfiction is crucial to strong comprehension. As suggested by Harvey and Goudvis (2000), I have had my students make a nonfiction conventions booklet (see Figure 4.9). Their awareness of blurbs, captions, indexes, tables of content, and other conventions of nonfiction was heightened considerably. I have always pointed out these conventions when we read nonfiction, but I was impressed at how much more information about conventions they integrated into their background knowledge when they created the conventions themselves in their own booklets. Having been exposed to these conventions and having some understanding of their purposes, my students will encounter nonfiction texts in the future with a stronger foundation for comprehension.

Just as picture books are distinguished from other books by the balance of text and illustrations, nonfiction or informational books are distinguished from fiction because of the balance of fact and fiction. Although storytelling can be used as a way to convey facts, as in *Magic School Bus* books, for the book to be considered nonfiction,

Figure 4.9 Jade enjoyed the process of learning about nonfiction conventions.

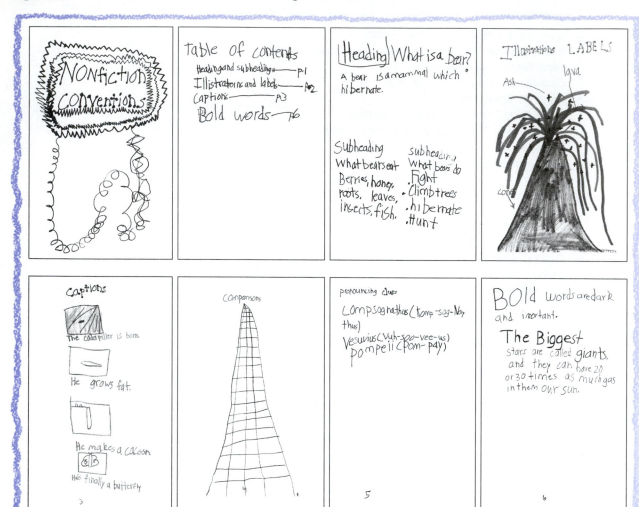

Nonfiction Conventions

Table of contents
Heading and subheadings ——— p.1
Illistrations and labels ——— p.2
Captions ——— p.3
Bold words ——— p6

[Heading] What is a bear?
A bear is a mammal which hibernate.

Subheading   subheading
What bears eat   What bears do
Berries, honey,   •Fight
roots, leaves,   •Climb trees
insects, fish.   •hibernate
                        •Hunt

Illustrations LABELS
Ash   lava
core

Captions
The catapiller is born.
He grows fat.
He makes a cocoon
He's finally a butterfly
3

Comparisons
4

pronouncing clues
Compsognathus (Komp-sog-Na-thus)
Vesuvius (Vuh-soo-vee-us)
Pompeii (Pom-pay)
5

BOld words are dark and inortant.
The Biggest stars are called giants, and they can have 20 or 30 times as much gas in them our sun.
6

glossary
Axis The imaginary line through the center of a star, plannet, or moon, around which it spins.
Core The center of a planet or star.
12

Index

Blurb
This book is about different nonfiction conventions. If you know about nonfiction conventions, you can write youre very own nonfiction book. YOu could learn a lot.

the facts must dominate. In children's literature, nonfiction books are becoming increasingly available, and their quality and appropriateness for younger children has improved. Many of the newest nonfiction books have exciting four-color photographs and illustrations, rather than black-and-white photographs and pen-and-ink drawings. Their text is less dense than that of older books; some have a single line of text on each page or only a short paragraph, making them appealing to beginning readers.

When we read nonfiction aloud, the opportunities for building our students' background knowledge are limitless. Nonfiction books present facts in the context of meaningful wholes and allow students to integrate new ideas into their existing schema. The students can create new categories of information in their schema and make new connections among existing concepts based on the books we read to them. You can find good nonfiction books on almost any topic. The excitement of finding a book on a topic that is interesting to them encourages students to grow. As they are read to or read these books on their own, students don't just dump facts into their brains; they respond to ideas, interpret the information for themselves, and construct their own understanding of it. The new ideas and information thus become a part of their whole way of thinking.

Nonfiction books are often a better way to teach concepts in science and social studies than the textbooks found in school. At the least, they support the textbook in ways that can deepen and enrich the students' understanding of the content area being studied. *A Seed Is a Promise* by Claire Merrill is an excellent example of nonfiction that provides accurate and comprehensive information about seeds and plants. A study of Antarctica is greatly enriched by reading *Antarctica,* by Helen Cowcher, in which the effect of humans on Emperor and Adelie penguins is examined thoughtfully, but not sentimentally. Nonfiction books pique students' interest in ways that textbooks cannot.

Biographies

Biographies are a convenient and fascinating way to introduce children to the concept of historical time; to help them compare their lives with the lives of those they read about; and to teach them social, cultural, and historical lessons, all in the context of one person's life. Biographies are often inspirational; children commonly learn from biographies that they, too, can make a difference in the world. They may also learn that the subjects of biographies are real people who not only made great achievements, but also made mistakes. In my classroom, I like to read aloud biographies in conjunction with the theme of civil rights, such as *A Picture Book of Martin Luther King, Jr.* by David Adler and *The Story of Ruby Bridges* by Robert Coles. Later the students add to the biography basket when they raid the library for biographies of sports figures, artists, presidents, inventors, and explorers. It's important for the teacher to provide balance in the collection by adding biographies of women and people from a range of cultures. I make it a point to read aloud a short nonfiction chapter book, *Helen Keller: Crusader for the Blind and Deaf* (Graff & Graff, 1991).

A selected list of biographies for children is given in Figure 4.10.

Math

Nonfiction can be used to support and extend all the curriculum areas. Even in math, picture books (both fiction and nonfiction) can be used to introduce, support, or

Figure 4.10   Biographies for the Primary Grades

Adler, David. *A Picture Book of Benjamin Franklin.*

Adler, David. *A Picture Book of Eleanor Roosevelt.*

Adler, David. *A Picture Book of Thomas Jefferson.*

Adler, David. *Jackie Robinson: He Was the First.*

Aliki. *The Many Lives of Benjamin Franklin.*

Bruchac, Joseph. *Crazy Horse's Vision.*

Burleigh, Robert. *Flight: The Journey of Charles Lindberg.*

Coles, Robert. *The Story of Ruby Bridges.*

Cooney, Barbara. *Eleanor.*

Giblin, James Cross. *George Washington: A Picture Book Biography.*

Gilliland, Judith Heide. *Steamboat! The Story of Captain Blanche Leathers.*

Hodges, Margaret. *Brother Francis and the Friendly Beasts.*

Jakes, John. *Susanna of the Alamo: A True Story.*

Le Tord, Bijou. *A Blue Butterfly: A Story About Claude Monet.*

Miller, William. *Frederick Douglass: The Last Day of Slavery.*

Poole, Josephine. *Joan of Arc.*

Ringgold, Faith. *My Dream of Martin Luther King.*

Rockwell, Anne. *Only Passing Through: The Story of Sojourner Truth.*

San Souci, Robert D. *Kate Shelley: Bound for Legend.*

Schroeder, Alan. *Minty: A Story of Young Harriet Tubman.*

Sis, Peter. *Follow the Dream: The Story of Christopher Columbus.*

Towle, Wendy. *The Real McCoy: The Life of an African-American Inventor.*

Venezia, Mike. (1993). *Georgia O'Keefe.*

Wallner, Alexandra. *Betsy Ross.*

Winter, Jeanette. *Sebastian: A Book About Bach.*

extend the mathematical thinking that the students are developing. For example, *The Doorbell Rang* by Pat Hutchins is a natural way to introduce division; children divide a plate of cookies into smaller and smaller portions as more and more people ring the bell and come into the kitchen. Jon Scieszka's *Math Curse* covers a wide range of mathematical problems, but the focus is on seeing math in everyday events and using them as a basis for problem solving. For excellent ideas on incorporating literature into math lessons, see *Math and Literature, Grades K–3* by Marilyn Burns. Additional titles are listed in Figure 4.11.

READING ALOUD TO DEVELOP STUDENTS' COMPREHENSION

When we read aloud with students we are able to teach them about responding to literature and building their background knowledge, but we are also able to teach them comprehension strategies that apply to all types of reading. Many terms are used in

Figure 4.11   Literature That Teaches Mathematics

Adler, David. *How Tall, How Short, How Faraway?*
Anno, Mitsumasa. *All in a Day.*
Anno, Mitsumasa. *Anno's Counting Book.*
Anno, Mitsumasa. *Anno's Magic Seeds.*
Axelrod, Amy. *Pigs Will Be Pigs.*
Bang, Molly. *Ten, Nine, Eight.*
Burningham, John. *The Shopping Basket.*
Burns, Marilyn. *The Greedy Triangle.*
Burns, Marilyn. *Spaghetti and Meatballs for All! A Mathematical Story.*
Crews, Donald. *Ten Black Dots.*
Ehlert, Lois. *Fish Eyes: A Book You Can Count On.*
Fleming, Denise. *Count!*
Friedman, Aileen. *A Cloak for the Dreamer.*
Friedman, Aileen. *The King's Commissioners.*
Hoban, Tana. *Count and See.*
Hoban, Tana. *Is it Larger? Is it Smaller?*
Hutchins, Pat. *Clocks and More Clocks.*
Hutchins, Pat. *The Doorbell Rang.*
Merriam, Eve. *12 Ways to Get to 11.*
Pinczes, Elinor. *A Remainder of One.*
Schwartz, David M. *How Much Is a Million.*
Schwartz, David M. *If You Hopped Like a Frog.*
Schwartz, David M. *If You Made a Million.*
Tompert, Ann. *Grandfather Tang's Story: A Tale Told with Tangrams.*
Walsh, Ellen Stoll. *Mouse Count.*

comprehension research, some of which are interchangeable. We will focus on five comprehension strategies that are effective and teachable: predicting, clarifying, questioning, summarizing, and evaluating.

PREDICTING

We naturally make predictions. Some people are so good at predicting a plot that they take all the fun out of going to a movie. Some people are very good at predicting how others will behave in certain situations. We want our students to predict, to make hypotheses about what the author will discuss next in a text, or how a character will react to an event, or what event will happen next. Sometimes students don't have enough background information to make a prediction or they don't access it. For example, as I was reading aloud *The Golden Compass* (Pullman, 1996) with Isaac, my 9-year-old son, one character poured a powder into a glass of wine that another character was going to drink. I asked Isaac, "What do you think the powder is?" He said, "I don't know." When we finished the chapter, I asked him, "Have you ever seen any movies or cartoons where someone pours powder into a glass?" "Yeah," he recalled, "in [the movie] *The Princess Bride*, a guy poisons both glasses, but he's been building up his immunity to the poison, so only the other guy dies." "Did you think of that when we read that part in the book?" "No."

As teachers, we want to model making predictions and show how we use our background knowledge to do that. We can then ask our students to make predictions; we ask them what they know about the situation and how that helps them to guess what might happen next. When we're thinking about the kinds of predictions we want our students to make, we're also thinking about how to ask questions that will solicit these predictions. These questions will, of necessity, be inferential. When we ask, "What do you think Sally will do when she sees Mark go into the cave?" there is no literal answer. There can only be conjecture and inference, basically the same thing. Readers constantly make predictions, conjectures, and inferences based on what they know, even while knowing they could be wrong. Of course, there are reasonable predictions and inferences and some not so reasonable. This is why we must make our students be accountable to the text. "What did the book say that made you think that?" "What do you base that idea on?" "Tell me or show me where in the story you began to think that this would happen."

DLTA–Directed Listening–Thinking Activity

Read aloud a story and stop at predetermined points to ask children to make predictions about what will happen next. With most stories, it works to stop after the title, shortly after the story begins, at one or two places of high interest during the story, and just before the story's problem is resolved. The questions you ask should be open ended. For example, "What do you think will happen next?" Students should be able to justify their answers and be accountable to the text when you ask, "Why do you think that? What in the story made you think that?" Here's an example from my own classroom:

After reading part of Eve Bunting's The Wednesday Surprise, *I paused and asked my students, "What do you think the surprise will be [the one that they're working on for Anna's dad]? "They're going to surprise the dad with a party," answered Megan.*

"They're going to give the dad a book, and they're trying to figure out which one to give him," said Ryan.

Lincoln said, "Anna might want to give him a birthday present that she knows how to read."

After we finished reading the book, I asked the class if they knew an older person who couldn't read. Only one student did. They didn't have the background knowledge they needed for predicting that the surprise was Grandma's being taught to read by 7-year-old Anna.

CLARIFYING

Background knowledge is also important when readers monitor their understanding by stopping to clarify what they've read. Clarifying is what readers do when they stop reading and ask themselves, "Did that make sense?" Perhaps they have read a word wrong and the sentence doesn't sound right, so good readers go back and reread to see whether they can figure out what went wrong. Or maybe they have read every word correctly, but don't know the meaning of a word and so the sentence doesn't make sense. Again, good readers might reread several sentences and see whether they can figure out the meaning from the context, or they ask someone else to help. Sometimes they read too quickly and realize they weren't paying attention to the meaning. Or they read aloud or in their heads with the emphasis on the wrong words, and the meaning breaks down. Rereading is the most frequent remedy good readers choose when a text doesn't seem to make sense.

When I read aloud to my students, I often stop to model clarifying. Reading *Duncan and Dolores* (Samuels, 1989) aloud to my second-graders, I stopped and said, "What is going on here?" Jared spoke up at once. "It's like Dolores always wants Duncan to play with her, and she says it really like mean, and he knows she's going to come and do something mean," he said. Evan added, "Whenever I want to play with my fish, he always goes to the back of his bowl. Unless he's hungry." Regina said, "We don't bother to play with my cat because he's fat and we're busy anyway."

Clarifying also happens when readers have completely understood a passage but stop to explain it to themselves in order to cement that understanding and perhaps attempt to store new ideas in their memory. Especially with nonfiction, I tell my students that it is important to stop and restate the ideas to myself. Then I show them how I monitor my comprehension and clarify what I've read. I ask myself aloud, "Do I understand what I've just read? Let's see . . . It says here that 'not all of these seeds will grow into plants. . . . A seed may not land on good earth. It may land on a rock or in your house.' Hmm . . . it may not land on 'good earth.' That's a funny way to say it. I think that means it might not land on real dirt, because then it says it could land on a rock or in your house, and that's not dirt so it won't grow." I tell the students that what I just did was clarifying—making sure things were clear to me.

Clarifying Frog and Toad

Even with a text as seemingly simple as Frog and Toad Are Friends *(Lobel, 1970), I take the opportunity to stop and model clarifying. "So there he is on the rock sticking his feet into the swimsuit."*

"No, he doesn't wear a swimsuit," Jordan reminds me.

"Oh, that's right. He's taking off his clothes. Oh that must be Frog, because Frog is just gonna go swimming in his frog skin."

"Yeah," reply several kids at once.

"You know what we're doing? We're clarifying. I'm making sure that I understand before I read more. I always get Frog and Toad mixed up."

"Frogs are green and toads are brown," says Jordan, helpfully.

"Well that helps me!"

If the students see that even an adult can be mixed up about a book like Frog and Toad, *then they understand how important it is to stop and clarify for themselves. We can also forgive them when they don't understand what seems obvious to us. Jordan thought it was obvious which was Toad and which was Frog, but she didn't make me feel dumb—she just reminded me how to tell the difference. She clarified for me.*

QUESTIONING

I have discussed questions as a way of having students respond to texts, but I want to touch on questioning again because it is such a powerful comprehension strategy. In fact, according to the National Reading Panel (2000), "the strongest scientific evidence was found for the effectiveness of asking readers to generate questions during reading" (p. 4-45). Proficient readers ask themselves questions before they read, while reading, and after they have read. We need to model for our students how to ask questions that clarify meaning and questions that speculate about what has not yet been read. Questions can also be about what the author intended to mean, the style of the writing, the content of the writing, and the format of the writing. Questions might also be **literal questions** that have specific answers in the text, or **inferential questions,** or even "wonderings"—questions that are not explicitly answered by the text.

During any kind of modeling, whether it's modeling questioning, clarifying, or predicting, we need to be sure that the students can see when we're reading the actual text and when we've stopped to discuss it. When we're thinking aloud, the students might think we're reading aloud unless we signal to them that we've stopped reading, either by looking at the students while talking or by saying something specific like, "Now, I'm going to ask some questions about what I've just read to you." The questions can be recorded on chart paper or whiteboard, which further clarifies that we're not reading aloud at that moment. Also, the questions can be grouped according to type and referred to later. It's important to point out that some of our questions may not be answered by a text. We might need to read a different book or find a recent article. Perhaps a question is not answerable, but rather is one that we might ponder, such as, "Does life exist on planets in other solar systems?" or "Would you eat the meat of a woolly mammoth found after being frozen for thousands of years?"

When we were reading *The Wednesday Surprise* (Bunting, 1989), the narrator, Anna, said, "I am sick from being nervous." I asked the class, "Why would Anna be nervous?" Jaren said, "She might be worried that her dad will look and find the present." Later, when Grandma is the one reading aloud, the book says, "Mom and Dad and Sam are all astonished!" I explain that astonished means very surprised. "Why would they be surprised to see Grandma reading?" Jaren answered, "Maybe it's not like her to read." Jordan said, "Maybe the grandma couldn't read for a long time and she practiced reading with Anna and now she can read." "Do you think she could read before and she forgot how?" I asked. "They've never seen Grandma read before," said Ryan.

It is more important to teach children to ask their own questions than to ask questions of them. Remember that comprehension questions don't *teach* comprehension, but only test it. Effective teachers encourage book discussions that focus on their students' authentic questions. We can provide children a structure for their wonderings by giving them ways to begin their questions. "I wonder . . . ." "Why does it say that . . . ?" "The part I don't understand is . . . ." "It confused me when it said . . . ."

Text Talk

Text talk (Beck & McKeown, 2001) is a way to help children not only improve their comprehension of texts, but also develop their use of language, because it focuses on helping children construct meaning from decontextualized language. Its components include the following:

> *Careful selection of texts:* The stories should have a series of events and enough complexity so that children can explore and explain ideas.

Initial questions: Through open-ended questions, the teacher asks children to talk about ideas, rather than recall specific words from the text. For example, using the story, *Julius, the Baby of the World,* the teacher might ask, "Why do you think Lilly changed her mind about Julius?" rather than "Who criticized Julius this time?"

Follow-up questions: Using students' initial responses, the teacher forms new questions to encourage students to elaborate on what they've already said.

Pictures: The teacher waits to show the pictures until after the students have heard the text and talked about it. Often children respond to the pictures, rather than the text, so for them to develop their ability to construct meaning from decontextualized language, it is important to reserve the pictures until after discussing the text.

Background knowledge: Students' background knowledge is not stressed except when it might be involved in a student's elaboration on an initial response. As with pictures, sometimes students focus too much on their background knowledge when responding to a text, and this can distract them from the work of constructing meaning from the text.

Vocabulary: Certain words are targeted for special attention. They should be somewhat unfamiliar to the children, yet words they can understand and possibly use in normal conversation.

SUMMARIZING OR RETELLING

Summarizing offers both the reader and the teacher a view of the reader's thinking process while reading. The reader learns to identify the most important ideas in a story or piece of text. Research on summarizing shows that, when students are taught to summarize, the quality of their summaries improves, their recall of the text improves, and they are better able to answer questions based on the text (National Reading Panel, 2000, p. 4–92).

When primary-grade students summarize, it often sounds like retelling, which is the logical place to begin teaching summarizing. Retelling is more detailed, but with young children who have just recently become efficient at decoding, retelling is an excellent way to assess whether they have understood what they read. Students who decode the words perfectly but have trouble retelling often resort to rereading instead of retelling. They seem to feel that finishing a book, having said or looked at all the words, is sufficient. We want them to understand that there's no point in reading the words if they don't get any meaning out of them.

I had a student one year—I'll call him Keith—who read very quickly and without expression and was unable to summarize or retell what he had read. Keith seemed to think that what I valued was reading lots of pages and finishing books. No doubt I had given him that impression somehow, so I had to work very hard to undo what I had inadvertently done. I said, "I don't care how many pages you read as much as I care that you understand what you read and can tell me about it." His head would nod, and I was never quite sure he believed me, but every day during reading workshop I asked Keith, "What just happened in your book?" Often the answers were vague, and often he claimed to have read far more than I thought possible. So I would ask him to reread while I listened. Every half-page or so, I would ask him to stop and summarize. I would also react with great interest to events in his book as they happened. This kind of coaching worked. He began seeking me out to tell me about his book, which indicated to me that he now understood what he was reading—indeed, understood the purpose of reading. By the end of the year, Keith was one of the best readers in the class.

Sometimes children can summarize what they just read, but they don't have an overall sense of the story. This happens frequently when a book is too difficult; the remedy is obvious—find a more appropriate book. When they can't retell, we ask the students, "Does this book feel comfortable to you?" Frequently, when asked, they can diagnose the problem themselves and save face by selecting an easier book. Sometimes the book isn't too difficult, but the child may need to retell frequently with a partner to practice monitoring his or her understanding and reinforce the idea that reading is supposed to make sense. In fact, we should have students retell with partners frequently, during a read-aloud or when they are partner-reading.

As we read aloud to our students, teachers also need to stop and summarize. We may begin the retelling and then hand it off to one of the students. "Okay, now it's your turn, Kimberly." If Kimberly leaves out an important portion of the story, we prompt her to go back or to ask another student to fill in what's missing. If she retells story events in the wrong order, we ask her or another student to try again. All this must be done in a way that doesn't embarrass the child. In fact, when we retell as teachers, we sometimes get things wrong, too. We need to point this out to our students so that they understand that we make mistakes, too, but that we are checking ourselves all the time. When our students catch our mistakes, and they often do, we admit freely that they're right and thank them. This way we're modeling how to receive feedback graciously and use it to enhance our understanding.

Retelling

I like to model retelling fiction using a story map as a guide. As I read aloud to the students, I stop and we add to the story map. The story map I use has five elements: characters, setting, problem, solution, and events. I write these elements on chart paper so that we have a record that can be saved and retrieved from day to day. This is especially important to do with texts that are too long to read in one sitting.

EVALUATING

Effective teachers encourage students to be critical readers on several levels. The first level is personal. Did they like the text and why? Was the sequel better than the first book and why? Who is their favorite author? What's their favorite genre? Rank this book on a scale of 1 to 10. Is the main character one that we can sympathize with? For example, after reading one of our guided reading books, Melissa said, "I liked it. I liked how it told how she had to get the water and it was heavy and then she would help her mom make breakfast. The best part was that she wrote 'Happy New Year' at the end." About the same book, Regina said, "I liked it because she put a lot of detail in like she put the date like 1866. I liked the drawings too. It kinda looks like a little kid drew it. I liked the writing [the font] too because it looks like a kid wrote it."

The second level is literary. Why did the author begin the story this way? Could the story have begun in a better way? Were there places that seemed confusing? Were there places where the action was too slow? Do long descriptive passages help you to enjoy the story, or do they get in the way?

Finally, we want our students to read texts on a social or political level. Why does a character describe Native Americans as savages? What can we do to help the homeless now that we understand what their lives are like? Is it okay for a boy to want a doll?

 ## CONCLUSIONS

Through reading aloud and discussing what was read, teachers encourage students to be critical, effective, and comprehending readers. It sounds simple, but of course it's not. Perhaps the hardest thing is keeping a balance between reading and discussing. And the next hardest thing is making sure that the talk is accomplishing one of the goals I've addressed here: responding to literature, increasing background knowledge, or improving comprehension skills. We want students to love literature, to love reading, and to grow intellectually from the encounters with literature that we create with them.

 ## SUGGESTED ACTIVITIES TO EXTEND YOUR LEARNING

1. Read aloud Taro Yashima's picture book *Crow Boy* (or any high-quality children's book) and write four columns on the whiteboard labeled: Feelings, Connections, Questions, and Favorite parts. Model your responses to each of these categories. On another day, with another book, invite students to model their responses to these categories.
2. Evaluate a classroom collection of books to see which genres are available.
3. Conduct a genre book hunt with students. Teach a minilesson on a particular genre, read aloud an example of this genre, and then ask students to find other books in the classroom that are of the same genre.
4. Based on the information in "Text Talk" on pages 96–97, develop a text talk lesson using a children's book with which students are not familiar.

 ## REFERENCES

Anderson, R. C., Hiebert, E. H., Scott, J. A., & Wilkinson, I. A. G. (1985). *Becoming a nation of readers: The report of the Commision on Reading.* Champaign-Urbana, IL: The Center for the Study of Reading.

Anderson, R. C., & Pearson, P. D. (1985). A schema-theoretic view of basic processes in reading. In P. D. Pearson (Ed.), *Handbook of reading research* (pp. 255–292). White Plains, NY: Longman.

Atwell, N. (2001). Keynote speech at the Spring 2001 Conference of the National Council of Teachers English, Birmingham, AL.

Beck, I. L., and McKeown, M. G. (2001). Text talk: Capturing the benefits of read-aloud experiences for young children. *Reading Teacher, 55*(1), 10–20.

Beck, I. L., McKeown, M. G., & Kucan, L. (2002). *Bring words to life: Robust vocabulary instruction.* New York: Guilford Press.

Burns, M. (1992). *Math and literature, grades K–3, book one.* Sausalito, CA: Math Solutions Publications.

Calkins, L. (2001). *The art of teaching reading.* New York: Longman.

Elley, W. B. (1992). *How in the world do students read?* Hamburg: International Association for the Evaluation of Educational Achievement.

Harste, J., and Burke, C. (1996). *Creating classrooms for authors and inquirers.* Portsmouth, NH: Heinemann.

Harvey, S., & Goudvis, A. (2000) *Strategies that work: Teaching comprehension to enhance understanding.* York, ME: Stenhouse.

Keene, E. O., & Zimmerman, S. (1997). *Mosaic of thought: Teaching comprehension in a reader's workshop.* Portsmouth, NH: Heinemann.

National Reading Panel. (2000). Teaching children to read: An evidence-based assessment of the scientific research literature on reading and its implications for reading instruction. *Report of the National Reading Panel.* Washington, DC: U.S. Department of Health and Human Services.

New Standards Primary Literacy Committee. (1999). Reading & writing grade by grade: Primary literacy standards for kindergarten through third grade. Washington, DC: National Center on Education and the Economy and the University of Pittsburgh.

Oczkus, L. D. (2003). *Reciprocal teaching at work: Strategies for improving reading comprehension.* Newark, DE: International Reading Association.

Palinscar, A. S., and Brown, A. L. (1984). Reciprocal teaching of comprehension—fostering and monitoring activities. *Cognition and Instruction, 1,* 117–175.

Pearson, P. D., Dole, J. A., Duffy, G. G., & Roehler, L. R. (1992). Developing expertise in reading comprehension: What should be taught and how should it be taught? In J. Farstrup & S. J. Samuels, (Eds.), *What research has to say to the teacher of reading,* 2nd ed. Newark, DE: International Reading Association.

Pearson, P. D., & Stephens, D. (1998). Learning about literacy: A 30-year journey. In C. Weaver (Ed.), *Reconsidering a balanced approach to reading.* (pp. 77–100). Urbana, IL: National Council of Teachers of English.

Rosenblatt, L. M. (1936/1978). *The reader, the text, the poem: The transactional theory of literary work.* Carbondale, IL: Southern Illinois University Press.

Rumelhart, D. (1980). Schemata: The building blocks of cognition. In R. J. Spiro, B. C. Bruce, & W. F. Brewer (Eds.), *Theoretical issues in reading comprehension* (pp. 33–58). Hillsdale, NJ: Erlbaum.

Short, K., Harste, J., & Burke, C. (1995). *Creating classrooms for authors and inquirers.* Portsmouth, NH: Heinemann.

Trelease, J. (2001). *The new read-aloud handbook,* 5th ed. New York: Penguin Books.

Children's Literature References

Ackerman, K. (1992). *When Mama retires.* Illus. A. Grace. New York: Knopf.

Adler, D. (1989). *A picture book of Martin Luther King, Jr.* New York: Holiday House.

Adler, D. (1989). *Jackie Robinson: He was the first.* New York: Holiday House.

Adler, D. (1990). *A picture book of Benjamin Franklin.* New York: Holiday House.

Adler, D. (1990). *A picture book of Thomas Jefferson.* New York: Holiday House.

Adler, D. (1991). *A picture book of Eleanor Roosevelt.* New York: Holiday House.

Adler, D. (1999). *How tall, how short, how faraway?* New York: Holiday House.

Aliki. (1982). *We are best friends.* New York: Greenwillow.

Aliki. (1983). *A medieval feast.* New York: HarperCollins.

Aliki. (1987). *The two of them.* New York: Morrow/Avon.

Aliki. (1989). *The many lives of Benjamin Franklin.* New York: Simon & Schuster.

Aliki. (1999). *Marianthe's story: Painted words/spoken memories.* New York: Greenwillow.

Anno, M. (1977). *Anno's counting book.* New York: HarperCollins.

Anno, M. (1990). *All in a day.* New York: Philomel.

Anno, M. (1995). *Anno's magic seeds.* New York: Philomel.

Axelrod, A. (1994). *Pigs will be pigs.* Illus. S. McGinley-Nally. New York: Macmillan.

Bang, M. (1983). *Ten, nine, eight.* New York: Greenwillow.

Bartone, E. (1993). *Peppe the lamplighter.* New York: Lothrop, Lee, & Shepard.

Blades, A. (1971). *Mary of mile 18.* Plattsville, NY: Tundra.

Blume, J. (1972). *Tales of a fourth grade nothing.* New York: Dell Yearling.

Brett, J. (1988). *The first dog.* New York: Harcourt Brace.

Brett, J. (1990). *The Mitten: A Ukrainian folktale.* New York: Putnam.

Bruchac, J. (2000). *Crazy Horse's vision.* New York: Lee and Low.

Bruchac, J., & Ross, G. (1995) *The story of the Milky Way: A Cherokee way.* New York: Dial.

Bulla, C. R. (1981). *A lion to guard us.* New York: HarperCollins.

Bunting, E. (1989). *The Wednesday surprise.* New York: Clarion.

Bunting, E. (1990). *The wall.* Illus. R. Himler. Boston: Houghton.

Bunting, E. (1991). *Fly-away home.* Illus. R. Himler. New York: Clarion.

Bunting, E. (1995). *Dandelions.* Illus. G. Shed. San Diego, CA: Harcourt.

Burleigh, R. & Wimmer, M. (1991). *Flight: The journey of Charles Lindberg.* New York: Philomel.

Burningham, J. (1980). *The shopping basket.* New York: HarperCollins.

Burns, M. (1994). *The greedy triangle.* New York: Scholastic.

Burns, M. (1997). *Spaghetti and meatballs for all! A mathematical story.* New York: Scholastic.

Carle, E. (1967). *Brown bear, brown bear, what do you see?* New York: Holt.

Cherry, L. (1992). *A river ran wild.* New York: Dutton.

Cleary, B. (1975). *Ramona the brave.* New York: Morrow.

Clifton, L. (1980). *My friend Jacob.* Illus. T. DiGrazia. New York: Dutton.

Coerr, E. (1986). *The Josephina story quilt.* New York: HarperCollins.

Coerr, E. (1995). *Buffalo Bill and the Pony Express.* New York: HarperCollins.

Cohen, M. (1967). *Will I have a friend?* Illus. L. Hoban. New York: Macmillan.

Cohen, M. (1989). *See you in second grade!* Illus. L. Hoban. New York: Greenwillow.

Coles, R. (1995). *The story of Ruby Bridges.* New York: Scholastic.

Conrad, P. (1989). *The tub people.* Illus. R. Egielski. New York: HarperCollins.

Cooney, B. (1996). *Eleanor.* New York: Viking.

Cowcher, H. (1990). *Antarctica.* New York: Farrar, Straus & Giroux.

Crews, D. (1986). *Ten black dots.* New York: Greenwillow.

Cronin, D. (2000). *Click, clack, moo: Cows that type.* New York: Simon & Schuster Children's Publishing.

Cullinan, B. (1996). *A jar of tiny stars: Poems by NCTE award-winning poets.* Honesdale, PA: Boyds Mills.

Dahl, R. (1982). *The BFG.* London: Puffin.

Demi. (1990). *The empty pot.* New York: Holt.

de Paola, T. (1973). *Nana upstairs, Nana downstairs.* New York: Putnam.

de Paola, T. (1981). *Now one foot, now the other.* New York: Putnam.

DiCamillo, K. (2003). *Tale of Despereaux: Being the story of a mouse, a princess, some soup, and a spool of thread.* Cambridge, MA: Candlewick Press.

Ehlert, L. (1990). *Fish eyes: A book you can count on.* San Diego, CA: Harcourt.

Fleishman, P. (1991). *Time train.* Illus. C. Ewart. New York: HarperCollins.

Fleishman, P. (1999) *Weslandia.* Cambridge, MA: Candlewick Press.

Fleming, D. (1992). *Count!* New York: Holt.

Florian, D. (1994). *Bing bang boing.* New York: Harcourt Brace.

Fox, M. (1985). *Wilfrid Gordon McDonald Partridge.* Illus. J. Vivas. Brooklyn, NY: Kane Miller.

Frasier, D. (2000). *Miss Alaneus: A vocabulary disaster.* New York: Harcourt.

Freeman, D. (1968). *Corduroy.* New York: Viking.

Friedman, A. (1994a). *A cloak for the dreamer.* Illus. K. Howard. New York: Scholastic.

Friedman, A. (1994b). *The king's commissioners.* Illus. S. Guevara. New York: Scholastic.

Frost, R. (1994) *Poetry for young people.* New York: Sterling Publishing.

Giblin, J. C. (1992). *George Washington: A picture book biography.* New York: Scholastic.

Gilliland, J. H. (2000). *Steamboat! The story of Captain Blanche Leathers.* New York: DK International/Kroupa.

Goble, P. (1992). *Crow chief: A Plains Indian story.* New York: Scholastic.

Goodall, J. (1979). *The story of an English village.* New York: Atheneum.

Graff, S., & Graff, P. A. (1991). *Helen Keller, crusader for the blind and deaf.* New York: Dell Yearling.

Greenfield, E. (1978). *Honey, I love and other love poems.* Illus. L. Dillon & D. Dillon. New York: HarperCollins.

Grifalconi, A. (1986). *The village of round and square houses.* Boston: Little, Brown.

Grimes, N. (1994). *Meet Denitra Brown.* New York: Lothrop, Lee & Shepard.

Grimes, N. (1999) *My man blue.* New York: Dial Books for Young Readers.

Haley, G. (1973). *Jack Jouett's ride.* New York: Viking.

Hall, D. (1994) *Lucy's Christmas.* New York: Harcourt Brace.

Hall, D. (1995). *Lucy's Summer.* San Diego, CA: Harcourt.

Hall, D. (1983). *Ox-cart man.* New York: Puffin.

Havill, J. (1999). *Jamaica and the substitute teacher.* Boston: Houghton.

Henkes, K. (1988). *Chester's way.* New York: Greenwillow.

Henkes, K. (1990). *Julius, the baby of the world.* New York: Morrow/Avon.

Henkes, K. (1991). *Chrysanthemum.* New York: Greenwillow.

Hesse, K. (1994). *Sable.* New York: Holt.

Hirschland, R. B. (1996). *How animals care for their babies.* Washington, DC: National Geographic Society.

Hoban, T. (1972). *Count and see.* New York: Simon & Schuster.

Hoban, T. (1985). *Is it larger? Is it smaller?* New York: Greenwillow.

Hoberman, M. (1991). *Fathers, mothers, sisters, brothers.* New York: Little, Brown.

Hodges, M. (1991). *Brother Francis and the friendly beasts.* Illus. T. Lewin. New York: Scribner's.

Hoffman, M. (1991). *Amazing grace.* Illus. C. Binch. New York: Dial.

Hogrogian, N. (1976). *The contest.* New York: Greenwillow.

Hopkins, L. B. (1988). *Side by side: Poems to read together.* New York: Simon & Schuster.

Houston, G. (1992). *But no candy.* New York: Philomel.

Hunt, J. (1989). *Illuminations.* New York: Bradbury.

Hutchins, P. (1970). *Clocks and more clocks.* New York: Macmillan.

Hutchins, P. (1986). *The doorbell rang.* New York: HarperCollins.

Hutton, W. (1992). *The Trojan horse: Retold.* New York: Simon & Schuster.

Hyman, T. S. (1986). *Little Red Riding Hood.* New York: Holiday House.

Jaffe, N. (1996). *The golden flower: A Taino myth from Puerto Rico.* New York: Simon & Schuster.

Jakes, J. (1986). *Susanna of the Alamo: A true story.* San Diego, CA: Harcourt.

Johnston, T. (1985). *The quilt story.* Illus. T. de Paola. New York: Putnam.

Joosse, B. M. (1995). *The morning chair.* New York: Clarion.

Joyce, W. (1985). *George shrinks.* New York: Harper & Row.

Kellogg, S. (1986). *Best friends.* New York: Dial.

Kuskin, K. (1980). *Dogs and dragons, trees and dreams.* New York: HarperCollins.

Lasker, J. (1974). *He's my brother.* Niles, IL: Whitman.

Lasker, J. (1978). *Merry ever after: The story of two medieval weddings.* New York: Viking.

Lears, L. (1998). *Ian's walk: A story of autism.* Illus. K. Ritz. Morton Grove, IL: Whitman.

Le Tord, B. (1995). *A blue butterfly: A story about Claude Monet.* New York: Doubleday.

Little, J. (1998). *Emma's magic winter.* Illus. J. Plecas. New York: HarperCollins.

Lobel, A. (1970). *Frog and Toad are friends.* New York: HarperCollins.

Lobel, A. (1991). *The dwarf giant.* New York: Holiday House.

Lucas, B. (1993). *Snowed in.* New York: Simon & Schuster.

Lyon, G. (1993). *Dreamplace.* New York: Scholastic.

Marshall, E. (1982). *Space case.* New York: Dial.

Martin, R. (1992). *The rough-faced girl.* Illus. D. Shannon. New York: Putnam.

Marzollo, J. (1984). *Ruthie's rude friends.* New York: Dial.

Marzollo, J. (1989). *Jed and the space bandits.* New York: Dial.

McClosky, R. (1941). *Make way for ducklings.* New York: Viking.

McDermott, G. (1993). *Raven: A trickster tale from the Pacific Northwest.* San Diego, CA: Harcourt.

McGel, A. (1999). *Molly Bannaky.* Illus. C. Soentpiet. Boston: Houghton.

McKissack, P. (1988). *Mirandy and Brother Wind.* Illus. J. Pinkney. New York: Knopf.

Merriam, E. (1988). *You be good and I'll be night.* New York: Morrow/Avon.

Merriam, E. (1993). *12 ways to get to 11.* New York: Simon & Schuster.

Merrill, C. (1973). *A seed is a promise.* Illus. S. Swan. New York: Scholastic.

Miller, W. (1995). *Frederick Douglass: The last day of slavery.* New York: Lee and Low.

Mitchell, M. (1993). *Uncle Jed's barbershop.* New York: Simon & Schuster.

Nickle, J. (1999). *The ant bully.* New York: Scholastic.

Norton, M. (1953). *The Borrowers.* New York: Harcourt Brace.

Nye, N. (1998). *The space between our footsteps: Poems and paintings from the Middle East.* New York: Simon & Schuster.

Onyefulu, O. (1994). *Chinye: A West African folk tale.* New York: Viking.

Oppenheim, S. (1992). *The lily cupboard.* Illus. R. Himler. New York: HarperCollins.

Osborne, M. (1992). *The magic tree house: Dinosaurs before dark.* New York: Random House.

Oughton, J. (1994). *Magic weaver of rugs: A tale of the Navajo.* Boston: Houghton.

Paek, M. (1988). *Aekyung's dream.* San Francisco: Children's Book Press.

Pinczes, E. (1995). *A remainder of one.* Boston: Houghton.

Pitcher, C. (2000). *Mariana and the merchild: A folk tale from Chile.* Illus. J. Morris. Grand Rapids, MI: Eerdmans.

Polacco, P. (1994) *My rotten redheaded older brother.* New York: Simon & Schuster.

Pomerantz, C. (1980) *The tamarindo puppy and other poems.* New York: Greenwillow.

Pomerantz, C. (1982). *If I had a Paka: Poems in eleven languages.* New York: Greenwillow.

Poole, J. (1998). *Joan of Arc.* Illus. A. Barrett. New York: Knopf.

Potter, B. (1902). *The tale of Peter Rabbit.* London: Warne.

Prelutsky, J. (1983). *The Random House book of poetry.* Illus. A. Lobel. New York: Random House.

Pullman, P. (1996). *The golden compass.* New York: Knopf.

Rappaport, D. (1988). *The Boston coffee party.* Illus. E. McCully. New York: HarperCollins.

Ray, M. (1994). *Alvah and Arvilla.* San Diego, CA: Harcourt.

Rinaldi, A. (1999). *My heart is on the ground: The diary of Nannie Little Rose, a Sioux girl.* New York: Scholastic.

Ringgold, F. (1995). *My dream of Martin Luther King.* New York: Crown.

Rockwell, A. (2000a). *Only passing through: The story of Sojourner Truth.* New York: Knopf.

Rockwell, A. (2000b). *The boy who wouldn't obey: A Mayan legend.* New York: Greenwillow.

Rosenberry, V. (1999). *Vera's first day of school.* New York: Holt.

Saenz, B. (1998). *A gift from Papa Diego/Un regale de Papa Diego.* Minneapolis, MN: Sagebrush Education Resouces.

Samuels, B. (1989). *Duncan and Dolores.* Scott Foresman.

San Souci, R. (1990). *The talking eggs: A folktale from the American South.* Illus. J. Pinkney. New York: Dial.

San Souci, R. (1995). *Kate Shelley: Bound for legend.* New York: Dial.

Say, A. (1999). *Tea with milk.* Boston: Houghton.

Schroeder, A. (1996). *Minty: A story of young Harriet Tubman.* Illus. J. Pinkney. New York: Dial.

Schwartz, D. (1985). *How much is a million?* Illus. S. Kellog. New York: Lothrop, Lee and Shepard.

Schwartz, D. (1989). *If you made a million.* New York: HarperCollins.

Schwartz, D. (1999). *If you hopped like a frog.* New York: Scholastic.

Scieszka, J. (1995). *Math curse.* New York: Putnam.

Sendak, M. (1963). *Where the wild things are.* New York: Harper & Row.

Sharmat, M. (1972). *Nate the great.* New York: Coward-McCann.

Sierra, J. (2000). *The beautiful butterfly: A folktale from Spain.* New York: Clarion.

Sis, P. (1991). *Follow the dream: The story of Christopher Columbus.* New York: Knopf.

Soto, G. (1993). *Too many tamales.* New York: Putnam.

Spooner, M. (1993). *A moon in your lunch box.* New York: Henry Holt.

Standiford, N. (1999). *Space Dog the hero.* New York: Random House.

Stevenson, J. (1992). *Don't you know there's a war on?* New York: HarperCollins.

Stevenson, R. (1947). *A child's garden of verses.* New York: Oxford University Press.

Tompert, A. (1990). *Grandfather Tang's story: A tale told with tangrams.* New York: Crown.

Towle, W. (1993). *The real McCoy: The life of an African-American inventor.* New York: Scholastic.

Turner, A. (1985). *Dakota dugout.* New York: Macmillan.

Turner, A. (1995). *Dust for dinner.* New York: HarperCollins.

Van Allsburg, C. (1979). *The garden of Abdul Gasazi.* Boston: Houghton Mifflin.

Van Allsburg, C. (1981). *Jumanji.* Boston: Houghton Mifflin.

Venezia, M. (1993). *Georgia O'Keefe.* Chicago: Children's Press.

Viorst, J. (1972). *Alexander and the terrible, horrible, no good, very bad day.* New York: Atheneum.

Viorst, J. (1974). *Rosie and Michael.* New York: Atheneum.

Wallner, A. (1994). *Betsy Ross.* New York: Holiday House.

Walsh, E. (1991). *Mouse count.* San Diego, CA: Harcourt Brace Jovanovich.

Walsh, J. (1982). *The green book.* New York: Farrar, Straus & Giroux.

White, E. B. (1952). *Charlotte's web.* New York: Harper & Brothers.

Wiesner, D. (1999). *Sector 7.* Boston: Houghton Mifflin.

Willner-Pardo, G. (1999). *Jumping into nothing.* New York: Clarion Books.

Winter, J. (1988). *Follow the drinking gourd.* New York: Knopf.

Winter, J. (1999). *Sebastian: A book about Bach.* San Diego, CA: Harcourt Brace.

Winthrop, E. (1993). *Battle for the castle.* New York: Holiday House.

Worth, V. (1987). *All the small poems.* New York: Farrar, Straus, Giroux.

Yashima, T. (1955) *Crow boy.* New York: Viking Press.

Yolen, J. (1980). *Commander Toad in space.* New York: Coward McCann.

Yolen, J. (1987). *Owl moon.* New York: Philomel Books.

Yolen, J. (1989). *Things that go bump in the night: A collection of stories.* New York: Harper & Row.

Yolen, J. (1992). *Encounter.* San Diego, CA: Harcourt Brace.

Yorinks, A. (1986). *Hey, Al.* New York: Farrar, Straus and Giroux.

Young, E. (1992). *Seven blind mice.* New York: Philomel.

Zelinsky, P. O. (1986). *Rumpelstiltskin.* New York: Dutton.

Zolotow, C. (1969). *The hating book.* New York: Harper & Row.

Zolotow, C. (1974). *My grandson Lew.* New York: Harper & Row.

Web Sites for Children's Literature

www.acs.ucalgary.ca/~dkbrown, searchable database at the University of Calgary, Canada

www.ala.org, American Library Association

www.bookwire.com, book reviews from *School Library Journal, Publisher's Weekly,* and Library Journal.

www.carolhurst.com, book reviews, suggestions for classroom use, thematic units

Word Study

John A. Smith

Tickle Words

I t's a Monday morning in mid-November in my first-grade classroom. My 23 students are seated together on the shag rug in front of my chalkboard, waiting to see what I'm going to come up with today.

My spelling pattern instruction task today is to introduce the spelling pattern CVCe, where the final silent e makes the preceding vowel say its long name. Behind me is a chart paper list of eight CVCe words.

time	same
made	side
Pete	hope
bone	dude

I point to the list of words and ask, "What's the same about all these words?" Francisco says they all have four letters. Jacque points out that they all end with the letter e. I thank Francisco and return to Jacque's comment. We look at the words together and notice all the final letter es. Then I point to and read the example words aloud to my students.

I then tell my students the "secret" to these words: "the final e reaches back over the consonant and tickles the vowel, which makes the vowel says its long name." My students are confused, so I point to the first example word time. "Watch how this works," I say. I cover up the final e and ask, "What's this word now?" "Tim," my students all shout, "We know it's Tim because it's a beginner word. That's easy."

Then I continue, "the final e reaches over the letter m, tickles the letter i, and makes it say its long name." At this point I nearly shout out a long i sound, as if I were being tickled. This startles my students, but it also gets their attention and makes the lesson fun. I repeat this overly dramatic explanation with each of the seven remaining example words. I always leave dude to the last. The students love it when the final e changes dud to dude.

I follow up this introduction of final silent e words with an activity designed to further cement the final silent e pattern into their heads. I send my students back to their desks, give each a handout with a dozen silent e words printed on it, and instruct them to cut out the words and spread them out across their desks. When *they are ready, I pronounce the final silent* e *words and ask students to find the same printed word on their desk and hold it up to show that they know it.*

After a few minutes of this, I show them how I can fold back the final e *on my paper word to make the word into a beginner word. Immediately, 23 students fold their final* es *back to see how the final* e *words have changed back to beginner words. Then I alternate pronouncing long and short vowel words (Tim, made, hop, side, pet, same, Sam, dude) and ask my students to hold them up. My students love finding the proper words and folding the final* es *back or out to make the vowel sound long or short.*

I conclude this introductory final silent e *spelling pattern lesson by projecting an overhead transparency onto the chalkboard of a paragraph that contains a large number of final silent* e *words. I read the paragraph aloud to my students and ask who can come to the chalkboard and underline some silent* e *words. My students study the transparency for a few seconds and then hands shoot up as they can't wait to come to the board, take chalk in hand, and underline one of the final silent* e *words. My students easily identify and underline all the silent* e *words in the paragraph.*

My final silent e *instruction for them tomorrow will be to review the example word chart together, give each a piece of paper, have them open their basal reading books, and with a partner make a list of all the final silent* e *words they can find in the book. After five to seven days of similar final silent* e *activities, my students will have no choice but to recognize the final silent* e *spelling pattern in virtually all the print they see.*

The purpose of this chapter is to familiarize you with the most common and useful spelling patterns and sight words with a simple three-step procedure for teaching them. This chapter will also describe the word identification activities that can be used interchangeably to teach the spelling patterns and sight words. Major topics of this chapter include the following:

- Understanding word identification
- Teaching word identification: in context and in isolation?
- Common spelling patterns
- Teaching spelling patterns: a three-step model
- Activities for teaching spelling patterns
- Structural analysis
- Sight vocabulary
- Conclusion

 ## UNDERSTANDING WORD IDENTIFICATION

OVERVIEW

In education, no single word may be as controversial and politically charged as *phonics*. Some people associate phonics with worksheets, meaningless drill-and-kill exercises, and generations of students who have been turned off to reading. Others genuinely believe that phonics is all that is really needed to read. The truth is that phonics is a necessary component of a balanced comprehensive reading instruction program, it can be taught in an enjoyable and effective manner, and it must be linked to meaningful aspects of reading.

Throughout the chapter I will often use the term **word identification.** I prefer this term because it goes beyond blending letter–sounds (phonics) to also include the important word identification contributions of context, syntax, and sight vocabulary.

WHAT DOES RESEARCH TELL US ABOUT WORD IDENTIFICATION INSTRUCTION?

A tremendous amount of educational research has been devoted to beginning reading instruction and specifically to the role of phonics. Three major conclusions from this research guide the word identification perspectives and instructional recommendations presented in this chapter:

1. Phonics instruction must be direct and systematic.
2. Phonics instruction must be linked to meaningful reading.
3. Phonics instruction must be simple, flexible, and enjoyable.

Phonics Instruction Must be Direct and Systematic

The cumulative findings of decades of beginning reading research support teaching word identification skills directly and systematically (Adams, 1990a, 2001; National Reading Panel, 2000; Stanovich, 2000). Direct phonics instruction, sometimes referred to as explicit phonics instruction, means that you present the phonics concepts to your students clearly and concisely. Systematic instruction refers to having a specific sequence of decoding concepts. Students learn the simplest decoding concepts first and then move to more complex concepts that build on and reinforce previous learning. An instructional sequence helps students to see the logic and structure of the alphabetic system (Adams, 2001).

Research studies continue to describe the benefits of direct systematic decoding instruction. Pressley, Rankin, and Yokai (1995) state that "explicitly teaching phonemic awareness, phonics, and letter–sound analysis have promoted improved performance on standardized tests and have proven superior to programs emphasizing meaning-making, such as whole language" (p. 3). The NRP's (2000) meta-analysis (combining and reanalyzing data from many studies) of the reading research data "provided solid support for the conclusion that systematic phonics instruction makes a more significant contribution to children's growth in reading" than do reading programs that provide unsystematic or no phonics instruction (p. 2–132).

It is also very interesting to note that, like the First Grade Studies described in chapter 1, the NRP concluded that no particular phonics program was the one and only best way to teach phonics. The NRP found that the various phonics programs they examined "do not appear to differ significantly from each other in their effectiveness" (p. 2–132). In other words, a number of phonics approaches can do the job effectively.

Phonics Instruction Must be Linked to Meaningful Reading

While word identification instruction is a very important part of a balanced instructional program, it must be kept in proper perspective. Sometimes word identification instruction is presented only as an isolated independent curriculum with little or no connection to the meaningful aspects of reading. Members of the National Reading Panel (2000, p. 2–135) wrote:

> Phonics teaching is a means to an end. . . . Programs that focus too much on the teaching of letter–sound relations and not enough on putting them to use are unlikely to be very effective. In implementing systematic phonics instruction, educators must keep the *end* in mind and ensure that children understand the purpose of learning letter–sounds and are able to apply their skills in their daily reading and writing activities.

Thus, phonics is only one aspect of reading instruction and must be integrated with other instructional components to provide comprehensive balanced reading instruction (Adams, 1990a; Anderson, Hiebert, Scott, & Wilkinson, 1985; Duffy, 1998; Fisher & Hiebert, 1990). Members of the National Reading Panel concluded that "phonics instruction is never a total reading program" (p. 2–97). Adams (1990b) did an exhaustive review of two decades of beginning reading research and concluded that "Approaches in which systematic code instruction is included along with the reading of connected text result in superior reading achievement overall, for both low-readiness and better prepared students" (p. 125).

A survey of 83 K–2 teachers from across the country who were identified as being effective, based on their students' reading achievement, provided important insights into the benefits of combining phonics with meaningful reading instruction (Pressley, Rankin, Yokoi, 1995; Pressley, Yokoi, Rankin, & Wharton-McDonald, 1995; 1997). The survey results suggested that effective teachers used instruction that is "multifaceted rather than based on one approach or another" (p. 3). These teachers allocated about 71% of their literacy instruction time to holistic practices, including providing a literate classroom environment, modeling comprehension and writing process strategies, flexible grouping for instruction, sensitivity to students' instructional needs, integrating reading instruction across the curriculum, and using extension activities. These teachers also reported spending approximately 27% of their time teaching a variety of word identification skills, including use of context and syntax cues, sounding out words, and using structural analysis cues and syllabication rules. Eighty-eight percent of the teachers who reported teaching word identification skills also reported providing "some isolated skills instruction, most often involving games and puzzles to teach the skill or provide practice with it" (p.15). Ninety-five percent of the teachers reported explicitly teaching phonics. Rayner, Foorman, Perfetti, Pesetsky, and Seidenberg, (2002, p. 91), in their research summary for the journal *Scientific American*, concluded that "indeed, recent work has indicated—and many teachers have discovered—that the combination of literature-based instruction and phonics is more powerful than either method alone."

Phonics Instruction Must be Simple, Flexible, and Enjoyable

Phonics instruction must be kept simple so that beginning readers will not be overwhelmed with an overabundance of meaningless and sometimes conflicting rules. Many phonics rules are inconsistent (Clymer, 1963, 1996; Johnston, 2001) or else apply to words that seldom appear in beginning reading texts. For example, as a first-year teacher I wasted half a teacher workday making a board game (suggested by the curriculum I was told to follow). The game was supposed to help students learn the rule that *g* is silent when it comes before *n*, so my students would be able to decode the words *gnu* and *gnome*. How often to you think these words appeared in my students' reading materials? Adams (2001, p. 75) suggests that we condense the amount of word identification concepts "from zillions of little things that must be rote memorized to relatively few big ones that the child can be reasonably asked to understand and think about." The next section of this chapter presents seven common spelling patterns that will help beginning readers to identify almost 1400 words. Anderson, Hiebert, Scott, and Wilkinson, (1985), in their national report *Becoming a Nation of Readers,* provided a great philosophy for phonics instruction: "Do it early. Keep it simple" (p. 43).

Reading instruction needs to be flexible. Some reading programs leave instructional decision making to the teacher; others script out virtually every word the teacher is supposed to say. Scripted programs run the risk of "reducing teachers' motivation to teach phonics" (National Reading Panel, 2000, 2–135) and focus on the program rather than the students. Teaching reading is not a one-size-fits-all endeavor. Students vary tremendously in their ability, maturity, background knowledge, interests, and preparation and support from home. Teachers must be able to balance the need for instructional consistency with the need to adapt their instruction to meet individual students' needs.

Finally, word identification instruction needs to be enjoyable for both teachers and students. When students are enjoying instructional activities, they will be more involved. When teachers don't enjoy instructional activities, they are less likely to implement them effectively, if at all. The National Reading Panel (2000) suggests that instructional activities should be "as relevant and motivating as possible to engage children's interest and attention to promote optimal learning" (p. 2–137). The NRP goes on to say that a lack of attention to motivation in instructional programs can be a serious problem.

> ### FOR ENGLISH LANGUAGE LEARNERS
>
> **Phonics Instruction**
>
> The best way to develop English language learners' beginning reading skills is through a combination of extensive and varied interactions with meaningful print and systematic and explicit instruction in phonemic awareness and phonics. Systematic phonics instruction can help English language learners develop word recognition and decoding skills to a high level even though their general knowledge of English is limited. However, the ability to decode does not automatically carry over into comprehension (Cummins, 2003).

TEACHING WORD IDENTIFICATION SKILLS: IN CONTEXT AND IN ISOLATION

Part of the controversy surrounding phonics instruction centers on how phonics should be taught. Many educators believe that phonics should be taught in context so that it makes sense. Others argue that phonics should be taught in isolation to better develop automatic recognition. I believe both approaches are necessary and complementary.

Many teachers who favor student-centered teaching prefer to teach word identification skills "in context," meaning that skills are taught spontaneously as they are needed in the process of shared reading with big books or other texts. For example, while reading the big book *Mrs. Wishy Washy* (Cowley, 1980), the teacher may focus on compound words by studying the words along the way as they appear in the book. The big book *Just This Once* (Cowley, 1987) provides an excellent opportunity for teaching about quotation marks as the book's characters speak to one another.

However, many teachers are uncomfortable with a purely contextual approach to word identification instruction, fearing that the lack of an established sequence of skills will make the instruction seem fragmented or hit and miss. The practice of jumping almost randomly from skill to skill based on the words in each new text (e.g., studying *ight* words with one reading book, then studying question marks with the next book, then studying suffixes with the next book) may provide inadequate opportunities for follow-up practice and developing automaticity.

Traditional reading programs (e.g., basal programs and **mastery teaching** programs) provide a specific sequence of word identification skills and practice opportunities that build one skill on another, thus enabling students to attain automaticity in identifying words. However, many teachers complain that such programs place undue emphasis on word identification skills and virtually ignore the meaning and esthetic aspects of reading. Other teachers fault such programs as being overly elaborate, for teaching too many word identification skills, many of which are very seldom needed, such as "xi sounds like /sh/ as in anxious."

Effective reading teachers have discovered that both contextual and isolated phonics instruction are needed for students to be able to recognize and apply spelling patterns in their reading (Pressley, 2001; Pressley et al., 1997). Sometimes teachers and students examine decoding concepts in isolation through word family activities and then apply them in reading connected text. At other times, unfamiliar words from reading materials can be taken aside, examined, and then reread in context.

This combining of isolated and contextual word identification has been likened to swimming instruction. A swimming instructor observes students swimming in the pool and then, noticing a student who needs some additional instruction, pulls the student out of the pool to practice or refine a certain swimming stroke out of the water. When the student shows proficiency with the stroke, he or she is put back into the water to practice the stroke "in context." Similarly, beginning readers benefit from word identification both in the context of meaningful reading and also in isolation to focus on specific spelling patterns and word parts.

Bear, Invernizzi, Templeton, and Johnston (2004, p. 4) highlight three keys to effective word identification instruction:

1. Teach word identification skills in a useful sequence.
2. Study the spelling patterns and word parts both in isolation and in context.
3. Develop students' automaticity by providing ample opportunities to practice recognizing and applying the patterns.

In their own words:

> The best way to develop fast, accurate perception of word features is to engage in meaningful reading and writing, and to have multiple opportunities to examine those same words out of context. The most effective instruction in phonics, spelling, and vocabulary, links word study to the texts being read, provides a systematic scope and sequence of word-level skills, and provides multiple opportunities for hands-on practice and application (p. 4).

COMMON SPELLING PATTERNS

Many reading programs and reading methods textbooks include lists of up to 200 or more phonics skills that beginning readers should be expected to learn or memorize. This is a rather daunting task for beginning readers. Based on my elementary classroom teaching experience, professional reading, and classroom research, I have organized the most common and useful spelling patterns and word parts into a cumulative instructional sequence of seven decoding concepts.

Beginning with simple three-letter CVC words (consonant–vowel–consonant: cat, Ted, big), the seven decoding concepts build on each other to help students to develop decoding fluency. Most of the seven concepts are groupings of multiple individual concepts that follow the same pattern. These seven concepts are common to virtually all methods texts and reading programs and provide a simple logical progression, from blending letter–sounds to recognizing more complex spelling patterns. Familiarity and practice with these seven concepts will enable beginning readers to recognize approximately 1500 single-syllable words and also parts of many multisyllable words.

Although there is no universally accepted instructional sequence for teaching decoding concepts, sequence is important so that teachers will have a place to start and a place to go next. Blevins (1998, p. 91) describes the importance of a sequenced cumulative system for presenting decoding skills.

> Systematic instruction follows a sequence that progresses from easy to more difficult. Systematic instruction includes constant review and repetition of sound–spelling relationships, applications to reading and writing, and focus on developing fluency through work with reading rate and decoding accuracy. Just because a program has a scope and sequence doesn't mean it is systematic. The instruction must be cumulative (p. 91).

The following sections of this chapter describe each of the seven common spelling patterns and suggest instructional activities for teaching them. The spelling patterns and word parts that I teach are listed in Table 5.1. Included are classroom names for the spelling patterns that I have used with my students to minimize reliance on confusing reading teacher jargon.

Table 5.1   Seven Common Spelling Patterns

Spelling Pattern	Classroom Name	Examples
Short Vowel Spelling Patterns		
1. Consonant–vowel–consonant	Beginner words	dad, ten, dig, mop, bus
2. Consonant blends	Blends	<u>pl</u>an, <u>sl</u>ed, te<u>nt</u>, <u>fr</u>og, ru<u>st</u>
3. Consonant digraphs	Digraphs	<u>ch</u>at, fi<u>sh</u>, <u>th</u>at, <u>wh</u>en
Long Vowel Spelling Patterns		
4. Final silent *e*	Tickle words	cake, pipe, rode, cute
5. Vowel digraphs	Vowel teams	r<u>ai</u>n, pl<u>ay</u>; t<u>ea</u>m, f<u>ee</u>d; g<u>oa</u>t, sn<u>ow</u>
Other Spelling Patterns		
6. R-Controlled vowels	Bossy R	c<u>ar</u>, f<u>or</u>; h<u>er</u>, s<u>ir</u>, f<u>ur</u>
7. Vowel diphthongs	Diphthongs	b<u>oy</u>, p<u>oin</u>t; l<u>ou</u>d, c<u>ow</u>; ch<u>ew</u>, str<u>aw</u>

I never could come up with a cute, less formal term for **diphthongs.** My students simply learned to call them diphthongs. One teacher colleague used the term "weird vowel teams" with her students. I hope that you and your students can come up with a term that you like.

 ## TEACHING SPELLING PATTERNS: A THREE-STEP MODEL

I have found much success teaching the seven spelling patterns through a flexible three-step procedure that combines both parts-to-whole and whole-to-parts approaches. This three-step instructional procedure can be applied to phonics skills that are part of your core reading program, supplemental programs, and intervention reading programs (Chapter 7).

A Three-Step Approach to Spelling Pattern Instruction

1.   Introduce *each spelling pattern to the students using word family examples.*

2.   Explore *each spelling pattern through follow-up classroom games and activities.*

3.   Apply *the spelling pattern while reading meaningful texts.*

STEP 1. INTRODUCE THE SPELLING PATTERN WITH WORD FAMILY EXAMPLES

I prepare for word identification lessons by writing a list of six to eight example words that contain the spelling pattern on the chalkboard or on a piece of chart paper. I prefer chart paper because I can reuse it for later lessons, and I often have students add their own words that contain the spelling pattern to the chart.

Step 1 has three simple components: (1) I read aloud to my students a list of example words that contain the spelling pattern and I explain the spelling pattern to them, (2) my students and I read the example words aloud in unison several times, and (3) small groups of my students read the chart words aloud to their classmates. I call this third component "show-off" reading.

To illustrate Step 1 of this procedure, I will describe a lesson in which I introduce **consonant digraphs.** The same procedure is used to introduce all the spelling patterns.

I begin the lesson by writing a list of example words on the board or displaying a chart containing lists of words with all four consonant digraphs (see Table 5.2).

I introduce the first column of words on the chart with the familiar question, "Whose turn is it to read first?" This reminds the students to listen quietly and follow along with their eyes as I point to each word in the first column and read them aloud slowly and clearly.

Next I ask, "What is the same about each of these words?" The students easily reply that the words all contain *ch.* (Some students point out that it says so at the top of the column.) I confirm this and then teach that when *c* and *h* are together in a word, they make the sound /ch/. I then lead the students in pronouncing the *ch* sound together several times, like a choo-choo train.

I also point out how the *ch* works together with other familiar letters to make words. For example, I cover up the *ch* on *match* and ask, "What word do you see

Table 5.2 A Sample Word Family Chart

Digraph Words			
<u>**ch**</u>	<u>**sh**</u>	<u>**th**</u>	<u>**wh**</u>
chat	cash	that	what
chip	ship	this	when
catch	shed	then	where
much	wish	moth	why
such	rush	bath	which
choke	shine	those	whine
match	shake	these	whale

now?" *(mat)*. I then say, "Let's say /mat/ and put the /ch/ on the end, slowly first, then fast." *(mat-ch, match)*. I repeat the process with *catch* and then do similar pattern explanations with *chip* and *chat*. My purpose here is to get my students to view words as combinations of familiar spelling patterns and word parts. Because of an enthusiastic and playful teaching style, my students take the same delight in connecting pieces of words that fit together as they do in connecting the pieces of a jigsaw puzzle.

I then ask if the students can think of other words that also have the *ch* sound. During the next 5 minutes, the chalkboard becomes filled with *ch* words as the students brainstorm: *chocolate, church, Chuck, chocolate chip, championship, chubby,* and *cheerleader*. I underline the *ch* in each of these as I pronounce them. One student excitedly points out that the word *championship* also contains an *sh* digraph.

I then move on to read the first column aloud with my students, choral fashion. I point to the words as the whole class reads them aloud with me in unison several times. I spice up the choral reading by asking the students to read in a variety of silly voices, including Daddy Bear and Baby Bear.

I move from whole-class choral reading to small-group reading by asking, "Who dares to be a show-off reader?" I organize small groups of my students to read the column of words aloud, first from top to bottom, then from bottom to top. For example, I call on "all students wearing purple" or "all students with shoelaces," or I'll invite a student to "choose three friends to be show-off readers with you." Occasionally, I'll enthusiastically say to a group, "You read that so well! You may get a free drink of water." A free drink of water is a big deal if you're in first grade. Depending on how well the students learned to read the words in the first column, I may repeat the procedure with another column or else move on to a follow-up game or activity designed to give the students further opportunities to explore and review the words.

One morning as my students and I were chanting the words in the *ch* column, Chelsea began waving her arm excitedly and calling out, "I'm a digraph, I'm a digraph." Chelsea had discovered that her own name began with the *ch* spelling pattern. So I happily grabbed my marking pen and added Chelsea to our list of *ch* words. About 30 seconds later, Whitney made the same discovery, so I added Whitney to our list of *wh* words.

After introducing a spelling pattern in this manner, I love to send my students on a word hunt. For example, after introducing digraphs, I instruct my students to keep a 3 by 5 index card handy during their reading group reading, independent reading, and reading at home and jot down words that contain digraphs. The next morning we fill up another piece of chart paper with digraph words the students have found.

I follow the same introductory procedures each morning, spending 5 to 7 minutes introducing, examining, or reviewing one or more word families displayed on chart paper. I may spend 1 to 2 weeks on a single chart, depending on how well the students grasp the concept. Following the introductory activities with the chart, the next step is to spend another 5 to 10 minutes in one of many fun word identification follow-up activities.

STEP 2. EXPLORE THE SPELLING PATTERN THROUGH FOLLOW-UP ACTIVITIES

The purpose of follow-up games and activities is to reinforce and deepen students' understanding by giving them additional opportunities to interact with and manipulate the spelling patterns and word parts. Students' understanding of the concepts is also strengthened by hearing and observing their peers provide additional examples and by discussing nonexamples. I also use the positive emotional atmosphere associated with these activities to promote the feeling that decoding is a pleasant challenge, much like assembling a jigsaw puzzle.

Sometimes these activities are games in which teams of students race to manipulate spelling patterns or word parts and win a big prize, like a verbal acknowledgment or lining up first for recess. For example, one morning I announced to my students that we were going to play the Airplane Game. I had the students bring their chairs and form three lines, side by side, sitting one behind another and facing the chalkboard. These three lines became the airplanes. I grabbed three headphones from our listening center and put them on the first student in each line and designated him or her as the pilot. I then went to the chalkboard and wrote the words *beginning, middle,* and *end* on the board in front of the three airplanes. I also placed a piece of chalk on the chalk tray beneath the three words. I told the students that I would pronounce a beginner word and that the pilot from the first airplane was to race to the board and write the first letter from the word beneath the word *beginning.* Likewise, the pilot from the middle airplane was to race the board and write the middle letter of the word I had pronounced, and the pilot from the third airplane was to do the same with the last letter. I pronounced a beginner word and counted "one, two, three, go," and the three pilots were off to the board, each writing his or her letter. The pilot or pilots who wrote the correct letter fastest got to go to the back of his or her airplane, and all the "passengers" moved up one chair. The first airplane to have the pilot make it back to the front was the fastest.

One of my favorite follow-up word identification activities is what my students and I call a "backward spelling test." Veteran teachers may know this activity as "sound spelling." In a backward spelling test I pronounce the *sounds* of the letters from a word, one sound at a time, and the students write the letter that makes each sound. For example, to further reinforce the concept of consonant digraphs, I begin by asking a student to distribute our spelling test sheet (see Appendix A) to the classmates, with the verbal reminder to put their names at the top of the page. Selecting the word *chip* from the word family chart, my instructions are as follows:

> *Word number one; the first sound has two letters, /ch/. Write the two letters that make the sound /ch/.*

The students begin writing *ch* on the first line of their spelling papers. Some students are already speculating that the word will be either *chat*, *chip*, or *choke*.

> *The second sound is /i/. Write the letter that says /i/.*

As the students write the letter *i*, they excitedly whisper to each other, "It's gonna be *chip*. I know it's gonna be *chip*."

> *The third sound is /p/. Now wait, don't say it yet. Wait until I count to three, then you may all say it together.*

At this point the students are almost unable to contain their desire to shout out the word they've written on line 1 of their spelling test sheet. When I determine that all students have completed writing the first word, I count aloud: "One, two, three." On the count of three, my students shout the word *chip* in unison.

> *You're right. The word is chip, /ch – i – p/. Raise your hand if you wrote ch – i – p.*

I then repeat the procedure with six other words from the chart, taken out of order. The eighth and final word is always designated as a bonus word. This is usually one of the students' names or a word from one of the many charts displayed around the room. For example, I once chose the word *allegiance* from the Pledge of Allegiance chart on the wall and teasingly said:

> *The bonus word today will be way too hard for you. Mostly only seventh graders can spell a word like this, but I'll let you try it anyway, just for practice; Word number eight, the first sound is /a/.*

Because the students saw and pronounced the word *allegiance* each morning during the pledge, it was familiar to them, and all but three of them recognized it as they spelled the bonus word.

Although the students view this as a fun "test" (with the appropriate delightful suspense), my purpose is to give my students an opportunity to practice blending the sounds of letters. Think of the instructional tasks that a backward spelling test asks the students to do. First they must listen for the sounds of the letters, then they must write the sounds, and finally they must blend the printed letter–sounds to pronounce the words. All these are necessary skills for reading and writing.

Other follow-up word identification activities involve students building words with letter cards or making individual word-part booklets.

STEP 3. APPLY THE SPELLING PATTERN IN READING MEANINGFUL TEXTS

Step 3 is critically important. This is where many beginning readers make the connection between the word identification lessons and real reading. This is where their eyes are opened to the fact that sometimes daunting pages of text simply contain words that are made up of the familiar spelling patterns and word parts that we are studying. It is exciting to see beginning readers, particularly those less prepared, begin to participate confidently in reading as they recognize and combine spelling patterns and word parts and identify previously unfamiliar words. Lines of text that were once beyond reach become accessible, because the students now hold and know how to use the pieces to the puzzle.

I do Step 3 of my spelling pattern lessons during our daily shared reading and guided reading lessons. During my shared reading lessons, we read from big books and from shortened versions of fables or fairy tales printed on four or five pieces of chart paper using the new large-format printer in the teacher workroom. We also read poems and stories from favorite "I Can Read" children's books (such as Lobel's *Frog and Toad Are Friends* and Rylant's *Henry and Mudge in Puddle Trouble*) copied onto overhead transparencies. I follow the same three-step procedure that I use when introducing the word family charts:

1. Read and explain a sentence from the story to the class.
2. Read the sentence aloud several times with the class.
3. Invite several small groups from the class to "show-off" read the sentence to me and their classmates.

Depending on the text and students' reading levels, I sometimes do two sentences at a time.

After the show-off reading of the sentences from the shared reading story, I ask my students, "Who can find some spelling pattern words in our sentences?" My students scan the day's sentences and previous sentences for words with any of the spelling patterns we've studied. As students identify the spelling patterns in the sentences, I invite them to use a marking pen or chalk and underline the spelling pattern on the chart or chalkboard. When using a big book for shared reading, I write the word on the chalkboard, and the student underlines the spelling pattern. After several minutes of finding and underlining familiar spelling patterns and word parts in the shared reading story, my students return to their seats to illustrate one or two pages in personal copies of the story.

Let's return to my classroom for an example of Step 3 of our decoding lesson (applying the concept in reading meaningful texts).

> *3. The mother duck looked around and saw one more egg, much bigger than the others. A large gray duckling hatched from the egg.*
>
> *4. The other ducklings chased and bit and pushed the ugly duckling all day long. They said, "You are so ugly. Go away."*

Having read these two sentences to the students and with the students and invited show-off readers to read aloud to their classmates and me, I ask my students to look for spelling pattern words. Aaron gets his hand up first and responds: "In sentence four, the word *chased* has a *ch* digraph." Melissa adds: "In sentence three, the word *hatched* has a *ch* in the middle." Erika points out: "In sentence three, the word *much* ends with a *ch*."

I invite these students to come to the chart and underline the *ch*s with a marking pen. Then I invite my students to look for other familiar spelling patterns from previous lessons. Other students respond with similar observations and take their turns underlining spelling patterns and word parts on the chart. For example:

> ❀ *In sentence four, <u>bit</u> is a beginner word.*
> ❀ *In sentence three, the word <u>than</u> begins with a <u>th</u> digraph.*
> ❀ *In sentence three, the word <u>hatched</u> starts with the beginner word <u>hat</u>.*
> ❀ *In sentence three, there are three <u>the</u>s that have <u>th</u>.*
> ❀ *In sentence three, the word <u>large</u> has an r-controlled vowel in the middle.*

Soon the chart is filled with many underlined familiar word parts. More spelling patterns will be underlined tomorrow and in the coming days. These underlined charts are displayed on the wall for a week or two and serve as a visual reminder for students that texts are comprised of familiar patterns. The process of reading the charts, examining them for familiar patterns, and then rereading them for practice and fluency is what Strickland (1998) calls whole–parts–whole instruction. It combines the benefits of both isolated and contextualized word identification instruction as students simultaneously process information from all three cueing systems while reading meaningful text.

 ## ACTIVITIES FOR TEACHING SPELLING PATTERNS

The following activities have been selected from leaders in the field and from my personal teaching experience. These activities can be adapted for teaching many of the spelling patterns and word parts described in this chapter. It is important to remember that these activities focus on spelling patterns and word parts in isolation and that students must have plentiful opportunities to connect these patterns to meaningful reading.

The following chapters describe many opportunities for students to apply word identification concepts in context. Instructional activities such as shared reading, guided reading, independent reading, and reading in the content areas provide meaningful opportunities for students to read for comprehension while seeing, processing, and reinforcing their knowledge of spelling patterns and word parts.

Addresses IRA Standard 2.2

Use a wide range of instruction practices, approaches, and methods, including technology-based practices, for learners at differing stages of development and from differing linguistic and cultural backgrounds.

SPELLING PATTERN 1: CONSONANT–VOWEL–CONSONANT (CVC) WORDS

About the CVC Spelling Pattern

The first spelling pattern that I teach is the CVC (consonant-vowel-consonant) pattern. This pattern provides the conceptual and instructional foundation for students learning how to blend the sounds of printed letters to form words. The CVC pattern includes the CVC short vowel word families for all five vowels. My beginning reading students and I refer to CVC words as "beginner words," because the six other spelling patterns build on these words. Table 5.3 is a brief list of common CVC or beginner words. (Complete lists of words that contain all seven spelling patterns are provided in Appendix A.)

Table 5.3 Beginner Words

a	e	i	o	u
dad	bed	did	job	cub
had	red	hid	rob	rub
ban	den	big	dog	bug
can	men	pig	fog	hug
map	bet	pin	hop	gum
nap	get	tin	mop	hum

The ability to blend the sounds of printed letters depends on two of the foundation concepts discussed in chapter 3: knowledge of letter names and sounds and phonemic awareness. Learning to blend the sounds of printed letters into CVC words is easy if students know the sounds associated with the printed alphabet letters and understand the principle that sounds can be blended to form spoken words.

The principle of blending the letter sounds is the same within and across vowels, so once the students have learned this principle and the letter names and sounds, they should with practice be able to read all possible CVC combinations equally well.

Ideas for Teaching the CVC Spelling Pattern

Say it slow, say it fast.   I like to introduce the concept of blending the sounds of printed letters using the "Say it slow, say it fast" technique. I write a CVC word (for example, *cat*) on the chalkboard or a piece of chart paper and say to my students, "Let's say it the slow way." I point to each letter individually, inviting the students to join me in pronouncing each sound in turn. After pronouncing the third sound, I say "Now, let's say it fast" and I sweep my hand left to right beneath the letters as the students pronounce the word. Some reading programs suggest pronouncing the three sounds individually (/c/ – /a/ – /t/) so that students can hear each of them. Other reading programs suggest linking the three sounds together as much as possible (ccc-aaa-ttt) to reinforce the concept of blending the sounds. I suggest that you try it both ways with your students. Some teachers like to begin teaching the blending concept with two-letter words, such as *ad, an, at, Ed, if, in, it, on,* and *up*.

Students chant "beginner words" in the first step of a word study lesson.

Blending letter–sounds with Post-It notes.   This is certainly one of the most fun activities I've used for teaching the concept of blending. I described this activity in chapter 3, so I'll provide just a brief review here. Write each alphabet letter on a Post-It note and stick them to the chalkboard. Then take three letters and make a CVC word. Invite the students to say it slow and say it fast. Then replace the initial letter with other Post-It note letters to form a variety of word family words. Invite students to come to the front of the class and change the Post-It note letters to make words you dictate.

There is a wonderful opportunity here for instructional playfulness. As the students get good at manipulating the Post-It note letters, call on a student to make a CVC word such as *top*. Just as the student is about to finish making the word *top*, pretend to change your mind and say something like, "Oh, wait, I didn't want *top*. We need to make the word *hop* first." Just as the student has almost finished making the change to *hop*, repeat the change-of-mind process by saying, "Oh no, my mistake, we really should make the word *mop* next because we need mops to clean the floor." I love to see how many times a student will put up with my changes of mind before he or she just stops and looks at me with that "will you make up your mind" stare. When students become proficient at manipulating the initial consonants *(cat* to *hat)*, we work on final consonants *(run* to *rug)* and then on manipulating both consonants *(dog* to *fox)*. The spelling pattern lists in Appendix A are very helpful for this and similar word identification games.

Decodable texts.   Decodable texts such as "Dan can fan Nan and Jan in the tan van" are often criticized as lacking meaningfulness and motivation for beginning readers. It is important to keep the use of decodable texts in proper perspective. Decodable texts should never be thought of as an entire reading program. In fact, I use them only to provide my students with extra practice with blending letter–sounds. I compare their use with my own children practicing the piano. Even accomplished pianists continue to practice musical scales so that the fingering patterns will remain automatic for them. Practicing scales is not like playing Rachmaninoff, but it helps a pianist to play Rachmaninoff fluently.

Beginning readers, particularly those who are struggling with word identification, will similarly benefit from the practice provided by reading decodable texts with teacher support. Limiting the spelling patterns in a text enables beginning readers to focus more of their attention on the structural aspects of the words and on the differences between the words (Adams, 2001). This focused practice enables readers to reach the ultimate goal of word identification instruction: to recognize and combine common spelling patterns automatically so they can free their attention to focus on what the words mean.

As described in chapter 11, I made it a goal for each of my struggling beginning readers to practice reading decodable texts for 10 minutes each day, one on one with me, a student teacher, or a parent volunteer. These struggling readers always participated in every other aspect of the entire reading and writing program, so there was a nice linking of the needed specific individual skills with meaningful stories and information texts.

SPELLING PATTERN 2: CONSONANT BLENDS

About Consonant Blends

A **consonant blend** occurs when two consonant letters come side by side in a word such as *flat* and *sand*. In a consonant blend, you can hear both consonant letter sounds. Say the words *flat* and *sand* slowly to yourself and listen. You can hear both consonant sounds. Be aware that consonant blends only occur within a single syllable.

Table 5.4 Blend Words

a	e	i	o	u
ba<u>nd</u>	<u>Fr</u>ed	fi<u>st</u>	<u>gl</u>ob	<u>st</u>ub
pa<u>st</u>	<u>sl</u>ed	<u>br</u>im	bond	<u>sp</u>ud
<u>br</u>an	be<u>lt</u>	gift	<u>fr</u>og	must
<u>pl</u>an	fe<u>lt</u>	lift	<u>dr</u>op	<u>pl</u>us
pa<u>nt</u>	be<u>nd</u>	<u>cr</u>ib	pond	du<u>nk</u>
la<u>nd</u>	ne<u>xt</u>	<u>sp</u>in	<u>sp</u>ot	<u>tr</u>u<u>st</u>

For example, in the word *Batman,* the *t* and *m* do come side by side, but they do not constitute a consonant blend because they are in separate syllables.

Teaching students to process words with consonant blends is easy. Once students have mastered the principle of blending three-letter sounds to form CVC words, simply adding a fourth letter-sound in the words is easy. For example, if students can blend three letters (f-a-t), by applying the same blending principle, they can just as easily blend four letters (f-l-a-t) or (f-a-s-t). My students and I refer to these as "blend" words.

Some reading programs teach consonant blends as distinct spelling patterns, such as the *cr* blend or the *sl* blend. My experience is that this is overly complicated and unnecessary. When students come to understand the principle of blending the letter sounds, they'll be able to produce the pronunciation of any consonant blend simply by applying the blending procedure.

Table 5.4 is a brief list of common CCVC or CVCC blend words:

Ideas for Teaching the Consonant Blend Spelling Pattern

I always begin teaching spelling patterns by introducing the pattern with lists of example words written on the board or a piece of chart paper, as described earlier. After reading the words aloud to my students, explaining the pattern, and having my students chant the list aloud together with me and in small "show-off" groups, I'll lead the class in an activity like the ones described here. Then I always finish the lessons by having my students search our reading books and other texts to find and list words that contain the spelling pattern we are studying.

Blending with an overhead projector.   This activity is a variation of the Post-It note activity described earlier. After the word family chanting activity, I pull the overhead projector to the front of my classroom and shine it on the chalkboard or screen. I gather the letters *a, e, u, b, c, d, l, m, n, r, s, t, t* from my tub of plastic magnetic alphabet letters and place them on the projector. I begin by demonstrating how to select and use the plastic letters to form a few blend words. Then I ask student volunteers to come to the projector and to select and use the letters to form blend words that I pronounce. For example, I'll model the blending process with the words *slab* and *crab* and then ask my students to make the words *bend, lend, blend,* and *bust, dust, must, rust,* and *trust.* Again, I love to playfully tease my students by saying things such as, "This next word will be way too hard for first graders" and then acting astonished as they form it correctly.

Spelling tests. Having students write and spell words is actually the flip side of having them decode words. In reading, readers visually perceive and then blend the letter–sounds. In spelling, writers audibly perceive and then write the sounds. An effective way to reinforce phonics spelling patterns is to give the students a spelling test with the words displayed on a word family chart in the front of the classroom. This way, the more accomplished students can write the words from memory, while other students use the chart for support. After the spelling test, grading the spelling test can serve as an additional reinforcement. Have students grade their own papers as you or invited students spell the words correctly on the chalkboard. Instruct students who misspelled a word to correct it on their paper. Spelling tests with the words displayed on chart paper serve as an instructional activity. More traditional spelling tests, those with the words hidden from view, serve more as an assessment activity.

The backward spelling tests described earlier are also great activities for reinforcing the concept of blending letter–sounds and word parts. Remember to always finish spelling pattern lessons by having students find words containing the pattern in their reading books.

SPELLING PATTERN 3: CONSONANT DIGRAPHS

About Consonant Digraphs

We know that there are approximately 44 sounds in the spoken English language. However, these 44 sounds are represented by only 26 alphabet letters. Thus, 18 sounds must be represented by letters that make more than one sound (e.g., vowels) and also some combinations of letters. Consonant digraphs (ch, sh, th, wh) help fill this need.

Unlike the consonant blends discussed earlier for which you hear both letter–sounds, you do not hear the letters make their sounds in consonant digraphs. For example *ch* doesn't sound like *c* or *h*. It makes an altogether different sound /ch/, which we hear at the beginning and end of the word *church*. The digraph *th* makes two sounds: /th/ as in *this* and /th/ as in *think*. Students must simply memorize the sounds of these four consonant digraphs and be able to blend them with the sounds of the other letters and spelling patterns to form words. My students and I refer to consonant digraphs as digraphs. Although some educators may worry about teaching beginning readers to use such academic sounding terms, I've found that my students learned the term *digraph* just as easily as the terms *consonant* and *vowel*.

Table 5.5 is a brief list of common digraph words.

Table 5.5 Digraph Words

a	e	i	o	u
than	shed	thin	chop	much
chap	them	chip	shop	such
bash	then	whip	gosh	thud
cash	when	dish	shot	hush
math	Beth	itch	shock	shut
chat	check	wish	moth	crutch

Figure 5.1 Pupil
Response Card

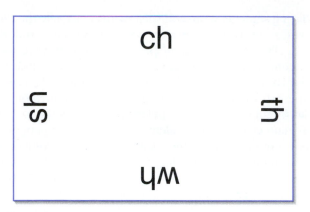

Ideas for Teaching the Consonant Digraph Spelling Pattern

Digraph with every-pupil-response cards.   After introducing and chanting digraph words on the word family lists, I distribute 5 by 7 inch index cards to my students with the four consonant digraphs arrayed on each card as shown in Figure 5.1.

I then tell my students that I will pronounce some words that begin with consonant digraphs, and their job is to rotate the index card so that the digraph that begins the word I pronounced is upright on the index card. This is called an every-pupil-response activity (Cunningham, 2000) because every student participates, rather than a few participating while others watch. Every pupil response activity allows me to quickly observe which students have mastered the concept and which have not.

Dictation.   Dictation activities are a natural follow-up to the spelling tests. After introducing and chanting a spelling pattern using a list of example words, dictate a few sentences that contain the spelling pattern. For example, dictate a few sentences such as *Chuck thanked Shelly in church* or *The white whale chased the shark*. Your students write the sentences on their regular writing paper. Then you write each sentence on the board and have the students check their sentences for accuracy. This dictation activity moves spelling one step closer to the genuinely meaningful activity it should be.

SPELLING PATTERN 4: FINAL SILENT E

About Final Silent E

At this point in my sequence of spelling pattern lessons, the focus switches from short vowel concepts to two long vowel concepts: **final silent *e*** and **vowel teams.** The final silent *e* spelling pattern (CVCe) is one of the most reliable spelling patterns. My students discovered that the pattern even works when an ending is added to a final silent *e* word (shines, shined). My students also understand that the pattern usually only works when there is one consonant between the final *e* and the preceding vowel.

My students and I refer to final silent *e* words as "tickle words," because the silent *e* on the end of the word reaches backward over the consonant and tickles the first vowel, making it say its long name. I enjoy dramatizing or hamming up the sound of a tickled vowel saying its name. I also point out that usually the *e* on the end is not strong enough to jump backward over more than one consonant.

Table 5.6 Tickle Words

a	i	o	u
face	dice	robe	cube
safe	hide	joke	dude
lake	life	home	mule
base	dime	note	tune
place	slice	smoke	prune
shade	while	choke	flute

Table 5.6 is a brief list of common final silent *e* or "tickle" words. Notice that there are very few single-syllable final silent *e* words when the first vowel is an *e* *(Pete)*. Notice also the cumulative effect of the spelling patterns as some of the tickle words also contain consonant blends (place) and digraphs (shade).

Ideas for Teaching the Final Silent E Spelling Pattern

Concentration.   This is one of the most versatile games I've used over the years. After introducing and chanting final silent *e* words from the example list, I prepare to play Concentration by obtaining 18 library pockets from the media center coordinator, a local librarian, or an office supply store (some of you from the "bar-code" generation may not remember library pockets). I rubber cement the 18 library pockets to a piece of posterboard (laid horizontally), with the word Concentration written across the top. I number the library pockets on the left side of the Concentration posterboard 1 to 9 and write the letters a through i on the nine library pockets on the right side of the posterboard. Then I list nine pairs of silent *e* words that work both with and without the final silent *e* (made–mad, Pete–pet, fine–fin, dude–dud, ride–rid, hope–hop, mane–man, ripe–rip, etc.). I write each word on a 3 by 5 index card and place the final silent *e* cards in the library pockets on the left side of the Concentration posterboard, and the corresponding short vowel words in the library pockets are on the right side of the posterboard.

With the Concentration board and final silent *e* index cards made, I'm ready to provide my students with practice on the final silent *e* spelling pattern. I like to introduce this game first as a whole-class activity and then later let students use it as a small-group or center activity. One word of caution is very important here. Games like Concentration can be very time consuming. Sometimes the time spent playing a game is not really worth the learning that results. I like to think of this as a time: learning ratio. Teachers need to decide if the learning from an activity justifies the amount of time that it takes. Games like concentration can be fun, but should be used judiciously.

Final silent *e* flashcards.   As described in the vignette at the beginning of this chapter, my students have enjoyed cutting out and using final silent *e* flashcards. (Appendix A shows final silent *e* words that I've made into flashcards on my computer.) The first step is to have my students cut out the flashcards and write their name on the back of each flashcard to minimize inevitable mix-ups. Next, I pronounce the final silent *e*

Students explore "tickle words" in a word study lesson.

words as my students find and hold them up until I'm certain that my students can easily recognize them. Then I have my students fold back the final *e* and I pronounce the short vowel CVC version of the words while they find and hold up the correct word.

My final step with the silent *e* flashcards is to make flashcard booklets. I instruct my students to put their final silent *e* flashcards in a stack (making sure all the words are facing the right direction). I come around to each student and put a couple of staples into the left side of the stack so that each student has a personal booklet. Of course, each student's booklet is in a different order, which makes it even more interesting as I alternately pronounce the short vowel CVC words and long vowel final silent *e* words that make up their booklets. As always, we finish each lesson with a final silent *e* word hunt through our reading books.

SPELLING PATTERN 5: VOWEL TEAMS

About Vowel Teams

Technically known as vowel digraphs, vowel teams refer to the old rule "When two vowels go walking, the first does the talking." The first of the two vowels says its "long" name; the second vowel is silent. Clymer (1963, 1996) found that the "when two vowels go walking" rule is in fact not very reliable. For example, *ie* and *ei* can be very confusing. *Oi* and *ou* don't follow the rule. *Ow* makes the long *o* sound as in *show* but also makes the vowel sound you hear in the word *cow*. Incidentally, I introduce *ow* first as a vowel team and then much later in the school year I will reintroduce the diphthong *ow*, making it very clear to my students that *ow* can also make the /cow/ sound.

Table 5.7 Vowel Team Words

A Teams		E Teams		O Teams	
maid	bay	bead	seed	load	mow
nail	day	leaf	meet	soak	low
gain	play	seal	seem	coal	tow
wait	stay	heat	jeep	boat	blow
brain	may	speak	fleet	coast	grow
chain	way	peach	teeth	throat	show

I teach six vowel teams that are the most common and reliable: *ai, ay; ea, ee; oa, ow*. I refer to them as *vowel teams,* rather than vowel digraphs, so that my students don't confuse them with consonant digraphs. Sometimes I refer to *ai* and *ay* as The A Teams, *ea* and *ee* as The E Teams, and *oa* and *ow* as The O Teams. As with the other spelling patterns, I introduce the vowel teams with many word family examples in lists and then follow up with activities and practice. Table 5.7 is a brief list of common vowel team words. Notice that some of them also contain consonant blends and digraphs.

Ideas for Teaching the Vowel Team Spelling Pattern

Long vowel pattern sort.   After introducing and chanting vowel team words using example word lists on the board or on chart paper, I often reinforce the vowel team spelling patterns with long vowel pattern sorts. I ask my students to brainstorm as many words as they can with the *long a* sound (main, game, freight, day, whale, bait, same, made, stay, scale, paid, great, play, etc.). I list these words on the chalkboard, bring my students' attention to the various spelling patterns represented among the words, and then guide my students in sorting the words into columns on the chalkboard. One long vowel pattern sort yielded the pattern categories shown in Table 5.8.

Notice that the first column is comprised of tickle words. Columns 2 and 3 are A Team words. Columns 4 and 5 are patterns that are so infrequent that I'll mention them, but not spend a great deal of time teaching them. I like to do the long vowel pattern sorts on a large piece of chart paper or butcher paper so that I can use them

Table 5.8 Long *a* Spelling Pattern Sort

a e	ai	ay	ei	ea
date	bait	day	freight	great
made	main	play	sleigh	
late	sail	stay	neigh	
skate	straight	away		
game	braid	say		
whale	chain	runway		
space	main			

for the follow-up Word Hunt activity. I assign my students to find vowel team words from their shared reading, guided reading, and independent reading materials and their reading at home. We add these additional *long a* words to the chart over the next several days. When my students are feeling confident with A Team words, I move on to E Team and O Team words.

Spelling pattern bingo.   I occasionally give each student a list of 24 vowel team words, along with a blank personal Bingo card (five rows and five columns, with the center cell is labeled FREE). My students write the 24 words in random order on their Bingo cards. Each student's list of 24 words can serve as a check-off sheet to help them avoid forgetting some words or writing other words twice on their Bingo cards. As I pronounce each word from my list of 24, my students use our math manipulatives, soda bottle twist-off caps, or other objects to cover the words on their Bingo page. After the first student has called "Bingo," I sometimes call out another two or three words to keep the game going a little longer. Like Concentration, Bingo is quite time consuming so I use it judiciously.

SPELLING PATTERN 6: R-CONTROLLED VOWELS

About R-Controlled Vowels

Having covered the major spelling patterns for consonants and short and long vowels, I want to include some additional common patterns. The first of these is the concept of **r-controlled vowels.** The letter *r* often follows a vowel, and when it does, it usually changes or eliminates the sound of the vowel. For example, in the word *bar* we only hear the sounds of *b* and *r* blended together. Say *bar* to yourself and listen. There is no long or short vowel sound in the word *bar*.

Like consonant digraphs, the r-controlled vowel sounds must simply be memorized. My students and I often refer to these as "bossy-r" words. It is interesting to note that *ar* and *or* make distinct sounds (as in *far* and *for*), while *er, ir,* and *ur* all make the same sound (as in *her, sir,* and *fur*). Additionally, some *or* words end with a final silent *e (more, shore)*. Students quickly learn that, although the word may look like a tickle word, it is pronounced like a "bossy-r" word. Many beginning readers will think of three-letter r-controlled vowel words (e.g., bar, car, her, fur) as beginner words because they do follow the CVC pattern. I simply tell them that these r-controlled vowel words cannot be beginner words because you do not hear the short vowel sound from the vowel. Table 5.9 is a brief list of common r-controlled vowel or "bossy-r" words. Notice that some of them also contain consonant blends and digraphs.

Table 5.9   Bossy-*R* Words

Same Vowel Sound				
a	**o**	**e**	**i**	**u**
bar	for	her	fir	fur
car	more	jerk	bird	surf
star	snore	germ	girl	burn
spark	porch	clerk	first	nurse
charm	horse	serve	thirst	hurt

Ideas for Teaching the R-Controlled Vowel Spelling Pattern

Word sorts. This is popular activity for giving students hands-on practice in identifying word families and spelling patterns (Bear et al., 2004; Morris, 1999). Simply put, individuals or small groups of students sort a deck of 12 to 15 words printed on index cards into two or three word families or spelling patterns. I generally have beginning readers sort words into families (at, bat, cat, mat; an, ban, fan, pan). I invite more experienced readers to sort words into spelling patterns (bone, code, home, poke; boat, goat, road, soap).

I prepare for a word sort by determining what word families or spelling patterns an individual reader or small group of readers needs to practice. I usually make this determination based on how well students can read the words on the word family chart and how well they can use the patterns in the follow-up word identification games.

Drawing on the Spelling Pattern Lists (see Appendix A), I select the words I want my students to sort and write each word on a 3 by 5 index card. I write one familiar word from each family in red marking pen to serve as a key word to help students in the sorting process. For example, to help a small group of beginning readers attend to the differences among the *ar, or,* and *er* word families, I chose the following words. The first word in each list served as the key word.

bar	*for*	*her*
car	more	germ
star	snore	jerk
yard	storm	clerk
smart	sport	serve

I began by placing the three key words (in red) side by side on the table and quickly teaching the students to recognize them. I pointed to, pronounced, shuffled, and otherwise played with the three key words until I was sure that each student could quickly recognize them.

Next, I modeled for them how to match the words from the deck to the key words and sort them into the proper columns. For example, I shuffled the deck of cards (in black) and drew the word *sport*. Thinking aloud to my students, I placed *sport* under the key word *bar* and said, "Let's see, does this black word in my hand have *ar* like the key word *bar*? No it doesn't. The word in my hand has *or*. Let's try the other two key words. It does not have *er* like the third key word *her*. OK, the black word in my hand has *or* like the middle key word *for*." I placed *sport* below the key word *for*. After repeating this think-aloud modeling procedure a couple of times, I let my students do the sorting.

I tend to use a simple three-step process for helping my students sort the words. I show one of the black word cards from the deck and ask the three following questions:

1. *Which key word has the same spelling pattern as this new word?* At this point one student takes the new black word card *sport* and places it below the key word *for*. Then I ask:
2. *What is the key word?* The students pronounce the key word *for*. This is easy because I've just taught them to recognize the key words. They pronounce the key word and then I ask:
3. *What is the new word?* The students pronounce the new word *sport*.

This activity teaches students to do what I want them to do all the time as readers: use parts of familiar words *(for)* to help to identify unfamiliar words *(sport)*. Cunningham (2000) calls this *reading by analogy*.

As the new (black) word cards are sorted into their columns, I ask my students to read the words aloud down the column for practice. Two additional follow-up activities further reinforce the students' attention to the word families and spelling patterns. First, after all the words in the deck have been sorted, I shuffle the deck, turn all cards upside down, and play a quick game of Concentration. Students who turn over a pair of word cards that contain the same spelling pattern get to hold the cards until the game is over.

The second follow-up activity is a dictation activity. I give each student a sheet of paper with the three key words printed across the top. Then I pronounce one new word from the deck and ask my students to write it on the paper beneath the appropriate key word. This combination of both recognizing and writing word families and spelling patterns is especially effective in helping students to understand aspects of the reading and writing connection.

When I've finished a word sorting activity, I gather all the word cards for that particular sort and store them in a snack-sized zipper-type plastic bag. I attach a small peel-off mailing label to each bag, number it, and write on it the word families or spelling patterns it contains. These bags of sorting cards store easily in a plastic storage container. Here is an example of a spelling pattern word sort (*r*-controlled vowel, final silent *e*, vowel team) for a more advanced reader.

bar	*fine*	*boat*
more	tone	read
wore	pride	main
storm	smoke	groan
horse	flute	seat

Bear et al. (2004) provide a sequential list of 117 word sorts. These include various short vowel sorts, spelling pattern sorts, and a variety of additional sorts, including sorts of inflections, multisyllable words, word roots, and word concepts. Notice that Bear's list of word sorts contains the same spelling patterns described in this chapter.

I Win—You Win

This is a simple flashcard game I use to reinforce my students' familiarity with spelling patterns and sight words. After teaching my students about r-controlled vowels with example word lists, I prepare a deck of flashcards with words containing r-controlled vowels. For slower readers I include only words from two r-controlled vowel families (e.g., bar, car, far, jar, tar; fir, sir, bird, girl, firm, dirt, first) in the deck and then gradually additional r-controlled vowel word families. I show the first card, and if the student correctly recognizes the word, he or she keeps the card. If the student misreads the word, I keep the card and put it back into the deck to be shown again. We continue until the student has all the cards. Sometimes, for fun, I reverse roles with the students after they have recognized all the words in the deck and let them be the teacher and "help" me to learn the words.

SPELLING PATTERN 7: VOWEL DIPHTHONGS

About the Vowel Diphthong Spelling Pattern

Vowel diphthongs (oi, oy; ou, ow; aw, ew) are additional vowel combinations that produce sounds different from the actual sound of either letter. Notice that *oi* doesn't

Table 5.10   Diphthong Words

oi	oy	ou	ow	aw	ew
oil	boy	ou<u>ch</u>	how	<u>dr</u>aw	few
boil	joy	loud	now	saw	new
soil	toy	rou<u>nd</u>	cow	hawk	<u>bl</u>ew
voice		house	<u>br</u>own	<u>cr</u>awl	<u>ch</u>ew
poi<u>nt</u>		<u>sh</u>out	<u>cl</u>own	lawn	<u>dr</u>ew

make either an *o* or an *i* sound. These diphthong vowel combinations are different from vowel teams in which you hear the first vowel's long sound and the second vowel is silent (rain, say, seat, soap). Diphthongs make two additional sounds /oy/ (also spelled *oi* as in boil) and /ow/ (also spelled *ou* as in proud) and also additional spellings of the existing sounds *short o* (aw) and *long u* (ew). When I introduce the diphthong *ow,* my students often point out that *ow* is a vowel team. I explain that *ow* is a vowel team when it makes a long *o* sound as in *blow* and *grow,* and *ow* is a diphthong when it makes the /ou/ sound as in *cow* and *flower.*

If you think this is getting complicated, imagine how your beginning readers feel when they have to learn it. This complexity is why I like to teach only common and useful spelling patterns and to teach the patterns inductively with spelling pattern word list activities.

Through the years that I've been teaching students to recognize diphthongs, I've not been able to come up with a student-friendly term for diphthongs, so my students have learned to call them diphthongs. (Maybe we should call them *dips.*) Notice that some of the diphthong example words in Table 5.10 also contain consonant blends and digraphs.

Idea for Teaching the Vowel Diphthong Spelling Pattern

Diphthong wall chart.   After doing the usual example word list explaining and chanting activities, I've explored and reinforced diphthongs by hanging a long piece of colored butcher paper on a classroom wall and writing across the top in big letters the sentence, *The boy pointed at the loud cow chewing straw.* This sentence contains the six diphthongs. Next we brainstorm on the chalkboard all the words my students can think of that make the /oy/ and /ou/ sounds. Like the long vowel pattern sort described earlier, this brainstorming gives me an opportunity to further explore diphthong spelling patterns with my students.

Next, I ask for a few student volunteers to come to me and get an index card, choose a favorite diphthong word from our brainstormed list, write the word in big letters on the index card with a fine-point marking pen, and then tape the diphthong word card to the diphthong wall chart below the corresponding diphthong word in the sentence. Finally, I send my students on a diphthong hunt, looking for diphthong words in their reading books and other print. The next day we list the diphthong words they found, write the words on index cards, and add them to the appropriate columns of diphthong words growing on the diphthong wall chart. Leaving the diphthong wall chart displayed prominently in our classroom helps to maintain my students' awareness of diphthong words and gives me a valuable reference tool for reteaching when necessary.

Table 5.11   Common Word Chunks

all	**ank**	**ing**	**ight**	**ink**	**old**
ball	bank	king	light	ink	bold
call	sank	sing	might	pink	fold
hall	tank	bring	tight	wink	gold
mall	thank	swing	slight	blink	told
wall	shrank	thing	fright	think	scold

SIX ADDITIONAL NONDECODABLE WORD CHUNKS

Toward the end of the school year we focus on six additional patterns *(all, ank, ing, ight, ink,* and *old)* that many teachers and my students refer to as **chunks.** These nondecodable spelling patterns consist of chunks drawn from Adams's (1990) list of the 38 most common phonograms (word endings), which were not included within the seven major spelling patterns. These chunks cannot be sounded out and must be memorized. For example, the *all* chunk actually makes the same *short o* sound you hear in *Bob, dog, doll,* and *fox.* Listen to the *short o* vowel sound in *ball* as you say it to yourself. The *ing* chunk is common both as a word part (s*ing*) and as an ending (end*ing*), yet it makes a *long e* vowel sound, rather than a *short i* vowel sound. The *ink* spelling pattern also makes a *long e* rather than a *short i* vowel sound. Students must also learn to recognize the *ight* chunk with its *silent gh* and *long i* vowel sound. The *o* in *bold* makes a *long o* sound, rather than the *short o* sound you would get if you applied phonics rules. Example chunk words are given in Table 5.11.

 ## STRUCTURAL ANALYSIS

Structural analysis refers to readers analyzing and putting together pieces of words as they read. The four most common structural analysis concepts are suffixes, prefixes, compound words, and contractions. My personal experience is that, when students have really mastered the seven common spelling patterns, we don't need to spend a lot of time teaching structural analysis. My students readily transfer their facility with letter sounds, the blending process, and common spelling patterns in decoding compound words, contractions, and words with affixes. For example, students who can successfully blend the sounds in *bat* should also be able to blend the sounds in *bats.* Similarly, students who can successfully blend the sounds in the word *can* can also blend the sounds in the word *can't.* Students' facility with **inflected** forms of words in their oral language helps them to identify printed words such as *it's, didn't, he'd, washes, rocked, unless,* and *report.*

I have used the same process of introduce, explore, and apply to teach my students to be aware of and to apply these structural analysis concepts. For example, I created a chart of the *all, ank,* and *ing* words listed above, explored and chanted the word lists, involved my students in some of the exploratory activities described above, and then sent them on structural analysis word hunts. We then repeated the process with a chart featuring *ight, ink,* and *old* words. I created similar charts for compound words and contraction words. By the end of the school, when I was teaching these concepts, my students had become very good at finding spelling patterns in words and easily came to recognize structural analysis words.

 SIGHT VOCABULARY

When teachers speak of sight vocabulary or sight words, they are often referring to one of two categories of words: (1) *high-frequency words,* such as *a, for, of, some, that, the,* and *very* that appear in virtually every sentence or (2) words that don't follow the "phonics rules," such as *a, because, come, does, give, of, said,* and *was* that simply must be memorized. The words that readers have come to recognize instantly are often referred to as their *sight vocabulary.* Much of the process of learning to read involves learning to identify words using their spelling patterns and then, soon after, adding these words to memorized sight vocabulary through seeing the words over and over in print.

High-frequency words appear in print so regularly that it only makes sense for students to learn to recognize them by sight. For example, 10 words, *the, of, and, a, to, in, is, you, that,* and *I,* make up nearly 25% of the words we see in print (Cunningham, 2000). It would be very cumbersome and counterproductive to have to sound out these words every time they show up. Happily, because these and other high-frequency words show up so often, most beginning readers learn to recognize them automatically simply from the amount of repetition. In fact, it is readily apparent to teachers that many words that students are learning from word family charts in September and October have become memorized sight words by January simply from repeated exposures in meaningful texts.

A second reason for helping students to quickly increase their sight vocabulary is that good readers use words in their sight vocabulary to help decode unfamiliar words (Calkins, 2001; Cunningham, 2000). Research suggests that students' recognition of familiar words accounts for 95% of their recognition of unfamiliar words (Moustafa, 1995). For example, a student who can automatically recognize the familiar word *big* will have an easier time recognizing the less familiar word *jig.* The unfamiliar word *shank* is less problematic for a student who can recognize the word *bank.* Sight words are generally learned through two avenues: wide reading and direct teaching (Cooper, 2000; NRP, 2000).

BUILDING SIGHT VOCABULARY THROUGH WIDE READING

It has been estimated that high school seniors have vocabularies of about 40,000 words (Cooper, 2000). Based on this figure, a minute or two with a calculator suggests that students are learning 3333 new words per school year, or about 92 new words per week (assuming 36 weeks in a school year). How many teachers do you know that can teach 92 new words per week? So where do college-level readers learn all these words? They certainly don't learn that many words from classroom vocabulary lessons. They learn them from seeing these words over and over during reading.

Wide reading is the most powerful way for beginning readers to increase the size of their sight vocabulary. Nagy (1988) states that "increasing the volume of students' reading is the single most important thing a teacher can do to promote large-scale vocabulary growth" (p. 32). Anderson et al., 1985, p. 38) concluded from their review of the research that "the best way to get children to refine and extend their knowledge of letter–sound correspondences is through repeated opportunities to read." All of us who have taught reading have had the experience of helping a student to decode a word during a reading lesson and then noticing that the student correctly identified the word the next time it appeared in the reading passage. Large amounts of meaningful reading give students the opportunities to encounter and scrutinize many words over and over, thus increasing their sight vocabulary. Calkins (2001, p. 212) asks, "Why not let children learn these high frequency words as they encounter them in texts that are funny, sad, or otherwise, memorable?" Procedures for organizing and promoting students' independent reading are described in chapter 6.

DIRECT TEACHING OF SIGHT VOCABULARY

Preteaching Sight Vocabulary

Although direct teaching of sight vocabulary is less effective than wide reading (Cooper, 2000), at times it is appropriate to identify specific vocabulary words for special instructional attention. For example, when examining reading passages prior to using them for instruction, I often notice words that my students might not know. Rather than risk interrupting the flow of the reading lesson, I have preintroduced a few words during the prereading introduction of the passage. This is very common practice when using a basal or core reading program. It is also something to consider when introducing information texts that contain content-specific vocabulary.

Direct teaching of vocabulary is as easy as writing the words on the chalkboard, pronouncing the words, underlining or highlighting familiar spelling patterns in the words, and then telling what the words mean. Have your students repeat the words aloud with you two or three times.

RIVET

Cunningham (2000) introduced a vocabulary activity she calls RIVET because it rivets the students' attention on the words being introduced. The steps for RIVET are as follows:

1. Select five or six key words or phrases from the passage. These can be selected because they are unfamiliar or are important to the passage.

2. Number down the left side of the chalkboard for the number of words you have selected, and write a blank line for each letter in each word so that the board looks something like this:

   1. __ __ __ __ __ __
   2. __ __ __ __   __ __ __ __
   3. __ __ __ __ __
   4. __ __ __ __ __ __
   5. __ __ __ __
   6. __ __ __ __ __ __

3. Begin filling in the blank lines with the letters from each word. Ask your students to try to guess what the words will be as you fill in the letters. As the

students guess each word, have them tell you what the remaining letters should be, and finish filling in the blanks.

4. Discuss the words. Highlight spelling patterns and discuss what each word means. Cunningham recommends having the students use the words to predict the content of the passage.

Word Wall

Displayed prominently across the back wall of my classroom is my word wall (Cunningham, 2000; Wagstaff, 1999), a very useful resource that my students and I use daily to study spelling patterns and to consult during writing workshop. A word wall is also an effective device for teaching students to recognize sight words, those irregularly spelled words that don't follow the phonics rules (see the italicized "outlaw words" in Appendix A).

To construct the word wall, I attached a piece of colored butcher paper long enough to stretch across the back wall of the classroom. I then wrote my students' first names in red marking pen on 3 by 5 index cards and taped them across the top of the butcher paper in alphabetically ordered columns. Then in alphabetical columns beneath my students' names I began taping words that students frequently used and misspelled during our writing workshop, written on index cards in black marking pen. I added about five or six words to the word wall each week so that, by the end of the school year, we had about 200 words.

I try to do a word wall activity each day so that my students will be cognizant of the word wall and use it regularly. For example, we chant a column of the words each day: top to bottom, bottom to top, and in random order to help them to become sight words. I often use words from the word wall for various spelling tests. I enforce the classroom rule that word wall words must be spelled correctly on writing workshop drafts.

Cunningham (2000) suggests a word wall activity she calls Be a Mind Reader in which you choose a word from the word wall and give your students five hints to see how quickly they can determine the word you have selected:

1. *It's on the word wall.*
2. *It has _____ (number of) letters.*
3. *It begins with the letter _____.*
4. *The vowel letter is _____.*
5. *It finishes the sentence _____.*

Some authors suggest highlighting the spelling patterns by underlining them or cutting the index card around the tall letters (b, d, f, h, k, l, t) and the letters that hang down (g, j, p, q, y) to emphasize each word's shape. However, I find such additional visual information to be confusing to some students. My preference is simply to write the words on the index cards so that my students will attend to the spelling patterns, rather than colors or shapes.

Calkins (2001) suggests a three-step say–spell–write procedure for teaching sight vocabulary from a word wall. Begin by selecting an irregularly spelled word such as *kind,* write it on the board, and pronounce it for the students. Then call on a student to spell the word aloud with his or her eyes closed. Then call on six to eight more students to do the same, one at a time. Often a cadence will develop as the students spell the word aloud over and over. Then ask the whole class to spell the word aloud in unison.

Next, have each student get out his or her whiteboard or a piece of paper and ask them to once again look at the word, spell the word aloud, and then write the word. Calkins suggests repeating this part of the lesson three times. A last step to this sight word teaching procedure is to explore word family derivations if applicable. For example, students brainstorm words that rhyme with *kind* (bind, blind, find, grind, mind, wind), you list them on the chalkboard, and then you dictate the words for the students to write.

Wagstaff (1999) provides descriptions and guidelines for constructing a variety of word walls for specific instructional purposes. For example, she describes how to develop and use an ABC wall, a chunking wall, a words-we-know wall, and a help wall.

 *ORAL READING FLUENCY*

The National Reading Panel (2000, p. 3–5) defines fluency as "the ability to read a text quickly, accurately, and with proper expression." Oral reading fluency is critically important to overall reading success because the ability to process printed words quickly, accurately, and effortlessly frees up a reader's congnitive resources to focus on the meaning of a text. The word study instruction strategies described in this chapter should give students the knowledge and skills they need to become fluent readers. However, while many students gain the word study knowledge and skills needed to recognize and process spelling patterns fluently and automatically, other students do not attain adequate levels of fluency. Their oral reading remains slow and laborious, diverting attention away from comprehension.

The National Reading Panel's review of research on fluency suggested that the most effective way to build students' oral reading fluency is to give them many opportunities for **guided oral reading** practice. In other words, students who need to improve their oral reading fluency need to read aloud daily from meaningful texts with ample teacher feedback, support, and guidance. The professional literature (National Reading Panel, 2000; Rasinski, 2003) suggests three major instructional approaches for developing oral reading fluency: teacher modeling, repeated reading, and performance reading.

TEACHER MODELING

Beginning readers, particularly those struggling to learn to read, need to learn what fluent reading sounds like and feels like. Unfortunately, struggling readers often have few opportunities to hear fluent reading in their reading groups and homes. Teachers must view teacher read-alouds as opportunities to provide students with models of smooth and expressive oral reading. Depending on the text, teachers need to vary the tempo, volume, inflection, expression, and intensity of their oral reading. Good oral reading should sound a lot like good oral storytelling.

Rasinski (2003) provides many suggestions for using teacher read-alouds to model oral reading fluency. He suggests that teachers read aloud to students at times during the school day that are most conducive to student attention and learning. Teachers should choose to read aloud personal favorites and books that build students' background knowledge and vocabulary. Teachers should practice reading aloud on occasion in order to maximize the effectiveness of reading aloud. Chapter 4 provides many suggestions for using teacher read-aloud for a variety of instructional purposes.

REPEATED READING

Samuels (1979) provided research data to demonstrate that reading passages multiple times produces gains in reading rate and accuracy. I have found the following repeated reading steps to be very helpful. First, I select a reading passage between 50 and 300 words in length. Passages may be selected from basal reading books, content area texts, song lyrics, and poetry. Next I read the passage aloud to a small group of my struggling readers to provide a fluent role model. Then I have my students take turns reading the passage aloud to me as I time them with a stopwatch. As each student finishes reading aloud to me, I note the elapsed time in seconds, convert it to words per minute, and plot the time on a line graph. I then assign each student to practice reading the passage aloud individually or with a partner in preparation for reading the passage aloud to me, and my stopwatch, again in a few minutes.

This approach to repeated reading is treated in depth in chapter 11. Other approaches include having students reread reading group lesson texts with a partner and using reading along with books on tape at a listening center. Books on tape can be purchased commercially, but I prefer to record them myself and invite guest readers such as the school principal, other teachers, parent volunteers, and local celebrities to also make the recordings.

PERFORMANCE READING

Performing texts as reader's theaters and mini-plays is highly motivating and takes advantage of children's instinctive desire to be on center stage. Rasinski (2003) describes a number of ways teachers can turn reading lesson texts into scripts. In *radio reading,* students are given portions of a text to practice at home and then perform in class with classmates as if they were professional radio announcers. Struggling readers in second or third grade can be assigned to prepare a brief picture book to read aloud to a *cross-age book buddy* in kindergarten or first grade. Perhaps the most popular form of performance reading is *readers' theater*. Many existing readers' theater scripts are available commercially and on-line, and teachers and students can also create scripts in class. After reading aloud and discussing a story thoroughly, I assign parts to students in a small group or involve my whole class by assigning three to five students to a single part. The fluency learning occurs as students practice reading their assigned parts over and over until it is ready for the performance. My students are highly motivated to perform their readers' theaters to classmates, students in other classrooms, and, of course, in front of a videocamera.

 ## CONCLUSIONS

My teaching of the seven major spelling patterns along with selected word chunks and structural analysis concepts took an entire school year at about 20 minutes per day. The largest amount of time was devoted to teaching the CVC patterns in the fall. Once my students had mastered the concept of blending letter–sounds, then the additional spelling patterns were learned more easily. One helpful classroom feature was our Word Parts We Use chart, which listed all the spelling patterns in sequence. This chart hung beside the chalkboard all year long and helped my students see the big picture, which spelling patterns they had already learned, and which patterns were coming up. These seven families of spelling patterns certainly do not contain every possible decoding concept. However, they do give students a manageable overview of the most common patterns.

While every published core reading program has its own **scope and sequence** of decoding skills, all programs include these seven major spelling patterns. Many teachers closely follow the sequence of decoding skills specified in the core reading program teacher's manual. Others use a supplemental decoding program to provide additional decoding instruction. What is important is to adopt a sequence of decoding skills that covers these major spelling patterns and to follow it carefully.

The instructional activities described in this chapter can be used interchangeably with a variety of spelling patterns. Additional instructional activities can be found in teachers' manuals and supplemental programs and through professional reading and presentations.

Word indentification instruction is often associated with meaningless drills. Many effective reading teachers know that decoding instruction can be gamelike and enjoyable. Effective decoding instruction makes use of both the specificity of studying spelling patterns systematically and the functionality of applying spelling patterns in meaningful reading.

 SUGGESTED ACTIVITIES TO EXTEND YOUR LEARNING

1. Interview a local first- or second-grade teacher about his or her philosophy toward teaching phonics. Does the teacher emphasize phonics in isolation, in context, or both? Do the spelling patterns to be taught come from the basal reading program, the state core curriculum, a supplemental phonics program, or some combination of these?
2. Find a child in your family or neighborhood and try a simple phonics lesson: (1) Select a spelling pattern, such as blending CVC words or final silent *e*, and *explain* the pattern to the child using a list of example words. (2) Engage the child in one or more of the *exploration* activities described in this chapter. (3) Help the child to find examples of the spelling pattern in meaningful print.
3. Get a copy of the book *Words Their Way* (2004) by Bear et al. Use the lists of word sorts in the Sample Word Sorts by Spelling Stage appendix to create your own file of words sorts on index cards organized in zipper-type snack-sized plastic bags.

REFERENCES

Adams, M. J. (1990a). *Beginning to read: Thinking and learning about print*. Cambridge, MA: MIT Press.

Adams, M. J. (1990b). *Beginning to read: Thinking and learning about print*. (Summary). Urbana-Champaign, IL: Center for the Study of Reading.

Adams, M. J. (2001). Alphabetic anxiety and explicit, systematic phonics instruction: A cognitive science perspective. In S. B. Neuman & D. K. Dickinson (Eds.), *Handbook of early literacy research*. New York: Guilford.

Anderson, R. C., Hiebert, E. F., Scott, J. A., & Wilkinson, I. A. G. (1985). *Becoming a nation of readers: The report of the commission on reading*. Washington, DC: National Institute of Education.

Bear, D. R., Invernizzi, M., Templeton, S., & Johnston, F. (2004). *Words their way: Word study for phonics, vocabulary, and spelling instruction* (3rd ed.). Upper Saddle River, NJ: Merrill/Prentice Hall.

Blevins, W. (1998). *Phonics from A to Z: A practical guide.* New York: Scholastic.

Calkins, L. M. (2001). *The art of teaching reading.* New York: Longman.

Clymer, T. (1963, 1996). The utility of phonic generalizations in the primary grades. *Reading Teacher, 50* (3), 182–187.

Cooper, J. D. (2000). *Literacy: Helping children construct meaning* (4th ed.). Boston: Houghton Mifflin.

Cowley, J. (1980). *Mrs. Wishy Washy.* San Diego, CA: The Wright Group.

Cowley, J. (1987). *Just this once.* San Diego, CA: The Wright Group.

Cummins, J. (2003). Reading and the bilingual student: Fact and friction. In Gilbert G. Garcia (Ed.), *English learners: Reaching the highest level of English literacy* (pp. 2–33). Newark, DE: International Reading Association.

Cunningham, P. M. (2000). *Phonics they use: Words for reading and writing* (3rd ed.). New York: Longman.

Duffy, G. G. (1998). Powerful models or powerful teachers? An argument for teacher as entrepreneur. In S. Stahl and D. Hayes (eds.), *Instructional models in reading.* Mahwah, NJ: Erlbaum.

Fisher, C. W., & Hiebert, E. H. (1990). Characteristics of tasks in two approaches to literacy instruction. *Elementary School Journal, 91*, 3–18.

Johnston, F. P. (2001). The utility of phonics generalizations: Let's take another look at Clymer's conclusions. *Reading Teacher, 55*(2), 132–143.

Lobel, A. (1979). *Frog and Toad are friends.* New York: Harper Trophy.

Morris, D. (1999). *The Howard Street tutoring manual: Teaching at-risk readers in the primary grades.* New York: Guilford Press.

Moustafa, M. (1995). Children's productive phonological recoding. *Reading Research Quarterly, 30*(3), 464–476.

Nagy, W. E. (1988). *Teaching vocabulary to improve reading comprehension.* Newark, DE: International Reading Association.

National Reading Panel. National Institute of Child Health and Human Development. (2000). *Report of the national reading panel. Teaching children to read: Reports of the subgroups.* Available online at www.nichd.Nih.Gov/publications/pubs/readbro.htm.

Pressley, M. (2001). *Reading instruction that works: The case for balanced teaching* (2nd Ed.). New York: Guilford.

Pressley, M., Rankin, J., & Yokoi, L. (1995). *A survey of instructional practices of primary teachers nominated as effective in promoting literacy* (Reading research report no. 41). Athens, GA: Universities of Georgia and Maryland, National Reading Research Center.

Pressley, M., Yokoi, L., Rankin, J., Wharton-McDonald, R., & Mistretta, J. (1997). A survey of instructional practices of grade 5 teachers nominated as effective in promoting literacy. *Scientific Studies of Reading, 1*(2), 145–160.

Rasinski, T. V. (2003). *The fluent reader: Oral reading strategies for building word recognition, fluency, and comprehension.* New York: Scholastic Professional Books.

Rayner, K., Foorman, B. R., Perfetti, C. A., Pesetsky, D., & Seidenberg, M. S. (2002). How should reading be taught? *Scientific American, 286,* 85–91.

Rylant, C. (1996). *Henry and Mudge in puddle trouble.* Fullerton, CA: Aladdin.

Samuels, S. J. (1979). The method of repeated readings. *Reading Teacher, 32,* 403–408.

Stanovich, K. E. (2000). *Progress in understanding reading: Scientific foundations and new frontiers.* New York: Guilford Press.

Strickland, D. S. (1998). What's basic in beginning reading? Finding common ground. *Educational Leadership, 55*(6), 6–10.

Wagstaff, J. M. (1999). *Teaching reading and writing with word walls: Easy lessons and fresh ideas for creating interactive word walls that build literacy skills.* New York: Scholastic.

Independent Reading

6

Sylvia Read

Engaging in Daily Independent Reading

The morning late bell rings, we stand and say the Pledge, and then every child in my second-grade classroom picks up a book and begins to read. José gets the rocking chair today because he is the leader of the day; Danny, Bethany, and Latesha have the couch today; and the rest of the class finds places to get comfortable on the floor or at their tables. The children have spent the time between their arrival at school and the bell carefully choosing the books they want to read from the many baskets and shelves placed throughout the room. The baskets of books are labeled with the names of authors or of genres and with other labels such as Caldecott books, Insects, Rocks, and Dinosaurs. For the next 20 minutes the

Shannon leans against the wall while reading *Junie B. Jones* by Barbara Park.

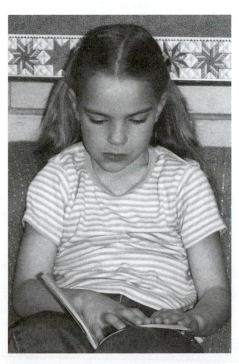

Bethany has couch privileges today!

sounds of independent reading pervade the room. Some children murmur the words as they read, some read a little louder, some make no noise at all except to talk quietly with me as I ask them about their reading, ask them to read aloud a few sentences, and answer any questions they have. This is my favorite time of day because I can concentrate on each child as an individual reader. I take anecdotal notes, including running records, in a spiral notebook, but I also store up my impressions of them as readers in my head. These informal assessments of their reading ability are extremely important. I draw on this information to give the children's families a practical sense of where these children are in their reading growth. I use other more formal assessments as well, but numbers don't reveal the joy these children experience when they read independently in my classroom.

Students need lots of time in school to read independently so that they can practice and solidify the skills and strategies they have been taught in whole-class reading lessons, small-group guided reading sessions, and individual conferences. This chapter addresses the issues associated with independent reading:

1. Building and organizing a classroom library by level and by genre
2. Matching books to student abilities and student interests
3. Independent reading
4. Time for, ownership of, and response to reading and books
5. Procedural, literary, and strategy and skills mini-lessons to support independent reading

Every child can experience the joy of reading when they have time to read real books (not contrived texts or worksheets). They need the opportunity to figure out what kinds of books they like to read and the authority to choose their own books most of the time. Give your students the time and power to choose books during independent reading and you will experience the joy of watching children grow as readers.

Independent reading can be called silent reading, SSR (sustained silent reading), DEAR (Drop Everything and Read), or a variety of other acronyms. Independent reading also happens during reading workshop or "just right" reading. Some teachers use independent reading as their time for conferencing individually with students, as in Patricia Cunningham's "4-block" approach (Cunningham, 1999), in which this time is called "self-selected" reading (p. 235).

I'll explain what independent reading looks like in my classroom and the purposes it achieves. But before you can get high-quality independent reading going on in your classroom, you'll need to build and organize a classroom library for your students.

 ## BUILDING AND ORGANIZING A CLASSROOM LIBRARY

It is important to have your own classroom library for a number of reasons. First, you want your students to have access to a large number of books. Recent research shows that access to books is a huge factor in literacy levels among schools (Smith, Constantino, & Krashen, 1997). The more books your students have access to the more they have to choose from, and choice leads to higher motivation. The usual recommendation is to have five books per child, minimum, in your classroom library. Frequent exposure to new books also allows students to put their growing reading skills into practice with unfamiliar texts.

Daily independent reading is one part of a comprehensive literacy program.

You also need a classroom library so that you can send home books for independent reading. Along with access to books, parent and family involvement in literacy development is correlated with higher language development and reading achievement (Snow, Burns, & Griffin, 1998).

There are a variety of ways to build a classroom library. The main source of many teachers' books is school book clubs like Scholastic and Trumpet Club. Even with only a few students ordering, over a few years you can build a substantial library of single titles. You can seek out grant opportunities to beef up your classroom library; small grants of $100 to $250 can go a long way toward building a good book collection. Other sources for books are thrift stores and garage sales; however, don't expect children to get very excited about extremely old or worn out books.

The other way to build a classroom library, though temporary, is to use your school and/or public library. School libraries often have no limit to the number of books that teachers can check out. Our local public library allows teachers to check out up to 30 titles at a time.

You can raid your home library. Our children are both past the age when they read certain picture books. Their books are still in the family though; I just keep them at school! I also purchase books with my own money for my classroom. In addition, I have received books and certificates to bookstores as teacher gifts and I use them to augment my collection.

By combining books from all these sources, you eventually should have a collection sufficient to read aloud to your students and for them to choose from for independent reading, with one caveat. Having a large collection of books does not guarantee having books at an appropriate level of difficulty for your students. Here's where you need to make a special effort to buy books that are or can be leveled according to difficulty. My leveled collection of books started with about 50 "I Can

Classroom library.

Addresses IRA Standard 2.3

Use a wide range of curriculum materials in effective reading instruction for learners at different stages of reading and writing development and from different cultural and linguistic backgrounds.

Read" and "Hello Reader" books. From there, I added other trade books. I also got samples of little books from textbook publishers who give them away to promote their current reading series. You can build your own library of leveled books, but it's more efficient to work with the other teachers in your school to build a schoolwide leveled book library, with multiple copies of books to use for guided reading lessons.

The bulk of the leveled books I use for instruction are in our school's guided reading book room. Over the past few years, using federal and state monies, our school has purchased over $10,000 worth of books that we have leveled, organized, and stored in a large room in our school library. These books were purchased from a variety of publishers, including Scholastic, Rigby, Modern Curriculum Press, and The Wright Group.

Organizing by Level

You can organize a portion of your classroom library by level and use this to guide students to books that are at their independent and instructional levels. Sometimes I call their **instructional level** their "just right" level. I like to use the Goldilocks analogy: she wanted a bed that was not too soft and not too hard, but just right. Similarly, I want my students to read books that are neither too difficult nor too easy, but just right. I would prefer that they read books that are a little too easy than too difficult. When children read books at their **independent level,** which is 95% to 100% accuracy, they have a chance to consolidate their reading skills, especially comprehension, because

Guided reading is supported by a leveled library of books.

they aren't using up all their attention to decode. Reading books that are somewhat easy also allows children to build fluency, which enhances comprehension.

The Fountas and Pinnell (1996) guided reading levels or Reading Recovery levels are useful for leveling and organizing books; however, you don't have to use lettered or numbered levels. You could opt for a color-coded system with only 5 or 10 levels, which is how I started. I caution against marking every single book in your room with a level (some libraries do this using Accelerated Reader levels or Lexile levels); some books, particularly picture books, can and should be enjoyed by all children regardless of their reading ability through emergent reading of the pictures, retelling the story based on having heard it, or rereading an old favorite that's fun and easy. We accept approximation in writing, and there is a place for it in reading as well. If you have ever read James Joyce's *Ulysses*, you'll know what I mean when I say that my reading of that book was certainly an approximation. We also, like children, enjoy reading books that do not challenge us, like the ones we buy in the airport to read on the plane or at the beach!

Read-alouds are often accessible to readers because of their familiarity. If I have read aloud *The Magic School Bus Inside the Earth* by Joanna Cole and Bruce Degen (1987) or we have watched a Magic School Bus episode, the book becomes accessible even to children who can't read these books with 95% accuracy. Conversely, many children enjoy revisiting *Hop on Pop* by Dr. Seuss (1963) even when they are able to read much more difficult books.

Figure 6.1 is a list of books that are representative of each guided reading level. You can use these books as benchmark books for assessing children's reading levels or as

Figure 6.1 Benchmark Books

Readily Available Books That Are Representative of Each of the Guided Reading Levels

Level		Title	Author
A	K	*Do You Want To Be My Friend?*	Eric Carle
B	K	*Lunch at the Zoo*	Wendy Blaxland
C	K/1	*Rainbow of My Own*	Don Freeman
D	K/1	*Bears on Wheels*	Stan and Jan Berenstain
E	1	*All by Myself*	Mercer Mayer
E	1	*The Foot Book*	Dr. Seuss
E	1	*Go Dog, Go*	Philip D. Eastman
F	1	*Cookie's Week*	Cindy Ward
F	1	*A Bug, a Bear, and a Boy*	David McPhail
F	1	*Who Will Be My Friends?*	Syd Hoff
G	1	*Just for You*	Mercer Mayer
G	1	*Mine's the Best*	Crosby Bonsall
G	1	*Sheep in a Jeep*	Nancy Shaw
G	1	*Spot's First Walk*	Eric Hill
H	1	*Sammy the Seal*	Syd Hoff
H	1	*Just Me and My Dad*	Mercer Mayer
H	1	*We Are Best Friends*	Aliki
I	1	*Dragon Gets By*	Dav Pilkey
I	1	*Father Bear Comes Home*	Else Holmes Minarik
I	1	*Hattie and the Fox*	Mem Fox
I	1	*Henny Penny*	Paul Galdone
J	1/2	*Cat in the Hat*	Dr. Seuss
J	1/2	*Danny and the Dinosaur*	Syd Hoff
J	1/2	*Henry and Mudge* books	Cynthia Rylant
J	1/2	*Mr. Putter and Tabby* books	Cynthia Rylant
K	2	*Arthur's Loose Tooth*	Lillian Hoban
K	2	*Dinosaur Time*	Peggy Parish
K	2	*Harold and the Purple Crayon*	Crockett Johnson
K	2	*Nate the Great* books	Marjorie Weinman Sharmat
L	2	*Amelia Bedelia* books	Peggy Parish
L	2	*Cam Jansen* books	David Adler
L	2	*George and Martha* books	James Marshall
L	2	*Horrible Harry* books	Suzy Kline
M	2/3	*Arthur* chapter books	Marc Brown
M	2/3	*Freckle Juice*	Judy Blume
M	2/3	*Junie B. Jones* books	Barbara Park
M	2/3	*The Littles*	John Peterson
N	3	*The Adam Joshua Capers* books	Janice Lee Smith
N	3	*Amber Brown* books	Paula Danziger
N	3	*The Leftovers* books	Tristan Howard
N	3	*Rumpelstiltskin*	Paul O. Zelinksky
O	3	*Baby-Sitter's Club* books	Ann M. Martin
O	3	*Baby-Sitter's Little Sister* books	Ann M. Martin
O	3	*The Boxcar Children* books	Gertrude Chandler Warner
O	3	*Can't You Make Them Behave?*	Jean Fritz
P	4	*Encyclopedia Brown* books	Donald and Rose Sobol
P	4	*Magic School Bus* books	Joanna Cole
P	4	*Time Warp Trio* books	Jon Scieszka
P	4	*Stone Fox*	John Reynold Gardiner
Q	4	*Wayside School Is Falling Down*	Louis Sachar
R	4	*Babe the Gallant Pig*	Dick King-Smith

Leveled books in baskets.

comparison books when leveling other books. They can also be used as a source of books for instruction. In addition, older basal readers, which are leveled already into preprimer, primer, and grade levels, can be used as a comparison. By examining features such as words per page, page layout, familiarity of vocabulary, and correlation between words and illustrations, you can determine for yourself whether a book should be considered a level D or a level G, for example. For more information on leveling books, see *Guided Reading: Good First Teaching for All Children* and *Matching Books to Readers: Using Leveled Books in Guided Reading, K–3* by Irene C. Fountas and Gay Su Pinnell.

In Figure 6.1, several examples are listed for levels E–P. However, I have listed only one book for each of levels A–D because these are mostly published by textbook companies, such as The Wright Group, Scholastic, or Rigby. The ones listed here are readily available trade books. Levels Q and up fall into a range of reading levels for which standard readability formulas are usually available. Primary grade students reading past level P probably do not need guided reading, but rather should be selecting books for independent reading and participating in literature discussions with other readers about a text they all have read.

At the beginning of the year, I purposely don't put out the more difficult levels. I like everyone to start out feeling comfortable. For my second-grade classroom this means that I put out baskets C through J. I make a point to read aloud a few books from each basket and then, as the weeks progress and we all become comfortable with reading again after what might have been a summer of little or no reading, I add higher levels and take away the lower ones. My biggest mistake over the years has been to make more difficult books available too soon. A few kids may be ready for them, but some kids panic, thinking that's where they're supposed to be, and they often attempt to read books that they aren't ready for. When children try to read books that are too difficult, they can learn that reading doesn't make sense. That's when students are "pretend reading." They flip pages quickly, glancing at the text and pictures. This is not a useful approximation of reading like the "pretend reading" of very young children. So I have learned to begin the year with familiar, easy books on display and the highest levels of books put away for a few weeks. This gives me time to get to know my students' interests, abilities, and dispositions. I notice and praise children for choosing books that are appropriate for their ability. I also have books in my classroom that are not leveled by difficulty, and they need to be organized in ways that help children to learn more about reading.

ORGANIZING BY GENRE

When you display books in your classroom library in baskets according to genre, you give students a chance to build an understanding of various genres. These books are

Books arranged according to topic.

Books arranged according to topic and genre.

usually ones you have either read aloud or done a book talk about. In addition, you may have taught the students the features of the genre in a mini-lesson. Some nonfiction baskets tend to change throughout the year as you study different content area topics. The basket containing books about rocks may make way for a basket of books about weather. Other genres, like poetry, biography, or fairy tales, stay out all year, though the books in them may change. In addition to organizing books by genre, I also have baskets labeled by author, such as Eric Carle or Mem Fox, which allows children to choose books by a familiar author and explore the topics this author writes about and the author's writing style.

MATCHING BOOKS TO STUDENTS

Because my students are allowed to choose much of their reading material, I teach them how to choose books with which they will feel successful and will enjoy. In fact, if students are not taught how to choose books, many will feel overwhelmed by the number and variety of available books. They need to learn how to choose books that match their reading abilities and personal interests.

MATCHING BOOKS TO STUDENT ABILITY

I begin the school year by teaching my students how to assess their reading ability. We discuss what a "just right" book is, and we talk about how it's okay to be reading harder or easier books than other students are reading. To emphasize that it's okay to be reading at different levels, I ask them silly questions like, "If you haven't lost any baby teeth yet, does that mean you're bad at losing teeth?" or "If you're shorter than the other kids, does that mean you're bad at growing?" I want them to accept their developmental differences in reading ability, just as they accept their physical developmental differences. I emphasize that the way they're going to improve their reading ability is through reading "just right" books instead of frustrating themselves with books that are too hard. I tell them that if I wanted to learn to play piano, I'd have to start with the easiest piano book I could find and that I accept this. Finally, I teach them to try out various levels and find the level that feels most comfortable for them.

When they are trying out different levels, I ask them to keep track of the hard words. If they run into five words on a page that they can't figure out, the book is not "just right." If they encounter only two or three difficult words, the book is probably "just right." I also tell them that, even though one book in a basket may seem just right, they need to try a few more to confirm this assessment. They notice that not all books in a given level are of equal difficulty. They sometimes recommend that I change a book's level because they have found it to be inappropriately leveled. I ask them to justify their evaluation and thus I get to hear their perspective, which teaches me a tremendous amount about them as readers and thinkers. I usually reward their initiative and thoughtfulness by accepting their evaluation and re-leveling the book.

After the students and I have established some procedures for their behavior and I'm relatively sure that I can begin to focus on individuals as readers, I begin estimating my students' reading levels by listening to them read from various books of their choosing. When I've got a rough idea of what they're able to read, I ask them to read from one to three of the benchmark books that our school has designated as representative of a reading level. As they read these books, I take a running record (Clay, 1985) and figure their accuracy level. I also listen for **fluency** and ask them to retell the book they've read or ask a few comprehension questions. If their accuracy is between 90% and 97% and their fluency and understanding are good, then this is their "just right" level. I then help them to choose books that are at this level (or easier) for independent reading. This is also the level at which they will read during guided reading groups. For example, Lincoln was happy reading *Arthur* picture books by Marc Brown (1993). Because these books are level K, I asked him to read *Watching the Whales* by Graham Meadows (1994), our school's benchmark book for level L. He was able to read it with 93% accuracy. I decided that he had judged his own ability fairly accurately.

Assessment is ongoing throughout the school year. (Assessment will be addressed more comprehensively in Chapter 10.) Periodically, I take a running record on students as they read a familiar book from a guided reading lesson. I use this information to decide whether I need to move students to different reading groups. I also take running records using our benchmark books, which are not familiar and must be read cold. This is done periodically to provide snapshots that show the progress a student has made over a period of time. During parent conferences, I share the results of these assessments. I may say to the parents, "When your second grader began the school year reading at level G, he was reading at a middle first-grade level. Now, in mid-October, he is reading at level I, which is the end of first grade. I'd like him to be able to read level L by the end of the year." This gives parents not only an idea of their child's progress over time, but also how that child compares to the "norm."

MATCHING BOOKS TO STUDENTS' INTERESTS

You can certainly pinpoint the level at which children read in terms of accuracy and provide a book that is at an appropriate difficulty level, but this means little if the child isn't engaged. Most students, thankfully, will read most of whatever you have available and be able to find their favorites among them. Reading aloud and doing book talks from your leveled collection helps students to decide what books interest them. Some students will have serious problems becoming engaged in their reading if the books aren't interesting to them. This is when you must really listen to them, not just during reading time, but all day. Sometimes you'll even need to eavesdrop as they talk with a friend to figure out what interests them. Interest inventories (Atwell, 1998; Ruddell, 1999) are available that can help you to figure out what most children like, but some children won't respond to them and you must take covert action!

I once had a student whose passion was snakes. It wasn't really hard to figure out. Damien talked a lot about wanting a pet snake. He latched onto the snake books

Addresses IRA Standard 4.1

Use students' interests, reading abilities, and backgrounds as foundations for the reading and writing program.

I had in my nonfiction book rack. I found more in the library. He exhausted my supply of snake books and those I had checked out from the library. After reading them multiple times, he began to be less interested in them and correspondingly less interested in reading. This is where I had to start doing detective work. I watched Damien chase butterflies at recess and provided jars for the crickets he caught and wanted to take home. So I made sure my insect books were out and found more in the library. He became interested in reading again. This cycle happened a few more times that year. If I asked him directly what kind of books he wanted to read, he couldn't answer. I had to be attentive to his interests. Damien grew as a reader because I made the effort to find books that kept him engaged.

When I taught first grade, several times each year I went to the public library and headed to the children's book section, specifically to the bookshelf labeled "I Can Read" books. I sorted through the books and placed exactly 25 in a box. The following morning at the beginning of our independent reading time I showed the box to the students and informed them that we had a new selection of books to choose from. The students' excitement was evident in their faces and chattering. I invited my students to sit on top of their desks, which were arranged in a horseshoe configuration with a shag rug on the floor in the middle. I sat in the old, overstuffed, fraying author's/reader's chair, pulled the books one by one from the box, and gave a 30-second book talk about each. These book commercials really whetted the students' appetites for the books, and I heard them whispering to each other, "I want Oliver Pig" or "I dibs the Little Bear book." I arranged the books on the rug and invited my students to come choose a book to read. Each ended up with a book, clutched tightly to his or her chest like treasure. They then returned to their seats to begin independent reading. At the end of independent reading time, my students placed the books carefully in a white plastic basket designated for this purpose. These books didn't go in their desks or get taken home. We kept them in our classroom for 2 weeks, and the students enjoyed reading and trading them. I have found this periodic activity to be a great way to supplement my classroom library and to maintain my students' high level of enthusiasm for books.

 INDEPENDENT READING

OVERVIEW

Research has confirmed that the more students read books at appropriate levels of difficulty, the better readers they become. Although the National Reading Panel (2000) did not find any research to support a causal relationship between silent reading and reading ability, correlation data show that there is a positive relationship between the amount of reading and reading achievement. Specifically, the highest achieving fifth graders in one study were found to read 200 times as many minutes as the lowest achieving fifth graders (Anderson, Wilson, & Fielding, 1988). Taylor, Frey, and Maruyama (1990) also found that time spent reading independently at school contributed significantly to reading achievement. *The Nation's Report Card: Fourth Grade Reading 2000* also showed that students who read 11 pages a day or more at school and at home achieved at levels far higher than students who read fewer than 5 pages (U.S. Department of Education, 2001). Independent reading has also been shown to improve the reading achievement of second-language learners and English-language learners (Elley, 1991; Flippo, 1999; Morrow, 1992).

Experienced teachers find that independent reading is an important component of the school day for all the same reasons that are shown by research, including motivation (Asher, 1980; Worthy, Moorman, & Turner, 1999). Personally, I find that independent reading is important for developing students' positive attitudes for reading. Choice is a crucial part of motivation, and motivation is a key aspect of learning. Children have to want to learn to read. They need to have reasons to reach and grow, and these reasons might be found in the pages of *Ranger Rick* or *Sports Illustrated for Kids*.

Beyond offering choice and increasing motivation, independent reading is a time for applying what has been learned during whole-class and small-group literacy instruction. For example, students apply phonics concepts as they decode new words. Many of my students point out the phonics concepts we have studied, such as vowel teams like *ea* and *oa*. Independent reading is also a literacy habit that needs to be established and maintained through daily practice. Older students and adults rarely read aloud to others (except their children, we hope!); reading alone needs to be practiced if it is ever to become a habit.

PROCEDURES FOR INDEPENDENT READING

Whatever you call your independent reading time, "it is important to maintain a simple, predictable structure, because it is the work children do that will be changing and complex. *How* we structure the reading workshop is up to each of us. The important thing is that we structure this time and that we do so in ways our students can anticipate" (Calkins, 2001, p. 66).

Just right reading is the carefully structured time when I meet with small guided reading groups and have conferences with individual students. In second grade, the year begins with a heavy emphasis on guided reading groups, but as the year moves along and the students are able to operate more independently and become more proficient readers, the emphasis shifts more toward reading independently, conferencing with individuals, partner reading, and literature circles. When I taught first grade, nearly the entire year was spent with guided reading groups. Kindergarten teachers may want to begin guided reading groups in January with those students who are ready.

What do the rest of the students do when I meet with guided reading groups or individuals? I do not have centers, but rather spend the first couple of weeks of school teaching the students how to operate independently and stay focused on reading. I have gone through several versions of these procedures. At one point, when I taught first grade, I told the students, "When I'm meeting with a small group, you may read by yourself, at your desk or on the floor, or you may read with a partner, as long as it stays somewhat quiet and as long as you are *reading*." In second grade, my students were able to read independently for longer periods of time, and so my instructions were even simpler. They had to read "just right" books, by themselves, at their desks, on the couch, or on the floor. Again, I emphasized that the point was to be reading. "If all we did in the independent reading workshop was to create a structure to ensure that every child spent extended time engaged in reading appropriate texts, we would have supported readers more efficiently and more effectively than we could through any elaborate plan, beautiful ditto sheet, or brilliant lecture" (Calkins, 2001, p. 68).

Independent reading time usually begins with a mini-lesson (more on this later in this chapter), which is followed by the activity time in which students read, respond, and conference with me or with peers. Procedurally, it works well to have the students choose their books for independent reading before teaching the mini-lesson. This way they have the time to choose wisely, rather than grabbing the first book that comes to hand. Choosing books is very important, and a certain amount of time needs to be set aside for this.

Another way I structured book selection time was to dismiss students one at a time from the rug after the mini-lesson. I would look at each weekly reading log and say something like, "Yesterday you read *Frog and Toad Are Friends* [Lobel, 1970] and *Owl At Home* [Lobel, 1945]. What do you plan to read today?" Then I handed them their weekly reading logs and sent them to choose their books and quiet reading places. The message here is that I know what they have been reading and I expect them to choose wisely today as well.

One thing I always watched carefully was the number of pages read by students reading chapter books. Two problems can occur. First, the number of pages may be inflated beyond what the student is capable of; in this case, conferencing needs to focus on real reading, rather than pretend reading. Occasionally, truly exceptional second-grade readers can finish a short chapter book in one sitting. Second, the student will indicate having read only two or three pages in a half hour of independent reading. In this case, conferencing needs to focus on either choosing just right books, if the book is too difficult, or on methods and places for concentrating and using the reading time wisely. All students need to feel that reading time is precious and not to be wasted.

While meeting with groups, the students read independently or with a partner. Sometimes they can choose their own partner and sometimes I provide them with partners. The beginning of partner reading time can be signaled with a timer. Initially, kindergarten or first-grade students might be able to read alone for 10 minutes; using the timer, you can gradually increase this.

For partner reading, they must read from one book (which means they must sit closely together and therefore are more likely to listen attentively while the partner reads), and they must trade off pages. I've tried having them read a whole selection to the partner and then the partner reads a whole selection, but attention wanders quite a bit this way. Trading off chunks of less than a page makes the reading too choppy and ruins the flow.

I've also experimented with partners who are somewhat equal in their reading ability versus having better readers model fluent reading and listen to and coach struggling readers. Some students are very good at this; they are attentive, patient, and don't interrupt to provide words too quickly. Others are not good at this and are better off with a partner who reads at basically the same level. It all depends on your students.

The key ingredients of independent reading are time, ownership, and response (Atwell, 1987). Students must have adequate time to read every day, they need to feel a sense of ownership about their reading, they need response from you, the teacher, and from their parents and peers, and they need to respond to what they've read.

 ## TIME, OWNERSHIP, AND RESPONSE

TIME FOR READING

To become proficient readers, students must read, read, and then read more. Just as we practice anything to improve and become proficient, we must practice reading. The term *practice* may sound dull; it might be better to think of it as playing. We get better at baseball by playing, by throwing the ball back and forth with a friend. So, too, children become better at reading through play. Reading independently becomes more playful when children are allowed an element of choice in what they read. Reading with a partner is inherently playful because of the social interaction that occurs during partner reading. Through choice and social interaction, we can increase the amount of time that children spend reading productively each day.

Bethany and Shannon partner read *The One in the Middle Is the Green Kangaroo* by Judy Blume.

This issue of time is crucial. When you look at how much time our students watch television compared to how much time they read, it is appalling. Literate fifth graders were found to spend 1% of their free time reading and 33 % watching television (Trelease, 2001, p. 6). In our classrooms, we can instill a love of reading by providing time for reading. We need to be sure we aren't wasting our students' time with worksheets or centers that merely serve to keep kids busy. We also need to send the message that if we expect students to read at home then reading is important enough to take time for in school. School is where we can get them hooked on reading.

Children need to read just right books for at least 30 minutes a day. They may begin the year, especially in first grade, only able to sustain independent reading for 10 or 15 minutes. The amount of time spent can gradually be increased throughout the year.

Figure 6.2 provides an overview of suggested reading amounts.

Figure 6.2   How Much Should Children Be Reading?

Kindergarten: Read or reread, independently or with another student or adult, two to four familiar books each day. Listen to one or two books read aloud each day at school and at home.

First grade: Read, independently or with assistance, four or more books a day. Hear two to four books or other texts read aloud every day.

Second grade: Read one or two short books or long chapters every day. Listen to and discuss every day one text that is longer and more difficult than what can be read independently.

Third grade: Read 30 chapter books a year. Listen to and discuss at least one chapter read aloud every day.

Note. From *Reading and Writing Grade by Grade: Primary Literacy Standards for Kindergarten Through Third Grade,* by the New Standards Primary Literacy Committee, 1999.

Source: Washington, DC: National Center on Education and the Economy. Copyright 1999 by NCEE Reprinted with permission.

Katie reads *Strega Nona's Magic Lessons* while lying on the floor.

It can be helpful to space the periods of independent reading throughout the school day. You might begin the day with silent reading for 15 minutes, have writing workshop, and then have reading workshop or just right reading later in the morning. Partner reading could occur after reading workshop or at the end of the day.

Occasional read-a-thons lend an atmosphere of celebration to independent reading. I ask my students to bring blankets, pillows, and stuffed animals to school on read-a-thon days. They spread out around the room reading with partners, reading to their stuffed animals, and reading alone. I read aloud periodically throughout the read-a-thon day.

OWNERSHIP OF READING

Ownership is about choice. Choosing is crucial to your sense of investment in what you're reading. Choice doesn't mean choosing from an infinite number of books; it can mean that the child gets to choose which books to read out of the appropriate leveled basket. It might mean he chooses to read his poetry folder today instead of the chapter book he has in his book bag. In guided reading groups, there usually isn't a choice. I choose what book the group will read based on my assessment of their needs and abilities. But the time they spend in a group is only a fraction of the time they spend reading, and they must have an element of choice woven into the balance of that time. The books I choose for the group to read help to reinforce what kinds of books are just right, which gives them power. The power of knowing your own abilities combined with choice leads to motivated readers who grow.

RESPONSE TO READING

Response to independent reading can take many forms. Children need the opportunity to have others respond to their reading and the opportunity to respond to the books themselves. Response may come in the form of feedback on the process of reading or of reflection on the content of what has been read. First I'll focus on response to readers, which occurs during conferences with the teacher, and when reading and sharing books with peers and family members. Then I'll focus on response to books as a way to reflect on what has been read.

Mrs. Navarro listens to Susana read.

Response to Readers

To get better at anything, we all need feedback. Feedback comes from the reader, the teacher, peers, or parents. After students become somewhat skilled at reading and understand how well their classmates read, they are able to evaluate their own reading. This happens all the time, naturally, but it can be enhanced by having them read into a tape recorder and playing it back. Over time, they can hear how they have progressed in fluency and in the difficulty of the reading material. Children know when they've made true progress; struggling readers especially need to become aware of their progress, because each increment needs to be celebrated, which motivates them to progress even more. Specifically, response happens during guided reading, through conferences with the teacher, sharing with classmates, and home reading.

During oral reading, feedback on verbal miscues has a strong effect on reading achievement (Hoffman, 1984; Schunk & Rice, 1993). In the Struggling Readers sidebar, Fountas and Pinnell (1996) offer a list of prompts to support the use of strategies, many of which are excellent for giving feedback about verbal miscues.

Conferences

Response occurs through informal and formal conferencing with my students. I provide the students with feedback on their reading skills and strategies, figure out what strategies they're using, assess their comprehension, and decide if the books they

FOR STRUGGLING READERS

- Read that again and start the word.
- Did you have enough words?
- Where's the tricky word?
- Check it. Does it look right and sound right to you?
- You almost got that. See if you can find what is wrong.
- Try that again.
- Does that make sense?
- Do you know a word that starts with those letters?
- Do you know a word that ends with those letters?
- You made a mistake. Can you find it?
- I like the way you worked that out.
- Put your words together so it sounds like talking.

Note: Adapted with permission from *Guided Reading: Good First Teaching for All Children* by Irene C. Fountas and Gay Su Pinnell. Copyright © 1996 by Irene Fountas and Gay Su Pinnel. Published by Heinemann, a division of Reed Elsevier, Inc., Portsmouth, NH. All rights reserved.

are reading are at an appropriate level of difficulty. During conferences, students are also able to reflect on their progress through self-evaluation.

To conduct *informal conferences,* I move around the classroom, visiting with as many students as possible during the independent reading time. During these brief conferences, I listen to the children read a few sentences, ask a few appropriate questions, or make comments on the content of what they're reading or their use of reading strategies, and listen to answers or comments from them on the content of the reading or how they feel about the strategies they're using. The questions I ask are open ended. Rather than asking, "Do you like the main character in this book?" I say, "Tell me about the main character in your book." If you ask a yes or no question, you will get a yes or no answer. If you discover that a student's comprehension of a book is imperfect, don't panic. It is normal for all readers to have imperfect comprehension of a book the first time they read it. Think about the first time (or the only time!) you read *Moby Dick* or *Julius Caesar;* you know that your comprehension was less than perfect, but that doesn't mean you understood nothing. Reading is a process, and when students are reading books at their instructional level, or just right books, then there will be a few challenges—decoding skills and comprehension may break down occasionally. If they only read books they fully comprehend and in which they accurately decode every word, there will be no opportunity for growth. Rereading books is a good thing and should be encouraged and demonstrated.

In *formal conferences,* I assess their reading accuracy on leveled benchmark books using running records or an informal reading inventory (IRI) to estimate their reading accuracy and comprehension. (More about assessment in Chapter 10.) I often tell students about what I'm recording; though some students become anxious about making mistakes, for the most part, I have found that being honest with them about their strengths and weaknesses as readers helps them to understand themselves as readers. However, if I am timing their reading as part of a fluency check, I try not to let them know, because they tend to rush and make more mistakes.

Reader's Chair

Another important sort of response comes through students sharing good books with classmates. When students recommend books to each other, they respond informally, but they also respond formally through a reading sharing time or reader's chair.

Addresses IRA
Standard 2.1

Use instructional
grouping options
(individual,
small-group,
whole-class, and
computer-based)
as appropriate
for accomplishing
given purposes.

With reader's chair, we provide time for children to share good books with their peers. This time is similar to the author's chair sharing that occurs after writing workshop. Two or three students are chosen or volunteer to read a page or two from their books or give a short book talk and explain why they think others might enjoy the book. The children practice what they know so well from television advertising—they sell the book to their classmates. The books they share inevitably become coveted reading material. This can promote a classroom culture of students recommending, sharing, knowing, and valuing books.

Small-Group Share

Small-group sharing is an alternative to reader's chair. Rather than having a few students share with the whole class, the students gather into groups of three to five members. They sit on the floor facing each other, and each person reads a passage or tells about his or her book. This is followed by the opportunity to ask questions or make comments. As the children talk in their small groups, the teacher moves from group to group, listening in, redirecting if necessary, and noticing children's reading and discussing behaviors.

Peer Conferences

Students may need or enjoy the opportunity to conference with a classmate about a book. They should only conference with a peer after they have spent a significant amount of time reading. Peer conferences allow children to share their reading one on one, to get help from a peer in order to understand a book, or to get ideas on new books to read. To limit the number of peer conferences going on at any one time, you can establish a peer conference corner or two or have a few cards displayed that the students take with them to their conference; when the cards are gone, no one else may have a peer conference. The cards should have the procedures for peer conferencing printed on them, along with some possible starter questions or unfinished sentences.

Home Reading

Through reading to and with their families, children get response from their parents or caregivers about what and how well they're reading. It is important to have some form of a home reading program; many children do not have reading material at home that is at an appropriate level of difficulty.

After the first couple of weeks of school have passed, I have a good idea about students' reading abilities and can begin to send home books to read to their families. I let them choose the book they want to take from the basket that matches their level. I record (and teach them to record) the book they've taken, which goes into a heavy-duty zipper-type bag, along with a letter from me explaining the homework and a reading log on which to record the date and title of the books they've read. I also provide a place on the reading log form for comments and parent initials. The students' job is to trade their homework book as often as possible, preferably every day. We trade books at the beginning of the day before the bell rings to begin school. As their reading ability progresses, the basket level from which they choose their books advances along with it. Reading books at home is often the only homework I require (especially in first grade); this allows both the parents and me to focus on making sure that the students' reading ability progresses as much as possible. Teachers need to provide guidelines for parents when reading with their children (see Figure 6.3). Sometimes parents can turn reading time with their children into a chore or a stress-provoking routine. With some guidance from teachers, parents can avoid these pitfalls.

Figure 6.3 Guidelines for Reading with Your Child

1. Read with your child before it is late in the evening when he or she is too tired to concentrate. Keep the reading session an appropriate length for your child. If 20 minutes is too long for your child, try breaking it up into two 10-minute sessions.

2. Keep the reading session enjoyable. If the book is too difficult, read it aloud to your child or take turns reading pages.

3. If your child cannot figure out a word in a few attempts, provide the word or show how you would figure it out.

4. Read short books several times, especially if your child still reads word by word. Repeated readings improve reading fluency.

5. Talk about the story and what it means. Reading is ultimately about getting the meaning, that is, figuring out the words is a means to an end, not the end in itself.

6. Read *to* your child sometimes, even if he or she can already read independently.

7. You are your child's first teacher. The one-on-one attention you can provide is invaluable. You are creating lifetime memories.

Figure 6.4 Tirzah responded to her reading by writing a letter to me about her book.

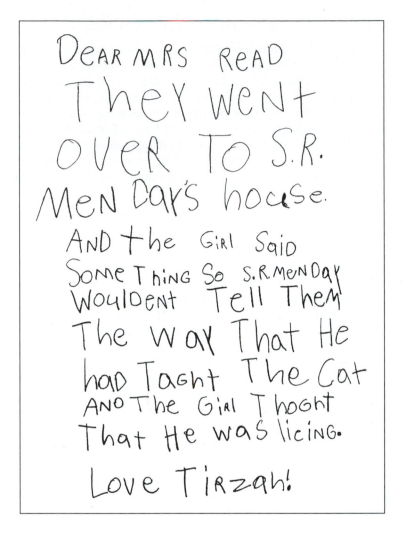

DEAR MRS READ
THEY WENT
OVER TO S.R.
MEN DaY'S house.
AND the GiRl SaiD
SomeThing So S.R.MeNDaY
WOulDeNt Tell Them
The Way That He
haD TaGht The Cat
ANDThe GiRl ThoGht
That He waS liciNG.
Love TiRzah!

RESPONSE TO BOOKS

All forms of response that serve as feedback can also serve as methods to promote reflection on books. Teacher-prompted conferences, readers' chair, peer conferences, and home reading are all avenues through which children can reflect on the ideas or content of their reading.

Response can also take the form of writing, art, or drama (see Figure 6.4). Keep in mind that none of these forms of response should take more time than it took to read the text. Often the most natural response to a book is to read another book. Sometimes, if I really enjoy a book by an author new to me, I read another one by the same author. Often, I find myself reading all the books an author has written as a response to reading the first book.

With young children, writing can be very labor intensive, and so writing as a form of response should be used judiciously until writing skills are more fluent. Even then, I would caution against the overuse of writing as a way to respond to books. If we, as adults, had to produce a written response to *everything* we read, we might very quickly begin to resent reading and try to avoid it. However, having said that, there are some guidelines for written responses to keep in mind and some forms of written responses that work well.

Keep the time for writing short, and make it a separate time in addition to the reading time. It might take the place of readers' chair or small-group share, for example. Before having students write any responses, demonstrate what you want them to do through a modeling mini-lesson. For example, show them how to use sticky notes to mark interesting passages that they might want to write about. Provide only one or two sticky notes for this purpose; otherwise, the students will mark too many things and not be able to focus on or decide what to write about. The sticky notes also help them to focus on the reading and worry about the writing later.

The kinds of writing students do can take many forms. Some teachers prefer a specific format; others allow students more freedom. With younger children, I have found it helps to have a more structured approach. For example, you can provide sentence starters as follows:

I thought it was interesting when . . .

I noticed that . . .

The part I found confusing was . . .

When I read this book, it reminded me of . . .

This author is really good at . . .

My favorite part was _____ because . . .

I felt . . .

My favorite character in this book is _____ because . . .

I love the way . . .

I can't believe . . .

I wonder why . . .

I learned . . .

If I were . . .

I wish that . . .

I post these for the students to refer to if they need to, or they can be stapled to the inside of a reading notebook.

Another helpful form of written response to use for fiction is a story map. You can use a graphic organizer for story mapping or you can use a paragraph frame with prompts built in and spaces for children to fill in the specifics of the book they have read. Reproducible forms are available in Appendix A.

Character maps are a way for children to explore a character's attributes (Taberski, 2000). A character map is much like a concept web, except the name of the character is in the center of the web and attributes of that character are listed next to lines that radiate out from the center. For example, Lilly in *Julius the Baby of the World* by Kevin Henkes (1990) has some obvious attributes, which makes it a good book to use when modeling the use of character mapping as a mode of response (see Figure 6.5).

Drawing or art projects can be used to respond to literature. The simplest form is to have children write responses accompanied by drawings. I use a response form that provides a rectangle at the top for drawing and lines at the bottom for writing.

More complicated art projects include creating artwork that mimics the style of a certain picture book illustrator. For example, using painted tissue paper, as Eric Carle does, my students like to create their own collages incorporating some of the signature images that he includes in his books, like the sun with rays. Recent Caldecott winner Simms Taback, author of *Joseph Had a Little Overcoat* (1999), uses collages of

Figure 6.5
Character Map for
Lilly in *Julius the Baby
of the World*

found objects to create illustrations. This is an interesting medium to introduce to students. Children can create their own birth story using Debra Frasier's book *On the Day You Were Born* (1991) as their model. Her use of bold shapes and colors in cut paper can be reproduced by children using construction paper. They can also use bold outlining around their drawings to produce an effect much like the artwork of Tomie de Paolo. The possibilities for responding through art are limitless.

Drama as a form of response comes naturally with younger children, who instinctively want to act out stories they've heard. Children can also use simple hand puppets with generic features to act out a wide variety of stories or they can create puppets using simple materials. With more developed readers, readers' theater is a way to respond to and extend the enjoyment of good literature. As a response to reading Judy Blume's *The One in the Middle Is a Green Kangaroo* (1981), my second graders and I wrote a reader's theater script that covers most of the elements in the story. They divided into three groups of eight to practice and then perform it for each other, their parents, and other classrooms in the school.

The **subtext strategy** (Clyde, 2003) is a dramatic way for children to infer what characters in picture books are thinking. To teach this strategy, it's good to begin with comic strips that use speech and thought bubbles to introduce how subtext is represented. Then, using a book like *Ruby the Copycat* by Peggy Rathman (1991), students act out the main parts of the story, and when the illustration indicates that their character might be thinking something to themselves, they say those thoughts aloud in the voice of the character. Later, students work in small groups and use Post-It notes to record the words that they, as a group, have decided the characters are thinking. This strategy is excellent for teaching **inferencing** and visualizing; in fact, it goes beyond visualization. Students enter the story fully, experiencing the feelings of the characters and making personal connections to the text.

 MINI-LESSONS TO SUPPORT INDEPENDENT READING

Mini-lessons are a way to teach students what they should be doing while they read alone or with a partner. The focus of mini-lessons ranges from issues of behavior, such as how to find a place in the room where they can concentrate and won't distract others, to more complex issues of what to do when they don't understand what they've read and how they can take action to repair their comprehension. Mini-lessons fall into three main categories: skills or strategies, procedures, and concepts of literature.

PROCEDURAL MINI-LESSONS

Procedural mini-lessons need to occur repeatedly throughout the school year. These lessons demonstrate or tell students the importance of finding a quiet place to read and staying in it, concentrating on the book, and not distracting others or being distracted. We may also review procedures like how to record the date, title, and pages read on a weekly reading log. The time I spend on teaching and reviewing these procedures pays off immeasurably in students' staying on task and focused. Here are some ideas for procedural mini-lessons:

- Where to sit during reading time
- Whisper reading to minimize distractions to others
- How to return books to their proper places
- What to do when you finish a book
- Keeping track of books
- Other rules for independent reading time
- How to give a book talk
- How to operate a small-group share session
- How to have a peer conference
- Being a good listener during sharing
- Evaluating your behavior during independent reading

During mini-lessons, as well as during many parts of the school day, it doesn't make sense to ask leading questions that force children to try to read the teacher's mind. Calkins (2001) has an excellent explanation of this in *The Art of Teaching Reading*. She compares the inefficiency of the leading question approach with the explicit approach of a simple reminder of other lessons taught, perhaps the day before, and an explanation of today's strategy or idea. However, a mini-lesson is not a mini-lecture. I want my students to listen and then do, not just listen.

Usually, the morning read-aloud is a springboard for the mini-lesson. In fact, children's literature is the best way to demonstrate most of what we need to teach. For example, as I demonstrate a strategy such as clarifying, I may stop four or five times during a read-aloud to explain something aloud to myself about what is happening in a story or information text. Then, just before the students go to their various quiet places in the room to read, I remind them of the strategy, name the strategy—"clarifying"—and ask them to notice whether they do that during just right reading. Later, at the end of reading time, I ask them to report on their use of the strategy. This cycle of teaching, practicing, and reporting should happen with most mini-lessons. Though you don't necessarily expect mastery of everything you teach in mini-lessons, children should know that you expect them to use the procedure or strategy, and they should expect to report back to you.

LITERARY MINI-LESSONS

Recently, I taught a mini-lesson to my second graders on genres within fiction. I explained briefly that Arnold Lobel's *Frog and Toad Are Friends* (1970) is considered fantasy because animals talk and animals do other things that animals don't do in real life, like wear clothing and receive mail. I reminded them of a few other kinds of fiction with which they were already familiar—science fiction, realistic fiction, and historical fiction—and gave brief descriptions of each. I asked them to notice that day which kind of fiction they read during just right reading and to be ready to bring an example and report to the class during our sharing time at the end. I don't expect "mastery" of this kind of information in second grade, but I do believe that, when children have a label and a definition, even a rudimentary one, of a genre, they have a powerful tool for enhancing their comprehension. Here are some ideas for literary mini-lessons.

- Differences between fiction and nonfiction books
- Genres within fiction
- Text structures of nonfiction (sequence, compare and contrast, cause and effect, description, problem and solution, combinations of these)
- Features of nonfiction (glossary, table of contents, index, headings, bold and italicized words, captions, etc.)
- First person and third person
- Characteristics of an author's writing style
- What setting contributes to the story
- Character development
- Leads and how they draw us into the story
- Titles and how they fit the story
- The use of dialogue
- Foreshadowing
- How to recognize the climax of the story
- The way illustrations add another layer of meaning
- Cliffhanger chapter endings in novels
- Surprise endings
- Mood

Mini-lessons are used to teach a variety of objectives: skills, processes, and procedures. Though you may think it would be nice to have a step-by-step lesson plan for every objective, this truly would prevent you from tailoring your teaching to your students' needs. Curriculum guides from our districts and states give us the concepts to teach; we, as professionals, need to decide how to teach these concepts based on our students' needs. We also, frankly, need to teach with personal integrity. Some methods for teaching work for some teachers and not for others; this has been demonstrated repeatedly in the research. Specifically, research has shown that it is the quality of the teaching, not the program, that matters most (Darling-Hammond, 2000). A good method of teaching implemented badly will not be effective. Our personal investment in how we teach can determine, in large part, how effective we are as teachers.

STRATEGIES AND SKILLS MINI-LESSONS

Mini-lessons often take the form of modeling or demonstrating a strategy that I want the students to use. I show them explicitly how I do something and ask them to do the same. I want to stress that mini-lessons should have one specific focus; more than that diffuses the power of the lesson.

I often follow up by having them report to the group their experiences with using the strategy. I want to make something very clear here: not all students will be ready to apply what I teach them that day. When I teach something to the whole class, I know that I will need to revisit the concept many times before everyone has been able to try it and certainly many times before everyone has used it successfully. But everyone deserves to be exposed to grade-level concepts and strategies whether or not they are ready to put them into practice. The differences in my students' abilities are due to differences in their developmental timetables, to some extent, and to differences in the number of exposures each child needs before something is learned. Some skills lessons need to be repeated often. For example, we review frequently what a just right book feels like when you're reading it and how pretend reading during this time does not lead to improvement. Here are some ideas for strategies and skills mini-lessons.

- Choosing a just right book
- Reading fluently (what it sounds like, how to reread for fluency, etc.)
- Figuring out unknown words using the sounds of blends, vowels, contractions, etc.
- Paying attention to whether the story makes sense
- Stopping to reread when it doesn't make sense
- Demonstrating emergent reader skills, such as knowledge of word boundaries, directionality of text, and one-to-one matching of voice and print (especially in kindergarten and early first grade)
- Retelling
- Looking for the main idea or important ideas
- Making predictions
- Inferring when the text is not explicit
- Stopping to clarify

I also want to stress here that really good mini-lessons grow out of observations of your students. I cannot offer a complete list of mini-lessons that every second grader should be taught. I can offer a more generic list of suggestions for the kinds of mini-lessons most students need and the general topics they should cover. Many schools are beginning to design curriculum calendars in which they outline the objectives that need to be taught during specific weeks of the school year. Each calendar is unique to each grade level in each school and is based on the specific strengths and weaknesses of their students. By getting together with the other teachers in your school who teach the same grade, you can cooperatively generate a list of mini-lessons you need for your classes. You also can build in the repetition needed to maintain the skills and strategies that are taught early in the year, and you can guarantee your school's community that all students have been taught grade-level objectives and been given the multiple opportunities they may need to truly learn these objectives.

I mapped out our state's curriculum objectives and correlated those with specific reading strategies. I use the map to decide where to focus some of my mini-lessons. For example, during the month of October I plan to demonstrate once or twice a week how I reread when something doesn't make sense. To reinforce the objective of rereading to repair comprehension, I ask students to notice when they find themselves reading for that reason and to mark the sentence or passage with a sticky note and be prepared to share that experience with the class. I also reinforce students individually for using this strategy during our guided reading groups.

In November, I will do a series of mini-lessons focusing on evaluating books. I could demonstrate writing book reviews, share book reviews from magazines, and have students write book reviews, which integrates with the writing curriculum because the genre focus for November is writing about books. The specific needs of my students in terms of evaluating books will emerge as they begin to talk and write critically about what they're reading. Perhaps they need to learn how to be accountable to the text by referring back to it, or perhaps they need to learn how to go beyond "I liked it." This is where the teacher must craft a unique approach for every class and, to some degree, for every student.

 ## CONCLUSIONS

When you first begin to conceptualize your classroom and how you will begin to organize for literacy learning, a chapter like this may seem daunting. There's so much here. How do you fit it all in? You don't. I personally can't fit all these instructional practices into a school day. You need to experiment with them to see what works with you, your students, and your schedule. You may need to rotate some of these activities in and out on a weekly or monthly basis. Independent reading must happen every day, however. How it happens and what activities surround it may differ over time, but to become better readers, students must read independently for a significant length of time every day.

 ## SUGGESTED ACTIVITIES TO EXTEND YOUR LEARNING

1. Observe in a classroom where independent reading is a structured part of the daily reading program. Write your observations and note how the teacher and students handle the independent reading routine.
2. Read independently yourself! Teachers who are readers communicate their enthusiasm for reading to students. Read 30 to 40 children's picture books or 8 to 10 longer young adult texts of various genres and by various authors and write short summaries of them.
3. Using the benchmark books listed in Figure 6.1 as your comparison guideline, evaluate the reading level of a set of texts.
4. Develop a set of literary mini-lessons for high-quality children's books.

 ## REFERENCES

Anderson, R. C., Wilson, P. T., & Fielding, L. G. (1988). Growth in reading and how children spend their time outside of school. *Reading Research Quarterly, 23,* 285–303.

Asher, S. R. (1980). Topic interest and children's reading comprehension. In R. J. Spiro, B. C. Bruce, & W. F. Brewer (Eds.), *Theoretical issues of reading comprehension* (pp. 525–534). Hillsdale, NJ: Erlbaum.

Atwell, N. (1998). *In the middle: New understandings about writing, reading, and learning.* Portsmouth, NH: Heinemann.

Calkins, L. (2001). *The art of teaching reading.* New York: Longman.

Clay, M. (1985). *The early detection of reading difficulties: A diagnostic survey with recovery procedures.* Auckland, NZ: Heinemann.

Clyde, J. A. (2003). Stepping inside the story world: The subtext strategy—a tool for connecting and comprehending. *Reading Teacher, 57*(2), 150-160.

Cunningham, P. M. (1999). *Classrooms that work: They can all read and write* (2nd ed.). New York: Addison-Wesley.

Darling-Hammond, L. (2000). Teacher quality and student achievement: A review of state policy evidence. *Education Policy Analysis Archives, 8*(1). Available: epaa.asu.edu/epaa/v8nl.

Elley, W. B. (1991). Acquiring literacy in a second language: The effect of book-based programs. *Language Learning, 41,* 375-411.

Flippo, R. F. (1999). *What do the experts say?: Helping children learn to read.* Portsmouth, NH: Heinemann.

Fountas, I. C., & Pinnell, G. S. (1996). *Guided reading: Good first teaching for all children.* Portsmouth, NH: Heinemann.

Fountas, I. C., & Pinnell, G. S. (1999). *Matching books to readers: Using leveled books in guided reading, K-3.* Portsmouth, NH: Heinemann.

Hoffman, J. V. (1984). Guided oral reading and miscue focused verbal feedback in second-grade classrooms. *Reading Research Quarterly, 19*(3), 367-384.

Morrow, L. M. (1992). The impact of a literature-based program on literacy achievement, use of literature, and attitudes of children from minority backgrounds. *Reading Research Quarterly, 27*(3), 251-275.

National Reading Panel, National Institute of Child Health and Human Development. (2000). *Report of the National Reading Panel: Teaching children to read. An evidence-based assessment of the scientific research literature on reading and its implications for reading instruction.* Washington, DC: National Institutes of Health.

New Standards Primary Literacy Committee. (1999). *Reading and writing grade by grade: Primary literacy standards for kindergarten through third grade.* Pittsburgh, PA: National Center on Education and the Economy and the University of Pittsburgh.

Ruddell, R. B., (1999). *Teaching children to read and write: Becoming an influential teacher* (2nd ed.). Boston: Allyn and Bacon.

Schunk, D. H., & Rice, J. M. (1993). Strategy fading and progress feedback: Effects on self-efficacy and comprehension among students receiving remedial reading services. *Journal of Special Education, 27*(3), 257-276.

Smith, C., Constantino, R., & Krashen, S. (1997). Differences in print environment: Children in Beverly Hills, Compton, and Watts. *Emergency Librarian, 24,* 8-9.

Snow, C. E., Burns, M. S., & Griffin, P. (1998). *Preventing reading difficulties in young children.* Washington, DC: National Academy Press.

Taberski, S. (2000). *On solid ground: Strategies for teaching reading K-3.* Portsmouth, NH: Heinemann.

Taylor, B. M., Frey, B. J., & Maruyama, G. (1990). Time spent reading and reading growth. *American Educational Research Journal, 27,* 351-362.

Trealease, J. (2001). *The read-aloud handbook* (5th ed.) New York: Penguin Books.

U.S. Department of Education: Office of Educational Research and Improvement. (2001). *The nation's report card: Fourth-grade reading 2000.* Jessup, MD: National Center for Educational Statistics 2001.

Worthy, M. J., Moorman, M., & Turner, M. (1999). What Johnny likes to read is hard to find in school. *Reading Research Quarterly, 34*(1), 12-27.

Children's Literature

Adler, D. (1980). *Cam Jansen* books. New York: Viking Press.

Aliki (1982). *We are best friends.* New York: William Morrow.

Berenstain, S., & Berenstain, J. (1969). *Bears on wheels.* New York: Random House.

Blaxland, W. (1996). *Lunch at the zoo.* New York: Scholastic.

Blume, J. (1971). *Freckle juice.* New York: Bantam Double Day Dell.

Blume, J. (1981). *The one in the middle is a green kangaroo.* New York: Bradbury Press.

Bonsall, C. (1973). *Mine's the best.* New York: Harper Collins.

Brown, M. (1993). *Arthur* chapter books. New York: Little Brown & Co.

Carle, E. (1971). *Do you want to be my friend?* New York: Harper Collins.

Cole, J. (1997). *Magic school bus* books. New York: Scholastic.

Cole, J., & Degen, B. (1987). *Magic school bus inside the Earth.* New York: Scholastic.

Danziger, P. (1994). *Amber Brown* books. New York: Putnam.

Eastman, P. (1961). *Go dog, go.* New York: Random House.

Fox, M. (1987). *Hattie and the fox.* New York: Simon & Schuster.

Frasier, D. (1991). *On the day you were born.* New York: Harcourt Brace.

Freeman, D. (1966). *Rainbow of my own.* New York: Puffin.

Fritz, J. (1977). *Can't you make them behave.* New York: Putnam.

Galdone, P. (1968). *Henny Penny.* New York: Houghton Mifflin.

Gardiner, J. (1980). *Stone fox.* New York: Harper Collins.

Henkes, K. (1990). *Julius the baby of the world.* New York: William Morrow & Company.

Hill, E. (1981). *Spot's first walk.* New York: Putnam.

Hoban, L. (1985). *Arthur's loose tooth.* New York: Harper Collins.

Hoff, S. (1959). *Sammy the seal.* New York: Harper Collins.

Hoff, S. (1960). *Who will be my friends?* New York: Harper Collins.

Hoff, S. (1985). *Danny and the dinosaur.* New York: Harper Collins.

Howard, T. (1996). *The leftovers* books. New York: Scholastic.

Johnson, C. (1955). *Harold and the purple crayon.* New York: HarperCollins.

King-Smith, D. (1983). *Babe the gallant pig.* New York: Random House.

Kline, S. (1989). *Horrible Harry* books. New York: Puffin Books.

Lobel, A. (1970). *Frog and Toad are friends.* New York: Harper & Row.

Lobel, A. (1975). *Owl at home.* New York: Scholastic.

Marshall, J. (1972). *George and Martha* books. Boston: Demco Media.

Martin, A. (1986). *Baby-sitter's club* books. New York: Scholastic.

Martin, A. (1988). *Baby-sitter's little sister* books. New York: Scholastic.

Mayer, M. (1975). *Just for you.* New York: Goldencraft.

Mayer, M. (1977). *Just me and my dad.* New York: Goldencraft.

Mayer, M. (1985). *All by myself.* New York: Goldencraft.

McPhail, D. (1998). *A bug, a bear, and a boy.* New York: Scholastic.

Meadows, G. (1994). *Watching the whales.* Auckland, NZ: Lands End.

Minarik, E. (1989). *Father Bear comes home.* New York: HarperCollins.

Parish, P. (1963). *Amelia Bedelia* books. New York: HarperCollins.

Parish, P. (1974). *Dinosaur time.* New York: HarperCollins.

Park, B. (1992). *Junie B. Jones* books. New York: Random Library.

Peterson, J. (1967). *The Littles.* New York: Scholastic.

Pilkey, D. (1991). *Dragon gets by.* New York: Orchard Books.

Rathman, P. (1991). *Ruby the copycat.* New York: Scholastic.

Rylant, C. (1987). *Henry and Mudge* books. New York: Simon & Schuster.

Rylant, C. (1994). *Mr. Putter and Tabby* books. San Diego, CA: Harcourt Brace.

Sachar, L. (1989). *Wayside school is falling down.* New York: Harper Collins.

Scieszka, J. (1987). *Time warp trio* books. New York: Viking Penguin.

Seuss, Dr. (1957). *Cat in the hat.* New York: Random House.

Seuss, Dr. (1963). *Hop on pop.* New York: Random House.

Seuss, Dr. (1968). *The foot book.* New York: Random House.

Sharmat, M. (1972). *Nate the great* books. New York: Bantam Doubleday Dell.

Shaw, N. (1986). *Sheep in a Jeep.* Boston: Houghton Mifflin.

Smith, J. (1981). *The Adam Joshua capers* books. New York: Harper Collins.

Sobol, D. (1963). *Encyclopedia Brown* books. New York: Dutton.

Taback, S. (1999). *Joseph had a little overcoat.* New York: Viking.

Ward, C. (1988). *Cookie's week.* New York: Putnam.

Warner, G. (1942). *The boxcar children* books. Morton Grove, IL: Albert Whitman.

Zelinksky, P. (1986). *Rumpelstiltskin.* New York: Dutton.

Guiding and Supporting Student Reading

7

John A. Smith

Gloria's Shared Reading Lesson

I't's early October in Gloria Bell's first-grade classroom. She has called together a group of eight students who are familiar with alphabet letter names and sounds, the concept of blending the letter–sounds to make words, and some print conventions. She's previously done a number of language experience lessons from which these students have learned to read their own dictated stories. These students are ready to move on. Gloria knows that shared reading is an effective strategy to transition students from reading their own text to reading text written by others. Students' reading enjoyable, meaningful texts is an important complement to the teacher read-alouds, word study lessons, independent reading time, and writing workshop experiences that Gloria provides her students each day.

Gloria selects a popular big book, Cowley's Mrs. Wishy-Washy (1980). It is a whimsical, predictable book about a woman who can't keep her three mud-loving farm animals clean. Because her students can't yet read this book on their own, Gloria decides to do a shared reading lesson. She'll read it aloud to her students first; then they'll all read it aloud in unison together several times with her; then, when they're ready, Gloria's students will read it aloud to her together as a group and then to each other in pairs.

Gloria begins the lesson with a picture walk to introduce the story's setting, characters, and events and to use the illustrations to preteach pertinent meaning vocabulary and background knowledge. Showing her students the book's cover, Gloria reads aloud the title and then asks, "What do you see here on the cover?" Liz immediately points to Mrs. Wishy-Washy. Gloria asks the group, "What do you notice about Mrs. Wishy-Washy?" Bryce says, "There's something in her hair." Gloria points to the scarf tied in Mrs. Wishy-Washy's hair and asks, "What's this called?" We discuss the words scarf, handkerchief, and neckerchief and several reasons why Mrs. Wishy-Washy might be wearing a scarf in her hair. Abbey points out that Mrs. Wishy-Washy is wearing an apron. Gloria points to the apron and asks, "Why do people wear aprons?" Becca points to Mrs. Wishy-Washy's fuzzy red slippers, and Gloria remarks that she has some fuzzy red slippers that she wears each evening at home. Finally, Cassie notices that Mrs. Wishy-Washy has her hands on her hips. Gloria asks and discusses together with her students, "What does it mean that Mrs. Wishy-Washy has her hands on her hips?" "How do you think she is feeling?" "What does it mean when your parents talk to you with their hands on their hips?"

Gloria continues the picture walk on the title page. She points to and reads the title aloud again, then points to the illustrations of the soap, bubbles, and scrub brush. She and her students name each item and together predict that Mrs. Wishy-Washy will be cleaning something, probably the bathtub, floor, or kitchen. As Gloria and her students examine the illustrations on subsequent pages, she points to the animals' body parts and gets her students to pronounce words like tail, hooves, udder, webbed feet, feathers, *and* beak.

Gloria's first step in the reading portion of this lesson is to read the text aloud to her students so that they'll be thoroughly familiar with the story's characters and events before she has them begin reading. She says, "Let's see what the words say," and asks her familiar question, "Whose turn is it to read first?" This question reminds her students that she'll read first; then they'll join her on subsequent readings. Gloria reads each page aloud, sweeping her hand beneath the words to help focus her students' attention on the print. Gloria especially delights in modeling expressive oral reading and hamming up the text: "Just look at you," she screamed, "In the tub you go!"

"Now, who's ready to read with me?" Gloria asks, and her students enthusiastically raise their hands. She points to the words as she and her students read them aloud together. Alex, Mark, Stevie, and Louis read along easily with her, while some classmates hang back a little, listening to Gloria and jumping in as they recognize words. Occasionally, Gloria leaves out predictable words and allows her students to read the words together on their own.

Away went the _____ *(cow).*
Away went the _____ *(pig).*
Away went the _____ *(duck).*

During this second reading through the book, Gloria also listens for words that give her students trouble. She and her students stop and examine the words away, along, *and* screamed, *pointing out print features that will help them to recognize the words on the next reading.*

Finally Gloria says, "You guys are doing so well. I bet you can read it to me!" She and her students begin their third reading of Mrs. Wishy-Washy. *This time Gloria points to the words and her students read aloud to her, following along as she sweeps her hands below the words. Because she's supported her students' reading by choosing a book at their instructional level, discussing all the illustrations with them, and reading the words aloud to them and with them, they are generally quite successful at reading to her.*

For a follow-up reading skills lesson, Gloria decides to do a mini-lesson on the irregularly spelled word said *that appears several times throughout the book. Gloria isolates the word* said *on the first page and asks her students if they can identify it. She explains that* said *is not spelled the way it sounds, but because it shows up in almost every story they'll read, her students will just have to learn to recognize it. Gloria writes* said *on her writing board, points to it, and has her students chant the letters. Then she shows them the printed word* said *as it appears in several other picture books and has her students chant the spelling. Gloria has her students reread the sentences in* Mrs. Wishy-Washy *that contain the word* said *and then reminds them to watch out for the word* said *in other books they read.*

Finally, Gloria has her students in this reading group pair up to partner read regular-sized copies of Mrs. Wishy-Washy. *Confident that her students know this story well enough to help each other read it successfully in pairs, Gloria is now free to have individual reading conferences with other students or to call another group together for a reading lesson.*

The shared reading lesson I've described here is one of four ways that teachers can run reading groups, depending on the amount of instructional support students will need to be successful with a particular text. Each of these four ways provides varying types and levels of instructional support to help students to read a text successfully. This chapter will discuss the concept of providing instructional support or scaffolding, present some issues associated with reading groups, and then describe four ways to run reading groups, in order of the most instructional support to the least.

Meeting with your students one on one and in small-group settings is your best opportunity to observe how well they can integrate and apply all components of the reading process as they read meaningful stories and information texts. This is also your best opportunity to provide your students with varying levels of instructional support that focus on the skills and concepts your students need at the moment they need them. You might say, this is where students are "taught in the act."

This chapter will provide information about the guiding reading strand of our literacy instruction framework and information about the following topics:

- Providing varying levels of instructional support as students learn to read
- Issues associated with reading groups
   1. Problems with traditional reading groups
   2. Alternatives to traditional reading groups
- Five kinds of reading group lessons
   1. Language experience lessons
   2. Shared reading lessons
   3. Guided reading lessons
   4. Literature circles
   5. Word study group lessons

PROVIDING VARYING LEVELS OF INSTRUCTIONAL SUPPORT AS STUDENTS LEARN TO READ

The shared reading vignette at the beginning of this chapter describes an instructional model some educators call **gradual release of responsibility** (Fountas & Pinnell, 1996; Pearson, 1983). In this intuitive instructional model the teacher (1) demonstrates the skill to be learned, (2) helps or supports students as they do the skill together, and (3) when the students are ready, the teacher gradually pulls back the instructional support until the students can do the skill alone. For example, a teacher may show students how to solve long-division problems by *demonstrating* solving some long-division problems on the chalkboard, *helping* as a small group of students work together to solve some long-division problems, and then having her students *practice* solving long-division problems independently at their seats. Former UCLA Lab School principal Madeline Hunter popularized this model in the 1970s, referring to these three steps as teacher modeling, guided practice, and independent practice.

Many reading educators now refer to this model as reading "to, with, and by" students (Mooney, 1990). In this model, the teacher models reading by reading aloud to the class, provides guided practice by helping the students to read in reading group lessons, and provides opportunities for independent practice as students read by themselves. Language experience reading lessons and shared reading lessons both incorporate the *to, with,* and *by* instructional support model.

During this chapter I will focus on five common reading lesson formats that provide varying forms and levels of instructional support. These include language experience, shared reading, guided reading, **literature circles,** and **word study group** lessons. These lessons often take place during reading groups, and the teacher selects which lesson format to use depending on the amount of support needed by the students in each group.

Table 7.1 shows a sequence of reading instruction lessons and experiences that provide gradually diminishing levels of teacher support as students take on increasing levels of responsibility for their reading.

Here is a brief description of the forms of instructional support associated with each of the reading instruction lessons and experiences. They are presented in a sequence of diminishing levels of teacher support. Language experience, teacher read-aloud, and independent reading were described in chapters 2, 3, and 4. This chapter will review language experience lessons and then describe shared reading, guided reading, and literature circle lessons. Additionally, this chapter will briefly describe temporary word study group lessons for students that need additional help with a similar word identification skill or strategy.

 ## ISSUES ASSOCIATED WITH READING GROUPS

A daily 2½- to 3-hour literacy instruction block of time usually begins with teacher read-aloud. This is generally very enjoyable for the teacher and students, gets the day off to a good start, and provides a "commercial" for reading, giving students a reason for learning to read. Word study instruction often comes after the teacher read-aloud, followed by the reading workshop part of the literacy instruction block in which students may participate in a variety of literacy activities, including reading independently or in pairs, learning center activities, literature enrichment projects, and personal writing. This is also a time for teachers to provide instruction to students in reading groups. This section of the chapter describes a number of issues associated with reading groups.

PROBLEMS WITH TRADITIONAL READING GROUPS

Grouping students for reading instruction has been the subject of much controversy over the years. Reading researcher Richard Allington (1980, 1983) pointed out many problems with reading groups based on reading ability, especially for the struggling readers. Struggling readers are generally given the least enjoyable texts to read. While their better reading classmates are reading Rylant's *Henry and Mudge* (1996) and MacLachlan's *Sarah, Plain and Tall* (1987) the struggling reading group is working its way through Dan can fan Nan in a tan van. Successful readers generally focus on constructing meaning from and responding to texts, while struggling readers are usually focused on word parts. Successful readers usually read many more words during a reading group than struggling readers. Successful readers listen to their successful

Table 7.1   Teacher Supports During Reading Instruction Lessons and Experiences

Instructional Supports During Teacher Read-Aloud	Instructional Supports During Language Experience Lessons	Instructional Supports During Shared Reading Lessons	Instructional Supports During Guided Reading Lessons	Instructional Supports During Literature Circles
Teacher selects an appropriate text based on student interest, listening comprehension levels, and curricular goals. Teacher introduces the text and provides motivation. Teacher provides necessary background knowledge. Teacher may have students predict the text's content based on the title and cover illustration. Teacher reads all the words. Teacher provides phrasing and expression. Teacher leads an appropriate amount of discussion before, during, and after the read-aloud.	Teacher writes students' dictated thoughts about the topic on a piece of chart paper. Teacher adjusts the length and pattern of the students' contributions to the text. Teacher draws students' attention to the letters and words as he or she writes them. Students are familiar with the text's content and vocabulary because they generated it. Teacher points to the words and models fluent reading as he or she reads the student-generated text aloud to the students. Teacher draws the students into the reading process as they read the text aloud together multiple times. Teacher provides follow-up word study activities from the student-generated text.	Teacher selects an appropriate-level text. The teacher introduces the text and provides motivation. Teacher provides background knowledge and vocabulary through a picture walk. Teacher models the text by reading it aloud to the students before they are expected to read it. Teacher and the students read the text aloud together. Teacher monitors and supports students' reading as they read the text. Teacher provides follow-up word study activities from the text.	Teacher selects an appropriate-level text. The teacher introduces the text and provides motivation. Teacher provides background knowledge and vocabulary as needed. Teacher observes students and supports their reading as they read the text. Teacher provides follow-up word study activities from the text.	Teacher guides students in selecting an appropriate level text. Teacher provides a response assignment for students to record their thoughts about the text. Teacher supports students during the literature circle discussion.

group mates read fluently with commendable phrasing and expression. Struggling readers listen to their group mates fumble slowly over many of the words they are given to read. Struggling readers also must put up with a higher percentage of distracting off-task behavior from their often disinterested and frustrated group mates.

Teachers' expectations can also influence the quality of the instruction they provide readers in differing ability groups. For example, when a student in a high reading group doesn't answer a question immediately, a teacher may be more inclined to provide a few seconds of wait time for the student to process the expected response. Conversely, when a struggling reader doesn't answer a question immediately, a teacher may simply assume that the student "doesn't get it" and quickly call on another student in a well-intended effort to avoid embarrassment. Struggling readers must also deal with the unpleasant social stigma of being in the low group. Reading group placement can become a self-fulfilling prophecy as successful readers gain confidence and experience, while struggling readers learn to feel dumb.

Finally, traditional reading groups are often associated with **round-robin reading,** the practice of having students in a small reading group each read a page aloud, one at a time, in order around the circle. I remember, when I was in first grade, I always found myself sitting next to my teacher in reading group. (Now I know why.) This meant that I was either the first or last student in my group to read aloud. If I read first, I tuned out of the lesson as soon as I was done with my turn. If I read last, I tuned out until the student next to me was reading; then I would hurry and find my place. Round-robin reading is a not good way to maximize student engagement during your reading lessons.

ALTERNATIVES TO TRADITIONAL READING GROUPS

Whole-Class Instruction

Due to the real problems with low reading groups, some teachers and reading programs moved away from ability grouping and focused on whole-class instruction or independent reading programs. In whole-class instruction, all students read the same grade-level texts and do the same instructional activities together. Whole-class instruction may be used effectively for reading instruction on an occasional basis, especially when the content is new and accessible to all your students. Teacher read-alouds and writing workshop mini-lessons are generally done in whole-class settings. Word identification lessons are often presented in whole-class settings.

Whole-class instruction carries the problem of one-size-fits-all reading instruction, which clearly does not meet all students' needs. It makes about as much sense to give all students in a classroom the same level of reading texts as it would to make them all wear the same-sized clothes. When we "teach to the middle," many struggling students are lost and confused, while advanced students are bored.

Independent Reading Programs

Independent reading programs (Veatch, 1968) are also a reaction to the problems associated with ability grouping. Independent reading programs are structured such that reading time consists of students reading appropriate-level books of their choice independently for extended periods of time, while the teacher provides reading instruction to students during individual teacher–student conferences.

While independent reading programs are better at getting students reading appropriate-level texts, providing adequate amounts of instruction is a problem. If a teacher does five or six teacher–student conferences each school day, each student only gets a few minutes of instruction once a week. This is not enough instruction, especially for beginning readers.

Flexible Grouping

So what's a teacher to do? Many teachers have hit on a compromise known as flexible grouping or dynamic grouping (Fountas & Pinnell, 1996). Flexible grouping is similar to ability grouping in that it involves pulling together groups of students with common instructional needs. However, it is different in two ways. First, flexible grouping is temporary. Students are not locked into the same group for months, if not the entire school year. Rather, group membership changes on a regular basis. A student may meet with three to five classmates in a reading group to read a book together, but the following week meet with other classmates in a different reading group for the next book. This fluidity and flexibility better allows students to progress through appropriate-level texts at their own rate.

The second difference between traditional ability groups and flexible grouping is that flexibility allows for a variety of purposes for reading instruction groups. A teacher may meet with four or five students for a guided reading lesson and then meet next with another group for a literature circle discussion. A few other students may meet together a few times with the teacher for word study group lessons to provide needed review of spelling patterns, rather than to read a story. Still other students may be grouped together in interest groups to study a content-area topic of common interest. The point is that students can and should be grouped together for instruction in reading groups that are temporary and changing.

In the following sections of this chapter, I will describe five well-established options for reading group instruction. You may select from among these instructional options depending on the needs of your students. For example, during a typical reading workshop while many students in your classroom are reading independently, reading with partners, or engaged in personal writing, you may do a language experience lesson with a group of your beginning reading students who still need to focus on spelling patterns and spaces between words. Then you may meet with a group of more advanced students for a literature circle discussion of a book they completed reading during their independent reading time. You might meet next with another slightly more advanced group of your beginning readers to do a shared reading lesson, focusing on reading fluency and expression. Finally, you may meet with a reading strategy or skills group and have the students practice constructing *ight* word families on their individual whiteboards.

PLACING STUDENTS INTO READING GROUPS

Teachers use a variety of techniques for placing students in reading groups. I'll mention a few here. More assessment information will be provided in chapter 10. Teachers strive to place students into groups reading text at their **instructional reading level.** This is the level at which the text is "just a little over their heads" and the students' reading ability will stretch and grow with teacher instruction and support.

Reading Program Placement Tests

When a school district adopts a basal or other reading program, the publisher generally includes a placement test. These tests often consist of a few pages of passages to read silently, accompanied by several multiple-choice questions after each passage.

Addresses IRA Standard 3.2

Place students along a developmental continuum and identify students' proficiencies and difficulties.

Teachers generally administer the program placement test sometime during the first week or two of school. Based on the number of correct responses on the placement test, students are assigned a preliminary reading level and placed in a group with other students at the same level.

Running Records

Many teachers use data from running records (Clay, 1993, 2000) to place students into reading groups. A running record is a quick procedure wherein a teacher listens to a student read aloud and records the student's oral reading errors (or miscues) on a scoring sheet. From the number of errors, it is easy to calculate the percentage of words read correctly. This percentage allows the teacher to determine whether the student is reading the particular text at an independent, instructional, or frustration level. From several running records, a teacher can estimate the text level at which the student reads at the instructional level. Running records will be described in greater detail in chapter 10.

Informal Quick Screening

Years ago when I relied more heavily on a basal reading program, I would go to the school's book storage room and check out a copy of the basal readers at each reading level. During the first several days of school, I kept the basal reading books stacked in a pile on my desk. Over several days' time, I invited each student to come to my desk and read aloud individually to me. I generally began by having each student read a page from the middle of a book one level below our grade level. As the student read aloud to me, I made a simple judgment that this particular level was either too hard, too easy, or just right for teaching (instructional level). If the level was too hard, I selected easier levels until I found the student's instructional level. If the initial level was too easy, I moved up through the levels until I found the student's instructional level.

Students' Actual Performance in Reading Groups

It's important to remember that placements into reading groups should always be seen as temporary. After placing students into initial reading groups at various levels of difficulty, teachers should always try out the placements for a couple of weeks or a couple of stories and fine-tune the placements by moving students to other reading-level groups as needed. Observing and analyzing students' reading behaviors during actual reading lessons is always the most valid form of reading assessment.

 ## FIVE TYPES OF READING GROUP LESSONS

In the following sections I discuss five types of reading group lessons and provide a lesson plan for each. Notice how the first four lessons gradually decrease the amount of teacher instructional support and increase the amount of student responsibility.

LANGUAGE EXPERIENCE LESSONS

Because I described language experience lessons in depth in chapter 3, I'll only give a brief overview here so that you may see it again in the context of reading groups. As you recall, language experience lessons are lessons in which you and your students discuss something of interest together and then you invite your students to help write

Addresses IRA Standard 2.2

Use a wide range of instruction practices, approaches, and methods, including technology-based practices, for learners at differing stages of development and from differing linguistic and cultural backgrounds.

a story about it by telling you about it (Nelson & Linek, 1999). As they talk, you write down what they say on a piece of chart paper, inviting them to watch and read along with you. After the language experience story is complete, you read it aloud to your students, pointing to the words; then you read it with your students aloud in unison several times; then you invite your students to read it back to you. You finish the language experience lesson by leading your students in several follow-up word study activities. A sample of a language experience lesson is given in Figure 7.1.

Language experience may be the easiest, most natural way to get beginning students reading text. Because they dictated the text to you, it is familiar to them. As they follow along with your hand pointing to the words, they are simply matching what is on the page to what is in their heads. Language experience is a wonderful opportunity for beginning readers to see the connections between oral language and print. They come to understand that what can be said can be written and that what can be written can be read.

Several years ago my students and I were happily anticipating our upcoming trip to the local fire station. I hung up a piece of chart paper, called five of my lower readers to a corner of the room, and said, "I'm so excited about going to the fire station. Before we go there, let's make a list of questions we have about the fire station." Because of their excitement for the field trip, they were instantly engaged. Their hands went up and I recorded the following questions:

> *How fast does the fire truck go?*
> *What do you do at the fire station?*
> *How many fires have you put out?*
> *Where do you get the water?*
> *How many spots are on the fire dog?*

I read the words aloud as I printed them on the chart paper; then I read the questions aloud to my group of students. I led them in choral reading of the chart and then pointed to the words as they read the chart back to me. For the next several days my students and I matched sentence strips and individual word cards and played with the text in a variety of ways to help them read it and to recognize the words and spelling patterns. Just before we left for our field trip, my group practiced reading the questions one more time, and then I took the chart down, rolled it up, and took it with me to the fire station. As we arrived, I announced to the fire fighters that we had some questions for them. My five students beamed as I displayed the chart and they read their questions to the fire fighters and in turn received answers to most of their questions. Sadly, the fire fighters had never counted the spots on their fire dog.

FOR ENGLISH LANGUAGE LEARNERS

Language Experience Lessons

Language experience lessons are very effective for English language learners. These lessons involve students in (1) using their English words to describe a personal experience, (2) seeing these words written by the teacher, and (3) exploring and learning to read these words.

SHARED READING

In shared reading, you select an appropriate-level text for your students and introduce it to them by discussing the illustrations. You read it aloud to them, pointing to the words as you read, and then invite them to read it aloud with you in unison several

Figure 7.1   A Language Experience Sample Lesson Plan

THE PRIMARY COLORS

PURPOSE

This lesson is designed for a group of five to six emergent readers. This lesson will:

(a) Reinforce the *conventions of print*: reading from left to right and top to bottom, capitalization, and periods.

(b) Reinforce the concept of *blending letter–sounds*.

(c) *Integrate visual arts content* into a literacy lesson.

1. BEFORE READING

(a) Gather the entire class together on the rug in front of the chalkboard. Hold up a blue, red, and yellow crayon and tell the students that these three colors, called the primary colors, can be combined to make other colors.

(b) Position the overhead projector in front of the chalkboard and place three petrie dishes on the projector. Fill each petrie dish with water. Then add three or four drops of blue food coloring to the first dish, three drops of red food coloring to the second dish, and three drops of yellow food coloring to the third dish.

(c) Tell the students that you will now mix the colors red and blue. Go to the chalkboard and write "Red and blue make _____." Ask the students to predict what colors they think will result. Then add three drops of red to the blue petrie dish. After the students finish ooooing and aaaaing, go to the board and complete the sentence with the word *purple*. Repeat this process by adding yellow to red and then blue to yellow. Write sentences on the board to describe these two mixtures.

(d) Send the students back to their seats to complete a follow-up art project using only blue, red, and yellow crayons. Show them an example design you did in advance in which you experimented with placing various colors on top of other colors.

2. DURING READING

Creating the Language Experience Chart

(a) Soon after the petrie dish demonstration, call a group of emergent readers together. Lead them in a brief review discussion of the demonstration and then tell them you would like them to help you write a story about the demonstration.

(b) Ask the students for a beginning sentence telling how the demonstration began. Aim for a sentence like "Teacher put food coloring in the dishes." Write the sentence on chart paper with the students watching carefully. Read the sentence aloud to the students (sweeping your hand below the words as you read) and then have them read it aloud together with you one or two times.

(c) Ask for more sentences about the demonstration, such as "Red and yellow make orange." Write these sentences below the first on the chart paper and read them aloud to the students and then together with the students.

(d) Ask for a concluding sentence, such as "We like mixing colors." Write the sentence below the others and read it aloud to them and then with them together.

Reading the LEA Chart

(a) Reread the entire chart (about five or six short sentences) aloud to the students, sweeping your hand below the words as you read.

(b) Invite the students to read the entire chart aloud together with you. Point out important aspects of print, such as capital letters, periods, and spaces between words.

3. AFTER READING

(a) *Conventions of print*. Invite the students to help you to count the number of letters in the words of the first sentence. Then invite them to help you to count the number of words in the first sentence. Help them to distinguish between letters and words. You may also want to teach them about the capital letters and periods on the LEA chart.

(b) *Blending letter–sounds*. Point to the word *red* on the chart paper and ask who can read it. Review with the students the process of blending the letter–sounds by leading them in reading it together "the slow way" and then "the fast way." Write the word *red* on the chalkboard and reread it with the students. Write the word *bed* below it and repeat the blending process. Repeat the process with the words *fed, led, Ted, wed, Fred*, and *sled*. Then reread the LEA chart sentences that contain the word *red*.

(c) *Make a book*. Lay three pieces of ditto paper on a piece of colored construction paper, fold in half width-wise with the construction paper on the outside, and staple along the fold to make a book. Make one for each group member. Type the text of the LEA chart (extra spaces between the sentences) and print a copy for each group member. Have them cut the sentences apart and glue-stick them onto the pages of the book. Have them illustrate each page. Practice reading the book until each student can read the book fluently. Send the books home to read with the family.

times. Finally, you do a variety of follow-up activities to focus on spelling patterns or other aspects of reading. Shared reading is different from language experience in that with language experience you are reading and studying a text generated by your students. With shared reading, you are reading and studying an existing text.

Shared reading began in New Zealand as an attempt to bring to the classroom all the personal warmth, enjoyment, and natural learning associated with parents and children reading together at home. Holdaway (1979) suggests that shared reading capitalizes on the enjoyable, relaxed, read-it-again characteristics of bedtime stories. Adams (1990) states that "big books, in short, allow a classroom equivalent of bedtime stories and, like bedtime stories, they are meant to be read over and over, as often as they are enchanting" (p. 369).

Many teachers use texts with repeating patterns for shared reading lessons. Text patterns such as "Would you, could you in a box? Would you, could you with a fox?" from Dr. Seuss's *Green Eggs and Ham* (1960) make it easier for beginning readers to predict upcoming words. This allows readers to match the text in their heads with the printed text on the page and thereby feel successful in the beginning reading process. For this reason, nursery rhymes, poems, and song lyrics make excellent texts for shared reading lessons. Many of the currently popular big books and first readers contain **predictable texts** with repetitive patterns.

Shared reading also builds on another instructional element missing in traditional basal instruction: repetition. Shared reading is much like music instruction in that readers have the opportunity to experience a text again and again until it can be read easily and fluently. This repetition enables students to focus on print features such as words, spelling patterns, and punctuation. Because of the repetition, it is important that texts for shared reading be very carefully selected. The texts must be interesting enough to sustain students' interest during the several rereadings. Holdaway (1979) recommends that shared reading texts have a well-defined plot, be predictable, include captivating illustrations, and make use of repeated language patterns.

During the successive readings of the text, the teacher can focus on a wide variety of reading skills. These include comprehension and listening skills, left-to-right orientation, sight vocabulary, punctuation, and intonation patterns. Activities including sentence strips, word cards, and cardboard masks that cover a text except for one selected word can help to bring students' attention to important features of print.

Another important benefit of shared reading is the community aspect of the learning. Unlike traditional round-robin reading, when students read aloud individually in front of their peers, the unison nature of shared reading allows students to read in a very nonthreatening, relaxed atmosphere. Students who don't recognize a word in the text will hear that word several times from their peers during the repeated readings and can begin to read the word aloud with classmates as the word is learned. Classmates' shared insights and comments during the follow-up word study portion of shared reading lessons are also very helpful.

Implementing Shared Reading

I think of shared reading as a two-step process: (a) *introducing* and learning the text through multiple oral readings and (2) studying important print characteristics through *follow-up* activities with the text. I introduce the text to my students by going on a picture walk through the illustrations, reading the text aloud to my students, reading the text aloud in unison with my students, and inviting my students to read the text aloud to me.

Picture Walk

The goal of the picture walk is to build my students' background knowledge and vocabulary and to thoroughly acquaint them with the text. I begin by pointing to the cover of the book and asking, "What do you see in this illustration?" I encourage discussion and comments as the students point to and name various objects in the illustration. I may follow up with questions like "What's another name for this?" "What is it used for?" "What is this person doing?" "What is he or she thinking?" "What else do you see?" "What do you think this story will be about?" I love doing picture walks. It's an enjoyable way to generate a lively discussion, and the students don't even realize that they're getting a vocabulary lesson.

After discussing the cover illustration, I have two options: (1) continue discussing all the illustrations and then return to introduce the text or (2) introduce the illustrations and text together, page by page. This choice depends largely on the students' reading level and ability to learn to read the text.

Teacher Reads the Text to the Students

After my students and I have discussed the illustrations, I point to the text and say, "Let's see what it says." I run my finger beneath the words as I pronounce them. This first time through the text I read aloud to the students. However, it is common for many students to join in spontaneously as I read. During this initial reading, I may involve students more heavily in the reading by asking them to make predictions or ask questions.

Teacher and Students Read the Text Aloud Together

When I feel that my students are very familiar with the text's content and vocabulary, I move to the next step, inviting the students to read aloud with me in unison. This is generally referred to as *choral reading*. The purpose of this step is to have the students imitate and adopt the fluent oral reading model I provide. This step is critical because it is where the students learn to read the book with phrasing and expression, as opposed to a labored word-by-word manner.

I point to the words as I read aloud, making sure that all my students are reading along with me. I have often stopped students in mid-sentence and said, "We're not all reading together. Let's start this sentence again. Follow my finger and let's stay together. Ready? One. Two. Three. . . . " More challenging pages may be read several times before going ahead. I sometimes involve the students further in the reading process by omitting selected words and allowing my students to say them.

This second step is also a good time for my students and me to explore together spelling patterns and decoding concepts. For example, I may point to an unfamiliar word and provide a spontaneous lesson on how that word might be decoded. Such lessons should focus on students' combined use of context, syntax, and graphophonic (letter–sound and structural analysis) clues. Richek, Caldwell, Jennings, and Lerner (2002) suggest four statements to guide students to use context, structural analysis, and phonics clues to decode an unfamiliar word:

1. If you don't know a word in your reading, first reread the sentence and try to figure it out (context clues).
2. If that doesn't work, sound out the first part and reread the sentence (phonics clues).
3. If you still don't know it, look for word endings and try to figure out the base word (structural analysis clues).

4. If you still haven't figured it out, sound out the whole word. Remember you may have to change a few sounds to make the word make sense (phonics clues).

During choral reading I sometimes use a **masking activity** to draw students' attention to word features. A mask is a piece of cardboard (a 5 by 7 index card works well) with a horizontal rectangular slot or window cut out of the middle. The height of the window is a little taller than the print. Attaching a movable slide to the back of the mask allows the length of the window to be adjusted. I use the mask to isolate specific words or parts of words for decoding lessons. For example, to study the word *anything,* I build the word backward by leaving only the suffix *ing* showing. After my students have pronounced the suffix, I uncover the digraph *th* and lead the students to pronounce *thing*. Then I add the word part *any* and encourage the students to combine the context, syntax, and structural analysis clues to identify the entire word.

Students Read the Text

When my students and I have read the text together a sufficient number of times for them to become fluent with the words, I launch into the next step by saying, "I'd like to see how well you can read the story to me." The goal of this step is for my students to read the book confidently and fluently on their own. I don't read this time, but continue to point to the words to keep my students reading aloud together. If my students read the text easily and fluently, it is time to move to the follow-up activities. If more practice is needed, I may read the text together with them a few more times. Bear in mind that these multiple readings may take place over several days so that the reading doesn't become tedious.

Other Text Formats for Shared Reading

Overhead Transparencies

We often associate shared reading with big books, but shared reading works equally well with other text formats. I regularly do shared reading lessons with transparencies and an overhead projector. For example, I may find a *Frog and Toad* story I really want for a shared reading lesson and use the copy machine to make overhead transparencies of it. My students sit together on the floor in front of the screen as I lead them through the shared reading process.

There are a couple of benefits to doing shared reading with overhead transparencies. By projecting the text onto the chalkboard, I can underline spelling patterns or other print conventions I wish to highlight. Also, I love having one of my students serve as the pointer. This student sits beside the overhead projector and points to the text with a pencil as the class reads along. This frees me to focus on my class's or group's level of participation in the shared reading. Poems also work well as transparencies for shared reading.

We have also enjoyed turning the transparencies into readers' theater scripts. After the students have learned to read the transparency story quite well, I underline each character's dialogue with a different colored marking pen. Nondialogue sentences are left unmarked for a narrator group to read. I divide my class into enough groups so that each character's dialogue and the nondialogue parts can be assigned to a group. Then each group is instructed to read only the words underlined in their color (and noncolor for the narrator group). A pointer student is designated, I count one, two, three, and a readers' theater is underway.

Big Books

Big books were designed for whole-class shared reading lessons so that all students can see the enlarged print and participate. I have enjoyed using big books to start the shared reading process with early readers at the beginning of each school year. They are fun to read and attractively illustrated. However, I have found that many students quickly advance beyond big books, which has left me searching for something more substantial for our shared reading lessons.

Leveled Readers

Leveled readers are very popular for shared reading and guided reading lessons. These small paperback books begin with just a few words per page and then very gradually increase in length and complexity up through the grade levels. Traditional basal reading programs provide very few gradients of difficulty within a grade level. For example, in first grade, most basal programs provided only five levels of difficulty: preprimer 1, preprimer 2, preprimer 3, primer, and first-grade reader. In contrast, alphabetically leveled sets of readers provide nine levels of difficulty in levels A–I. In grade 2, most basal programs provide only two levels of difficulty, the 2^1 and the 2^2 readers, whereas sets of leveled readers provide 14 levels of difficulty in levels B–P. Fountas and Pinnell (1996, 1999) provide extensive lists of beginning reading books organized according to their alphabetic reading levels. The more finite gradations provided by leveled readers make it easier to select shared and guided reading texts that are more closely matched to students' reading levels. The two most widely recognized publishers of leveled readers are The Wright Group (*Wrightgroup.com*) and Rigby (*Rigby.com*). I suggest going online to their Web sites and requesting a catalog from each publisher to get lists of leveled reading titles.

Teacher-Made Shared Reading Charts

I have also created my own shared reading texts by writing stories on chart paper. For example, one morning I read aloud a picture book version of Hans Christian Andersen's *The Ugly Duckling* (1999). After reading and discussing the story, I announced that later that morning we would learn to read it. After our word study and independent reading, I displayed five pieces of chart paper on which I had written my own condensed version of *The Ugly Duckling* and pinned them to the wall. I then asked my standard question, "Whose turn is it to read first?" Having reminded them that I read first during a shared reading lesson, we were off learning to read *The Ugly Duckling,* usually about two sentences per day. I have made a number of approximately 200-word summaries of familiar fairy tales and some popular contemporary books. Constructing teacher-made charts for shared reading and other purposes has become much easier due to new large-format printers now available. Hewlett-Packard makes a very nice one.

Follow-up Teaching

Highlighting Spelling Patterns in Text

This may be the most important follow-up activity because it is where students make the critical connection between word identification activities and real reading. When my students have learned a shared reading story, I like to ask them, "Who can show us some word parts in the story?" and then invite them to identify examples of the spelling patterns we have been studying. Students raise their hands, and as I call on them they identify the page or sentence, which word, and then the pattern in the word. For example, Tania would raise her hand and say, "On page two, the word *pushed* has an *sh* digraph and an *ed* ending." Then either Tania or I would use a marking pen to underline the word parts on the chalkboard or chart paper or point to the word if we're reading from a big book. Leaving the marked-up chart papers in view provides a helpful resource. I've noticed many students studying the charts, reinforcing the combinations of spelling patterns in the words.

Being the Words

Cunningham (2000) popularized this activity. You make word cards from one sentence in the shared reading text. Then invite several of your students to come to the front of the class and give each student one of the word cards, in random order. Have them hold the word cards up so all can see them. Then invite the students to rearrange themselves so that they reconstruct the sentence.

Reproductions

Another favorite activity for reinforcing shared reading lessons is to create personal-sized versions of the text, often known as reproductions, for students to partner read, illustrate, and then take home to read with the family. These personal versions of the text provide opportunities for students to practice reading the text multiple times. I have found it effective to limit my students to illustrating two pages per day so that they don't hurry through the illustrating and do a sloppy job.

Reproductions are an important part of my shared reading lessons. After reading a story together in a shared reading group, I distribute the personal copies of the story to my students. I tell them which pages they may illustrate that day and then have them practice reading the personal copy of the story independently and then to me or a classmate for more practice. Sometimes I reproduce the text in booklet format, with individual pages to illustrate. Other times I reproduce the entire text on a single page.

Concepts of Print

The enlarged print format of big books provides great opportunities for teaching and reinforcing beginning readers' familiarity with concepts of print. For example, after reading a page in a big book, I often ask a student to point to the cover, the back, and the title page. I'll ask, "Can you point to a letter?" "Can you point to a word?" "Can you show me a sentence?" I may choose to focus on punctuation by asking my students to point to a period, comma, question mark, or exclamation point. I also ask students to point out upper- and lowercase letters.

Print-Matching Activities

These activities help beginning readers focus on printed letters as they match word cards to printed text. A common activity is to make a deck of word cards that correspond to one or more pages of the shared reading text. During a shared reading lesson, I distribute a few of the word cards to my students and ask them to bring the cards to the big book one at a time and hold them next to the same word printed on the big book page. I also give my students the entire deck of word cards and ask them to use the cards to reconstruct the text. A pocket chart is handy for this purpose. For

Figure 7.2   A Shared Reading Sample Lesson Plan

JUST THIS ONCE
by Joy Cowley

Story Overview

Much to her parents' consternation, Liz wants to bring her pet hippopotamus everywhere they go.

PURPOSE

This lesson is designed for a small or large group of beginning readers. It will focus on:

(a) Building students' *oral reading fluency*.

(b) Introducing students to *quotation marks*.

1. BEFORE READING

(a) *Motivation*. Lead the students in a brief discussion of what they like to do with their pets.

(b) *Background knowledge and vocabulary*. Lead the students in a brief *picture walk* through the cover and subsequent illustrations. Build students' vocabulary and background knowledge by pointing to and discussing objects in the illustrations. For example, on the cover, discuss the girl and the bows in her hair and the hippo, leash, and travel posters. On the first page, discuss the conductor, his whistle, the suitcase and identification tag, and the woman passenger.

2. DURING READING

(a) Begin by asking the students, "Whose turn is it to read first?" Then read the book aloud *to the students*, sweeping your hand beneath the words as you read.

(b) Invite the students to read the book aloud *together with you*. Model expressive reading of the dialogue. Occasionally leave out some words for the students to pronounce without you. Listen for words the students have difficulty pronouncing. Stop as appropriate and provide some brief, spontaneous decoding lessons for these difficult words.

(c) When the students are ready, invite them to read the book *to you* as you continue to sweep your hand beneath the words. Add variety by inviting individual students, pairs, or small groups of students to read a page ("show-off" reading) to you and the whole group.

3. AFTER READING

(a) *Quotation marks*. Return to page 1, point to the quotation marks in the sentence, "No Liz," said Dad, "You can't take the hippopotamus on vacation." Ask the students if they know what the marks are called and what their purpose is. Explain this concept. Read the book through again, this time as a readers' theater. Have the students read the dialogue parts with much expression, and you read the "narrator" parts outside the quotation marks.

---

a center activity, I have made two photocopies of a page from a shared reading text we have learned, laminated both copies, and cut the words from one copy into individual word cards; then the students matched the cut out words to the uncut page.

A shared reading sample lesson plan in shown in Figure 7.2.

GUIDED READING

Overview

Guided reading is most similar to the traditional reading group lessons many of us recall from our own elementary school days. Guided reading is very flexible and works well with leveled readers, with basal reading program stories and texts, and with children's literature selections. The before, during, and after flow of a guided reading lesson also applies very well to content area textbooks as you *prepare* the students before reading, *guide* them during reading, and *enrich* their learning after reading.

Guided reading is for students who need less instructional support than shared reading provides. In guided reading I provide a brief focused introduction to the text, but do not read the text to the students in advance. Guided reading is often thought of as the heart of a reading program, because this is when a teacher sits together with a small group of students and helps them as they read. Guided reading lessons are also an important opportunity for teaching students to apply reading comprehension strategies such as prediction, questioning, making images, seeking clarification, and constructing summaries (Block, Gambrell, & Pressley, 2002; Block & Pressley, 2002; Cunningham & Allington, 2003; Pressley, 2002). Fountas and Pinnell (1996) describe guided reading as a lesson in which:

> The teacher introduces a text to this small group, works briefly with individuals in the group as they read it, may select one or two teaching points to present to the group following the reading, and may ask the children to participate in an extension of their reading. (p. 2)

Procedures

Selecting a Text

I select a book that group members can read with at least 90% accuracy and that will be interesting or entertaining. I may choose the book on the basis of its level of difficulty or because it contains a particular print concept my students need to learn.

Introducing the Text

An effective introduction to a story or information text is very important because it helps students get off to a running start. There are several components to an effective introduction that I try to cover as I briefly introduce a story or information text to a guided reading group. I selectively pick and choose from the introduction components discussed next based on the characteristics of the particular text and the levels of instructional support my students will need to read successfully.

Build background knowledge and vocabulary. I begin each introduction by building or activating my students' background knowledge and vocabulary associated with the topic of the story or text. There are several ways I can do this. Often I use the cover illustration and subsequent illustrations to generate a group discussion of the topic. Sometimes I bring an object related to the text and use it to stimulate a discussion of the topic. Often I write the theme or topic of the text on my writing board and do a **webbing** or **mapping** activity to generate a group discussion. This component is also an important time to provide motivation for the students to read the passage if necessary.

Point out features of the text structure. I generally let my students peruse the text during the introduction and help them to decide if it is a story or an information text. If it is a story, I tell them to pay attention to the story elements: setting, characters, events, and ending. If it is an information text, I tell them to pay attention to information text elements: main ideas and details. If an information text contains sections or subheadings, I point these out so that my students can better mentally organize the information as they read. Sometimes I write the applicable text structure elements for the text we're reading on my writing board or a piece of chart paper and then fill them in as an after-reading follow-up activity.

Provide a brief word study lesson.   If I notice that the text contains words and reoccurring spelling patterns that may be confusing to my students, I do a very brief minilesson to prepare them to navigate these words successfully. For example, if I notice that the potentially confusing spelling pattern *ight* occurs a number of times in the text, then I write *ight* on my writing board and lead my students in studying some familiar "*ight* family" words: *fight, flight, fright, light, might, night, right, sight, slight, tight*. Then I invite them to look through the pages of the text we're about to read to find and point out the *ight* words that we'll be reading.

Set a purpose for reading.   There are two ways that I set a purpose for my students' reading. Often I simply say, "Let's read this to find out . . . " and provide my students with an important *where, why, how,* or *when* topic to focus on as they read. My favorite way for setting a purpose for reading, however, is to have my students examine the title and cover illustration and then predict the content of the story or information text. Usually I model how to make a prediction by making one myself and then invite the students to make their own predictions. Predicting involves students' using available information about the text to formulate a knowledgeable prediction, and then they read to see how accurate their prediction was. Predicting is the first step of the **reciprocal teaching** comprehension strategies instruction method discussed in chapter 4. The other reciprocal teaching steps of clarifying, questioning, and summarizing take place during the next step of the guided reading lesson as students read the text (Oczkus, 2003).

Reading the Text

There are several options for teachers during this portion of a guided reading lesson. Sometimes I like to read the first page to my students to provide a fluent role model and get the reading off to a good start. Sometimes I instruct all group members to read a page or two silently and then stop and discuss what they've read. Other times I invite individual students to read a paragraph or two aloud while others follow along silently so that I can hear my students' oral reading. I like to combine these three modes of reading to inject variety into our reading group lessons. You can also use different instructional approaches depending on the length of the text.

Guided reading with shorter selections.   Fountas and Pinnell (1996) have popularized an approach to guided reading for use with shorter leveled reading texts. When using the Fountas and Pinnell approach, I provide the introduction to the text and then ask my students in the guided reading group to read it softly aloud to themselves at an individually comfortable rate. As my students do this, I listen in on each student for a few minutes, noticing any reading problems and providing help when needed. As some students finish reading before others, I invite them to return to their desks and continue reading a self-selected book independently, partner read with a classmate, participate in a learning center activity, work on some personal writing, or do some other genuine reading or writing activity. Sometimes I may invite those members who finish early to begin rereading the text for practice so that they will still be with the group for some follow-up instruction or discussion.

A strength of this approach, as opposed to the traditional practice of having students read the story one at a time aloud, round-robin fashion, is that no student's instructional time is wasted waiting for other students. Each student reads through the entire story at his or her own pace. Each student's time is productively spent reading a text at the appropriate level, while I observe their reading, listen in, and provide support as needed. As my students puzzle over a word or ask for help, I may provide both contextual or print cues as appropriate to build each student's independence in using reading strategies. This guided reading time is also an excellent opportunity for me to take a running record on one or two students in the guided reading group to monitor their reading level and use of reading strategies. Running records will be described in detail in chapter 10.

Teaching reading comprehension skills with longer texts.   Longer stories and information texts provide excellent opportunities to teach students how to apply reading comprehension strategies. The first thing I do is to look through the selection and identify two or three stopping points where we can have a brief discussion. In stories, stopping points often occur naturally after the author has described the setting and after each major event. Information texts often provide natural stopping points in the form of subheadings. In this approach, I remind students to (1) check the predictions we made, (2) look for words or phrases they don't understand, and (3) think of questions they might want to ask about the story's characters and events or the information text's content. I invite them to read to my predetermined stopping point and either begin reading aloud myself, inviting all group members to read to the stopping point silently to themselves, or we take turns reading paragraphs or pages aloud.

At the first stopping point, we comment on the accuracy of our predictions. Sometimes, I ask my students to go back, find, and read aloud a sentence that supports the prediction. Next I ask if any group members came across confusing words or phrases that we should clarify. Again, I often model this step by saying, "I found a word in that section that I think we should clarify." I then tell my students the word, ask if any of them know what it means, and provide an explanation of my own as well. Then I ask if any group members have questions about the content of the section that we just read. I model this strategy too by asking a question of my own, discussing it with the group, and then inviting group members to ask their own questions. Finally, I ask a group member to summarize the section we just finished reading. Sometimes I ask another group member to add information to the first student's summary. After we've had a complete summary of the section's content, I may choose to ask for another round of predictions for the next section.

At each subsequent stopping point, we repeat the same basic process of (1) checking predictions, (2) clarifying confusing words or phrases, (3) asking questions, (4) summarizing the section, and (5) making new predictions. It's important to remember that the purpose for these activities is to systematically and explicitly teach students to apply reading comprehension skills. When you and your students become proficient at this, you'll notice a marked difference in their level of involvement with the texts. They won't be reading just to pronounce words. They'll be actively mentally involved with the content of the text. Guided reading group discussions will become much more lively. Students will notice when their reading doesn't make sense and will reread to fix the problem or seek clarification from you and classmates.

After Reading the Text

I like to do several things after my guided reading students have finished reading a text. I select from the activities discussed next based on the level of my students' understanding of the text, word identification or comprehension problems that may have arisen, my students' continued level of engagement with the text, and the time available.

Summarize the text.   The first is to summarize the entire text in just a few sentences so that all group members have a shared understanding of the content of what we've just read. This is not a long, detailed retelling of the text, but rather a brief wrapping up.

Discuss the text's theme or content.   I also like to focus on the theme of the text if it is a story or the content of the text if it is an information text. For example, a story may have a theme such as making friends in a new town or sticking up for someone who's being picked on. First, I ask my students if they can think of a theme or lesson that we can learn from the story. We discuss the theme and how the characters handled the situation. Then, as appropriate, I may ask group members to share personal experiences based on the theme.

If we've just completed reading an information text, I ask my students to help me to list the main ideas we learned and discuss some of the supporting details. If time permits, this is a good time for a mapping or webbing activity to generate a good follow-up discussion and visually cement the information in your students' minds.

Follow-up word study lessons.   After my students have finished reading the text, I often bring them together for a follow-up lesson focused on a spelling pattern. For example, I select a word from the text that contains a spelling pattern that my students need to practice, such as *make*. I give each student an individual white board and ask them to write *make*. Then I ask them to write other words on their white boards that follow the same pattern such as *bake, cake, lake, rake, take, wake, brake, flake,* and *shake*. Such lessons are like the word study lessons I sometimes teach before reading a text. The only difference is that these follow-up word study lessons are based on problems that occurred during reading.

Extension activities.   Occasionally I may choose to involve my students in an extension activity designed to get them back into the text to deepen their understanding of it. Over the years I've come to categorize extension activities as art, drama, writing, making, and research. These will be described in detail in the next section of this chapter. It is important to remember that extension activities must be used selectively. Every minute spent drawing or performing is a minute not spent reading. You must decide if the instructional benefits of the extension activity outweigh the benefits of reading.

Browsing boxes.   Finally, I put the texts we've just completed in one of our classroom browsing boxes for students to select and reread during independent reading time over the next few weeks. Browsing boxes filled with books that my students can read easily greatly facilitate my students' being able to quickly select books for independent reading.

Basal Reading Programs

Many teachers use basal reading program materials to teach their guided reading lessons. Descended from the old Dick and Jane readers, basal reading programs are intended to provide a complete classroom reading program. They tend to follow popular trends in reading instruction. In recent years, basal reading programs emphasized literature-based reading instruction and then balanced reading instruction. These programs currently emphasize research-based reading instruction and feature the essential elements of instruction identified in the Report of the National Reading Panel (2000).

Basal reading programs published by prominent publishing companies, including Harcourt, Holt, Merrill, Open Court, and Scott-Foresman, are built on a "scope and sequence," the list of the program's reading skills and the sequence in which they are introduced and taught. All basal reading programs feature the same essential spelling patterns and **comprehension strategies,** but their organization and sequence will vary from company to company. Basal reading programs consist of student reading books, workbooks and reproducible worksheets, and a teacher's manual that contains lesson plans for all the reading selections in the student reading books.

Basal reading programs offer a number of advantages. Basal programs, currently referred to as core reading programs, provide instructional consistency from classroom to classroom and grade to grade. New teachers who don't yet have extensive instructional experience can rely on a basal or core reading program for a road map of skills to teach and the activities to teach them. When a school district adopts a basal reading program, the publisher will send trainers to make sure that teachers understand the program's organization and procedures. One concern with basal reading programs is that some teachers focus too much on teaching the program and not enough on teaching the students. Teachers should realize that a well-designed basal reading program can be a valuable instructional resource, but that the responsibility for determining students' instructional needs and selecting and implementing techniques to meet these needs will always rest with teachers.

Guided reading lessons may be taught with basal reading program selections, leveled reading texts, children's literature, or any other text that provides appropriate-level opportunities for students to enhance their reading skills. A sample lesson plan is given in Figure 7.3.

LITERATURE CIRCLES

Overview

Over the years, my wife and I have belonged to a number of neighborhood book clubs. Each month the five or six couples select a new book of common interest and obtain a copy. During the month we each read the book; then on a selected Friday evening we all assemble at a couple's home. We sit around the fireplace, munch on snacks, talk about our kids and the news, and finally, when everybody was ready, the host couple ask, "Well, what did everybody think of the book?"

The next 40 to 50 minutes are generally spent in a very stimulating discussion of peoples' responses to the book, personal connections to the book, questions about the book, and favorite parts of the book. One person's comment sparks connections for other people, and the discussion weaves spontaneously in and out of the book as

Figure 7.3 A Guided Reading Sample Lesson Plan

THE GREAT BLUENESS AND OTHER PREDICAMENTS
by Arnold Lobel

Story Overview

In an all-gray world, a wizard invents three colors that eventually mix to become many more colors.

PURPOSE

This second-grade level story also complements a study of the primary colors.

1. BEFORE READING

(a) *Motivation.* Display a number of Arnold Lobel's well-known children's books, such as *Frog and Toad* and *Fables.* Tell your students how much you enjoy his books because of the connections to everyday situations we all face.

(b) *Background knowledge and vocabulary mapping activity.* Write the word *wizard* on the writing board and ask students to tell you all they know about wizards. Add their information to the writing board and discuss the items as you write them. You might want to stimulate their thinking by asking lead-in questions, such as "What do wizards look like?" "What do wizards do?" "Where do wizards live?" "Who are some famous wizards we already know about?"

(c) *Word study lesson (consonant blends).* List the following consonant blends and words on your writing board.

bl	gr	st
black	gross	stop
blind	grandma	start
blend	great	best

Read the words to your students and explain how you can hear both consonant sounds in a blend. You or a student should underline or circle the blends as you do so. Then see if your students can generate additional words that begin with these three consonant blends. Finally, have your students skim through the pages of the story and locate additional words that begin or end with any consonant blends. Add these to the list on your writing board. Some students may confuse consonant blends with consonant digraphs (*ch, sh, th, wh*). In such cases, I write the digraph words in a separate column and explain that these consonants do not make their own sound, but an altogether different sound.

(d) *Set a purpose for reading.* Read the title to your students and explain that the word *predicament* is a synonym for *problem.* Read the first two paragraphs about the all-gray world and the wizard; then make a model prediction of what the story might be about. Invite your students to make a few predictions of their own. Record these on your writing board.

2. DURING READING

(a) Invite students to read (silently or aloud in turns) through the section about the Great Blueness. Tell them to stop after the sentence that reads "But the Great Blueness wasn't so great." Remind them to look for words and phrases they don't understand, and remember questions they might have. After they have finished reading this first section, help them to review their predictions for accuracy. Clarify concepts such as an all gray world (like an old black-and-white TV show) and words like *potions* and *spells.* Invite your students to share any questions they might have. Finally, review the concluding sentence "But the Great Blueness wasn't so great," and ask students to predict what problems might arise from an all blue world.

(b) Repeat this process with the two story sections describing the Great Yellowness and the Great Redness.

(c) Read the final section where the three colors spill on the floor and mix to make many more colors, to the end of the story. Review any final predictions, clarify any confusing words and phrases, discuss any questions students might have, and summarize how the story ended.

3. AFTER READING

(a) *Summarize the entire story.* Write the four words *setting, characters, events,* and *theme* on your writing board in the configuration shown next and have your students help you to fill in the details.

Setting	Characters
back in the "castle days"	the wizard
in a small town	the neighbors

Figure 7.3   Continued

> **Events**
> the world was all gray
> the wizard made blue . . . sadness
> the wizard made yellow . . . headaches
> the wizard made red . . . angry
> the colors mixed . . . a beautiful world
>
> (b) *Discuss the theme (variety).* Ask the questions "What would it be like if we only had one kind of food to eat, one kind of clothes to wear, one TV show to watch, one song to listen to on the radio, or only one friend to play with? Discuss how variety enriches our lives in many ways.
>
> (c) *Curriculum integration.* Join with other classmates to participate in the follow-up demonstration of mixing primary colors as described in the language experience lesson plan.

we explores multiple layers of meaning. For me, the best part of these discussions was hearing people comment on aspects of the book that had totally eluded me. My own understanding of the book was invariably deepened as I listened to and participated in the discussion.

Many teachers, generally in grades 2 and above, have capitalized on the motivational and educational benefits of such book clubs and adapted them for classrooms (Daniels, 2002; Peterson and Eeds, 1990; Samway, 1991). Some teachers refer to these groups as literature circles, literature study groups, or book clubs. I will use the term *literature circles* here.

The purpose of literature circles is to move students beyond simply being able to read. Literature circles help students to consider themselves to be readers, part of the literate community. Calkins (2001) describes how children's discussions of literature help them to see the purposes and rewards of being a reader:

> they help our children know that readers have reasons to read. We read to laugh out loud, to get advice, to feel less alone, to learn about new places, to walk in the shoes of people who are different from ourselves, to be reminded of other lives, to take pleasure in something lovely, and yes, to get the tears out. How good it is for children to learn, right from the start, that literacy and life go together. (p. 330)

Literature circles are different from reading groups in a couple of ways. In reading groups, students read the story during the group meeting. A literature circle is a time when students get together to discuss a book or a section of a book that they have already finished reading. Literature circles are also different from reading groups in that they are very student centered. In traditional reading groups the teacher runs the show. He or she selects the story, guides the pace of the reading, asks the predetermined comprehension questions, and selects the follow-up lessons and activities. In literature circles, the students choose the books and set the pace of their reading. The spontaneous student-to-student literature circle discussions center on the students' responses, connections, questions, and favorite parts. Finally, literature circle members select the follow-up enrichment activities.

Literature circles are the icing on the reading instruction cake. They are a time for students to enjoy the genuine benefits of all that word identification and comprehension strategy instruction and practice. Literature circles are a time for readers to do what real readers do. The following sections describe the basic steps of organizing literature circles.

Procedures

Selecting Books for Literature Circles

To have literature circles in your classroom, you need sets of books. Some will be picture books. Others will be easy chapter books. My single most important criteria for choosing literature circle books is theme. I look for books that students can relate to and make connections with. The books have to be substantial enough in content to support a discussion. *Mrs. Wishy Washy* (Cowley, 1980) is a cute book, but as one astute student pointed out, "There's just not very much to talk about."

I usually purchase books for literature circles in sets of 10. My personal experience suggests that the ideal size of a literature circle is about five to seven students. Literature circles with fewer than five students can lack some of the energy and synergism needed for a vibrant discussion. With more than seven, the circle may be too large. It may be hard for some students to hear other students in the circle, especially with the ever-present background noise of a classroom. A large group provides fewer opportunities for students to participate. I purchase 10 copies of each title because invariably a few will become lost or destroyed. It's a small price to pay for creating genuine readers.

Introducing the Books

I begin my literature circles by first giving a book talk, a commercial, to the class about each book. I usually introduce five titles at a time. This allows for groups of five to six. I read the title and show the cover. I tell briefly about the setting and characters and maybe the problem the characters are facing. I often read one or two paragraphs aloud so that my students can get a feel for each author's writing style. I show them a few pages, because some students select books in part on how daunting the print appears to be.

Allowing Students to Choose

A major element of literature circles is choice. Choosing which book to read builds student ownership of the process. Because students get to choose the books, they are more committed to the process.

After I've done a book talk on each book, I invite students to choose which book they want to read. I've done this a number of ways. Sometimes I write the five titles across the top of the chalkboard and ask for a show of hands for each title. I then write students' names below the title they want. Sometimes I simply pick up five or six copies of a title, ask students to raise their hands if they want that title, and hand those students a copy of the book. I've also had students write their first and second choices on a slip of paper, but this can be cumbersome for some primary-grade students.

The Initial Literature Circle Group Meeting

Once the membership of each group is established, I call the groups one by one to meet with me in a corner of the classroom. I do three things with each group during this initial meeting. First, I give each student a copy of the book. With younger students, I put the book in a zipper-type freezer bag for protection because the book will be going home with the student after school. With younger students I include a note to Mom and Dad explaining that their child's reading group will be discussing the book on a certain day and ask the parents to read the book with their child at home. My note also asks the parents to discuss their own responses and connections with their child as they read and to help with any writing or illustrating assoicated with the response assignment. Finally, the note reminds the parents to send the book back to school on the appointed day.

While many students have supportive parents who will follow through, helping their child to read and discuss the book, too many students do not. You must be able to anticipate which students will need extra support in the classroom for their literature circle discussions. I have provided this by reading the book in advance as a teacher read-aloud so that the student is familiar with it prior to the discussion. Teacher aides and classroom volunteers can also help here.

My second task is to help the students set a reading schedule. I ask them, "How long will it take us to read this book and get ready for the discussion?" Younger students will often ask for two or three days to read a simple picture book. With older students reading easy chapter books, I may suggest reading three chapters at a time and having several discussions. Setting their own reading schedule is another student-centered aspect of literature circles. Once we have all agreed on a day to have the discussion, I move to the third task, giving the students a response assignment.

A response assignment is a means for students to record their thoughts and feelings about the book. Students bring the response assignment to the discussion and refer to it as a reminder of what they have to say. The most common response assignment, and perhaps the most appropriate for younger readers, is to give each of them three or four Post-it notes and ask them to attach the notes to their favorite pages. I also instruct my students to write on the Post-its why they chose each page. Another response assignment appropriate for younger readers is called sketch to stretch (Harste & Burke, 1996). I simply ask my students to "draw a picture of what the book makes you think about." I don't want pictures of the book's events and characters, but rather pictures of the connections the students make. Another of my favorite response assignments is to give each student a page divided into four quadrants labeled responses, connections, questions, and favorite parts. As the student reads the book or after the reading, the student fills in each quadrant on the paper. Daniels (2002) suggests assigning students specific literature circle roles, such as leading the discussion, making connections, generating questions, looking for interesting vocabulary words, and sketching an aspect of the story, until students become comfortable with all the roles and can maintain a literature circle discussion spontaneously.

Reading the Book

With a copy of the book in hand, a reading schedule, and a response assignment, the students are ready to begin reading. My students usually read their literature circle book during independent reading time in class, at home with the family, or in both settings. As mentioned earlier, some students will need extra support to read the book successfully. In addition to doing the book as a teacher read-aloud or using classroom aides and volunteers, I've also tape-recorded literature circle books and put them in the classroom listening center. Parent volunteers and local celebrities, such as the school principal, make wonderful readers for listening center books on tape. Make sure your volunteer readers know to read slowly enough so that the students can follow along and also to ring a bell or provide some other signal for page turns.

The Literature Circle Discussion

My favorite way to begin a literature circle discussion is to call the group together and simply say, "Well, what do you think about the book?" I then sit back and let the students talk to each other about the book. I do not dominate the discussion or over-structure it by asking for all students' responses, then connections, questions, and favorite parts. I let the discussion evolve naturally and genuinely from the students' interests and comments.

I encourage my students to talk freely about the book at first and to save their response assignment comments for later. My goal here is to encourage student-to-student discussion. This is quite different from the teacher-ask, student-answer inter-rogations that most students are used to. Students must be taught how to respond to literature before they can be expected to carry on and sustain a stimulating literature circle discussion.

Teacher's role.   As teacher, I am an equal member of the literature circle. I tend to save my comments for those moments when the discussion wanes a bit. I have found it very helpful at those moments to read aloud one of my favorite paragraphs from the book and then share with the students why I value that paragraph or what connec-tions it holds for me. This provides a good opportunity for me to model referring back to the text to make appropriate thoughtful comments, a behavior I very much en-courage. I also encourage referring back to the text by occasionally asking a student to find and read to us the passage that stimulated a comment.

I also try to help the students to learn to get beyond just sharing their own feel-ings and, instead, to listen carefully to their classmates and together enjoying a mean-ingful dialogue. My colleague Debbie Hobbs and I have found over the years that students are generally very excited to share their own thoughts in a literature circle, and often this has to happen first before they can relax and start listening to others. Calkins (2001, p. 242) suggests a few helpful phrases to encourage students to "pig-gyback" on each others' comments:

> ❀ *I'd like to add on to what David said . . .*
> ❀ *I have an example of what David just said . . .*
> ❀ *Another thing that goes with David's comment is . . .*
> ❀ *I liked David's comment because . . .*

After initial comments have been shared, I often invite students to refer to their response assignments and share what they brought to the literature circle. I ask them to show the pages they have tabbed with their Post-it notes and explain why they chose those pages. Other students will show their sketch-to-stretch illustrations and explain the connections they represented in their drawings.

One other thing I do during literature circle discussions is to take very brief notes on the topics that bubble up to the surface. For example, during a literature cir-cle discussion of the touching book *Fly Away Home* by Eve Bunting, my students were curious about the fact that the young homeless boy wasn't going to school. From my notes I was able to hint at the connection between unemployment and education and help my students to discover additional layers to the story.

I've found over the years that most literature circle discussions last about 20 minutes, regardless of grade level. As it becomes apparent that the book has become talked out, I use my notes to briefly summarize the discussion and to occasionally guide my students in developing an appropriate postreading enrichment activity,

Figure 7.4   A Literature Circle Sample Lesson Plan

THE JOSEFINA STORY QUILT
by Eleanor Coerr

Story Overview
Faith's father reluctantly allows her to bring her pet chicken Josefina on their covered wagon journey to the West. Josefina and the family experience adventures and close calls.

PURPOSE
To heighten students' awareness of the personal challenges, sacrifices, and joys experienced by pioneers in the 19th-century American West (part of the class social studies unit).

1.   BEFORE READING

(a)   Meet together with the students in this literature circle group. Preview the book with students, pointing out a few important elements of the story's setting, major characters, and events.

(b)   Discuss with the students in the literature circle how long it might take them to read the book, and establish an agreed upon date when all students will have finished the book.

(c)   Give each student four Post-it notes and instruct them to attach each note to a favorite page or where the student has a question about the story. Also, instruct the students to write on the notes the reason why they chose each page or the question they have about each page.

(d)   Give each student in the literature circle a copy of the book and tell them to begin reading it during independent reading time, at home, or both.

2.   DURING THE LITERATURE CIRCLE

(a)   Begin the literature circle discussion by asking the question, "Well, what did you think of *The Josefina Story Quilt*?"

(b)   Encourage students to comment on each others' responses and connections, answer each others' questions, share favorite parts, and generally develop a genuine student-to-student discussion of the book.

(c)   Take brief notes on the topics that seemed of most interest to the students. Use these notes to summarize the discussion and to suggest follow-up enrichment projects as appropriate.

3.   AFTER THE LITERATURE CIRCLE

(a)   *Drawing.* Invite students to draw a side-view outline of a covered wagon and draw all the things they would want to take with them packed into the wagon. Share these in a subsequent group meeting.

(b)   *Writing.* Invite students to write about a family trip they remember. It might be a local outing or a trip to a faraway location. Have students illustrate these written accounts. Read them aloud and show the illustrations to the class. Display them in the classroom.

(c)   *Drama.* Produce a brief readers' theater based on the book. Assign students to parts and have them read and reread their parts until they are ready to put the parts together and perform the theater for their classmates.

(d)   *Research.* Create an Immigration Bulletin Board. Have students ask their parents (perhaps with a simple printed survey) how their family came to live in the town where your school is located. Where did their parents or other ancestors travel from? How long ago did they make the trip? For what reasons did they make the trip? What interesting experiences did they have associated with the trip? Use a world or U.S. map and some yarn to show where each students' family came from. Point out that much of history is about people moving from one place to another and the challenges they faced.

one that will take them back into the book. A sample literature circle lesson plan is shown in Figure 7.4.

Follow-up Enrichment Activities

People learn better by doing. This axiom holds true with literature as well. For some books and literature circles, student learning can be extended by having students go back into the book, dig deeper into the text, and then represent their learning through a group enrichment project or a series of individual enrichment projects. The enrichment projects I've done over the years tend to fall into the categories of art, drama, writing, making, and research. Art projects might include drawing pictures of the book's setting, characters, and events. Some teachers help their students to create artworks in the same medium as the book's illustrator, such as charcoal drawings or tissue paper illustrations like Eric Carle's. Students can cut photographs from magazines to create a collage that represents a book's theme.

Drama seems to be a perennial favorite follow-up enrichment activity. Hot Seat is an activity in which selected students assume the persona of characters from the book and answer questions from others in the group. I've made several readers theaters from picture books rich in dialogue and used them to turn books into group performances. More advanced students can write their own scripts for plays based on the books they read.

Writing follow-up activities can include having students keep personal response journals, write letters to or from book characters, or write original poetry or song lyrics about books. Chapter 9 provides detailed information about students reading information books together and then writing about what they learned. Making activities include making and collecting artifacts and displays related to the books. For example, second-grade teacher Laura Stewart, after reading the book *Dakota Dugout* by Ann Turner, helped her students to make a miniature sod house and also to convert their desks into covered wagons, along with pioneer songs and meals. Research activities include supplying students with information books on related topics or having them develop questions about the topic and finding answers through interviews or other resources.

WORD STUDY GROUP LESSONS

Overview

These 10-minute lessons are an opportunity to pull together small groups of students who need reteaching or extra practice on a particular reading skill or strategy. These small-group lessons also provide an opportunity to provide oral reading fluency instruction and practice for those students who need it. These groups are temporary in nature and may only meet one time or a few times as needed.

FOR STRUGGLING READERS

Word Study Group Lessons

Word study group lessons are particularly appropriate for struggling readers. These lessons give you an opportunity to provide additional focused instruction to students who need it. The word study group lessons may be a review of instruction provided earlier, or they may present the word study concepts in a different way that may help your struggling readers to better connect the new concepts to prior understandings.

Procedures

Based on record-keeping procedures described in chapter 10, identify one to five students who evidence a need for additional instruction or practice with a previously introduced word study concept. During Reading Workshop time, when all other students are reading independently, reading in pairs, working at learning cen-

Figure 7.5 A Word Study Group Sample Lesson Plan

QUOTATION MARKS

1. INTRODUCING THE SKILL

(a) Write three or four sentences that contain quotation marks on your writing board.

"I would like some candy," said Marie.

Jermaine said, "I will get some candy for you."

"That's very nice of you," said Marie.

(b) Ask the students in the group if they notice what is the same about all these sentences.

(c) Bring your students' attention to the quotation marks.

(d) Explain the purpose of quotation marks. Ask questions such as "Who wants some candy?" "Who will get some candy for Marie?" "What did Marie say to Jermaine?" and have students point to the words in the sentences that answer the questions.

2. EXPLORING THE SKILL

(a) Ask a student in the group to compose an oral sentence that contains dialogue. Write this sentence on your writing board for the students to see, filling in the quotation marks. Ask the group to read the sentence with expression. Repeat this process with dictated dialogue sentences from other group members.

3. APPLYING THE SKILL

(a) Invite group members to look through a reading text that they will read soon in their reading group that contains dialogue. Have them find dialogue sentences. Have group members read these sentences aloud to the group, with expression.

---

ters, or doing personal writing, invite these students to meet with you at a table designated for small-group instruction.

When you and the students have assembled, simply follow the same lesson steps involved in the word study instruction that were introduced in chapter 5: (1) introduce the reading skill to the group members, (2) explore the skill with the group members, and (3) help group members to apply the skill.

A sample lesson plan for a word study group is shown in Figure 7.5.

Using Word Study Groups to Develop Oral Reading Fluency

Word study groups are designed for students who need additional time and instruction in order to recognize and process spelling patterns and word parts effectively. Some students will process spelling patterns accurately, but not quickly or expressively. These students will need additional oral reading fluency instruction. As you rotate students through LEA lessons, shared reading and guided reading groups, literature circles, and word study groups each day, you may also want to create oral reading fluency groups. Whereas students in word study groups focus on spelling patterns and word parts, students in oral reading fluency groups participate in repeated readings, radio reading, cross-age buddy reading, reader's theater, and other activities designed to help readers to develop oral reading fluency (Rasinski, 2003; Samuels, 1979).

 *CONCLUSIONS*

Effective sports coaches carefully observe their protégés during practices and competitions and strive to improve their performance by modeling correct procedures and giving corrective feedback, along with healthy doses of well-deserved encouragement. Effective reading teachers like Gloria do much the same. During reading group instruction, they listen to their students read and ask them questions to assess and improve reading comprehension. They help students to learn and apply word identification strategies as opportunities arise during meaningful reading. Nowhere else during reading instruction does a teacher have this focused opportunity to carefully observe and support students as they read meaningful texts.

Based on students' reading ability and instructional needs, teachers may provide varying levels of support through group activities, including language experience lessons, shared reading lessons, guided reading lessons, literature circle discussions, and word study group lessons. It is important to recognize that these activities are not mutually exclusive lesson formats. Experienced teachers can skillfully adjust the levels of instructional support for each reading group, based on the group members' various reading abilities and the difficulty of the text, to move almost seamlessly among these lesson formats. Reading with students in instructional groups provides opportunities to focus on word identification and comprehension skills and also builds students' positive attitudes toward reading by providing high success experiences with highly engaging texts.

 SUGGESTED ACTIVITIES TO EXTEND YOUR LEARNING

1. Have class education members share recollections and impressions of ability grouping from their own primary-grade years. What was it like to be assigned to the low group? Were there opportunities to move from group to group? Were there group-to-group differences in the quality of reading materials? Was that an effective way to manage reading instruction?

2. Find a beginning reader in your family or neighborhood and teach him or her a shared reading lesson. Gather a selection of picture books at the child's level and let the child choose one. Do a picture walk of the cover and inside illustrations. Read the story aloud to the child and then again aloud with the child in unison. Then ask the child to read the story aloud to you. Finish up with some follow-up teaching activities.

3. Meet with a small group of education classmates, select a story from a basal reading program, and develop a guided reading lesson plan for the story. Generate a list of *before reading* activities, including building background knowledge, introducing vocabulary, identifying and teaching a spelling pattern, and setting a purpose for reading. Prepare activities for the *during reading* portion of the lesson, including identifying stopping points for discussions, a list of questions to discuss, and words and concepts that might need clarification. Finally, develop some *after reading* activities, including summarizing the story content, following up on spelling pattern instruction, and extending student learning through writing, dramatizations, projects, research, and other curriculum integration activities.

REFERENCES

Adams, M. J. (1990). *Beginning to read: Thinking and learning about print.* Cambridge, MA: MIT Press.

Allington, R. L. (1980). Poor readers don't get to read much in reading groups. *Language Arts, 57,* 872–877.

Allington, R. L. (1983). The reading instruction provided readers of differing abilities. *Elementary School Journal, 83,* 548–559.

Block, C. C., Gambrell, L., & Pressley, M. (2002). *Improving comprehension instruction: Rethinking research, theory, and classroom practice.* San Francisco: Josey-Bass.

Block, C. C., & Pressley, M. (2002). *Comprehension instruction: Research-based best practices.* New York: Guilford Press.

Bunting, E. (1991). *Fly away home.* New York: Clarion.

Calkins, L. M. (2001). *The art of teaching reading.* New York: Longman.

Clay, M. M. (1993). *An observation survey of early literacy achievement.* Portsmouth, NH: Heinemann.

Clay, M. M. (2000). *Running records for classroom teachers.* Portsmouth, NH: Heinemann.

Cunningham, P. M. (2000). *Phonics they use: Words for reading and writing* (3rd ed.). New York: Longman.

Cunningham, P. M., & Allington, R. L. (2003). *Classrooms that work: They can all read and write.* Boston: Allyn and Bacon.

Daniels, H. (2002). *Literature circles: Voice and choice in book clubs & reading groups.* Portland, ME: Stenhouse.

Fountas, I. C., & Pinnell, G. S. (1996). *Guided reading: Good first teaching for all children.* Portsmouth, NH: Heinemann.

Fountas, I. C., & Pinnell, G. S. (1999). *Matching books to readers: Using leveled books in guided reading, K-3.* Portsmouth, NH: Heinemann.

Harste, J., & Burke, C. (1996). *Creating classrooms for authors and inquirers.* Portsmouth, NH: Heinemann.

Holdaway, D. (1979). *Foundations of literacy.* Sydney: Ashton-Scholastic.

Mooney, M. E. (1990). *Reading to, with, and by children.* Katonah, NY: Richard. C. Owen.

Nelson, O. G., & Linek, W. (1999). *Practical applications of language experience: Looking back, looking forward.* Boston: Allyn and Bacon.

Oczkus, L. D. (2003). *Reciprocal teaching at work: Strategies for improving reading comprehension.* Newark, DE: International Reading Association.

Pearson, P. D. (1983). Changing the face of reading comprehension instruction. *Reading Teacher, 38,* 724–738.

Peterson, R., & Eeds, M. (1990). *Grand conversations: Literature study groups in action.* New York: Scholastic.

Pressley, M. (2002). *Reading instruction that works: The case for balanced teaching.* New York: Guilford Press.

Rasinski, T. V. (2003). *The fluent reader: Oral reading strategies for building word recognition, fluency, and comprehension.* New York: Scholastic.

Richek, M. A., Caldwell, J. S., Jennings, J. H., & Lerner, J. W. (2002). *Reading problems: Assessment and teaching strategies* (4th ed.). Boston: Allyn and Bacon.

Samuels, S. J. (1979). The method of repeated readings. *Reading Teacher, 32,* 403–408.

Samway, K. (1991). Reading the skeleton, the heart, and the brain of a book: Students' perspectives on literature study circles. *Reading Teacher, 45* (3), 196–205.

Veatch, J. (1968). *How to teach reading with children's books.* New York: Richard C. Owen.

Children's Books

Andersen, H. (1999). *The ugly duckling.* New York: Morrow Junior.

Coerr, E. (1986). *The Josephina story quilt.* New York: HarperTrophy.

Cowley, J. (1980). *Mrs. Wishy Washy.* Auckland, NZ: Shortland.

Cowley, J. (1987). *Just this once.* San Diego, CA: The Wright Group.

Dr. Seuss (1960). *Green eggs and ham.* New York: Random House.

Lobel, A. (1979). *Frog and Toad are friends.* New York: HarperCollins.

Lobel, A. (1983). *Fables.* New York: HarperTrophy.

Lobel, A. (1987). *The great blueness and other predicaments.* New York: HarperCollins.

MacLachlan, S. (1987). *Sarah, plain and tall.* HarperTrophy.

Rylant, C. (1996). *Henry and Mudge: The first book.* New York: Alladin.

Turner, A. (1985). *Dakota dugout.* New York: Macmillan.

Writing Instruction

8

Sylvia Read

Luis's Story

Luis sat proudly in the author's chair ready to share his story about the talking dog. The class sat in a circle so that everyone could see him clearly. When Luis finished reading, several classmates raised their hands to make comments. "I heard that the dog was black with white spots." "I heard that when the boy figured out his dog was gone, he cried." Questions and comments followed. "What are you going to write next?" "Did the dog run away or did someone steal him?" "I like how you wrote 'big tears went down his face.' That sounds like Tomie de Paola." The next day during writing workshop, Luis finished his story and began to proofread it so that he could get it published. He read it out loud to himself and put in a few periods and some words he had left out accidentally. He circled five words he thought were probably spelled wrong and then asked a friend to help him spell those words. When I found it in the publishing basket next to the computer, I was able to type it for him after school so that he could begin illustrating it the next day. He spent two days drawing detailed pictures to go with his story. Then I put a comb binding on it and he took it home that night to share with his family. At parent conference time, Luis's mom and dad told me how much they enjoyed his story and how proud they were of him. Luis's smile told me that writing workshop is worth every minute it takes.

This chapter discusses the importance of writing instruction for children who are learning to read. Specifically, it addresses the reading–writing connection, the writing workshop, and writing in many genres.

 ## THE READING–WRITING CONNECTION

Many children write before they read. They play with writing using scribbles and perhaps random letters to represent "real" writing. Because they use symbolic representation, drawings are also an early form of writing. When asked to tell about a drawing, many children tell an elaborate story. Eventually, they begin to represent the beginning sounds of words. ILMM might be read, "I love my mom." They can read their own writing long before they read words written conventionally. Children tend to use temporary

Addresses IRA Standard 1.1

Demonstrate knowledge of psychological, sociological, and linguistic foundations of reading and writing processes and instruction.

Kristen wrote SSW:
Spiders spin webs.

Addresses IRA
Standard 1.3

Demonstrate
knowledge of
language
development and
reading acqui-
sition and the
variations related
to cultural and
linguistic
diversity.

spellings such as M for mom, MK for milk, or PICSHR for picture. While writing is important on its own, it is also a natural way to begin the process of learning to read (Harste, Woodward, & Burke, 1984).

When they write, children learn how print works, and what they write shows us something about what they've noticed and internalized about print. When they write, children must look and think carefully about the specific features of letters; write words, one letter at a time; place letters spatially on a page; think about how to place letters in a specific order; and pay attention to the smallest details of forming letters, while also keeping in mind the words and sentences they create (Clay, 1991).

The relationship between reading and writing has been well documented and analyzed in a number of important ways (Fitzgerald & Shanahan, 2000). When children are beginning to write, they are learning about "universal text attributes," one of which is graphophonics:

> Readers, to read words, must learn to deal with letters and phonemes and how they combine. Writers, likewise, must learn about letters and sounds if they are to spell accurately. (Fitzgerald & Shanahan, 2000, p. 40)

Later, as children become more adept at using graphophonics, they begin to use more and more conventional spellings and begin to memorize the spellings of phonetically irregular sight words such as *their* (Weaver, 1996). The National Research Council's

B. J. wrote SPMKWB:
Spiders make webs.

report, *Preventing Reading Difficulties in Young Children* (Snow, Burns, & Griffin, 1998), recommends the following about writing:

> Once children learn to write letters, they should be encouraged to write them, to use them to begin writing words or parts of words, and to use words to begin writing sentences. Instruction should be designed with the understanding that the use of invented spelling is not in conflict with teaching correct spelling. Beginning writing with invented spelling can be helpful for developing understanding of phoneme identity, phoneme segmentation, and sound–spelling relationships. Conventionally correct spelling should be developed through focused instruction and practice. Primary-grade children should be expected to spell previously studied words and spelling patterns correctly in their final writing products. Writing should take place on a daily basis to encourage children to become more comfortable and familiar with it. (pp. 323–324)

I have found that writing is the most personal and active way that my students strengthened their knowledge and use of phonics.

PHONICS, SPELLING, AND THE BEGINNING READER AND WRITER

Phonics knowledge is acquired through the process of becoming a reader and writer (Weaver, 1996). Young children often begin writing using scribbles to represent letters and words. If young children are writing every day, they can think deeply about sound–letter relationships as they use phonetic, transitional spellings to record their thoughts and stories. As they learn to read, they use the same understanding of letter–sound relationships to decode unknown words. Young children begin to spell sight words such as *was* or *they* as they have seen them repeatedly in the books they read. By writing, children learn how print works. Through reading their writing back to themselves, either as part of the writing process or during the sharing time of writing workshop, students learn to decode their own writing. They quickly learn that they can't read what they've written if they haven't left themselves enough phonetic or contextual clues to figure out a word. At the end of first grade, children sometimes look back at their writing from the beginning of the year and wonder what it says and why they ever wrote it that way!

As the number of words they can spell conventionally grows, they continue to need to use phonetic spellings for less frequently used, but important, words. If they felt comfortable using temporary spellings early in their writing history, they will feel comfortable using them later for difficult words like *exciting* or *Disneyland*. I want my students to know that, while spelling is important, it is more important to get your ideas down first and worry about the spelling of difficult words later. They learn to circle words they think are misspelled as they write and look them up later during the editing and proofreading phases of the writing process. They begin to gradually phase out their use of temporary spellings of frequently used words while they write and use phonetic spellings only for words they know they'll want to look up later. They learn to judge which kinds of words they should know how to spell and which can be represented phonetically. For example, Jordan asked me how to spell *could* during January of second grade. At this point in the year, she knew that *could* was a word she ought to know how to spell and I was willing to spell it for her and remind her quickly of other words with the same spelling pattern (*would*, *should*).

Research on invented spelling shows that, if students are reading and writing a lot and also thinking and learning about spelling patterns, they will advance through stages toward conventional spelling (Henderson, 1990). The words they write most frequently are the ones they need to learn correctly, because it is possible to get them embedded incorrectly (Cunningham, 1995). Children need to know that we expect them to spell phonetically irregular words such as *they* correctly after they have had some teaching and practice with these words.

Figure 8.1 describes the CASL program to help struggling spellers.

Dictation and the Language Experience Approach

Though children are perfectly capable of using phonetic spellings to write independently, taking dictation from children through the Language Experience Approach (Allen, 1999) is an efficient way to teach children about the conventions of language they might not yet be using. Taking dictation takes advantage of the relationships among thought, oral language, reading, and writing. Students quickly and easily see that what they think can be said, what they say can be written down, and what has been written can be read. This can be an inspiring discovery to a young child! Students who may not understand or value writing when they come to school quickly see how

Figure 8.1 Supporting Struggling Spellers

The Center to Accelerate Student Learning (CASL) has designed an intensive spelling program that speeds the spelling development of poor spellers. It teaches children basic sound–letter combinations, spelling patterns involving long and short vowels, and common spelling words that fit the patterns. Activities include word sorting, "graph busters," simple games like tic-tac-toe in which a student produces the correct written spelling of a word in order to complete a move, identifying initial sounds of words associated with a picture card, and word building by changing the onset for a particular rime. The program also includes unit tests and a review of previous units.

Spelling Patterns Taught in Each Unit of the Spelling CASL Program

Unit	Spelling Patterns
1	Short vowel sound for /a/, /e/, and /i/ in CVC-type words.
2	Short vowel sound for /o/ and /u/ in CVC-type words.
3	Short vowel sound for /a/ in CVC-type words. Long vowel sound for /a/ in CVCe-type words.
4	Short vowel sound for /o/ in CVC-type words. Long vowel sound for /o/ in CVCe-type words.
5	Short vowel sound for /i/ in CVC-type words. Long vowel sound for /i/ in CVCe-type words.
6	Short vowel sound and /ck/ at the end of monosyllabic words. Long vowel sound and /ke/ at the end of monosyllabic words.
7	Adding the suffix *ed* to monosyllabic words with a short vowel or a long vowel sound.
8	Adding the suffix *ing* to monosyllabic words with a short vowel or a long vowel sound.

writing is a powerful tool for expressing themselves. For a more in-depth description of the Language Experience Approach, see chapter 3.

INTERACTIVE WRITING EXPLICITLY CONNECTS READING AND WRITING

Interactive writing is a technique developed and named by McCarrier, Pinnell, and Fountas (2000). With small groups or the whole class, the teacher engages the children in composing and constructing written message on chart paper. Many aspects of writing can be addressed in a typical interactive writing lesson:

- Deciding on a topic
- Spelling individual words
- Formation of letters
- Spacing between words
- Constructing a sentence
- Punctuation
- Paragraphing
- Adding interesting words to jazz up a sentence
- Deciding on a title
- Formatting a friendly letter

Interactive writing can consist of a short daily message. Miss Roundy and her bilingual class wrote "Today is pajama day."

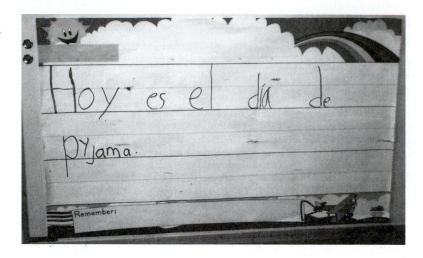

Once the teacher and student have decided on the first sentence of the writing, the teacher selectively invites students to come up and "share the pen." Students write anything from single letters to whole words. While one student is writing a letter or word on the chart paper, other students write the same thing on individual whiteboards or paper, which keeps them attending to the lesson and makes it more likely that the learning will transfer to their individual writing.

Part of the goal of interactive writing is to produce a text suitable for students to read, so the writing needs to be as conventional and legible as possible. This means that formatting mistakes, such as backward or incorrectly formed letters, are corrected using white-out tape or "Band-Aids" made out of computer labels. During the production of the text, the teacher has children refer to the writing tools in the room: labels, name chart, alphabet chart, word wall, and any other writing displayed in the room.

It takes several days to produce a complete text, because children must come up to the chart paper to write and each contribution they make can take a while to write; but it's important to know that the children *do not* need to have a turn to write every day nor should they write every word of the text. This would take too long and make the process tedious. Instead, the teacher selects the focus of the lesson carefully, choosing to have students write the parts that they're just beginning to have control of. Anything they've already mastered can be written quickly by the teacher, which will keep the lesson flowing more smoothly and help the pacing of the lesson. The teacher can also write words or word parts that students do not need to know yet.

Here are some steps for teaching an interactive writing lesson on clouds:

1. Read aloud *The Cloud Book* by Tomie de Paola.
2. Observe clouds outside.
3. Gather students on the rug in front of an easel. Each student should have an individual whiteboard or a piece of paper on clipboard so that they can write what's being written on the chart. This keeps everyone engaged.
4. Explain that you're going to write a book together about clouds. Ask students for a title. Invite students to come to the easel to write sounds they hear or letters they know are in the words of the title.

Example of interactive writing.

5. Negotiate and compose sentences, inviting students to write sounds or words. The teacher writes words that everyone already knows (e.g., *and*) or words that none of them should be expected to spell yet (e.g., *cumulus*).

6. Remind students to say the words slowly and connect them to names on the class name chart or words on the word wall. The teacher models, "Cloud starts with C just like Calvin," or "We have the word *are* on the word wall."

7. An alphabet strip is posted near the easel so that children can refer to it when they're unsure about how to form a particular letter or when the teacher needs to correct their formation of a letter.

8. Reread the message so far.

9. The next day, reread the previous day's text. Add more text until you and the students are satisfied.

10. Post the text in the classroom. Students can add illustrations to make a bulletin board about clouds. Students should be encouraged to read the text during "read around the room."

SCAFFOLDING EMERGENT WRITING

Scaffolded writing (Bodrova & Leong, 1998) is a method for supporting emergent writers' work so that it moves from one developmental stage to another more quickly. The theory is based on Vygotsky's idea of the **zone of proximal development,** as well as materialization and private speech. Materialization refers to the use of objects or actions to represent a strategy or concept that we want the child to learn. Private speech is self-directed, regulatory speech or talking to yourself about what to do.

Example of
Scaffolded writing.

I HV A DOG

HR NM IZ CORKY

SHE DOST HV A

TAL.

Here's how it works. The teacher asks the child to say aloud the message she wishes to write, and then the teacher repeats the message so that the child can confirm its accuracy. Then the teacher and the child repeat the message together as the teacher draws a highlighted line to stand for each word in the message. The highlighted line is the materialization of the concept of word. The child and teacher repeat the message together while pointing to each highlighted line, which models private speech for the child. The child then writes the message by writing the word on each line drawn by the teacher in whatever form he or she can: a letterlike form, a letter, or a combination of letters. While the child is writing, the teacher may help the child with sounding out the words or encourage the child to use the class name chart and alphabet chart or word wall to aid in figuring out how to write the word. The teacher–child interaction can happen in a brief one-to-one interaction or when working with a group of four to six children. Eventually, the children use the scaffold on their own as they transition to independence. Scaffolded writing is a temporary tool that, like training wheels on a bike, is eliminated when it's no longer needed.

The research on scaffolded writing (Bodrova & Leong, 1998) shows that at-risk kindergarteners were significantly better able to write more words and more complex messages than a control group. They also spelled more accurately and read their messages back more accurately.

Luis gets help with his writing from Mrs. Bilbao.

SPELLING PHONETICALLY IRREGULAR WORDS AND METACOGNITION

A second-grade student once told me that he deliberately pronounces words incorrectly that he's learning to spell. For example, when spelling "listen," he pronounces the /st/ blend, rather than saying /lissen/. Or he overemphasizes a vowel sound in a word like *invitation*. He explained to me that it is usually pronounced in-vuh-ta-tion, but that he says it with a strongly pronounced short /*i*/ sound: in-vi-ta-tion. I pointed out that the *i* comes from the root word *invite*, but that didn't make much of an impression. At this point in his development, his awareness of the spelling was based on visual cues, not semantic ones.

I have often told children to do this with words like *Wednesday* and *friend*, but after making a casual comment in the hallway to the whole class about mispronouncing words so that I can spell them, Daniel, during our word study time, told me his metacognitive spelling strategies. I don't know if he had already begun to use these strategies before I made the comment or if my comment led him to do this; but he confirmed that this strategy of mispronouncing words allows him to use phonics to spell them conventionally.

I asked Daniel to explain his strategy to the class and solicited examples from them as well. He used the word *island*, to illustrate his strategy, explaining that he pronounces it to himself as /iz-land/. This simple modeling inspired other students to share their strategies or invent new ones for themselves. Ryan says *probably* as pro-babe-ly, which is similar to Braden's strategy for *invitation*. Those tricky /uh/ sounds can be overpronounced or wrongly pronounced so as to emphasize their unique vowels.

Silent letters also can be emphasized or pronounced separately. Sydney told us that for *beautiful* she spells the first three letters and then says the rest normally: b-e-a-utiful. Katie says pee-oh-ple for *people*.

Some children are still using phonetic strategies to spell and thus spell words like *orange* O-R-N-A-G-E because they hear the /n/ that follows the /r/, but know there is an A in there somewhere! So Evan taught himself to say or-ange with an emphasis on pronouncing a short /a/ sound before the /n/.

There are two powerful reasons for asking students to share their spelling strategies. First, this develops their ability to think metacognitively—to think about their own thinking processes. Second, it encourages them to construct their own understandings of phonics, spelling, writing, and reading. These understandings are strong, and they can build on these while they develop new spelling strategies, even as they are decoding words while they read. This is one way that children begin to read like writers and write like readers.

READING LIKE A WRITER AND WRITING LIKE A READER

Beyond noticing spellings as they read and incorporating these into their writing, students will notice, borrow, and imitate literary language from what they read. "I like how you said 'it was a frightful noise.' That sounds like a book!" remarked Jordan. Sitting in the author's chair during the sharing time that ends writing workshop every day, Megan looked pleased that Jordan had pointed this out. Other children experiment with dialogue to make their writing sound more like the books they read. Their use of dialogue ranges from "Where is Ryan?" in a simple mystery story about a missing classmate to taunting jibes back and forth between sibling characters Sam and Samantha in Brock's new spy story. Sometimes the dialogue advances the plot, or helps to develop a character, but the degree to which the student is consciously crafting his or her writing at age 7 depends on the development of the student as a writer. Sometimes students decide to use dialogue just because others are trying it out, which why building a community of writers who are willing to share their writing with each other can help all of them grow and develop.

My second-grade students have begun to notice word choices in each others' writing; their comments reflect the discussions we have during read-alouds about specific word choices authors have made.

Brock	I like how you put the word "suffocated."
Evan	Thank you.
Braden	I like how you said that Frodo was furious.
Me	Did you like the word "furious?"
Braden	Yeah.
Me	It's a much more descriptive word than mad, isn't it? (Braden nods.)
Sydney	I like how you said Frodo was getting the creeps.
Evan	That's 'cause he gets scared easy.
Me	What do you like about that Sydney?
Sydney	I just like how it says, "getting the creeps."
Me	You like the phrase, "getting the creeps."
Sydney	Yeah.

Sydney and Braden's comments sound much like the kinds of comments we make during read-alouds of professionally written books. I encourage my students to make these connections between what they have read and what they write.

Jared made his reading–writing connections clear for me in a writing conference.

Me	Tell me what you're working on.
Jared	Well, it rhymes. I wanted to try writing something that rhymes.

My eyes were scanning his text, which was titled "The Mountains," and I noticed that he was writing descriptive nonfiction about the animals and plants in the mountains around us. I also noticed that he was writing in rhyming couplets.

Me   Wow, Jared! How did you decide to do that?

Jared   Well, my mom and I were reading Shel Silverstein and I thought I'd like to try writing something that rhymes, but something more serious.

We had also had a guest in our classroom recently who read aloud Shel Silverstein to the students. He asked the kids to tell him which poems they wanted to hear and he read their requests aloud. Now Jared was telling me that Shel Silverstein had been the inspiration for his more lyrical descriptive poetry about the mountains. Jared had been reading like a writer at home with his mom. Now he was writing like a reader at school.

Kids do borrow from literature and from each other. Graves documented this in his seminal work, *Writing: Teachers and Children at Work* (1983). For example, Megan, one of my second graders, began writing a *Magic Tree House* mystery using the same characters, Jack and Annie, but writing a new adventure for them. Jared wrote several versions of the three little pigs that incorporated ideas from the original and from parodies. Many children wrote their own versions of *Nate the Great* stories, with themselves as lead detective looking for various lost items. Stevie used the word *impertinent* in her writing after hearing *Tale of Peter Rabbit* read aloud. I like to call attention to these connections and celebrate them with the students; it shows that their writing and reading lives are interwoven. What we read aloud in class and what they read to themselves will have a direct impact on what children write during writing workshop.

 ## WRITING WORKSHOP

Writing workshop is a structure, not a theory, for teaching writing. In my classroom, it is a structure within which students are encouraged to write personally meaningful texts every day, though the structure could be misused by "laminated teachers" who trot out the same writing assignments year after year. Daniels and Bizar (1998) pointed out how the term *workshop* has:

> drifted away from the careful and narrow definition of its inventors, until by the late 1990s almost any activity involving student reading or writing, including methods totally contradictory to the original model, were being blithely labeled workshop. (p. 8)

Teachers who structure their students' writing lives around a writing workshop usually believe that writing instruction should balance both process and product, which means that students are encouraged to write first drafts, revise, and edit at a level appropriate to their age and ability, and publish selected pieces of writing through reading aloud to their peers and through having some pieces typed for them and formatted in various ways, some of which they can illustrate.

KEY CONDITIONS OF WRITING WORKSHOP

The key conditions of writing workshop are time, choice, response, demonstration, expectation, room structure, and evaluation (Graves, 1994). Students have

Shaylee chooses to write while sitting on the floor.

time in school every day to write. If I value writing, I will provide *time* for writing. If I value it, the students will value it too. Graves's data on children showed that, even when students were not actively writing, putting pencil to paper, they were still composing.

Students make *choices* about their writing and thereby take ownership of their writing. They choose the topic, when to put a piece aside for a while, what to publish, and when to share. I put limits on the range of choices, for example, by asking them to focus on writing in a particular genre, but I never remove the element of choice entirely. Choice and motivation are inextricably tied.

Students need *response* to their writing from both the teacher and their peers. Without an audience, many students will not be motivated to write. The main forms of response occur during conferencing and sharing. Many times the students and I respond with wonder and delight. Sometimes we are confused and need the author to clarify for us. Other times we have suggestions for the author to consider. Always our responses occur within the safety of our classroom community. One time, when too many students wanted to share, I experimented with small sharing groups among which I floated, listening in and monitoring. But it wasn't enough monitoring. One group in particular had two girls, Shaylee and Emma, who weren't listening attentively. When I asked the students to tell what they thought of having small group sharing, it was Shaylee who objected saying, "It wasn't as good because you weren't with us to make sure that people were listening." The

1-23-03

My game boy Advanced.
I got my game boy
Advanced for my 9th
birthday. my mom and
dad gave me a
game. They gave
me Harry Potter and
the Chamber of Secrets
for my game boy Advanced
then aftar awyl I
Metroid Fusion.
My oldised brother
Tyler got to this one
port wen yuo can got this
suit that can
increase hip and love
timachers, yuo git abilities
When yuo dete best
boses. yuo can git three difret
cinds of misls regulor misls
nuclear misls and frost misls.
and you can git 5 difrent cinds
bomes regulor boms and super bomb.

Talan chose to write about his Game Boy Advanced.

Reading!
By Tirzah Earl.
age#7.
9-27-02

Reading is
fun. you can
Get a Lot of
Smart ideas.
I like Reading.
it isfun.

Tirzah chose to write a little book called *Reading!*

teacher's presence is more crucial than I thought, even though much of the time it seems like the students can conduct sharing sessions without much intervention from me.

Through *demonstration* we show our students how we value writing, make decisions about writing, incorporate the conventions of print, and can accomplish different goals by writing in different genres, and more. Demonstrations are the heart of mini-lessons; this is how we mentor our students as apprentice writers.

We foster students' writing growth by having high *expectations*, and we communicate this over and over again through all our interactions with students. We let kindergartners know that their drawings need to be accompanied by a form of writing. These expectations grow incrementally until the end of second grade, when we expect their writing to be punctuated correctly most of the time and that commonly used words are spelled correctly. As an aid in spelling, students can use dictionary cards such as the one shown in Figure 8.2. Along with higher expectations for writing conventions, we also expect that their thoughts will be explained more thoroughly, they will be making some decisions about word choice, their writing will have some organizing features, and they will have some sense of their own voice in their writing.

Room structure is the safety net that we create by having predictable procedures and routines. I teach my students how to plan for their writing time, get their writing folders, and find a good place to write. I teach them what to do when their pencil breaks, when they finish a piece of writing, when they want to have a peer conference, and when they need a bathroom break. This room structure pervades the day, which is what makes it work during writing workshop. When students know what to do and what to expect, they are free to explore and grow as writers and learners.

Figure 8.2 Students can have words they want to use in their writing added to their dictionary cards by the teacher or by looking up the correct spelling in a dictionary.

Dictionary Card

Aa	Bb	Cc	Dd	Ee	Ff	Gg	Hh
a	baby	came	Dad	eat	father	get	had
after	back	come	day	each	for	girl	have
all	be	can	did	every	found	go	he
am	because	could	do	enough	friend	going	her
and	big	cousin	down		from	good	him
are	boy	can't	didn't		favorite	got	his
Aunt	brother	chapter	don't			Grandpa	home
any	but		dedicated			Grandma	house
animal							
away							
again							

Ii	Ji	Kk	Ll	Mn	Nn	Oo	Pp
I	jump	know	like	made	no	of	people
if	just	knew	little	me	not	on	place
in	joke	king	look	mother	now	one	play
into			love	Mom	never	our	put
is				my	night	out	
it					neighbor	over	
						off	
						other	

Qq	Rr	Ss	Tt	Uu	Ww	Xx	Zz
queen	ran	said	that	Uncle	was	x-ray	zoo
quickly	run	saw	the	up	we		zipper
quiet	rabbit	school	them	us	went	**Yy**	
	really	see	then		were	yes	
		she	there		when	you	
		sister	they	**Vv**	will	your	
		so	this	very	would	yellow	
		some	to	volcano	who	yesterday	
		should	threw		where	year	
		surprise	through		why		
					write		
					writing		

For years, *evaluation* was the teachers' job only. But lately, through evaluation procedures like collecting writing in a portfolio and reflecting on the writing, students have become part of the process. Much of students' time is spent alone with their writing, and they need to be taught early on to self-assess. How is my writing going? Am I accomplishing what I set out to do? Will my readers understand me?

"I am going to my cousin's house" was written by Lorena, an English language learner. She liked to use her dictionary card to help her spell as she wrote.

10-23-02

I am going to my cousins.
House. Her Name is
Alexa. Yesterday Was
her Birthday.
I'm giring her a
surprise. The
surprise is
a water gun.
I Pled tag
I said to my sister
to GOTO the zoo

These self-assessing habits are taught through many interactions with students during conferencing and sharing. I have been teaching my students the language of the six traits (Spandel, 2001), as Spandel recommends, so that they are able to think about their writing in these terms. Spandel recommends not using the numbers of rubric scoring with young children; "[There is] plenty of time for that beginning in third or fourth grade" (p. 324). (See Spandel, 2004, *Creating Young Writers: Using the Six Traits to Enrich Writing Process in Primary Classrooms*, for a wealth of primary-grade specific advice and demonstrations.) She also advocates focusing on ideas and voice primarily, then on conventions. As children experiment with conventions, they will make mistakes, sprinkling apostrophes and quotation marks, and we should be glad to see this, according to Spandel. I have always celebrated children's use of new conventions, however inexpertly they apply them, because it is a sign of growth. Just like a baby's first steps are wobbly, so are children's first steps in each new literacy skill or tool. So, while evaluation is important, it should be used gently and judiciously with young children's writing.

Writing folder crate.

THE ROUTINE

The daily writing workshop routine in my classroom consists of a mini-lesson, time for writing (during which conferences occur), and a sharing time; this is consistent with how workshop was originally defined by Graves (1983), Calkins (1994), and Atwell (1987). My daily ritual for writing workshop has certain repetitive aspects. For example, the mini-lesson lasts for 5 to 10 minutes, and then I ask the students to tell me what their writing plans are for the day. Atwell called this taking the "status of the class." For the few children who aren't sure what they will write about, it helps to hear others' plans; also, as I ask, "What are your writing plans today?" I convey to them the importance of having a plan. Everyone is swept along in the tide of getting down to the important work of writing.

Children are dismissed one at a time from the group area after telling me their writing plans. Then they get their writing folder and find a good place to write (at a table, on the floor, on the couch, in the rocker) and begin to write for 20 to 30 minutes. During this time, I conference with individual students, and students sometimes engage in peer conferences. This time is quiet, but by no means silent, because I want the students to ask each other how to spell words. In addition, through peer conferences, I want them to discuss their writing with each other to get ideas or other kinds of help. I have laminated cards they take when they want to conference with another student. On one side of the card are listed the reasons to have a peer conference (see Figure 8.3), and on the other side are the steps to follow when conducting a peer conference (see Figure 8.4).

MINI-LESSONS

Through mini-lessons, I can demonstrate a wide variety of writing skills and strategies and also introduce and explore a wide variety of ideas that young writers need to ponder. Here are the steps to follow:

1. Introduce the topic or skill.
2. Share an example or demonstrate the skill.
3. Ask students to use the skill or notice other examples similar to the example given during the day's independent writing.

Figure 8.3 Reasons to Have a Peer Conference

1. To get encouragement.
2. To get ideas.
3. To get help so your story will be more interesting.
4. To get help with spelling or punctuation or capital letters.
5. To see if your story makes sense.

Figure 8.4 Steps for Having a Peer Conference

1. Only two people can have a conference.
2. Tell your partner why you need to have a conference.
3. Read aloud your writing to your partner.
4. Ask for questions or comments.
5. The other person gets a turn to read aloud and get comments.
6. Get back to writing!

Quinten and Lincoln having a peer conference.

4. Reflect on learning. Did the students use what you taught them that day? During sharing time, ask students to report on their use of what was taught in the mini-lesson. Be aware that not all students will be ready to use what you taught. Mini-lessons are repeated as necessary for the whole class or through individual conferencing or small-group instruction.

Procedural Mini-lessons

At the beginning of the school year, I focus on teaching procedural mini-lessons. This is when I get students into good work habits like dating their writing, numbering

Writing center.

pages, writing on one side of the paper, and skipping lines. I also teach them where to store their writing folders, what to do when their pencils need to be sharpened, what to do when they need more paper, or how to organize their writing folders so that precious pages of writing are not destroyed or lost. The following are some suggested procedural mini-lesson topics:

- Writing name and date on pieces of writing
- Getting writing folders
- Stapling finished pieces
- What to do when you've finished a piece of writing
- Using one side of the paper and skipping lines on lined paper so that revision is possible
- How to conduct a peer conference
- How to find a quiet place to work

Skills Mini-Lessons

Skills mini-lessons should grow out of the needs you perceive among your students and your district's or state's core objectives for your grade level. Kindergartners and beginning first graders will need skill lessons focusing on how to orient print on a page and how to put space between words, whereas second graders will need to see you model how to figure out where periods go in text that has no punctuation. Skill lessons are most effectively taught through modeling or interactive writing in which the students come up and are part of the creation of a shared text. Skills mini-lesson topics might include the following:

- Top-to-bottom and left-to-right orientation of print
- Putting spaces between words and concept of word
- Using capital letters at the beginning of sentences and for proper names
- Using quotation marks to indicate character talking out loud (use your own writing or let a student teach this lesson using his or her writing)
- Adding *ing* and *ed* to verbs
- Concept of sentence and listening for where punctuation goes (role play putting periods at the end of lines)

❀ Writing left to right, top to bottom (role play the wrong way)
❀ How and when to use various spelling resources, such as a word wall, dictionary, book, peer, or adult

Strategy Mini-Lessons

Writers sometimes have tricks or strategies they use during the writing process. We can demonstrate these in strategy mini-lessons. They include simple ideas like lining out words instead of erasing, because it is both quicker and allows us to see the revisions we've made and possibly change back to our original text. I have even taught one or two students the proofreader's term *stet,* which literally means "let it stand," so that they can indicate that they want to ignore a change they've made to their writing. Strategies are also more complex and abstract, such as focusing on what's important in a piece of writing, which is an idea that overlaps into the craft of writing, that is, the ways that we can increase the quality of writing. Here are some suggested strategy mini-lesson topics:

❀ Using a caret to insert words
❀ Lining out instead of erasing when you want to make a change
❀ Rereading own writing at the beginning of writing time
❀ Rehearsing ideas at home or with friends through talk
❀ Figuring out the important part of one's writing and concentrating on that
❀ Topic selection or what to do when you can't think of anything to write; for example, look at the class's published books or other books for a short time, read through your folder for a piece of writing you haven't finished or would like to try rewriting, write about not knowing what to write

Craft Mini-Lessons

I also introduce ideas about what makes high-quality writing through craft mini-lessons. Though I'm thrilled when I can help children write fluently and produce lots of writing, I also want them to see that there are things they can try that will make their writing better or more interesting. It's very important to talk positively with young children about their writing, though I sometimes tell them I am confused by what they have written or that they might add or change words that could help their reader understand the writing better. As teachers we are clearly writing experts compared to our students (though we may not feel like we're writing experts), and we need to make sure we don't overwhelm them with all the growth they have ahead of them or make them feel as if they will never measure up. So, while I introduce ways that authors make their writing more effective, I don't expect that my students will use the ideas that day, week, or even year. But I've planted the seeds and made them aware of the qualities of good writing; they will continue to grow as writers and the seeds I've planted may take a while to germinate, but one day they will think about the ideas I introduced and try them in their writing. These are not discrete skills that I expect them to master in a finite period of time; these are ideas, techniques, and strategies that may one day prove to be useful tools.

For example, *Voices in the Park* by Anthony Browne is written from the point of view of four different characters. Using this book, I show my students how the point of view changes the story. Young children can see how this works even if they aren't ready to write from different points of view.

Katie enjoys writing poetry.

Craft mini-lesson topics could include these:

❀ Making a picture in the mind of the reader
❀ Considering the effective leads in familiar books
❀ Using words to advance a story (other than "and then"); for example, "the next day," "two weeks later," "later that night"
❀ Considering how point of view affects the way a story is told
❀ Letting the writer's personal voice come through
❀ Using your senses when adding description

Figure 8.5 provides a list of suggested titles to use as aids in teaching children writing skills.

CONFERENCING

Almost all experienced writers discuss their writing with others at some stage in the writing process. I belong to a writing group that meets monthly to respond to pieces written by members of the group. We read the pieces before we meet so that our entire time can be spent talking about the writing, telling the author what worked, what was confusing, and offering suggestions. I shared chapters of this book with the group and came away with ideas about how to improve my writing, but also feeling validated as a writer. Adults in many situations bounce ideas off each other, getting feedback, before deciding how to proceed. Children need to do this too.

Some children need to talk through their stories, rehearsing them aloud, before they can write them down. Some children will find they have so much more to say after they've explained what they're writing. When I am conferencing, I try to focus mostly on the content, but spelling, punctuation, or other conventions are legitimate concerns that children have, and I do try to help them while their writing is in process. Though I try to listen as much as possible in a writing conference, I also want to walk away from a conference knowing that I've helped a child in some specific way. Maybe I've expressed some confusion and the child has decided to go back and add a word or sentence to clarify something. Or maybe I've read through a page of their writing with them, letting them hear the rhythm and pauses that help them figure out

Figure 8.5 High-Quality Literature to Teach the Craft of Writing

Aliki. *Fossils tell of long ago.* Use of sequenced drawings in information text to visually explain a process.

Berger, M. *Do all spiders spin webs?: Questions and answers about spiders.* Using a question and answer format for writing information text.

Brown, M. *Arthur's computer disaster.* All the Arthur books have great examples of dialogue and alternate words for *said.*

Browne, A. *Voices in the park.* Great for showing multiple points of view of the same event.

Casely, J. *Bully.* Problem and resolution structure of fiction.

DuTemple, L. (1997). *Polar bears.* Using a table of contents to organize information text.

Guiberson, B. *Cactus hotel.* Using chronological narrative structure to relay information.

Henkes, K. *Julius, the baby of the world.* Effective word choice for characterization.

James, S. *Dear Mr. Blueberry.* Letter writing between characters as a narrative structure.

Lester, H. *Author: A true story.* Various strategies authors use.

Lowery, L. *Martin Luther King day.* Elements of a good biography.

Nixon, J. *If you were a writer.* Various writing strategies.

Pallotta, J. *The icky bug alphabet book.* Pallotta's series of alphabet books are all useful for modeling the alphabet book as a nonfiction writing structure.

Spooner, M. *A moon in your lunch box.* Good examples of concrete poetry, free verse, and subtle rhyming verse.

Steig, W. *Sylvester and the magic pebble.* Word choice for description.

Viorst, J. *Alexander and the terrible, horrible, no good, very bad day.* Using a repeating phrase to add humor to a story.

where periods go. Sometimes I tell them how to spell a word that they're eager to spell right, or I've encouraged them to try it for themselves and confirmed their instincts about how to spell the word. Here is an example of showing a student how to brainstorm titles.

Me	You were saying that you were trying to think of a title? Is that right?
Ryan	Uh huh.
Me	Can I show you a strategy for thinking up titles?
Ryan	Okay.
Me	Okay. What's your story about?
Ryan	It's a story about a detective.
Me	Uh huh. A detective story? And what's the problem in your story?
Ryan	Um, he gets a phone call and he goes and tries to find her cat and he finds her cat. It was in the. . . . I forget where it was.
Me	Okay. So, it's a lost cat story. It's a detective story. It's a mystery?
Ryan	(nods head)
Me	Okay, let's think of about three different titles and then you could probably choose one of them. Let's just think of one first. It doesn't have to be interesting.
Ryan	The Case of the Missing Everything?
Me	The Case of the Missing Everything. Why do you say everything?

Ryan   'Cause everybody's calling me and all their stuff is lost.

Me   Oh, okay. There's one idea. Let's think of another one. (long pause) Does your detective have a name?

Ryan   Mmm, no.

Me   What if he did? Let's call him Detective Ryan. That could be a title. (I left Ryan to think of a third title, which he did, and came back a few minutes later.) You don't have to decide which title you like now, but is there one you like better than the others? Which one do you like best?

Ryan   The Deep Dark Night.

Me   Hey, good, I'm glad 'cause that's one you thought of. Great!

Whatever you focus on, when you are conferencing with a student, keep it short. You don't want to overload the writer with advice; young writers can usually only attend to one teaching point. If I keep all my conferences short, I can try to touch base with as many students as possible during the open writing time; I keep track of who I've conferenced with so that across several days I am sure to get to everyone. Often several students need something from me at the same time. I teach my students what to do about pencils, bathroom, and other routine tasks so that they don't need to interrupt a writing conference. If they have questions about writing, I ask them to check with other students first, then raise their hand and I'll come help them as soon as I can. If you truly keep conferences short, this works well. Some teachers have assigned students to certain days of the week, which ensures that they meet with everyone; however, I wouldn't want a student to sit for three days waiting for a conference with me and getting nothing written. I prefer a needs-based approach that keeps me zigzagging around the room; my proximity keeps many on task, and my availability is reassuring to needy writers.

Prompts to Begin Writing and Extend Conferences

Here are questions you can ask to help students get started and follow-up questions to help them extend or reflect on their writing:

- How's it going?
- How can I help you?
- What's going to be the most important thing?
- Tell me about the most important part.
- How do you do that?
- What's happening in this piece?
- What are you writing about?
- What was the best part?
- Are you going to write about that?
- What are you going to say about it?
- Tell me what you're going to do.
- Tell me about the picture in your head.
- Are you going to write all this?
- What are you going to write next?
- What do you particularly like?
- Any surprises in your writing?

As young writers talk, they discover what they have to say and are then able to write or elaborate on what they have already written. You are validating their ability to think and solve their own writing problems (soon they may be able to have a conference with themselves). You need to listen and be genuinely interested in what they have to say. Really listening means being open to the child's agenda. You show the child you've listened when you try to restate what he or she has said before you offer your response.

Me	What's happening in your story?
Shannon	They came home and they're like going to eat supper.
Me	Mm hm.
Shannon	Then they're going to bed. Then wake up.
Me	Okay, so what are you going to write right now?
Shannon	I can't decide.
Me	So you're trying to make a decision. Tell me what you're trying to decide.
Shannon	If they're going to set the table or if it's all set and they're going to eat.
Me	So you're trying to decide how much detail to put in?
Shannon	(nods)
Me	Like whether to have the characters set the table or have it all set and not worry about that?
Shannon	(nods)
Me	Which do you think would keep your audience more interested? Do you think they want to hear about setting the table or would they rather get going further along in the story?
Shannon	Get going in the story.
Me	Did that help you make a decision?
Shannon	Yeah.
Me	Okay.

Try (and this is difficult) to teach your students not to interrupt a writing conference; ignore those who try to interrupt and stay focused on the writer. If students know the procedures in your classroom, most routine matters can be taken care of independently, without adult intervention. At times they truly do need me, such as when I've let the paper supply run low and we run out during writing workshop or someone feels sick and needs to call home. You don't want to coldly ignore the genuine needs of your students, but you do want the writers you are conferencing with to feel important enough that you will focus your attention on them.

SHARING WRITING

Writing workshop ends with a sharing session that lasts for 15 to 20 minutes. A few students read part or all of their writing and take comments and questions from their classmates. Writing workshop in my classroom lasts for 45 minutes minimum, usually longer, every day. I can't stress enough how important it is to have writing workshop every day, preferably at the same time. When students know that they will write every day, they come mentally prepared to do that. The predictability of the routine makes them feel safe and secure; they know what to expect and what is expected of them. Students in my classroom rarely run out of ideas to write about because they know that when one piece is finished they are expected to write another, and they usually have a list of ideas written down or ideas lurking in their minds that they're eager to begin. They think about writing when they're home and they come to school prepared to write more.

Sharing their writing is crucial to young writers. Knowing they will have an audience is very motivating. Also, their peers are an authentic audience for their writing. Writing for the teacher's eyes only is a sure way to develop writing that meets only minimal standards of quality.

Author Concerns

Who should share? Someone who's had a good writing day. Someone who's tried something new. Someone who hasn't shared recently. I keep track of who has shared writing in any given one- or two-week period so that everyone has a fair chance to share during that time. Sometimes I ask particular students to share, and sometimes they ask me if they may share. I limit the numbers of students who share each day because, if more than two to four writers share, the focus becomes too fragmented and students' attention spans reach their limit. I choose how many will share based on the length of writing to be shared, the length of time available, and my estimate of students' ability to listen attentively at that point in the school year.

I ask the students to sit in a sharing circle so that everyone can see everyone else. The author sits in a chair, sometimes labeled the author's chair, and reads his or her piece of writing loudly and clearly enough to keep the audience engaged. Afterward, the audience asks questions or makes comments. If the author seems really motivated to incorporate suggestions or add in information that the audience asked about, I ask if they want to go to their seat and get the ideas down right away, before they forget. Some say they will do it the next day, and I make a note on a Post-it to help them remember. In any case, it is the author's decision whether to make any changes based on the class's responses.

Listener Concerns

At the beginning of the year, I emphasize careful listening to those who share, so we always begin with what we've heard. The students must begin their response with "I heard . . ." or "I learned. . . ." This teaches the children to listen for the meaning and lets writers know if their writing is clear. It emphasizes to the audience the importance of listening, which in turn encourages and validates the writer.

Later in the year, after careful listening has been established, students are ready to begin their responses with questions or comments and sometimes suggestions for the writer. In the following examples, I've only left out the author's words when calling on the students who want to ask a question or make a comment.

Shannon	Are you gonna describe, like, what color the unicorn is?
Bethany	White with a gold mane and a silver horn.
Jared	What's the unicorn's name?
Bethany	Good question. Maybe I'll name it Audrey.
Brock	I like that one sentence.
Bethany	You mean "through brambles, across little streams, under low branches of trees, finally the two found what was making the noise."
Me	That *is* an amazing sentence. It is very descriptive.

Questions for the author should clarify meaning. "I was wondering. . . . " "I was confused when you said. . . . " "I want to know. . . . " Sometimes I have to steer my students away from focusing on unimportant details because they do not really add anything to the writing. Of course, this means modeling and discussing what kinds of details are important and what kinds are not. Good questions can help the author generate ways to extend the writing the next day.

Comments for the author about the writing should be specific. "I liked your story" is too vague and not helpful. Comments should focus on the author's story, not the person who's commenting (many children have a tendency to want to tell their own experience that is similar to what the author has written).

Shannon	Where did you get the idea that Bessie got sucked into the book? (Shannon asked this about Brock's time travel historical fiction, "Bessie the Colonial Girl.")
Brock	Um, I got it from *Scooby Doo and the Cyber Chase* [McCann, 2001] and I also got the colonial idea from *If You Lived in Colonial Times* [McGovern, 1992].
Bethany	What does Bessie look like?
Brock	I'll probably add that in here. She has long, to her shoulder length, dark brown hair. And she has kind of a stubby nose, which means small. She has big eyes, like me. She wears this yellow dress with an apron and a bonnet. Oh, and just to tell you, they're ten years old.
Regina	I'm excited for your story.
Lincoln	What's gonna happen next?
Brock	They're gonna meet Helen and then Maria doesn't hate Helen and then Bessie and Maria aren't friends anymore, but then Bessie has to rescue her father from jail because he was arrested. And so Maria calls Bessie her hero because Bessie's dad is Maria's great-, great-, great-, great-grandmother's son.

Sharing time often needs its own mini-lessons. Sometimes I have the students begin their comments with "I heard" or "I'm wondering" or "I liked." On this day, I was trying to get the kids not to ask things like "When did you start writing this?" or "What's going to happen next?"

Me	I want you to be listening for things that you like about Alex's writing, about the way he wrote it or the information that he included. That's what I'd like for you to make comments about. Right now there's still some rattling going on. Any movements that you make make it hard to hear Alex. Are you ready to listen? Okay, read loudly.
Jaren	I liked the sentence where you used the word *smaller*.
Me	So he used comparison words, *smaller than*?
Jaren	Yeah.
Lincoln	I liked how you said *than* instead of *then*. (The difference between *than* and *then* was difficult for some of the students earlier in the year, and I had worked hard with a few of them to impress on them that the word *than* was used when comparing things.)
Me	Yes, we've talked about that haven't we? Alex did a good job with that.

Braden   I like how you put descriptive words like Mercury is smaller than Earth and Pluto is smaller than Mercury.

In some ways, sharing is more important than formal publishing, because students get more feedback that helps them to improve the piece they're working on or to write differently the next time; but publishing is also important, because students gain the satisfaction of creating a finished product that they can share with their parents and that can take its place in the classroom library.

PUBLISHING

Publishing can take many forms. The simplest is when students read their writing aloud to the class. More permanent forms of publishing include bulletin board displays, letters (i.e., when they are actually sent to the recipient), student-written classroom newsletters, posters, books, single poems, and class anthologies of poetry.

Each student publishes at least one book during the year. With first graders, whose pieces were shorter, I published much more of their writing to keep their

Dalton's published poem.

My Dogs
by Dalton Childs

Otis is the wild one.
He runs around the
yard chasing
his tail. He jumps on
me when I get home.
Shadow just lays around.
One time Shadow jumped on
a chair and on the counter
and slept there.
Taz look puffy.
He loves his little
basketball. He looks for
it all
the time. He knocks over couches
and lamps and knocks
over chairs.
And Romeo,
he's a weiner dog
and he jumps
high and he eats
cat food and chases the cat.
Romeo is fun.
He drinks
out of the sink.
He climbs up the drawers.
When he gets down he jumps

Writing portfolios.

motivation for writing high and to give them personalized reading material. After they have edited it to the best of their ability, I keyboard their writing with conventional spellings and punctuation. They illustrate the pages, and I bind it with heavy card stock for the front and back covers and laminate their cover illustration to the front. I can produce these quickly with the materials and tools at my school. Every book has a title page and cover, and some books have dedication pages or about-the-author pages. Including these real-book features is important because it gives their book an authentic feel; they know that real books have these elements. Pages are numbered for everyone's convenience. Most children want to illustrate the whole book like a picture book, but some prefer a more chapter book-like look with no interior illustrations. I allow them to illustrate during writing workshop for two days, and then they must use free time to finish illustrating (illustrating can also be integrated into the art curriculum; teaching children about horizon lines, for example, improves their illustrations considerably). These books are valuable to the children; they take them home to share with their families, but they bring them back to be part of our classroom collection until the end of the year. Pieces of writing that are not published, but are finished, go into the students' portfolios.

Tips on Publishing

1. As a mini-lesson, I discuss what they need to do before they can publish their work. First, they must have at least three pieces to choose from. They must read all three of them in their entirety and then choose which one they want to publish. Then they need to proofread. Typically, I ask them to circle any words they think might be misspelled and check for capital letters and punctuation.

2. Before I keyboard their writing, I check to see if they have proofread to the best of their ability. If they haven't, I ask them to check again. For spellings, I pair them up with a parent volunteer or with a more advanced speller to work on just the words they've circled. When they've done all that, a classroom volunteer or I will keyboard it. We fix the rest of their errors as we type. "Real" authors have editors too.

About the auther

Tirzah EarL lives in Utah. aS he has a baby brother, & her mom is going to have a baby girl. I am the oldest. My baby brothers name is Micah. My mom's name is Robyn. My dad's name is Bryan. I was born in Logan, Utah. I am eight years old. I go to school at North Park Elementry.

Tirzah wrote an About the Author page for one of her published books.

3. With more advanced writers, I decide what they are ready to do in terms of revising and editing their own writing:

Are they ready to find some correct spellings in a picture dictionary?

Are they ready to add periods and capital letters?

Are they ready to add quotation marks?

Are they ready to change the sequence of their writing?

Are they ready to cut extraneous material?

Are they ready to figure out where paragraphs should go?

As my second graders become more fluent writers, their writing pieces get quite long. I couldn't possibly publish everything they write. They have to pick and choose, and they understand that, as their publisher, I have the right to reject their manuscript. I ask them to wait until they have three pieces of writing before they publish. They must reread these three pieces of writing carefully and consider which is their best or favorite. If they've followed these steps, I almost always publish their writing. Parent volunteers can be very useful in the publishing process!

I also like to publish shorter pieces of writing during the year: class books about field trips, interactive writing pieces, New Year's resolutions, poems, biographies of classmates, and book reviews. Writing in these other genres is important to the overall development of writers.

WRITING IN MANY GENRES

As a part of mini-lessons, I teach the students about many different genres of writing, some of which I expect them to try. For example, I have taught second graders to write book reviews, poetry, nonfiction information writing, friendly letters, personal narrative, and fiction. Perhaps because of the **expressivist tradition** out of which writing workshop was born, teachers have tended to overemphasize personal narrative as the genre of choice in writing workshop. While I agree that it is important to write about what you know best, I don't believe that means we should limit children to writing personal narratives. As long as students have some element of choice, there is no reason that we should not expect or assign specific forms of writing. (Nonfiction, specifically information writing, will be addressed in depth in Chapter 9)

NONFICTION GENRES OF WRITING

With nonfiction forms of writing, as with all the genres I teach, modeling is the main instructional mode.

Letters

Letters, or the "friendly letter," are interesting to write and have built-in motivation. I begin my teaching of the friendly letter with a need-based opportunity. For example, the local volunteer firemen came to our school to show us their trucks and take us through the smoke house where they demonstrate various fire safety lessons. We all wrote letters to thank them for coming and to let them know what we learned from their visit. The following week our computer lab teacher took a job at the local high school, and the students wrote her goodbye letters letting her know what they would miss about her, that they might see her again when they get to high school, what they liked about computer class, and how they hoped she would enjoy her new job. Not every letter touched on all these topics, of course; each student wrote a unique letter. With two assigned letters under their belts, the students were ready to write letters to each other. These tend to be shorter and more task oriented.

Book Reviews

Unlike traditional book reports, book reviews have a definite purpose beyond fulfilling a teacher's requirement. Book reviews are meant for other students to read and look to for recommendations about what might be appealing to read. Through modeling, I teach the students that a book review usually has a short summary of the book (though the ending isn't always revealed) and a statement or two of evaluation. We also find examples of book reviews in magazines and examine their features. Students usually accompany their book reviews with a copy of the book itself or a hand-colored photocopy of the cover of the book. This is an excellent way to introduce persuasive writing.

Autobiography and Biography

My students begin the year writing autobiography and then later in the year we pair up and write biographies of each other. Both are forms of nonfiction that do not require reading any source materials but rather allow students to draw on their knowledge of themselves as they write or tell a peer about themselves. Our biography writing began with a discussion of what a biography should have in it. Then we read many biographies to see if they fit our expectations. We revised our list of what a good biography should include, and I engaged them in a group writing experience

The Life of Tylor by Alexis Harris.

in which in teams of two they interviewed me and my son about six different aspects of our lives. We found that the categories overlapped and compressed them into four final categories. We took these four categories and created a web for them to use while interviewing each other.

POETRY

Poetry has been the most exciting genre that I've taught recently. I like to teach poetry near the end of the year when students are feeling adventurous about life, but a little tired of their usual writing. Regie Routman's book *Kids' Poems: Teaching Second Graders to Love Writing Poetry* (2000) transformed the way I thought about teaching poetry to young children. (She also has versions of this book for kindergarten, first grade, and third and fourth grades.)

We had been immersed in reading lots of poetry one year when a student, who had a particular zeal for reading poetry, wrote a poem with no demonstration or prompting from me. I was excited that she had ventured into this territory on her own and had her share her poem with the class. Another student tried poetry with similar success. Both were nonrhyming poems. I shared these two girls' poetry and some of the student-written poetry Routman provides with my class, and my students were off and running. Every student wrote a least one poem, but most wrote many more. One student, who had been a reluctant writer all year, found his voice in his short, focused poetry. I published, copied, and bound a copy of a class anthology of poems for each child to keep.

FICTION

Fiction is a difficult genre to teach young children to write because it is so complex. It can be frustrating because they get part of the way into a story and don't know what will happen next. Or they can't figure out how to end a piece. I try to address this partially by asking them to plan their fiction writing using a simple story map, as shown in Figure 8.6. The map helps them formulate a plan for their writing and reins in the infinite possibilities. I am not adamant that they use a story map, but I make positive comments about those who do. Some students enjoy "making it up as they go along" and I don't want to suppress the joyfulness of that kind of writing adventure.

Figure 8.6   Story Map

Characters:

Setting:

Problem:

Solution:

Events:

Conclusion:

CONCLUSIONS

Writing workshop needs to take place every day. It works best when teachers make writing part of the daily classroom schedule, preferably at the same time every day. Children thrive on the structure and predictability of writing workshop. They know what to expect and are prepared for it.

Don't skip any part of it. Mini-lessons are your chance to teach new skills and strategies. Students' writing will improve if you don't teach mini-lessons, but only through maturity and osmosis. Conferencing is your chance to listen carefully and provide some individual writing coaching. Finally, sharing is crucial. The children need an audience, other than you, for their writing. Their peers are their natural audience.

Be responsive to your students. Much of writing workshop cannot be planned very far in advance. You are continuously making decisions about what to teach, say, and do. If you really listen to the students, watch what they're doing and reflect on your observations; you will know what to teach, say, and do.

Page 13 of Emily's five-chapter fiction piece called *The Secret Shortcut.*

Daisy counts on having time to write every day.

 SUGGESTED ACTIVITIES TO EXTEND YOUR LEARNING

1. Observe in a classroom where writing workshop happens on a daily basis. Take note of the management routines and the nature of the mini-lessons. If possible, talk to the students about their writing and look at writing samples.
2. Select two or three pieces of high-quality children's literature that would be useful for demonstrating a certain quality of writing. Develop mini-lessons for each.
3. Develop an interactive writing lesson plan based on a content area topic from your state's curriculum and a high-quality nonfiction children's book. See page 206 for steps for teaching an interactive writing lesson on clouds for an example.

 *REFERENCES*

Allen, R. V. (1999). Using language experience in beginning reading: How a language experience program works. In O. Nelson & W. Linek (Eds.), *Practical classroom applications of language experience*. Boston: Allyn and Bacon.

Atwell, N. (1987). *In the middle: Writing, reading, and learning with adolescents*. Portsmouth, NH: Heinemann.

Bodrova, E., & Leong, D. J. (1998). Scaffolding emergent writing in the zone of proximal development. *Literacy Teaching and Learning, 3*(2), 1–18.

Calkins, L. M. (1994). *The art of teaching writing*. Portsmouth, NH: Heinemann.

Clay, M. (1991). *Becoming literate: The construction of control*. Auckland, New Zealand: Heinemann.

Cunningham, P. M. (1995). *Phonics they use: Words for reading and writing*. New York: HarperCollins.

Daniels, H., & Bizar, M. (1998). *Methods that matter: Six structures for best practice classrooms*. Portland, ME: Stenhouse.

Fitzgerald, J., & Shanahan, T. (2000). Reading and writing relations and their development. *Educational Psychologist, 35*(1), 39–50.

Graham, S., Harris, K. R., & Fink-Chorzempa, B. (2003). Extra spelling instruction: Promoting better spelling, writing, and reading performance right from the start. *Teaching Exceptional Children, 35*(6), 66–68.

Graves, D. (1983). *Writing: Teachers and children at work*. Portsmouth, NH: Heinemann.

Harste, J. C., Woodward, V. A., & Burke, C. L. (1984). *Language stories and literacy lessons*. Portsmouth, NH: Heinemann.

Henderson, E. (1990). *Teaching spelling*. Boston: Houghton Mifflin.

McCarrier, A., Pinnell, G. S., & Fountas, I. C. (2000). *Interactive writing: How language and literacy come together, K–2*. Portsmouth, NH: Heinemann.

Routman, R. (2000). *Kids' poems: Teaching second graders to love writing poetry*. New York: Scholastic.

Snow, C. E., Burns, M. S., & Griffin, P. (1998). *Preventing reading difficulties in young children*. Washington, DC: National Academy Press.

Spandel, V. (2001). *Creating writers through 6-trait writing assessment and instruction* (3rd ed.). New York: Addison-Wesley Longman.

Spandel, V. (2004). *Creating young writers: Using the six traits to enrich writing process in primary classrooms*. New York: Pearson.

Weaver, C. (1996). Facts on research on the teaching of phonics. In C. Weaver, L. Gillmeister-Krause, & G. Vento-Zogby (Eds.), *Creating support for effective literacy education*. [Online]. Available: www.heinemann.com/shared/onlineresources/08894/08894f2.html

Children's Literature

Aliki. (1990). *Fossils tell of long ago*. New York: Harper & Row.

Berger, M., & Berger, G. (2000). *Do all spiders spin webs?: Questions and answers about spiders*. New York: Scholastic.

Brown, M. (1997). *Arthur's computer disaster*. Boston: Little, Brown.

Browne, A. (2001) *Voices in the park*. New York: DK Publishing.

Casely, J. (2001). *Bully*. New York: HarperCollins.

De Paola, T. (1985). *The cloud book*. New York: Holiday House.

DuTemple, L. (1997). *Polar bears*. Minneapolis, MN: Lerner.

Guiberson, B. (1991). *Cactus hotel*. New York: Henry Holt.

Henkes, K. (1990). *Julius, the baby of the world*. New York: Morrow.

James, S. (1991). *Dear Mr. Blueberry*. New York: Simon & Schuster.

Lester, H. (1997). *Author: A true story*. Boston: Houghton Mifflin.

Lowery, L. (1987). *Martin Luther King day*. New York: Scholastic.

McCann, J. L. (2001). *Scooby Doo and the cyber chase*. New York: Scholastic.

McGovern, A. (1992). *If you lived in colonial times*. New York: Scholastic.

Nixon, J. (1988). *If you were a writer*. New York: Simon & Schuster.

Pallotta, J. (1986). *The icky bug alphabet book*. Watertown, MA: Charlesbridge Publishing.

Spooner, M. (1993). *A moon in your lunch box*. New York: Henry Holt.

Steig, W. (1969). *Sylvester and the magic pebble*. New York: Simon & Schuster.

Viorst, J. (1972). *Alexander and the terrible, horrible, no good, very bad day*. New York: Macmillan.

Nonfiction Reading and Writing

9

Sylvia Read

Learning About the Natural World in a Writing Workshop

I t's writing workshop time in Mrs. Read's second-grade classroom. Jeff and Tony are hunkered down over a book about snakes. They stop to point at things in the illustrations and talk animatedly. They turn the book face down on the floor; then Jeff dictates and Tony writes, "Snakes have jaws that can open real wide so they can swallow stuff that's bigger than their head." Taisia stands by the rack of nonfiction books looking for the one about butterflies that we read aloud yesterday. She finds it and carries it over to the chrysalis of a monarch butterfly that we have hanging upside down in a canning jar. She finds the picture of the chrysalis in the book and says to Jaime, who is drawing a picture of the chrysalis, "The real one is much more shiny than this picture. I think the author of this book should have done a better picture. She should have used real gold 'cause the real one has those dots that look like real gold." Jaime nods and keeps drawing. Jaime is drawing the life cycle of the butterfly by showing the different stages of the metamorphosis. So far, he's labeled them with numbers showing the order in which they happen.

 ## READING NONFICTION

Research tells us that in most primary-grade classrooms, students aren't exposed to much nonfiction (Kamberelis, 1998; Yopp & Yopp, 2000). In basal readers, the percentage of nonfiction varies from as low as 12% (Hoffman et al., 1994) to a high of 33.8% (Schmidt, Caul, Byers, & Buchmann, 1984). Yopp and Yopp (2000) found that teachers reported that only 14% of read-alouds were nonfiction.

Children gravitate toward nonfiction, checking it out from their neighborhood library more often than fiction (Kamil, 1994). They can retell it (Pappas, 1991) and they can write about it (Read, 2001). Reluctant readers and writers often become engaged in reading and writing when they are given the opportunity to work with nonfiction texts (Caswell & Duke, 1998).

Often teachers assume that fiction is read for pleasure and nonfiction is read for information, which means the choice is pleasure versus information. The thought that

Mrs. Kendrick reads nonfiction aloud to her kindergarten class.

information can be pleasurable is left out of the decision. But children find facts and information interesting and fun—in fact, their strong curiosity about the world is fed with nonfiction. Patricia Lauber, a well-known children's author of nonfiction, says that she wants to show readers that "it is possible to read science for pleasure, that a good science book touches the mind, the heart, the imagination" (Lauber, 1992, p. 15).

When teachers *do* read aloud nonfiction, the conversations that occur are often better for fostering comprehension than the conversations during fiction read-alouds (Smolkin & Donovan, 2001). Because students will be asked to read and write nonfiction kinds of texts so often in the intermediate, middle school, and high school grades, it only makes sense to be sure that we offer young children a balanced diet of fiction and nonfiction.

PURPOSES FOR READING NONFICTION ALOUD

We need to read nonfiction aloud to young children so that they are exposed to a variety of text features and structures. Children also learn specialized vocabulary and new concepts, which builds their background knowledge (Yopp & Yopp, 2000). When they are asked to read nonfiction independently, their comprehension is highly dependent on their level of background knowledge, which is why we need to make a special effort to build their knowledge base through read-alouds. When we read nonfiction aloud to students, they often note discrepancies between texts. Texts do not always present the "facts" the same way and may even contradict each other. The discussions about the contradictions help students to become critical readers. Finally, nonfiction texts can be a catalyst for literacy (Caswell & Duke, 1998), drawing in reluctant readers and writers because the content is interesting to them.

NONFICTION IN SHARED READING AND INTERACTIVE READ-ALOUDS

Shared reading is a way to read books aloud with students that allows the students to participate interactively. Rather than a read-aloud straight through, an **interactive**

read-aloud (Smolkin & Donovan, 2001) allows for lots of discussion to take place during the reading. If charts, big books, basal anthologies containing nonfiction selections, or photocopies of articles are used, students can read aloud along with the teacher.

Students will have questions, comments, and connections with other media (books, magazine, television programs) as the nonfiction text is read. An effective teacher will use an interactive style of reading and discussion that capitalizes on students' curiosity and wonderings to make the experience of the text deeper and more complete. This is how students will be able to build their vocabulary and background knowledge, which is crucial to their comprehension of all kinds of texts.

For example, during an interactive read-aloud, the teacher should be modeling and scaffolding an understanding of how texts have links between and within sentences. In the text *Sunken Treasure,* (Gibbons, 1988), the sentence "Divers descend and crewmembers lower baskets over the side to them" contains an example of a link within a sentence. The teacher can stop and explain briefly that "descend" and "lower" are linked in this sentence and that "lower" provides the meaning for "descend."

Teachers can also model summarizing. First, you read a bit of the text. This is from Gibbon's book *Beacons of Light: Lighthouses* (1990) : "Waves thrash and winds swirl, tossing a ship about in the darkness. Then, in the distance, a light appears. It flashes three times, disappears, then flashes again. On board, the ship's crew recognizes that this is a lighthouse signal. It is telling them to veer away from something hidden beneath the water. The captain locates a rocky ledge on his chart and uses the light signal to plot their position." Then you need to signal to the students that you are not reading anymore, but rather you are now thinking aloud. You might put the book in your lap or put your hand over the text. Then say something like, "Okay, I see. The light tells the ship to stay away from rocks underneath the water. It's good to stop and make sure you understand what you've read by telling it back to yourself in your own words."

By pointing out the features of nonfiction you're reading aloud, you give students a chance to see how these features can be used to understand the ideas in the text. For example, if a book has pictures with captions, you can point out which captions go with which pictures and how the captions give you information about the picture. Headings and subheadings are also useful features to point out. Once students understand that headings and subheadings tell them the main idea or topic of the text that follows, they will be more likely to read and use them to help themselves to focus on the important parts.

Creating mental imagery and using analogies are two strategies for promoting comprehension that can be modeled during an interactive read aloud. Petty's book, *Pandas,* shows a close-up of a newborn panda and the text says, "The babies are the size of kittens." You can help students to better understand how small newborn pandas really are by saying, "Hold out your hands and cup them together. Imagine a baby panda nestled in your hands. That's how small they are when they're born. Amazing, isn't it?" Later the book says, "The young panda is fully grown toward the end of its second year. It is over 220 lb in weight and about five and a half feet tall when it stands upright." Here you can show students how tall five and half feet is by telling them how tall you are and making the analogy or by showing them on a wall chart that you use for measuring the students' height.

Inferring or inferencing can be modeled when the text and what you already know can be put together into a hypothesis. In Gibbons's book, *Fire! Fire!*, the text says, "A man is trapped. A ladder tower is swung into action. The man is rescued quickly." The illustration shows a six-story apartment building. You might say, "I think that if the building is too tall, the ladder might not reach the person who is trapped. That must be when they use those trampoline things. Let's see if the text tells us." In this case, the text doesn't tell what happens with taller buildings, but the hypothesis can be pursued by finding and reading other resources that might answer the question.

Teachers also need to model using fix-up strategies when comprehension breaks down. For example, sometimes when you're reading aloud, you may make a mistake. It's good to acknowledge that mistake aloud and explain how you're going to go back and reread so that you can be sure the text makes sense. Also, when you've read aloud a fairly complex passage, stop and think aloud about your comprehension process. "Did I understand that right? Let's see . . . ."

All these comprehension strategies should be modeled, though not in every read-aloud. Eventually, your students will interrupt the reading to make similar sorts of comments. Your job then is to validate their use of the strategies and praise them for their efforts to make sense of what is being read. You also want to ask them to reflect on their comprehension in a similar fashion during guided reading sessions and independent or partner reading. You also need to be sure to expose your students to a variety of types of nonfiction.

TYPES OF NONFICTION TO READ ALOUD

Because there are different kinds of nonfiction, it is important to read aloud from a variety of them, partly so that you can demonstrate the different features they have and the different ways they can be read. Short magazine articles can be read in their entirety. Books with indexes and tables of contents can be read selectively, depending on the kind of information you're looking for, or they can be read cover to cover if you're hoping to get some background knowledge on a subject you don't know much about yet. Encyclopedic kinds of books especially lend themselves to selective reading. Question and answer books like *Do Stars Have Points? Questions and Answers About Stars and Planets* by Berger and Berger (1998) can be read selectively also. Informational alphabet books such as *Amazon Alphabet* by Jordan and Jordan (1996) lend themselves to cover-to-cover reading because it can be a great fun to predict what will be the featured subject of each letter. Later, alphabet books can be used selectively to go back and reread the parts the class is most interested in hearing again.

Different books also use different expository text structures (see Figure 9.1). As you read aloud, you can point out the places where the books use these text structures to achieve their purposes.

NONFICTION IN GUIDED READING

Because basal readers contain so little nonfiction (Hoffman et al., 1994), it is especially important to find and use nonfiction texts during guided reading lessons. If your school has a guided reading book room, actively seek to have an equal number of nonfiction and fiction titles. If you collect multiple copies of books for your own instructional use, be sure to include nonfiction. If your budget is limited and the basal is all you have, use magazine articles from magazines like *Ranger Rick*. The following is a list of magazines that include nonfiction articles written for children:

> *ASK (Arts and Sciences for Kids)* *www.cobblestonepub.com*
> *Kids Discover* *www.kidsdiscover.com*
> *National Geographic Kids* *www.nationalgeographic.com/ngkids/*

Figure 9.1   Expository Text Structures

Description: Authors provide lists and examples to describe the characteristics, features, or traits of a person, place, or thing. Metaphor and simile are also used to describe. Seymour Simon, in *Whales*, (1989) compares the length of a humpback whale with the length a large bus.

Sequence: Authors write about certain kinds of phenomena sequentially when it is important to show the order in which something happens. For example, history is often written in chronological order. Life cycles of animals and plants need to be written about sequentially. *Desert Giant: The World of the Saguaro Cactus* by Bash (1989) uses sequence to describe the life cycle of the saguaro cactus.

Compare and Contrast: Authors use comparison and contrast when they want to describe the similarities and differences among people, places, or things. Sometimes visuals are used to illustrate the comparison and contrast. Gail Gibbons, in her book *Frogs,* compares frogs and toads using diagrams.

Cause and Effect and Problem and Solution: Authors often use these structures together. *A River Ran Wild,* by Lynne Cherry, describes in detail the causes of pollution and its effect on the river. She also describes the pollution as a problem and how the river was cleaned up as the solution.

Combination of Structures: Most texts do not use just one text structure. For example, a book describing the life cycle of a butterfly will use both sequence and description. Another common combination is description and compare and contrast. *Christmas in the Big House, Christmas in the Quarters* by McKissack and McKissack (1994) uses both sequence and compare and contrast as it shows the ways that Christmas is celebrated by the white people in the plantation house and by the slaves who worked the plantation.

Mixed Genre: Some authors combine a fictional narrative with information. Children enjoy the *Magic School Bus* books by Joanna Cole and the *Magic Tree House* books by Mary Pope Obsorne, which combine a fantasy story structure with fact. Historical fiction uses historical facts to support a fictional narrative. Biography employs a narrative structure to tell the story of someone's life.

Nonlinear Structures: Books published by Dorling Kindersley often have a nonlinear structure. There are short paragraphs, extended pieces of text, pictures with captions, time lines, and diagrams combined on a page. The text can be read in any order and seems to invite the reader to skip around in a hypertextual sort of way. From my observation, when children read this sort of text, they often concentrate on the pictures and sample the text itself in a highly selective way.

Ranger Rick www.nwf.org/kidspubs/rangerrick/

Sports Illustrated for Kids www.sikids.com

Time for Kids, Big Picture Edition for grades K–1, News Scoop Edition for grades 2–3 www.timeforkids.com/TFK/class/index.html

Weekly Reader www.weeklyreader.com

Zoobooks www.zoobooks.com

When students read nonfiction in guided reading lessons, you can use the features of nonfiction to guide the lesson. For example, to introduce the book, begin with a picture walk of the book, but also notice and read aloud any headings. Look at the table of contents to anticipate what the children will be reading about in the book. As a follow-up to their reading of the text, ask them to respond to the reading by using the index to find their favorite part of the book. The next day you can revisit the book and concentrate on one section of the book. Talk together to determine which ideas were most important and use these ideas to form a verbal summary.

In a guided reading leveled library there should be a wide selection of books, including nonfiction book sets.

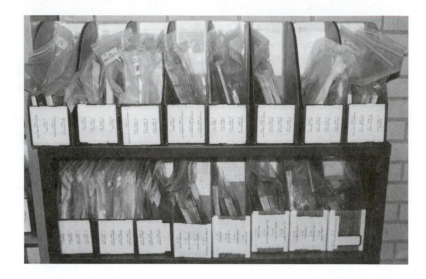

NONFICTION IN INDEPENDENT READING

Nonfiction books need to have a prominent place in your classroom library. You should strive to have nearly equal numbers of nonfiction and fiction books. Have your students organize the books into categories that interest them. The books can then be stored in baskets with labels that the students make. This increases their ownership of the classroom library and facilitates their search for books.

Children are also drawn to books that are displayed with their covers facing outward, as they are in bookstores. Rain gutters are an inexpensive way to increase the amount of space you have to display books this way.

Children should be encouraged to read independently in a wide variety of genres. You can model this for them by what you read aloud. This also gets and keeps them interested in nonfiction, because children gravitate toward the books the teacher has read aloud (Robinson, Larsen, Haupt, & Mohlman, 1997). Their literary diets can also be tracked by having them record the genre on a simple reading log. They can either color code the book by coloring a square on the reading log or write N, F, C, or P for nonfiction, fiction, combination, or poetry.

 ### WRITING NONFICTION

In writing workshop, teachers encourage young children to write about what they know, which often turns out to be personal narratives about the children's lives. Personal narrative is a form of nonfiction writing, but it is only a small fraction of the nonfiction writing realm. In a survey of the instructional practices of primary teachers who are considered effective by their supervisors and administrators, the researchers found that these teachers had their students write mostly stories, responses to reading, and journal entries (Pressley, Rankin, and Yokoi, 1995), but they didn't mention nonfiction specifically. Daniels (1990) believes:

> [T]he writing curriculum experienced by many American students as they go up through the grades is essentially: story, story, story, story, story, story, story, story, story, story, story, term paper. . . . A predictable outcome of this unbalanced cur-

riculum is that today's students write much better stories than they write reports, arguments, or essays. (p. 107)

In the primary grades, teachers can balance story writing with opportunities for young children to explore nonfiction writing. Keep in mind that most young children are not ready to learn the technical aspects of report writing like paragraphs and footnotes, but they are full of curiosity about real things, and they're definitely ready to explore them through reading, talking, writing, and drawing.

Sometimes it is the reluctant writers in the classroom who are especially drawn to nonfiction writing. Both boys and girls find nonfiction writing stimulating and a way to express themselves that doesn't involve writing a personal narrative. Some children are uncomfortable with personal narratives for various reasons, and when encouraged to write nonfiction, they enjoy immersing themselves in the particulars of a topic that fascinates them personally, but doesn't expose them emotionally.

When we integrate writing into all the areas of the curriculum, we are also integrating critical thinking. Thinking skills need not be taught in a vacuum as a separate skills program; it only makes sense to think, read, and write across all areas of the curriculum.

Teachers are just beginning to understand the value of having young children write various forms of nonfiction. There are several ways to infuse nonfiction writing into writing workshop and other curriculum areas. Before having young children write nonfiction independently, it is important to model nonfiction writing through various whole-class experiences.

Whole-Class Nonfiction Writing

You can begin a whole-class experience of writing nonfiction simply by choosing a topic that makes sense for your students in terms of what you're currently studying. For example, if you are studying insect life cycles, then you would model information writing with the whole class through **interactive writing, language experience approach,** or **shared writing.** You would be modeling a basic report—a traditional kind of nonfiction writing. This is where you do most of the actual teaching—through modeling.

- After reading a book (or part of a book) aloud to the class, deliberately close the book and set it aside (do this in an obvious way and explain why you're doing it).
- Then model writing what you learned or what was important about what you just read.
- Think aloud as you write.
- Make mistakes. Line out words and write in your revisions.
- Insert information using a caret.
- Change the order of the information using a numbering system.
- Throughout this process, let the students tell you things to write that they learned or thought were important. This process can take several days. When you're done, you have a text that can be:
  - Read as a chart
  - Typed and copied for all the children to have as reading material
  - Typed so that each child's contribution is on a separate page that they can illustrate, thus producing a class book
  - Displayed on a bulletin board in the classroom or hallway.

Figure 9.2   Language Experience Approach Text

ALL ABOUT PRAYING MANTISES

Written by Mrs. Read's Class

Praying mantises look like they are praying. (Montana)

But they aren't really saying their prayers. (Isaac)

They are just waiting to catch some bugs for food. (C. C.)

They stay up all the time and never rest. (Jordan)

Praying mantises don't drink nectar like bees. (Lauren)

They eat other insects and sometimes other praying mantises. (Mrs. Read)

Praying mantises snatch their food faster than you can see. (Colin)

They don't eat big grasshoppers when they are little. (Courtney)

They don't hunt their food. They wait for it. (Brooke)

Praying mantises are good climbers. (Laura)

They crawl in your house. (Christina)

They go on top of your roof. (Celestia)

Praying mantises have an exoskeleton on the outside instead of inside like us. (Eryn)

They shed their skin as soon as they come out of the egg case. (Jessica)

They shed every bit of their exoskeleton. (Michael)

When they come out of the egg case, they have a little string, kind of like a thread, attached to them. (Lorna)

When they come out of their egg case, they are orange. (C. C.)

They have to wait for their exoskeleton to harden. (Taylor)

When the mothers make their egg case, the fathers spread their wings and the mother makes a signal back to him. (Kyle)

The girls are bigger than the boys. (Ashlyn)

They bite hard. (Jimmy)

They bite until you bleed. (Edward)

Some kinds of praying mantises that are white. (Jonathon)

Some praying mantises are black. (Landon)

Some praying mantises are pink. (Brendan)

They have good camouflage. (Jason)

Once you've modeled this a few times (and I would do this at the beginning of any new unit of study), the children may be ready to begin writing information individually or in pairs.

When I taught in a multiage class of 6- and 7-year-olds, we studied insects, with a special focus on the praying mantises that lived in our school's native garden. We observed the praying mantises closely and read a high-quality nonfiction book about praying mantises called *Backyard Hunter* (Lavies, 1990). I read the book aloud slowly over about a week's time. Each day we put the book aside and the children told me what was important about what we'd read that day. I wrote it down in note format, sometimes using complete sentences and sometimes not. Each day we reviewed our notes from the day before. The day after we finished the book we reread all our notes. Then I turned to a fresh piece of chart paper and, through the language experience approach, each child dictated to me while the rest of the class listened (see Figure 9.2). Composing aloud as a group made it possible for the children to follow up on each other's statements so that the piece was basically coherent. The children's names are written next to their contributions.

When the mothers make their egg case,
the fathers spread their wings
and the mother makes a signal
back to him. (Kyle)

19

Kyle's page from our class book about praying mantises.

EXTENDING NONFICTION WRITING INTO INDEPENDENT AND SMALL-GROUP WORK

To provide children with a chance to write individually or in pairs about an information topic, it helps to choose an umbrella topic, such as weather, animals, rocks, insects, or ocean life. Any topic in the core curriculum can be used as an umbrella topic. Based on the resources you have available, you can determine some subtopics for children to choose from when they write alone or with a partner. Occasionally, you might want to let the children choose any topic for which you have resources. For example, you might have two children who want to study knights, two children who want to study cheetahs, and so on.

You can also choose a genre of writing to explore, such as biography, how-to writing, or persuasion. You need to make that genre authentic for your students by connecting it with something else you're studying or finding some other hook. For example, my second graders wrote book reviews, which allowed them to respond to literature (an important part of reading) and practice persuasive writing (the reviews were written for their peers to read and decide whether to read a particular book). We also wrote biographies by interviewing each other, which taps into the inherent social nature of learning.

When you have students work in pairs, you can choose partners or let the children choose a topic and then pair them up. When you decide how to pair up students, you need to keep in mind the social dynamics of your class and the academic strengths and weaknesses of your students. The advantage of pairing them yourself is that you can put good readers with less able readers or good writers with reluctant writers. You can also make sure that a socially problematic child isn't left out. If you pair them up, let them choose their subtopic after they've been paired so that it's a joint choice for the partners. If you want to increase the students' ownership of the topics, then you should have them choose a topic and then pair them up.

The first day of research can be done without reading anything. The children can begin by writing what they already know about their topic. Meanwhile, you can gather library books and other materials (Web pages, magazines, guest speakers, videos, etc.) that the children will need for their research. These materials, along with a folder for their writing, can be placed in hanging files or boxes so that the children can have easy access to them. With young children, it is helpful to scaffold the research process by preselecting books, magazines, and other materials that are written at a useful readability level.

When children start using their resource materials, give them time to read and look at pictures without any pressure to write or draw anything. The goal here is for them to internalize the information, become experts, and make the learning their own. Even the youngest students can glean information from pictures and draw or write about what they see.

When they begin to read their resource materials, volunteers or older students can spend time with younger students to read and reflect on source materials. You can also pair students so that strong readers are with beginning readers. If I only have a couple of students who need help reading their resources, I circulate among them reading aloud a paragraph or two and leaving them to write down what they thought was important.

Some teachers find it useful to help students to organize their writing by giving them notecards or pieces of paper that have been folded into fourths. On each card or section, the students write one sentence. Later, these can be organized before the sentences are keyboarded or rewritten in a book or report format. I have found that when students use a web to brainstorm, their writing is more organized, but not all students can predict what they will find interesting or want to write about. Students can also write their ideas on sticky notes, which can then be rearranged over and over again until the order is logical and pleasing to the writer. A research-proven effective organizational structure for report writing is the I-chart or inquiry chart (Viscovich, 2002). Figure 9.3 provides an example of an I-chart that students could create to organize their research on dinosaurs.

I often publish their nonfiction work by keyboarding it for them (correcting spelling, punctuation, and other errors of convention) and binding it as a book that they can illustrate. It's also possible to integrate art by having them produce a watercolor painting, clay figure, or other art form to go with their information.

Information Text Written by First Graders

The following is an example of nonfiction writing done by a pair of children, both first graders. One was a proficient reader and one was reading below grade level. Over the course of two weeks, Isaac read several books aloud to Landon, and they looked at pictures as they wrote. They tended to draw first and then write. Drawing was an important part of the writing process for both of them. They also engaged in various forms of dramatic play while reading and writing. They each wrote their own

Figure 9.3 I-Chart on Dinosaurs

Dinosaurs	When did dinosaurs live?	Why did the dinosaurs die?	What did dinosaurs eat?	Where did dinosaurs live?	Some cool dinosaurs we like.
What we know					
The World of Dinosaurs by Melvin Berger					
My Visit to the Dinosaurs by Aliki					
The Magic School Bus in the Time of Dinosaurs by Joanna Cole					
Video on dinosaurs					

parts and made no attempt to put the parts together in any way. I put together their separate pages of writing into a published book, and they each got their own copy to illustrate and keep. Each line break indicates a page break in their published book.

Knights by Isaac and Landon

Swords were used very often when a knight was knocked off his horse.

These are the helmets that the knights have. The helmets are made out of metal.

These are the weapons that the knights sometimes use.

Knights from stories fight dragons. . . . Well, sometimes. And save princesses.

Knights fight a lot. Sometimes on horseback and sometimes on the ground.

Knights save people from dragons in stories. In Saint George, George kills a dragon. Sir Lancelot fought good. King Arthur pulled the sword from the stone.

Charge! Many knights did tournaments. They use blunt weapons. It is a fake battle. They have feast after that. Excalibur can break rocks. Excalibur is the best sword. Excalibur can break any sword. King Arthur pulled Excalibur from the stone.

These are weapons that the knights use. But the knights still have the weapons.

These knights are fighting with each other.

One dragon is on the ground.

The kids practice being knights.

Addresses IRA Standard 4.1

Use students' interests, reading abilities, and backgrounds as foundations for the reading and writing program.

Addresses IRA Standard 4.2

Use a large supply of books, technology-based information, and nonprint materials representing multiple levels, broad interests, and cultural and linguistic backgrounds.

Page from Isaac and Landon's published book on knights.

These are weapons that the knights use. But the knights still have the weapons. And the shield.

These knights are fighting with each other.

Dragons in stories have fire to kill knights.
The knights have pretend war. They sit on horses and fight each other with lances.
Knights steal money from dragons. They give it to the poor.
One guy tied up another guy but the guys' swords fell into the ground.
People tell kids dragons and knights stories. They are tales.

INTEGRATING NONFICTION WRITING INTO THE WRITING WORKSHOP

Nonfiction writing can occur throughout the school day in math, science, and social studies. Children can choose to write nonfiction during writing workshop, and information writing should always be mentioned as one of the choices during a topic brainstorming lesson. ("Hmm, I could write about my dog and then I could write about dogs . . . or I'm really interested in knights. I have knight Legos and I like to read books about knights, so maybe I could write about that.") You can also make nonfiction the genre focus for a few weeks and require all students to write one piece of nonfiction.

Austin reads aloud his nonfiction book about birds. He wrote it during writing workshop.

A writing workshop unit focusing on nonfiction writing would form the basis for a variety of mini-lessons, such as these:

- Teach the idea of information writing as a way to teach others *what you know* and what you've learned. Some kids get stuck on the idea that they should only write the new information that they've learned.
- Semantic mapping as a way to brainstorm and organize information.
- I-charts as a way to organize information.
- Read a short passage, close the book, and write what you understand; then compare.
- Voice issues: Does it sound like me? Does it sound like the book? Have I accidentally copied?
- Features of nonfiction such as pronunciation keys, captions, headings, labels.
- How to look for books on your topic in the library, in an encyclopedia, or on the Web. The younger the students you work with, the more you need to scaffold this.
- Model modes of information writing as invitations; for example, the alphabet book, informational poster, question and answer book, *The Important Book* (Brown 1949), poetry, biography, and so on.

When students choose to write information, I like to reinforce their decision by choosing them to share it, encouraging them to publish it, and publicly praising them for choosing to try a new kind of writing.

One of the most useful sets of mini-lessons I have taught is on the conventions of nonfiction. I got the idea for this from *Strategies That Work* (Harvey & Goudvis, 2000). We began with three sheets of 8 by 11 copy paper folded in half and stapled with a blue copy paper cover. We wrote "Nonfiction Conventions" on the cover and then we began the process of reading lots of nonfiction books and noticing and discussing their special features. For example, we noticed right away that many nonfiction books have a Table of Contents, so we began ours on the front inside cover of our book. We went on to create examples of headings, subheadings, illustrations with labels, captions for pictures, subheadings, illustrations with labels, captions for pictures, comparisons such as the Statue of Liberty next to the Great Pyramid at Giza, pronouncing clues, bold words, glossary, index, and finally a blurb on the back cover of the book. For nearly every feature we noticed in the books we read, we created an example in our booklets. Every child made one and I made one right along with them. Through this activity they became very conscious of the features in the books they read and also began to put them into their nonfiction writing. One child wrote this for her blurb on the back of her nonfiction conventions booklet: "This book is about different nonfiction conventions. If you know about nonfiction conventions, you can write your very own nonfiction book. You could learn a lot."

Student work sample of Paisley's "volcano" writing.

A Volcano is so hot that it could melt a car. Hot lava can be 2100°F. The lava can flow at 6 miles per our. There are two kinds of lava pahoehoe and aa. Pahoehoe is smooth. aa is rough and Jaged

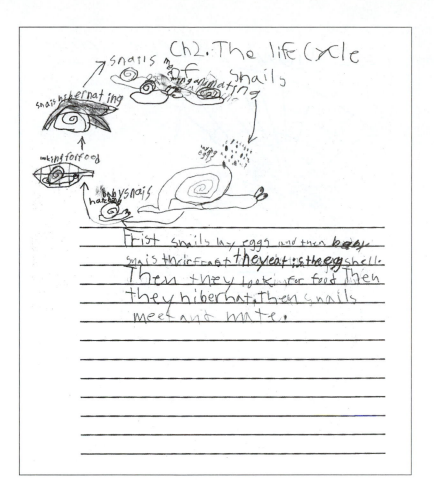

Daniel's life cycle of a "snail" writing sample.

Students Choose to Write Nonfiction in Writing Workshop

The following examples were written by second graders during writing workshop. They chose to write nonfiction and they chose their topic. Both of these students read multiple sources to gather information. Jaren's reading ability was below grade level, while Braden's was above grade level.

Out in Space by Jaren

When you're in space there is no gravity, but did you know the hottest planet is Mercury?

And the coldest planet is Pluto and Pluto is the farthest planet from the Sun.

The Sun is 27,000,000 degrees F. The crust of the Sun is ten million degrees F.

That's it for today.

What Is a Mammal? by Braden

A mammal does not lay eggs, except the monotremes, which are platypuses, and echidnas. A mammal gives birth to its baby like we do. It gives birth to live babies.

Jonathan's "How Spiders Eat" writing sample.

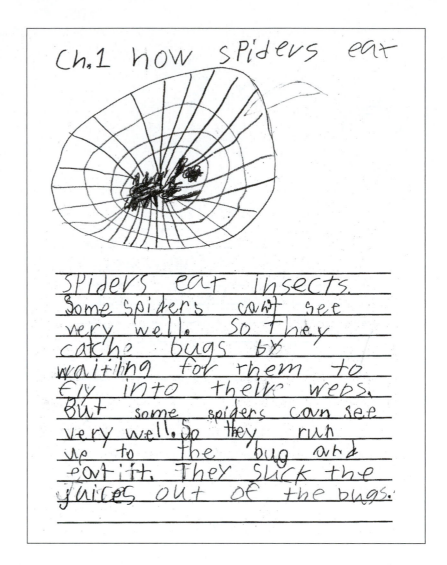

Ch. 1 how spiders eat

Spiders eat insects. Some spiders cant see very well. So they catch bugs by waiting for them to fly into their webs. But some spiders can see very well. So they run up to the bug and eat it. They suck the juices out of the bugs.

The world's smallest mammal discovered is a bat. The bat's name is the bumblebee bat. It is the size of a jelly bean and weighs as much as a penny. Can you believe that? It must have a really small wing span.

The second smallest mammal is a pygmy shrew. I am not sure how much a pygmy shrew weighs.

The biggest mammal weighs about three hundred thousand (300,000) pounds. That means that you would have to get 27 elephants and put them on a scale. Then you will have the weight of one big blue whale. Blue whales are amazing. They're like all mammals except they don't have hair. Most mammals grow hair, but the blue whale does not. Lots of animals and mammals have hair that live in the sea.

Why are insects not mammals? Insects are not mammals because all insects lay eggs, are not homothermic, which means warm-blooded, and all insects have six legs. So there is a big difference between mammals and insects.

Alex chose to write nonfiction during writing workshop.

Mammals also have endoskeletons (end-oe-skel-uh-tuns) and insects have exoskeletons. Endoskeleton means that they have meat around their bones. And exoskeleton means the opposite—the bones are around the meat.

Is a dolphin a fish? No, a dolphin is a sea mammal. It kind of looks like a fish, but it is not because it doesn't have gills and all fish have gills. The dolphins have lungs instead of gills.

INTEGRATING NONFICTION WRITING INTO MATH

Math is a form of communication that conveys what we are thinking about mathematical ideas. We want students to be able to actively construct their understanding of mathematics, connect new ideas to familiar ones, and develop new understandings about the interconnections among ideas. Even though we are teaching more than the abstractions of pure math in school, the curriculum often emphasizes the abstract more than the practical. When students only compute problems with numbers and mathematical symbols, they are only working with a small portion of mathematics. We need to provide them with personally meaningful contexts for using mathematical ideas and procedures. Furthermore, they need to communicate their thinking either through talking, writing, and/or drawing. Writing, in conjunction with talking and drawing, is a powerful way to lead kids to a deeper understanding of the concepts.

Metacognition, or thinking about our thinking, is also important for a deeper understanding of math. Writing is a way for your students to find out what they are thinking about math as a subject, about concepts they're learning, and about how they gather, organize, and clarify their thoughts. Writing is a way for the teacher to both develop and assess students' mathematical understanding. Before asking students to write for assessment purposes though, it is important to have them write about math for a variety of other reasons.

Writing Story Problems

I have students write their own story problems or math riddles to make math learning relevant to their lives. The numbers in the stories and riddles have meaning for them when they or their classmates have designed the problem. For example, when exploring two- and three-digit addition, I asked them to write story problems with two- and three-digit numbers. I wanted to know what kinds of things they deal with in real life that involve numbers that high. I found out that sometimes they think of these numbers realistically: "I have 90 Pokemon cards and my friend has 40. How many do we have all together?" But sometimes they think of these numbers abstractly and don't care what kind of object they write about using numbers that large. For example, "Roman has 800 fish and Shane has 100 fish. Shane gives Roman 80 fish and Roman gives Shane 80 fish. How many fish do they have left, in all?" Nevertheless, the students are motivated to write and solve these problems, knowing that their classmates will be solving them too.

Writing as an Extension of Math-Related Children's Literature

I use writing as an extension from children's literature that contains mathematical ideas. For example, in response to *Math Curse,* my students wrote story problems like those they encounter in real life.

❈ *This morning I got dressed in 5 minutes. It took me 10 minutes to eat breakfast. How many minutes did it take me to eat breakfast and get dressed?*

❈ *My sister is going to get a puppy and say it is 2 feet long and it grows 4 more feet. And in each foot is 12 inches. Then how many inches will he be?*

❈ *I am going to the dentist in 2 weeks. My cousins are coming in 5 weeks. How many days until I see my cousins?*

Table 9.1 lists books and Web sites that address mathematical concepts. Writing in response to these books can extend the students' understanding of the main concept.

Scaffolding Math Writing Using Sentence Frames

As part of our study of division, we read and discussed Pat Hutchins's *The Doorbell Rang*; I wrote a sentence frame on the board, "They each get _____ cookies. I figured it out by _____." The students copied the sentence frame or wrote their own sentence to tell their answer and, more importantly, how they arrived at their answer. I also encouraged them to draw a picture to go with their writing.

When I ask students to respond to a riddle or story problem, I find that it helps to use a sentence frame. It gives many students a starting place for their writing, but it is open ended enough to allow them to express their ideas in their own way. Some children don't need the frame and I do not require that they use it. I do require that they explain their thinking as fully as I think they can. Just as in writing workshop, I roam the room holding brief conferences. Many children need to discuss their thinking aloud before they can write it down, and by conferencing with them, I am able to draw their thinking out of them by asking questions and reflecting their answers back to them. The drawing that I ask them to do also serves as a way to clarify their thinking and provides an anchor for their writing. I don't make them do a literal, repre-

Table 9.1   Children's Literature and Math

Concept	Title	Author
Division	*The Doorbell Rang*	Pat Hutchins
Counting, size, comparison, and ratio	*Counting on Frank*	Rod Clement
Measurement	*Measuring Penny*	Loreen Leedy
Measurement	*How Big Is a Foot?*	Rolf Myller
Counting, patterns	*I Can Count the Petals on a Flower*	John and Stacey Wahl
Number sense	*How Much Is a Million?*	David M. Schwartz
Counting	*One Monkey Too Many*	Jackie French Koller
Money	*A Chair for My Mother*	Vera B. Williams
Money	*Alexander, Who Used to Be Rich Last Sunday*	Judith Viorst
Estimation	*Moira's Birthday*	Robert Munsch
Multiplication	*Two of Everything*	Lily Toy Hong
Place value	*Number Art: Thirteen 123s from Around the World*	Leonard Everett Fisher
Money	*"Smart" from Where the Sidewalk Ends*	Shel Silverstein
Measurement	*Inch by Inch*	Leo Lionni
Shapes, spatial sense	*Grandfather Tang's Story*	Ann Tompert
Addition	*Annie's One to Ten*	Annie Owen
Addition	*12 Ways to Get to 11*	Eve Merriam
Problem solving	*A Million Fish . . . More or Less*	Patricia McKissack
Measurement	*Twelve Snails to One Lizard: A Tale of Mischief and Measurement*	Susan Hightower
Shapes	*Architecture Shapes*	Michael J. Crosbie
Symmentry, geometry	*Reflections*	Ann Jonas
Addition and subtraction	*Rooster's Off to See the World*	Eric Carle
Addition and subtraction	*Splash*	Ann Jonas

Math Web Sites

www.enc.org/topics/across/lit

www.terc.edu/investigations/resources/html/ MathChildLit.html

illuminations.nctm.org/index_o.aspx?id=83

sci.tamucc.edu/%Eeyoung/literature.html

fcit.usf.edu/math/resource/bib.html

www.geocities.com/Heartland/Estates/4967/math.html

sentational drawing (because that can be distracting and time consuming), but rather I encourage the children to use circles, Xs, or whatever symbol they prefer to represent the objects in the problem. After all, what's algebra if not symbolic!

Writing Survey Questions

I want students to understand and experience writing about math that doesn't involve solving a problem. When we studied graphing, I asked students to write a survey question and collect data from the class. I began by modeling the process of thinking through how to word a question so that a limited number of answers was possible. I showed them how it would turn out if I asked too broad a question, such as what is your favorite movie? Then I showed them how I could narrow the range of possible answers by either writing a question that could only be answered with a yes or no, writing a question and providing a multiple-choice array of answers, or using a Likert-type scale of 1 through 5 or 1 through 10. I usually opted to model a multiple-choice question. I collected my data from the kids and then showed them how to take these raw data in the form of tally marks or whatever they chose to indicate answers and create a bar graph. I modeled how to create the scale, label the categories, and write a title for the graph. When I was done, I asked them lots of questions about the graph; these questions involved an overall interpretation of the graph and also focused on specific categories.

The next day they began the process of writing their questions, gathering the data from their classmates (or other classes), and recording it. It's a bit chaotic to have them all asking and answering each other's survey questions simultaneously; but it's also interesting to see how they manage the problem of knowing who they have asked and who they haven't asked, and they're so engaged in what they're doing that they behave very well. Sometimes I provide a class list for them so that they can keep track of who they have surveyed; other times I don't because the problem-solving opportunity is so real that I don't want to jump in with my own solution. The next day, after we have reviewed the parts of a graph, they graph the data and I again model how to create one. Finally, they write questions about their graph for the other students to answer. The graphs and their questions are displayed throughout the room, and the next day they read and record their answers to their classmates' questions. The thinking and writing that go into this week-long activity are invaluable.

Students can also be asked to write summary statements that require them to analyze and interpret the data they gathered. If the class gathers data over a period of time, such as daily temperatures, a line graph can be created and students can write questions or summary statements about the line graph.

Writing Fermi Questions

Fermi questions are named for Enrico Fermi, who liked to pose impossible mathematical questions and come up with approximate, but reasonable, answers. These kinds of questions can be a lot of fun for young children to explore concretely. After they have played around with ways to answer the question, they can write their answer and how they arrived at it. The students need to be encouraged to think of answers that come close, since Fermi questions really don't have any set answers. They also need to understand that their answers should be reasonable. Here are some examples of Fermi questions:

❀ *How many jelly beans could you hold in both your hands cupped together?*
❀ *How many jelly beans would it take to fill a gallon milk jug?*
❀ *How many steps will it take to walk across the classroom?*

🦋 *How many students could fit into this classroom if we took out all the furniture?*

🦋 *How many meals will you eat in a year? (Hyde and Bizar, 1989)*

For more on Fermi questions, see mathforum.org/workshops/sum96/interdisc/shiela1.html.

Assessing Students' Math Understanding

Assessing Students' Understanding of Math Concepts

I use writing to assess students' understanding of math concepts. For example, I have created a worksheet with doubles addition facts paired with their multiplication counterpart. For example, $6 + 6$ is paired with 6×2. They answer the problems. Then, at the bottom of the worksheet, is this question: "How are adding and multiplying alike?" They wrote things like these:

🦋 *Well, if I ask you what $6 + 6$ is then it has to be 12. So . . . it's 2 groups of six so it's $2 \times 6 = 12$.*

🦋 *If you count 5 twice you are multiplying and you do not know it. You are working on 2×5 and $5 + 5 =$.*

🦋 *Well, I know that all you have to do is add that number 2 times and you did multiplication like $5 + 5 = 10$. So that is just like doing $2 \times 5 = 10$.*

After introducing and studying division for about a week near the end of second grade, I also ask my students to write in response to the question "What is division?" This helps me to assess their understanding of division as a math concept. Here are a few of their answers:

🦋 *What is division? Division is dividing something equally. Division can be fractions too. It's how many times one number goes into another number. $8 \div 4 = 2$. When you divide you practically regroup. Regrouping is if you have a group of 4 and you break it into 2 groups. Division is also like splitting a pizza. If there are 4 people in your family and the pizza has 8 pieces you would first take 4 out of 8 so there are 4 left. So everybody would get 1 piece and there would be 4 more left and everybody would get one more piece. So everyone would get 2 pieces.*

🦋 *What is division? O.K. It was after supper and my big sister was over from Illinois. It was time for our 6:45 dessert. I got out the cookie jar. There were 3 cookies left and 4 of us. How could we divide the 3 cookies equally? You would cut each cookie into 4 quarters so we would each get 3 parts.*

Using Writing to Assess Students' Understanding of Math Processes

I use writing to assess students' understanding of a math process. Subtraction with regrouping is a difficult, but crucial, skill for second graders to learn. After we have been working on it for a couple of weeks, I ask them how they would solve the problem $63 - 35 = $ _____. I have gotten answers like this:

🦋 *First I checked to see if I need to borrow. I do so I cross out the six and write a 5 and I make the 3 a 13. Then I get 10 fingers and count up from 3 to 5 and I get 8. And then I go to the 5 and then take away 3 of the five and I get 28.*

Using Writing as an Overall Math Assessment

I use writing for overall assessment and general reporting to parents. I asked the students before a student educational progress (SEP) conference to write a letter to their parents telling them about some of the things they have learned this year in math. First we brainstormed the topics we had covered and then I set them free to write.

> *Dear Mom and Dad,*
>
> *I want you to know I have begun to learn algebra! I am going to show you some.*
>
> $4 + n = 9$
> $n = 5$ *and* $12 \div 2 = 6$
>
> *I love you!*

SCIENCE AND WRITING

Elementary teachers are fortunate to be able to integrate reading and writing with all areas of the curriculum. In fact, to fit everything into a packed school day, we must integrate. When integrating science and writing, I try not to use our writing workshop time when students should choose their own topics. Science writing should happen during another time of day, which could be called inquiry, science workshop, research, or anything that conveys to students and parents that this is a time of day when the class will be focusing on science.

Shannon writes "What I Have Learned About Rocks."

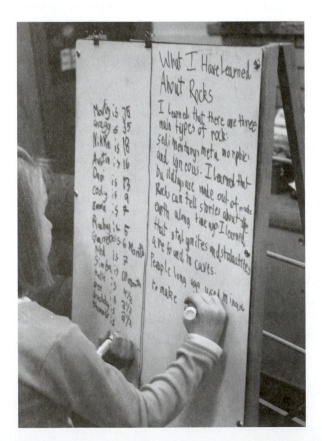

The way we set up the writing moment is crucial. We cannot ask students to write in a vacuum, but if we bring in a frog or leaf, boil a pot of water, or scrape some cheek cells onto a slide and put it under the microscope, and *then* ask our students to write, we have given them something real to focus on. This doesn't mean the writing will be easy to do and wonderful to read every time, but it does mean that there is true content to be grappled with. We want our students to be able to observe, collect data, predict, analyze, and communicate about scientific artifacts or phenomena. These processes of scientific inquiry need to be structured so that students are not left to flounder and feel frustrated. If we provide structure and guidance, students can think about something, explain it to themselves, and communicate it to others. When this occurs, they have truly internalized that knowledge and claimed it as their own.

In the early grades, I focus on teaching students to be scientists who write from observation. We are confronted daily with the phenomena that scientists study, and yet we don't often take the time to reflect on them. Learning logs provide a place for students to draw and write in response to a variety of situations that cause them to think about scientific ideas or phenomena, such as these:

- Predict what they might learn from a read-aloud of *Red-Eyed Tree Frog* by Joy Cowley
- Write what they learned after hearing and seeing *Red-Eyed Tree Frog* by Joy Cowley
- After a floating and sinking experiment, write about the process of creating a clay boat and filling it with pennies
- Draw and write about a leaf gathered from a neighborhood walk
- Draw and write daily over a period of a few weeks about the growth of a bean seed

The artifacts and phenomena that children can observe are numerous. Simple field trips to the playground can be fodder for writing about and drawing what they have observed. Students can draw and write about:

Tree bark, leaves, and the like

A Hula-Hooped area of grass

Insects

The heat of the blacktop compared to the heat of the grass

The sky

Shadows

Cardinal directions (When I look north I see . . .)

Puddles

Heart rate after running the perimeter of the playground

Artifacts can be brought into the classroom for close observations. For example,

Feather

Frog, insect, spider, fish, or other creature

Classmate's pet, such as a guinea pig

Fossils

Shells

Batteries and bulbs

Electromagnet

Magnets

Pond water

Onion skin

Alexis wrote: Coal rock doesn't look like rock. Coal rock burns. Scientists say coal rock is rock. Coal looks black and brownish.

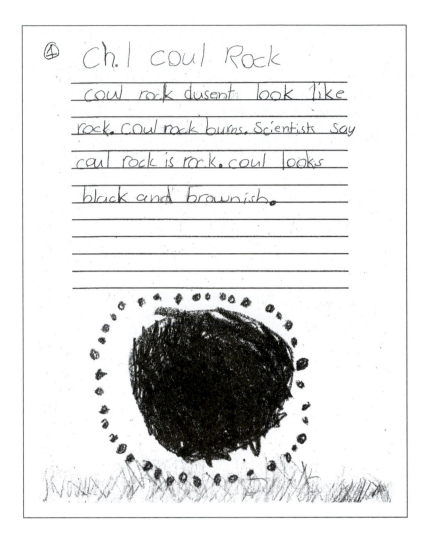

When students are writing, it can be helpful to provide a prompt. For example, after exploring the school grounds looking for objects of certain shapes or colors, students can finish the sentence, "I think things outside are green (or brown, or whatever color) because . . . . " After a session where students focus on using their senses of sight, hearing, smell, and feel, they might write about which sense they think is most important and why. After collecting hitchhiker-type seeds on socks that are worn over their shoes, students can write about what kind of seeds they collected, why they think seeds are important, or what they learned about how seeds travel. I like to provide two or three prompts for students to choose from; choice is always crucial for keeping motivation high.

Ellen Doris, in her book *Doing What Scientists Do: Children Learn to Investigate Their World* (1991), recommends the use of worksheets that are both structured and yet open ended. The worksheets she uses are designed by the teacher (not a publisher) to fit the nature of the activity, help define the activity, and provide the children with a way to approach a task. As she says, "simply sending them off to observe can be too open-ended or vague for some children. The worksheet can suggest a way to proceed without narrowing children's responses to 'one right answer.' It can say, 'Tell

Jared chose to read nonfiction for independent reading.

your name and what you looked at. Draw what you see in this space. Notice some things and write about them here'" (pp. 31–32). Though recording their observations is important, she stresses that the finished product is only one aspect of the work of science. Because writing and drawing are demanding tasks, especially for young children, they need to have time just to look. As teachers, we need to make sure that we provide these times for looking and sharing, free from the requirement to record; otherwise students will equate scientific observation with filling in a worksheet, which, even if the worksheet is open ended, is not the overall message we want children to receive about science.

Science Meeting and Seminars

When you have students create a product, it is important to provide a way for students to publish their work through sharing or display. When they know they will be sharing their findings with an audience, students feel that there is a reason for recording their observations other than obeying the teacher. Rather than calling it sharing, the way we do when it follows writing workshop, you can have a science meeting or seminar where students present their findings. This isn't just cute; it's a way to teach students that scientists have official ways that they share their research with other scientists. Doris explained it to a group of 5- and 6-year-olds this way:

> After scientists have been working on a project for a while, they might go to a meeting. Sometimes scientists work on their own or with a team and sometimes they get together with lots of other scientists at a meeting. Sometimes the meeting has a special name, like "seminar" or "symposium" or "conference." We'll call ours a "Science Meeting." (Doris, 1991, p. 65)

Science meetings need to be actively managed by the teacher so that children understand how to behave respectfully while others share their work and how to respond appropriately. The teacher models how to do this over and over, and in some ways these behaviors are more important than the content of what is shared. Having a predictable format is also important. Young children will be better able to think, talk, and pay attention when they know that the meeting won't last longer than a specified amount of time—they won't miss recess or lose any free time.

Interactive Writing and Science

Young children, especially kindergartners and first graders, need to have writing modeled for them frequently. A powerful way to model, while also involving the students in the writing, is called **interactive writing.** A thorough description of interactive writing can be found in chapter 8.

Briefly, interactive writing is a form of shared writing in which students come to the easel and write letter sounds, parts of words, and whole words. "Sharing the pen" with students is the most obvious way that interactive writing differs from shared writing, but it also differs from shared writing in its emphasis on involving students in all parts of the writing process: writing the easy-to-hear sounds of our language; writing whole, memorized sight words; using left-to-right and top-to-bottom directionality; keeping handwriting proportional to already written text; deciding the purpose of a text; deciding what to write; rereading to check their writing; summarizing what was written; revisiting the text to notice particular details; and extending the writing to its intended purpose (e.g., a recipe could be used to cook with the students).

Interactive writing can be used with the whole class or a small group who needs to focus on particular skills. For science, whole-class interactive writing is best because, through the process of creating a text using interactive writing, you build a community of learners with a common core of knowledge and the desire to explore together new ideas and concepts.

Specifically with science writing, interactive writing can be used to teach students how to take notes, label drawings, describe something in detail, organize information into charts or diagrams, and compare and contrast. Writing is also modeled as a tool for inquiry. As an example, before exploring the schoolyard for certain shapes or colors, the students can write their predictions of what they might find. While outside, they keep a tally sheet and write a few words to describe what shapes and colors they saw. Upon returning to class or the next day, they can create a chart that includes all the things they saw and also write an analytical statement about them, such as "We saw lots of green leaves because it is spring."

Writing is a flexible tool to support science inquiry. It can be used in all content areas, including social studies.

SOCIAL STUDIES AND WRITING

Good social studies instruction assumes that writing will be a part of instruction and assessment. Answering the questions at the end of a textbook chapter is not the best way to incorporate writing, however. The subject matter for discussing and writing should be much more than a textbook. Quality children's literature and powerful ideas are the basis for meaningful classroom discourse. Students should be engaging in "cooperative learning, construction of models or plans, dramatic recreations of historical events, role-play and simulation, interviews of family members, and data collection in the local community" (Brophy and Alleman, 1996, p. 48). With young children especially, the writing need not be the major part of social studies learning, but it is a way to record learning, process an idea, or explore possibilities.

Storypath (McGuire, 1999) is a structure for learning social studies concepts through story, dramatic play, reading, writing, talking, and listening. Each unit lasts two to three weeks, but doesn't take over the entire day. Writing workshop, reading workshop, and math continue as usual, with Storypath allocated to a separate time of day. For example, in a kindergarten unit on "Neighborhood," the teacher reads a story about a neighborhood or a description of a neighborhood setting, and the class adds their own ideas about what a neighborhood should be like. Then the students create a mural representing their neighborhood. They populate their neighborhood with characters, including themselves and their families, and the teacher leads them in some shared writing about their neighborhood. A social context is built through having the students experience the everyday events that might occur.

Eventually, the teacher introduces a problem, or "critical incident," such as the discovery of litter in the neighborhood. The students discuss what to do about it, make decisions, and act accordingly. They can also explore ideas like what to do when a new student comes to the classroom and how to incorporate this new neighbor into their neighborhood. Each time a problem is encountered and solved, the teacher leads the class in shared or interactive writing about it. These writings can be compiled into a book of writing and photographs that can be sent home with the children to share with their families. Sometime during the unit, it may be appropriate to go on a field trip or invite a guest speaker to the class to find out more about the situation. The unit ends with a positive experience such as a ceremony, festival, or parade.

Storypath also has units that explore other social studies concepts and incorporate other kinds of writing. For example, in "Main Street," the setting is a business district or shopping mall, the characters are the employers and employees of the businesses, and the plot involves the problems of public safety and the needs of the workers. Writing activities include writing advertisements to persuade people to come and shop at their stores.

Other language activities that can be integrated into a Storypath unit are developing word banks, writing poetry about the setting, writing descriptive paragraphs about the setting, drawing and writing postcards, writing character biographies, introducing characters to the class, writing about significant events in characters' lives, writing captions for pictures depicting events in the history of the context, creating a time line, writing flyers or newsletters, interviewing an expert regarding the critical incident, writing a persuasive speech in response to the critical incident, and creating advertising flyers or invitations for the culminating event.

 ## CONCLUSIONS

Writing can and should be incorporated into all areas of the curriculum. In a way, writing is not a separate curriculum; however, writing workshop is the main way that children will learn to write fluently. Throughout the school day, we need to be careful not to let narrative writing dominate the curriculum. The way to keep the writing curriculum balanced is to focus on the various kinds of nonfiction writing that can be part of math, science, social studies, health education, and all other parts of the curriculum.

 ## SUGGESTED ACTIVITIES TO EXTEND YOUR LEARNING

1. Use a nonfiction book as the basis for a language experience approach lesson. Develop a multiday plan for how you will read the book and how you will take notes with the students, and conclude with having the students dictate the contents of a nonfiction book.

2. Write down the steps for solving a word problem or doing long division. Notice your thought process as you do this, and analyze the benefits for students of writing about math.

3. Bring reality into the classroom related to a subject of study in science or social studies. Set up an observation table where students can go in ones or twos to observe and write about the objects. When everyone has observed and written, hold a science conference so that students can share.

4. Take students on a field trip to the playground. Have them pick a place to sit. Give them a loop of string (or a Hula-Hoop) to define the space that they will observe and write about. Model first using your own space and hoop so that students understand how much detail they can see and write about in their defined space. Follow up with a science conference as described in this chapter.

 *REFERENCES*

Brophy, J., & Alleman, J. (1996). *Powerful social studies for elementary students*. New York: Harcourt Brace.

Caswell, L., & Duke, N. (1998). Non-narrative as a catalyst for literacy development. *Language Arts, 75,* 108–117.

Daniels, H. (1990). Developing a sense of audience. In T. Shanahan (Ed.), *Reading and writing together: New perspectives for the classroom* (pp. 99–125). Norwood, MA: Christopher-Gordon.

Doris, E. (1991). *Doing what scientists do.* Portsmouth, NH: Heinemann.

Harvey, S., & Goudvis, A. (2000). *Strategies that work: Teaching comprehension to enhance understanding.* York, ME: Stenhouse.

Hoffman, J., McCarthey, S., Abbott, J., Christian, C., Corman, L., Curry, C., et al. (1994). So what's new in the basals? A focus on first grade. *Journal of Reading Behavior, 26,* 47–73.

Hyde, A. A., & Bizar, M. (1989). *Thinking in context: Teaching cognitive processes across the elementary school curriculum.* New York: Longman.

Kamberelis, G. (1998). Relations between children's literacy diets and genre development: You write what you read. *Literacy Teaching and Learning, 3*(1), 7–53.

Kamil, M. (1994, April). *Matches between reading instruction and reading task demands.* American Educational Research Association.

Lauber, P. (1992). The evolution of a science writer. In E. B. Freeman & D. G. Person (Eds.), *Using nonfiction trade books in the elementary classroom: From ants to zeppelins* (pp. 11–16). Urbana, IL: National Council of Teachers of English.

McGuire, M. (1999). *Storypath foundations: An innovative approach to social studies.* Chicago: Everyday Learning.

Pappas, C. (1991). Fostering full access to literacy by including information books. *Language Arts, 68,* 449–461.

Pressley, M., Rankin, J., & Yokoi, L. (1995). *A survey of instructional practices of primary teachers nominated as effective in promoting literacy* (Reading research report no. 41). Athens, GA: Universities of Georgia and Maryland, National Reading Research Center.

Read, S. (2001). "Kid mice hunt for their selfs": First and second graders writing research. *Language Arts, 78*(4), 333–342.

Robinson, C., Laresen, J., Haupt, J., & Mohlman, J. (1997). Picture book selection behaviors of emergent readers: Influence of genre, familiarity, and book attributes. *Reading Research and Instruction, 36,* 287–304.

Schmidt, W., Caul, J., Byer, J., & Buchmann, M. (1984). Content of basal selections: Implications for comprehension instruction. In G. G. Duffy, L. R. Roehler, & J. Mason (Eds.), *Comprehension instruction: Perspectives and suggestions* (pp. 144–162). New York: Longman.

Smolkin, L., & Donovan, C. (2001). The contexts of comprehension: The information book read aloud, comprehension acquisition, and comprehension instruction in a first-grade classroom. *Elementary School Journal, 102* (2), 97–122.

Viscovich, S. (2002). The effects of three organizational structures on the writing and critical thinking of fifth graders. In P. E. Linder, M. B. Sampson, J. R. Dugan, & B. Brancato (Eds.), *Celebrating the faces of literacy: The twenty-fourth yearbook of the College Reading Association.* (pp. 44–67). Readyville, TN: College Reading Association.

Yopp, R., & Yopp, H. (2000). Sharing informational text with young children. *Reading Teacher, 53*(5), 410–423.

Children's Literature

Aliki. (1985). *My visit to the dinosaurs.* New York: Harper & Row.

Bash, B. (1989). *Desert giant: The world of the saguaro cactus.* Boston: Little, Brown.

Berger, M. (1996). *The world of dinosaurs.* New York: Newbridge.

Berger, M., & Berger, G. (1998). *Do stars have points? Questions and answers about stars and planets.* New York: Scholastic.

Brown, M. W. (1949). *The important book.* New York: Harper & Row.

Carle, E. (1972). *Rooster's off to see the world.* New York: Scholastic.

Cherry, L. (1992). *A river ran wild.* New York: Harcourt Brace.

Clement, R. (1991). *Counting on Frank.* Milwaukee, WI: Gareth Stevens.

Cole, J. (1994). *The magic school bus in the time of the dinosaurs.* New York: Scholastic.

Cowlcy, J. (1999). *The red-eyed tree frog.* NY: Scholastic.

Crosbie, M. (1993). *Architecture shapes.* New York: Wiley.

Fisher, L. (1982). *Number art: Thirteen 123s from around the world.* New York: Four Winds Press.

Gibbons, G. (1984). *Fire! fire!* New York: HarperCollins.

Gibbons, G. (1988). *Sunken treasure.* New York: HarperTrophy.

Gibbons, G. (1990). *Beacons of light: Lighthouses.* New York: Morrow.

Gibbons, G. (1993). *Frogs.* New York: Scholastic.

Hightower, S. (1997). *Twelve snails to one lizard: A tale of mischief and measurement.* New York: Simon & Schuster.

Hong, L. (1993). *Two of everything.* Morton Grove, IL: A. Whitman.

Hutchins, P. (1986). *The doorbell rang.* New York: Greenwillow.

Jordan, M., & Jordan, T. (1996). *Amazon alphabet.* New York: Kingfisher.

Jonas, A. (1987). *Reflections.* New York: Greenwillow.

Jonas, A. (1995). *Splash.* New York: Greenwillow.

Koller, J. (1999). *One monkey too many.* New York: Harcourt Brace.

Lavies, B. (1990). *Backyard hunter: The praying mantis.* New York: Dutton.

Leedy, L. (1997). *Measuring Penny.* New York: Henry Holt.

Lionni, L. (1960). *Inch by inch.* New York: Aston-Honor.

McKissack, P. (1992). *A million fish . . . More or less.* New York: Knopf.

McKissack, P., & McKissack, F. (1994). *Christmas in the big house, Christmas in the quarters.* New York: Scholastic.

Merriam, E. (1993). *12 ways to get to 11.* New York: Simon and Schuster.

Munsch, R. (1987). *Moira's birthday.* Toronto: Annick Press.

Myller, R. (1991). *How big is a foot?* New York: Dell.

Owen, A. (1988). *Annie's one to ten.* New York: Knopf.

Petty, K. (1991). *Pandas.* Hauppauge, NY: Barron's.

Schwartz, D. (1985). *How much is a million?* New York: Lothrop, Lee & Shepard.

Silverstein, S. (1974). *Where the sidewalk ends.* New York: HarperCollins.

Simon, S. (1989). *Whales.* New York: Morrow.

Tompert, A. (1990). *Grandfather Tang's story.* New York: Crown.

Viorst, J. (1978). *Alexander, who used to be rich last Sunday*. New York: Atheneum.

Wahl, J., & Wahl, S. (1976). *I can count the petals on a flower.* Reston, VA: National Council of Teachers of Mathematics.

Williams, V. (1982). *A chair for my mother.* New York: Greenwillow.

Reading Assessment

John A. Smith

10

Using Assessment Data to Guide Daniel's Reading Instruction

When I was a Title 1 reading teacher, a third-grade classroom teacher in my school asked me to test her student Daniel, who she felt was falling behind in reading. I happily agreed to help and began the testing by giving Daniel the first-grade word list from my informal reading inventory (IRI) reading test and asking him to read the words aloud to me. This list was easy for him (independent level). He only missed one word. Then I had him read the second-grade word list to me. He struggled with four or five words. This placed him at the instructional level for second-grade word recognition. When I asked Daniel to read the third-grade word list aloud to me, he missed 11 words, placing him in the frustration level. I concluded that his sight word recognition was at the second-grade level, approximately 1 year behind his classroom grade level.

Next, I handed Daniel first- to third-grade level reading passages from my IRI reading test and asked him to read the passages aloud to me and answer comprehension questions about them. I recorded the words he misread. Daniel's performance on the reading passages was very similar to his performance on the word lists. First-grade reading was easy; third-grade reading was too hard. Daniel was reading at the second-grade level. However, when I administered the listening comprehension part of the IRI to Daniel, he easily answered the comprehension questions through the sixth-grade level passage.

Based on these IRI data, I created a bar graph of Daniel's reading ability (Figure 10.1) to share with his classroom teacher. Using the bar graph, I pointed out to her that Daniel was a year below grade level in sight word recognition, oral reading fluency, and reading comprehension. I also pointed out that his listening comprehension level was very high, meaning that his vocabulary and background knowledge were very strong. This profile of Daniel's reading abilities suggested that his reading problems centered around his lower ability to recognize and read words fluently. I also suggested to Daniel's teacher that, if she worked carefully with Daniel and his word recognition and reading fluency levels improved, his reading comprehension level would improve, because it was his word recognition and reading problems that were constraining his comprehension level. Daniel knew the word meanings, as evidenced by his high listening comprehension level on the IRI.

Figure 10.1 Graph of Daniel's Reading Ability

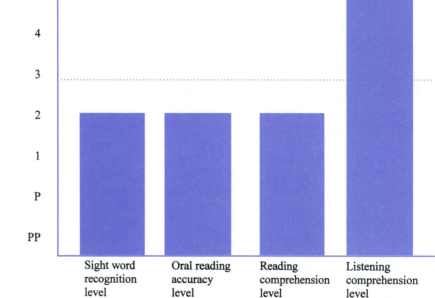

Comments: Daniel's IRI shows that he has very good vocabulary and background knowledge, as suggested by his strong listening vocabulary score. However, his sight word recognition and oral reading accuracy levels are below grade level. I suggest more instructional time and attention to Daniel's ability to recognize and apply common spelling patterns and to his oral reading fluency. When these areas improve, I expect that his reading comprehension will improve as well.

Daniel's word recognition and reading fluency problems were holding back his overall progress in reading.

Accordingly, Daniel's classroom teacher and I worked out a plan for her to (1) focus Daniel's phonics instruction on those particular spelling patterns he hadn't yet mastered, as identified by the IRI, (2) connect Daniel's phonics instruction directly to his reading of connected text by having him underline spelling patterns on photocopies of his reading group texts, and (3) increase the amount of time that Daniel received phonics and fluency instruction each day through participation in an "extra" reading skills group each day.

The data-based instructional intervention plan that Daniel's classroom teacher and I developed was successful, and Daniel was able to catch up and keep up with his classmates. He was never again referred to or needed support from the Title 1 reading program.

I begin the school year each August with the goal that all my students will leave my classroom in June reading at or above grade level. Having this goal is extremely important because, when some of my students begin falling behind, I know that I will have to make some instructional changes, such as providing differing kinds of instruction and extra amounts of instruction for my struggling readers, if I am to accomplish my goal.

I assess each student during the first 2 weeks of school with quick and reliable reading tests and note their levels of alphabet knowledge, phonemic awareness, phonological knowledge, and oral reading fluency. I give follow-up assessments in these areas each month and chart each student's growth. This testing allows me to identify which students are reading well and which will need extra support. These assessment data also allow me to determine the specific reading skills that I need to teach (Reutzel & Cooter, 2003). Some students will need extra support with phonemic awareness and phonics. Others will need extra attention to building their oral language skills.

This process of gathering early, ongoing assessment data on my students, analyzing classroom trends in their reading achievement, and providing extra instructional support where needed is known as the *assessment–instruction cycle*. Over the years, this linking of instruction to assessment data has enabled me to enjoy substantial success in leading my young learners to literacy.

It is important to understand that the assessment procedures and instructional **interventions** described in this chapter are applicable to all students, not just struggling readers. However, when students are failing to make adequate progress, these assessment and intervention strategies become even more important. This chapter will describe ways to gather data on students' reading strengths, needs, and progress and how to link this information to the reading instruction you provide, with an emphasis on struggling readers. Specific chapter topics include the following:

- Understanding factors associated with reading problems
- Assessing students' needs and progress in reading
  - Standardized testing
  - Informal assessments
- Developing an annual assessment plan
- Communicating assessment information

UNDERSTANDING FACTORS ASSOCIATED WITH READING PROBLEMS

No competent physician would perform surgery or prescribe medication without first developing a thorough understanding of the underlying causes of a patient's medical problems. Physicians receive years of training in medical diagnosis procedures and have many reliable tests available for diagnosing illnesses. Unfortunately, reading teachers all

Addresses IRA Standard 1.1

Demonstrate knowledge of psychological, sociological, and linguistic foundations of reading and writing processes and instruction.

Addresses IRA Standard 1.3

Demonstrate knowledge of language development and reading acquisition and the variations related to cultural and linguistic diversity.

too often apply instructional treatments to students' reading problems without first determining their source. For example, a teacher may place a struggling reader in a skills group to receive extra phonics instruction when in fact the student may already be proficient in phonics and his reading problem is really a lack of sufficient vocabulary and background knowledge to comprehend the meaning inherent in the words. Teachers should avoid making assumptions about the cause(s) of a student's reading problems. Rather, a few minutes of assessment can quickly identify factors responsible for a student's lack of progress and suggest appropriate instructional interventions.

Environmental factors.   Title 1 (sometimes called Chapter 1) is a federally funded program that provides additional reading teachers for schools in low-income communities. During the 5 years that I was a Title 1 reading teacher, I visited my students' homes to meet their parents and build home support for reading. I visited homes where there was no print in sight: no newspapers, books, magazines, or even mail. However, there was always a television. My students struggled learning to read, but they could always tell me about the guests on the late-night talk shows.

Educational research is very clear about the strong link between home environment and educational achievement. Adams (1990, p. 8) summarized research studies showing that parents in many U.S. homes read to their preschoolers daily, "resulting in hundreds and thousands of hours of literacy exposure prior to school entry," while other preschool children "rarely even see a storybook." Adams points out that most children who struggle learning to read in the early grades don't lack the ability to learn; they lack the preparation to learn.

Physiological factors.   I remember standing in a grocery-store checkout line one day. Behind me was a young mother who was feeding her infant child what appeared to be Kool-Aid from a baby bottle. I remember wondering to myself if Kool-Aid constituted the majority of that child's diet and what effects the lack of nourishment would have on the child's physical and particularly, mental growth.

A variety of physiological factors can affect students' ability to learn to read. Students with *hearing problems* will be less able to recognize and distinguish between the sounds (phonemes) of spoken language and to make the connections between the spoken sounds and the printed letters that represent them. Perhaps more importantly, students with hearing problems have difficulty acquiring language: the vocabulary, speech patterns, and background knowledge necessary for learning to read.

A variety of *vision problems* (see Figure 10.2) can prevent students from seeing letters clearly and accurately (Richek, Caldwell, Jennings, & Lerner, 2002). Teachers should watch for the signs associated with vision problems, such as squinting at texts, inattention to board work, and holding texts too close or at arm's length.

Neurological problems, associated with levels and areas of brain activity may make it difficult for some students to recognize letters and words. Problems such as brain damage, delayed neurological development, and congenital brain defects can cause both learning and emotional problems (Block, 2003).

Figure 10.2 Vision Problems

Myopia (nearsightedness) is difficulty seeing objects from a distance.

Hyperopia (farsightedness) is difficulty seeing objects up close.

Astigmatism is a general blurring of objects at any distance.

Binocular problems are associated with difficulty focusing both eyes simultaneously on an object.

Emotional factors. Imagine the effects on your ability to concentrate and learn, knowing a bully is waiting for you after school. Worries such as this or something much more severe, like child abuse, can interfere with learning. Self-esteem can also be diminished by being placed in the low reading group for the third straight year. Emotional problems related to feelings of anxiety and low self-worth can affect a student's ability to learn and the amount of effort a student will put into learning. Pressley (2002) describes the role of students' beliefs in their own ability to learn as the level of *persistence* they will exert during a challenging learning task. Some students believe that academic achievement is attributable to *intelligence,* or "being smart." Others believe it is the result of *effort,* or "working hard." When faced with a difficult academic task, students who believe in effort will tend to increase their level of effort ("try harder") until they succeed. Students who believe in their own lack of ability are more likely to give up trying, because they believe that they are not smart enough to learn and any amount of effort would be a waste. There is a powerful cyclical effect in learning. Students who experience success early in school gain confidence and tend to apply themselves to learning. Students who experience failure early in school are more likely to become discouraged, give up trying, and, as a result, experience even more failure (Pressley, 2002).

Language factors. Oral language is the foundation on which learning to read printed language is built. Nonnative English-speaking students whose level of English language is minimal or whose language patterns or dialect are different from the language of instruction are more likely to have problems learning to read. Many students easily learn to recognize and apply spelling patterns and can pronounce most of the words they see in print. However, if they don't have the requisite vocabulary to know what the words mean, they will be unable to match a word from their oral vocabulary to the word they are pronouncing. They might have a correct pronunciation and not even know it. Even a simple phonetically regular but less familiar word like *cog* can be difficult for a student who has never heard the word before. Students who lack background knowledge in a specific area are more likely to encounter difficulty reading about that topic. A student from a small rural farming community can be expected to have problems reading about elevated trains running among skyscrapers. Students whose own language patterns ("Me and my mom was . . . ") are different from "book language" will find it harder to use syntax as a means of identifying unfamiliar printed words. Finally, students who grew up saying *casa grande* or *perla negra*

FOR ENGLISH LANGUAGE LEARNERS

Don't Do This!

Concurrent translation is *not* an effective way to teach ELL students. This method provides both English and the native language in written and oral forms. It is not effective because it allows students to focus only on their native language and ignore the English. Also, the teacher has no need to make the English comprehensible (Krashen 1992).

may be confused when they encounter adjectives in English text where they would expect to see nouns.

Instructional factors.   Of all the factors associated with reading problems, by far the most common factor leading to reading difficulties is simply poor instruction (Pressley, 2002). Too many students don't learn to read well because they have not been taught well. For example, in some classrooms students don't receive very much direct instruction, as in the case of programs in which students spend the majority of reading instruction time sitting at their seats reading independently. Sometimes reading instruction is hit and miss, as when teachers only provide decoding instruction based on words that students struggle with. Such instruction can result in students learning about one spelling pattern on Monday, another on Tuesday, and still another on Wednesday, with no consistency or follow-up.

Sometimes reading instruction is one dimensional: one component of reading instruction is overemphasized and other necessary components are left out. Sometimes reading lessons don't match students' instructional needs. Students who can already apply spelling patterns effectively in their reading may have to sit through frequent and unnecessary spelling pattern lessons.

Alternatively, students may be given reading instruction in texts that are so easy that nothing new is learned or so hard that the major outcome of the lesson is frustration. In some classrooms the management of classroom routines and student behavior is so poor that instruction is constantly interrupted. And in far too many schools, instructional safety nets are not in place, so struggling students are left to sink or swim on their own. Looking at reading problems from an instructional perspective will allow me to share how the source of most reading problems and their remediation is the one reading problem over which teachers have the most control.

 ## ASSESSING STUDENT NEEDS AND PROGRESS IN READING

Addresses IRA Standard 3.1

Use a wide range of assessment tools and practices, from individual and group standardized tests to individual and group informal classroom assessment strategies, including technology-based assessment tools.

An effective educational program, in any discipline, requires a three-way alignment among (1) educational *goals,* (2) *instructional* methods and materials, and (3) *assessment* measures and practices. Once clear educational goals are established, instructional programs must be selected and implemented to help students reach these goals, and an assessment plan must be developed and put in place to determine how well students are reaching the goals and what instructional modifications must be made to improve students' achievement if necessary.

My own goals for reading instruction have always focused on teaching my students to (a) recognize and read words fluently, (b) comprehend the content of what they read, and (c) enjoy reading for information and recreation. Therefore, I have provided my students with instruction in recognizing and applying spelling patterns to build reading fluency, building vocabulary and learning and applying reading comprehension strategies, and providing regular opportunities for students to enjoy discussing literature and learning from text. To monitor how effectively my instruction was in helping my students achieve reading goals, I employed a variety of frequent assessment measures, including recording and charting my students' reading rate and accuracy, asking questions about and having my students retell what they read, and discussing with my students what kinds of books they like to read and how they can broaden their reading repertoire. Effective reading assessment includes using a variety of assessment instruments and engaging in ways to gather, analyze, and use assessment data to guide instruction.

TYPES OF READING ASSESSMENT

Any discussion of the purposes of assessment must begin with the concepts of validity and reliability. **Validity** refers to the appropriateness of an assessment. **Reliability** refers to the accuracy and consistency of an assessment. When considering whether to use any assessment measure, teachers must ask themselves if the measure is appropriate for the intended purpose and if it will provide accurate data. For example, the Oral Reading Fluency subtest (ORF) of the Dynamic Indicators of Basic Early Literacy Skills test (DIBELS: Good & Kaminski, 2002; Good, Simmons, & Kame'enui, 2001; Kaminski & Good, 1996) is a very good test for monitoring students' growth in reading rate and accuracy. It was designed for this purpose. However, it would not be appropriate to use this subtest to diagnose a student's reading strengths and weaknesses. It was not designed to do this and is not valid for that purpose. Assessments must also be reliable; they must provide data that are accurate and consistent. The DIBELS Oral Reading Fluency subtest is reliable because the scoring procedures are precise and relatively simple. If 10 teachers who are experienced in DIBELS used it to test the same student for oral reading fluency, the likelihood is high that all 10 will get the same score.

To obtain useful assessment data that will guide instruction and help students reach reading goals, it is important to be clear on the purposes for assessment and then to select appropriate assessments. Teachers must be familiar with early literacy assessments that can be used for (1) **screening** students for reading problems, (2) **diagnosing** students' reading strengths and needs, (3) **monitoring** students' reading progress, and (4) **measuring** students' reading achievement outcomes.

Screening assessments. Screening assessments are given to all K–3 students at the beginning of each school year to identify students who may have or develop reading problems or who are likely to need additional instructional support to achieve reading goals. The DIBELS subtests each come with **benchmark** scores and indicate the levels below which students are considered to be at risk for reading difficulties. For example, a second-grade student who reads below 26 words correct per minute at the beginning of the school year may need additional instructional support to reach the goal of reading at or above grade level by the end of the year.

Diagnostic assessments. Diagnostic assessments are more comprehensive tests that provide in-depth data on students' reading strengths and needs. For example, an **informal reading inventory (IRI)** begins with a student reading a word list at each grade level to estimate the student's word recognition level. The student then reads a passage aloud to the teacher, who records the words from the passage that the student misreads. These records are later analyzed to identify how well the student is using phonic, syntactic, and semantic information to read words. Finally, the student is asked to answer comprehension questions about the passage to determine the student's ability to understand literal information, make inferences, and evaluate the quality of texts. The teacher then analyzes all this diagnostic information about the student's reading to assemble a profile of the student's reading level and reading strengths and weaknesses. Diagnostic assessments are often given at the beginning of a school year to gather in-depth data on students identified by the screening instrument as needing extra instructional support.

Progress monitoring assessments. Students in schools all across America take state-mandated standardized tests at the end of each school year to see how well they can read. Unfortunately, results from these tests often come back to schools a week before summer vacation (if not during summer vacation), so the data are of no use to teachers in planning instruction for students during the year that they teach those students. Progress monitoring assessments are quick tests that are given on a recurring basis (weekly, monthly, quarterly) that allow teachers to track students' rates of progress and identify students who are not making adequate progress. Selected DIBELS subtests, in addition to serving as screening assessments, function well as progress monitoring assessments, because they are quick and easy to administer and there are enough same-level DIBELS passages for each subtest. Students' progress monitoring scores can be graphed by computer to create charts showing exactly how well students are progressing throughout the school year.

Reading achievement outcome assessments.   At the end of each school year, teachers, administrators, parents, and others in the education community need to know how well students did during the school year in learning and progressing in reading. Reading achievement outcome assessments are the end-of-year assessments, standardized and informal, that provide the final indication of how well students achieved. Reading achievement outcome assessments allow teachers and others to determine which students excelled, achieved at grade level, or failed to make adequate progress during the year. Reading achievement outcome assessments may be end-of-year standardized tests, but the final data gathered from progress monitoring assessments may also be used for outcome assessment.

Table 10.1 provides a sample list of reading assessments suitable for screening, diagnosis, progress monitoring, and outcome measuring. The list is based on and adds to a review of assessments conducted by literacy educators at the Institute for the Development of Educational Achievement (IDEA) at the University of Oregon (Kame'enui, 2002). Notice that many of the assessments may be used for multiple assessment purposes.

STANDARDIZED TESTING

Types and Purposes of Standardized Tests

When educators discuss standardized testing, they're usually referring to commercially published tests that are generally given at the end of the school year to determine how well students have learned (outcome measuring). Tests such as the *California Achievement Test,* the *Iowa Test of Basic Skills,* the *Comprehensive Test of Basic Skills,* and the *Stanford Reading Test* are referred to as standardized tests because they are given under standardized conditions, such as (a) during prescribed weeks of the school year, (b) with prescribed time limits for each test subsection, and (c) with uniform test administration and test-taking instructions.

In many school districts around the country, standardized reading tests are only given in grades 2 and up, because it is felt the kindergarten and first-grade students haven't yet had sufficient opportunity to learn to read. Additionally, many educators express concern about the emotional stress that high-stakes standardized tests may place on young students. Standardized tests are usually given in the spring as an outcome measure of students' reading achievement. They are sometimes given in the fall as screening and diagnostic measures.

Standardized tests generally come in two formats: **norm-referenced** tests and **criterion-referenced** tests. The purpose of norm-referenced tests is to *compare* the

Table 10.1   Sample Reading Assessments

Assessment Purposes	Recommended Assessments
Screening	Dynamic Indicators of Basic Early Literacy Skills (DIBELS)
	Early Reading Diagnostic Assessment (ERDA)
	Gray Oral Reading Test IV (GORT IV)
	Phonological Awareness Literacy Screening (PALS)
	Peabody Picture Vocabulary Test (PPVT-3)
	Texas Primary Reading Inventory (TPRI)
	Woodcock Reading Mastery Test, Revised
	Yopp/Singer Test of Phoneme Segmentation
Diagnosis	Analytical Reading Inventory
	Basic Reading Inventory
	Critical Reading Inventory
	Early Reading Diagnostic Assessment (ERDA)
	Flynt–Cooter Reading Inventory for the Classroom
	Gray Oral Reading Test IV (GORT IV)
	Iowa Test of Basic Skills
	Phonological Awareness Literacy Screening (PALS)
	Qualitative Reading Inventory (QRI) III
	Texas Primary Reading Inventory (TPRI)
	Woodcock Reading Mastery Test, Revised
	Yopp/Singer Test of Phoneme Segmentation
Progress monitoring	Dynamic Indicators of Basic Early Literacy Skills (DIBELS)
	Texas Primary Reading Inventory (TPRI)
Outcome measuring	Dynamic Indicators of Basic Early Literacy Skills (DIBELS)
	Early Reading Diagnostic Assessment (ERDA)
	Gray Oral Reading Test IV (GORT IV)
	Iowa Test of Basic Skills
	Peabody Picture Vocabulary Test (PPVT-3)
	Slosson Oral Reading Test (SORT)
	Stanford Achievement Test (SAT-9)
	Woodcock Reading Mastery Test, Revised
	Yopp/Singer Test of Phoneme Segmentation

academic performance of each student, school, district, and state against others taking the same test across the country. For example, the National Assessment of Educational Progress (NAEP: The Nation's Report Card) is designed to show how well students in grades 4, 8, and 12 in each state perform academically compared to students in other states. Based on NAEP test scores, states are rank ordered from highest to lowest performing. NAEP scores also allow for comparisons across socioeconomic and cultural groups. NAEP testing allows us to see which regions of the country and which groups are doing well and which are not and where precious educational resources are most needed.

The purpose of criterion-referenced testing is to see how well students are meeting educational goals. For example, the Utah State Office of Education creates and updates its **core curriculum** and educational objectives in each subject area. Core curriculum documents and objectives are distributed throughout the state and local districts, and schools are expected to "cover the core." The state of Utah has also created End-Of-Level criterion-referenced tests that are given to all students at the end of each school year. Rather than placing the emphasis on comparing schools against schools and districts against districts (Utah uses another standardized test to do that), the scores from the End-Of-Level tests reflect to what extent each individual student has mastered the objectives in the Utah Core Curriculum. Sometime during the summer, each parent of a Utah school student receives a letter from the local school district containing the student's End-of-Level test scores. These scores are represented as a list of instructional objectives and a statement that the student has achieved mastery, near-mastery, or minimal mastery for each objective. Norm-referenced test scores are most useful to politicians, educational policymakers, special-interest groups, and real estate agents who use the scores for political and economic purposes. Criterion-referenced test scores are instructionally useful to teachers, because they show where each student is performing well and where additional instructional support is needed.

Using Standardized Tests Appropriately

In this era of increased educational accountability, the pressure on educators to generate high test scores is intense. Serious consequences for students are attached to standardized test scores, including promotion to the next grade, high school graduation, and placement in mandatory summer school programs. Likewise, there are also serious consequences for educators. Under the federal government's current education initiative, No Child Left Behind, schools where students don't achieve at acceptable levels or who don't show acceptable levels of progress face sanctions, including paying for remedial instruction for students, paying transportation costs for students to attend other schools, and reassignment of the principal and teachers to other schools. This national obsession with standardized test scores, also known as *high-stakes testing,* has raised serious concerns among educators about the misuse of test scores. In July 2000, the American Educational Research Association (AERA) released a position statement acknowledging the high-stakes nature of standardized testing and outlining considerations that must be addressed in order for standardized testing to be fair, accurate, and useful.

Don't make high-stakes decisions based on the results of a single test. A score from a single test should always be considered together with other pertinent information about a student's academic performance, including classroom teacher observations of the student in the classroom setting, scores on other tests, and, if appropriate, testing by another educator such as a resource teacher or school psychologist. If evidence exists that the low standardized test score may not represent a student's true academic ability, other means should be made to allow the student to demonstrate his or her ability, such as retaking the test or taking another similar test.

For example, for several years I served on my elementary school's Special Services Committee that reviewed student achievement data and made decisions about placing students into programs such as Special Education, Chapter 1 Reading, the Gifted and Talented program, the Speech and Hearing program, and the Behavioral and Emotional Disorders program. The meeting was always attended by the school principal, the student's classroom teacher, representatives of each special program, and the student's parents. The committee reviewed the student's standardized test scores, listened to the classroom teacher describe the student's classroom performance, and heard about any additional academic or psychological testing that had taken place. The committee then reviewed placement options and described these options to the parents. Finally, the committee made a decision about which combination of classroom and or special services would best meet the student's needs, always with the caveat that the committee would monitor the student's progress to determine if additional modifications were needed.

Ensure alignment between the test and the curriculum. It is not fair and provides no useful information when students are taught content ABC during the school year and then tested on content XYZ on an end-of-year standardized test. One of the first things I did when I became a classroom teacher was to ask the principal for a list of the reading objectives that would be covered on the end-of-year standardized test. This list did not control my teaching, but I did make sure that the objectives were covered. It would have been unfair to my students not to provide instruction on objectives for which they were going to be held accountable. There must be a seamless three-way alignment among the education objectives, classroom instruction, and the content of the testing.

Provide opportunities for remediation for those who fail. One purpose of standardized testing is to determine which students are succeeding academically and which are not. It is both unethical and illogical, when standardized testing identifies failing students, not to provide remedial instruction to help these failing students to "reach the bar." If a second-grade student generates a low reading test score that would require retention in second grade, a summer reading program or individual tutoring should be made available during the summer and the student should be given the chance afterward to demonstrate his or her level of readiness to advance to third grade.

Provide appropriate accommodations for students with language differences or learning disabilities. If a student who is learning English (ELL: English language learner) cannot read the instructions or the items on a standardized test, the test results become a reflection of the student's level of English knowledge rather than content knowledge. A student who reads very well in her native language may be classified as a nonreader because of her inability to read the test in English. Similarly, a **learning disabled** student who has strong knowledge of science or social studies content may not be able to demonstrate his level of knowledge because of reading skill problems. In the case of students with language differences or other learning disabilities, special accommodations may be needed to obtain valid test scores. The NAEP test results Web site designates those test scores where accommodations were made.

Standardized test scores have an important role to play in education. There is a genuine need to know which schools are not doing well so that necessary changes can be made to improve students' educational opportunities. However, standardized tests must be administered and interpreted properly. It is incumbent on teachers to be familiar with the curriculum objectives that are required and on which their students will be tested and to bring into alignment the objectives, instruction, and assessment. And it is essential to always consider multiple indicators of educational achievement whenever important educational decisions are being made.

INFORMAL ASSESSMENTS

Effective teachers are constantly assessing students informally, often in their heads, less frequently on paper. Effective teachers continuously reflect on how students are responding to instruction, and they adjust their teaching accordingly (Pressley, 2002). In my experience, if I had to use a paper and pencil assessment tool for every decision I made about young readers, I would be an *ineffective* teacher because I wouldn't be able to respond to students' needs in a timely manner. Even so, it is important to document students' progress, and there are some very useful and informative ways to assess reading achievement. Informal reading inventories (IRIs), running records, phonemic awareness tests, word lists, conferencing with readers, and attitude inventories are the essential assessment tools effective teachers have in their repertoire. Any assessment you use should eventually lead to a decision about what to teach to an individual, a small group, or the whole class. The following assessment descriptions provide examples of commonly used informal assessments that can inform the assessment–instruction cycle. As you read through the descriptions, look for the fundamental reading behaviors that are being measured, such as reading rate and accuracy, patterns in student reading errors, background knowledge and vocabulary, and levels of reading comprehension.

Phonological Awareness Literacy Screening (PALS)

PALS is a series of early literacy assessments developed at the University of Virginia for children in grades K–3. PALS-K and PALS 1–3 are designed to help teachers *screen* for students who are lagging behind in reading and would benefit from additional literacy instruction. Additionally, PALS can serve as a *diagnostic* assessment by helping teachers gather detailed information about individual students' reading strengths and instructional needs.

PALS-K

PALS-K is a series of seven subtests that measure young children's alphabet recognition, phonological awareness, concept of word, and knowledge of letter–sounds and spelling. The *Rhyme Awareness*, subtest is administered in small groups and measures students' ability to identify which of three pictures rhymes with a target picture. Those students who struggle with this task may be tested individually. The *Beginning Sound Awareness* subtest is similar to the Rhyme Awareness subtest; however, students are asked to identify which of three pictures has the same beginning sound as the target picture. The *Alphabet Knowledge* subtest measures how many of the lowercase alphabet letters a student can identify. This is followed by the *Letter Sounds* subtest in which students are asked to produce the sounds of 23 uppercase letters and three digraphs. The *Spelling* subtest asks students to spell five CVC (beginner) words. Students receive credit for every correct letter or acceptable substitutions (k-a-t). The *Concept of Word* subtest measures students' word tracking ability by asking them to (a) touch words as they follow along with a printed memorized nursery rhyme and (b) identify individual words in the text and outside the text. The final PALS-K subtest, *Word Recognition in Isolation,* is optional and asks students who have some beginning reading skills to read preprimer, primer, and first-grade word lists.

Teachers administering the PALS-K record the number of each student's correct responses on scoring sheets provided for each PALS subtest. Individual subtest scores are summed to produce a total score that is compared to grade-level benchmarks established for both fall and spring of the kindergarten year. Students whose total PALS-K score falls below the established benchmarks should receive additional or intervention instructional activities. The PALS Web site (*pals.virginia.edu*) contains very helpful lists of instructional activities and lesson plans that correspond to the PALS subtests.

Pals 1–3

PALS 1–3 begins with two *Entry Level* subtests: Spelling and Word Recognition in Isolation. The *Spelling* subtest asks students to spell lists of words that contain spelling patterns that students should master at each grade level. Like the PALS-K spelling subtest, students receive credit for each spelling pattern spelled correctly. The *Word Recognition in Isolation* subtest measures how many words students recognize while reading graded word lists. Students who do well on the Entry Level subtests go on to two additional Level A subtests. Students who do less well on the Entry Level subtests go on to subtests at Level B or if necessary Level C.

There are three Level A subtests: *Oral Reading in Context, Passage Reading,* and *Comprehension.* The *Oral Reading in Context* subtest measures a student's oral reading fluency based on indexes of accuracy, rate, and phrasing and expression. The *Passage Reading* subtest gives the teacher an opportunity to determine each student's reading level by taking a running record as students read leveled passages aloud. Finally, the *Comprehension* subtest measures students' comprehension through multiple-choice questions provided after the reading in context passages.

Students who do not meet the benchmarks on the Entry Level subtests will be asked to take three Level B subtests that measure students' alphabet recognition, knowledge of letter sounds, and concept of word. Students who do not meet the benchmarks for Level B will also be asked to take the Level C *Blending* and *Sound-to-Letter* subtests that measure students' ability to blend phonemes to produce spoken words and conversely to segment and identify individual phonemes within spoken words.

PALS Data Management

An attractive feature of the PALS assessment framework is that teachers can send their PALS data via computer to PALS headquarters and instantly receive back a variety of useful data summaries. For example, teachers can receive PALS class reports that list which students scored high on the subtests and which scored low and will need supplemental instruction. PALS class reports also group students by reading level and knowledge of spelling–phonics concepts. PALS also produces Student Summary Reports that show each student's performance on PALS subtests compared to grade-level benchmarks. Student History Reports provide individual students graphs that plot each student's growth over time on each PALS subtest. PALS also provides Back to School reports for each class based on data gathered the previous spring and Year-End Reports that provide an outcome measure of each student's reading achievement.

PALS is a very conceptually simple yet complete assessment of students' early literacy skills. PALS student subtest data and the accompanying instructional resources support teachers in knowing where each student is in literacy growth and the activities and resources that are appropriate to support continued growth. PALS data can also be very useful in grade-level teaching team instructional planning meetings and in parent conferences.

Dynamic Indicators of Basic Early Literacy Skills

The Dynamic Indicators of Basic Early Literacy Skills (DIBELS: Good & Kaminski, 2002; Good, Simmons, & Kame'enui, 2001; Kaminski & Good, 1996) is a series of individually administered reading subtests for students in grades K–3 that can be used for screening, progress monitoring, and outcome measurement in the areas of phonemic

Table 10.2   Recommended K–3 Schedule for DIBELS Subtests

Literary Skill	Subtest
Kindergarten	
Phonemic awareness	Initial Sound Fluency
	Phoneme Segmentation Fluency
Phonics	Letter Naming Fluency
	Nonsense Word Fluency
First Grade	
Phonemic awareness	Phoneme Segmentation Fluency
Phonics	Letter Naming Fluency
	Nonsense Word Fluency
Fluency	Oral Reading Fluency
Second Grade	
Phonics	Nonsense Word Fluency
Fluency	Oral Reading Fluency
Third Grade	
Fluency	Oral Reading Fluency

awareness, phonics, and fluency. DIBELS subtests were designed to be quick and easy to administer so that teachers can measure and analyze their students' reading achievement on a continuous basis throughout the school year.

Table 10.2 provides a schedule of which DIBELS subtests are appropriate for grades K–3. Notice that the phonemic awareness subtests that begin in kindergarten are replaced by the oral reading fluency subtests in grades 2 and 3.

Administration and Scoring DIBELS Subtests

To administer the DIBELS *Initial Sound Fluency* subtest, the teacher or other examiner shows the student four pictures, names the pictures, and then asks the student to point to or say the picture that begins with the sound pronounced by the teacher. For example, the teacher shows pictures of a boat, horse, kite, and tiger; names the four pictures; and asks "Which one starts with /b/?" The teacher calculates the number of initial sounds the student can name in 1 minute and records the score. To administer the *Phoneme Segmentation Fluency* subtest, the teacher pronounces a list of words one at a time, asking the student to pronounce the individual phonemes from each word. For example, the teacher says the sounds *mud* and the students says /m/ /u/ /d/. The teacher calculates the total number of phonemes the student can pronounce in 1 minute and records the score. To administer the *Letter Naming Fluency* subtest, the teacher shows the student a page of alphabet letters and asks the student to name them. The teacher records the number of letters the student can name in 1 minute. For the *Nonsense Word Fluency* subtest, the teacher gives the student a page of phonetically regular **nonsense words** such as *vig*, *pav*, and *et*. The teacher records the number of nonsense words the student can pronounce correctly in 1 minute.

Table 10.3 DIBELS Oral Reading Fluency Benchmark Scores

	Beginning of Year	Middle of Year	End of Year
First Grade CWPM			
At risk		<8	<20
At some risk	NA	8–20	20–40
At low risk		>20	>40
Second Grade CWPM			
At risk	<26	<52	<70
At some risk	26–44	52–68	70–90
At low risk	>44	>68	>90
Third Grade CWPM			
At risk	<53	<67	<80
At some risk	53–77	67–92	80–110
At low risk	>77	>92	>110

Note. From DIBELS Data System, http://dibels.uoregon.edu. Reprinted with permission.

Perhaps the most well known DIBELS subtest is the Oral Reading Fluency (ORF) subtest. Designed to be introduced toward the middle of first grade, the ORF involves the teacher listening to a student read a grade-level passage and determining the number of words the student can read correctly in 1 minute. As with all DIBELS subtests, the ORF is administered frequently throughout the year, and the increases in student performance are graphed so that the rate of improvement can be monitored for instructional planning.

DIBELS also provides benchmark scores for each subtest so that teachers may determine which students are At Risk, At Some Risk, or At Low Risk for reading problems based on their subtest scores. For example, Table 10.3 shows DIBELS Correct Words Per Minute (CWPM) benchmark scores for the Oral Reading Fluency subtest.

In an effort to enhance reading assessment and instruction for all students, the DIBELS creators (Good & Kaminski, 2002) have put all DIBELS assessment materials along with the DIBELS *Administration and Scoring Guide* on the DIBELS Web site in English and Spanish for teachers to download and use *at no cost.* The DIBELS Web site (*dibels.uoregon.edu/*) provides multiple forms of the testing materials for repeated testing in order to monitor students' fluency growth throughout the year. Additionally, teachers may choose to send their DIBELS data online to DIBELS headquarters, where the data will be analyzed, graphed, and returned to the teacher for a very nominal fee. Figure 10.3 is an example of an online DIBELS student report, and Figure 10.4 is an example of an online DIBELS class report from the DIBELS Web site.

Informal Reading Inventories

An informal reading inventory (IRI) is an individually administered, commercially published reading test composed of two parts: (a) word lists or screening sentences

Figure 10.3 Sample DIBELS Student Report

Name: G, JERAME
ID: 15288
Class: Adams 3rd #1
Grade: Third
Year: 2001-2002
School: Adams
District: Test District

Dynamic Indicators of Basic Early Literacy Skills
Student Report

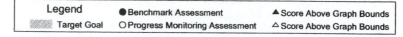

Legend
● Benchmark Assessment   ▲ Score Above Graph Bounds
▨ Target Goal   ○ Progress Monitoring Assessment   △ Score Above Graph Bounds

PHONEMIC AWARENESS

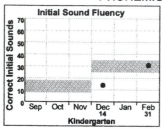
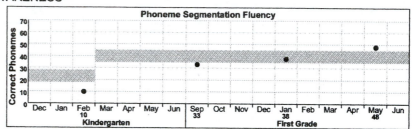

ALPHABETIC PRINCIPLE

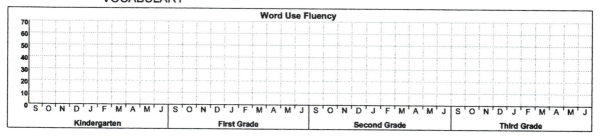

VOCABULARY

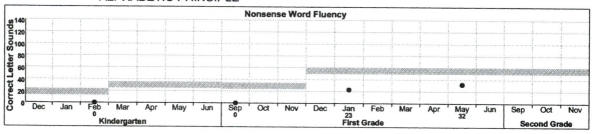

FLUENCY AND COMPREHENSION

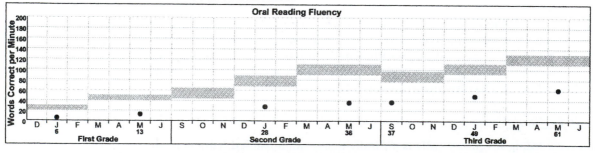

Note. © 2000–2004 DIBELS Data System, http://dibels.uoregon.edu. Reprinted with permission.

04/09/2004, 9

Figure 10.4 DIBELS Data System Sample Class Report

Dynamic Indicators of Basic Early Literacy Skills
Kindergarten Class List Report

District: Test District
School: Adams
Date: January, 2001-2002
Class: Adams K #2

Note: Scores provide an indication of performance only. If there is any concern about the accuracy of scores for an individual student, performance should be verified by retesting to validate need for support.

Student	Initial Sound Fluency			Letter Naming Fluency			Phoneme Segmentation Fluency			Nonsense Word Fluency			Instructional Recommendations
	Score	Percentile	Status	Score	Percentile	Status	Score	Percentile	Status	Score	Percentile	Status	
D, BRITTANY	12	11	Emerging	0	<1	At risk	3	7	At Risk	4	11	At Risk	Intensive - Needs Substantial Intervention
V, JOHNATHON	13	12	Emerging	18	37	Some risk	27	35	Low Risk	16	45	Low Risk	Strategic – Additional Intervention
B, MATHEW	14	14	Emerging	18	37	Some risk	16	24	Some Risk	12	34	Some Risk	Strategic – Additional Intervention
V, SHANIA	14	14	Emerging	37	73	Low risk	42	63	Low Risk	22	60	Low Risk	Benchmark - At Grade Level
M, RACHEL	19	28	Emerging	12	22	At risk	36	50	Low Risk	8	22	Some Risk	Strategic – Additional Intervention
B, SARAH	19	28	Emerging	16	32	Some risk	7	11	Some Risk	10	28	Some Risk	Strategic – Additional Intervention
E, SERENA	21	35	Emerging	7	12	At risk	32	43	Low Risk	0	3	At Risk	Strategic – Additional Intervention
G, BENJAMIN	23	41	Emerging	40	78	Low risk	42	63	Low Risk	29	75	Low Risk	Benchmark - At Grade Level
S, KYLE	24	47	Emerging	9	16	At risk	34	47	Low Risk	10	28	Some Risk	Strategic – Additional Intervention
P, CHRYSALICE	24	47	Emerging	39	76	Low risk	40	59	Low Risk	33	83	Low Risk	Benchmark - At Grade Level
J, MADISON	24	47	Emerging	59	95	Low risk	50	79	Low Risk	43	94	Low Risk	Benchmark - At Grade Level
D, FAYTH	26	54	Established	22	46	Some risk	50	79	Low Risk	26	69	Low Risk	Benchmark - At Grade Level
S, KYLER	29	63	Established	36	71	Low risk	14	21	Some Risk	30	77	Low Risk	Benchmark - At Grade Level
F, KARLEE	30	66	Established	25	53	Some risk	48	74	Low Risk	7	19	Some Risk	Benchmark - At Grade Level
H, KENDRA	30	66	Established	32	65	Low risk	30	40	Low Risk	25	66	Low Risk	Benchmark - At Grade Level
G, TEVIN	30	66	Established	80	>99	Low risk	52	85	Low Risk	59	98	Low Risk	Benchmark - At Grade Level
S, BRIANA	32	72	Established	69	99	Low risk	59	95	Low Risk	27	71	Low Risk	Benchmark - At Grade Level
C, ZACHARY	34	77	Established	28	58	Low risk	50	79	Low Risk	27	71	Low Risk	Benchmark - At Grade Level
J, SARAH	34	77	Established	68	99	Low risk	50	79	Low Risk	53	97	Low Risk	Benchmark - At Grade Level
E, MELISSA	38	85	Established	51	91	Low risk	55	90	Low Risk	26	69	Low Risk	Benchmark - At Grade Level
W, LAURA	41	89	Established	44	83	Low risk	33	45	Low Risk	20	55	Low Risk	Benchmark - At Grade Level
	60	98	Established	55	93	Low risk	55	90	Low Risk	40	91	Low Risk	Benchmark - At Grade Level
	26.9 Mean			34.8 Mean			37.5 Mean			24 Mean			

Note. © 2000-2004 DIBELS Data System, http://dibels.uoregon.edu. Reprinted with permission.

at each grade level for estimating a student's sight word recognition level and (b) reading passages at each grade level for estimating a student's reading comprehension, oral reading fluency, and listening comprehension levels. Informal reading inventories are often given by reading **resource teachers,** rather than classroom teachers, because a complete IRI can be time consuming. Many classroom teachers choose to administer an informal reading inventory (as a diagnostic assessment) only to those students identified by a screening assessment as likely to need extra instructional support in reading. Data from an informal reading inventory can be used to estimate a student's reading level, identify a student's reading strengths and weaknesses, match students with appropriate reading materials, group students for instruction, and select instructional concepts.

Assessing student performance in four aspects of reading.   When I give an informal reading inventory, I use it to examine a student's reading abilities in four areas of reading: sight word recognition, oral reading fluency, reading comprehension, and listening comprehension. I obtain an estimate of a student's *sight word recognition level* by listening to the student read the word lists or screening sentences (part 1 of the IRI) aloud to me. I estimate a student's *oral reading fluency level* by listening to the student read the passages aloud and by noting the percentage of words read correctly. I estimate the student's *reading comprehension level* by asking comprehension questions about the passage or by asking the student to retell passage content to me. Finally, I read a passage or two aloud to the student and ask comprehension questions or request a retelling to estimate a student's **listening comprehension** level. Listening comprehension provides an estimate of the level of a student's vocabulary and background knowledge.

Assessing a student's levels of reading.   Informal reading inventories are designed to help a teacher to classify a student's reading levels into one or more of the following three reading levels: independent, instructional, and frustration (see Table 10.4). Just as Goldilocks discovered the three bowls of porridge were too hot, too cold, and just right, an IRI can help a teacher determine if a particular text is too hard, too easy, or just right for teaching.

Table 10.4   Independent, Instructional, and Frustration Reading Levels

Reading Levels	Description	Performance Ranges
Independent level	A student can read text at this level successfully and independently.	95%–100% oral reading accuracy
	The text is too easy for instruction.	Approximately 90% reading comprehension
Instructional level	A student can read text at this level successfully, with teacher support.	90%–94% oral reading accuracy
	The text is just right for instruction.	Approximately 75% reading comprehension
Frustration level	A student cannot read text at this level.	Below 90% oral reading accuracy
	The text is too hard for instruction.	Below 50% reading comprehension

Preparing for IRI Testing

Before I begin IRI testing, I like to identify a time and quiet location for testing where my student and I can be as free of distractions as possible. Before and after school work well. So does a recess break or planning period when other students are out of the room. A complete IRI may need to be given in smaller increments over two or three testing sessions. To get the IRI off to a good start, it is important to have the testing materials ready. This will include the graded word lists and passages for the student to read and photocopies of the passages for marking the student's misread words. I also like to have a clipboard to write on. Some teachers like to tape record the IRI sessions so that they can listen to the student's oral reading again at a later time to confirm the accuracy of their markings of the student's misread words. Finally, I like to put the student at ease before I begin the actual testing. My favorite way to do this is with simple comments like, "Thank you for helping me to figure out what a good reader you are. What I would like you to do is just read some words and short stories to me. I know you'll do very well!"

Administering and Scoring the IRI Word Lists

Administering the IRI word list.   I begin the IRI testing by asking the student to read a word list that is 1 or 2 years below her grade level. I want the student to get off to an easy start. I place the first word list in front of her and say, "I'd like you to read this list of words out loud to me, starting here at the top and reading down" (I point to the starting and stopping places).

As the student begins to read the word list aloud to me, I mark the words that the student **miscues** on my separate photocopy of the word list. These miscues usually fall into one of the four categories listed in Table 10.5.

Also, I like to shield my marking of the student's miscues as much as possible in order to minimize distracting the student or causing the student undue anxiety about his or her performance. Placing an opened file folder between us works well to shield my marking of the student's miscues.

Scoring the IRI word list.   Most commercially published IRIs include 20 words on each grade-level word list. Some informal reading inventories use brief phrases or sentences in lieu of word lists to better approximate reading connected text. Although there will

Table 10.5   IRI Word List Marking Format for Misreadings

Miscue Category	Description	Recording Format
Correct pronunciation	Student pronounces the word correctly.	Write C or make a checkmark beside the word.
Word or nonword substitution	Students pronounces a nonword or a different word from what is written.	Write what the student says beside the word.
Doesn't know the word	Student was unable to generate any pronunciation of the word.	Write DK (doesn't know) beside the word.
Self-corrections	Student mispronounces the word, then self-corrects it.	Write SC (self-correct) beside the word and count it as correct.

be some variation in scoring procedures from one IRI to another, they all stick pretty close to the following scoring criteria:

0–1   miscues indicate an *independent* reading level for that level word list.
2–5   miscues indicate *instructional* reading for that level word list.
6   or more miscues indicate *frustration* level for that level word list.

If the student misreads between 0 and 5 words (independent or instructional reading level for that word list), record the student's score and ask the student to read the word list at the next higher grade level. Continue having the student read the word lists until he or she reaches the frustration level. Record the highest level at which the student scores within the instructional level as the student's word recognition level. If the student scores at the frustration level on the first word list, ask the student to read an easier word list. Watch the student for other signs of frustration level, such as fidgeting and anxious tone of voice. Don't force a student to finish a word list when it's clearly evident that the list is too hard.

Administering the IRI Reading Passages

Once you have determined and recorded the student's instructional word recognition level from the word lists, give the student a reading passage that is one level below his or her instructional word recognition level. This will help to get the student off to a running start with the passages.

Some IRIs are designed to have the student read each passage one time aloud and then answer the comprehension questions based on the student's oral reading. Other IRIs invite the student to read each passage twice, first silently to measure the student's reading comprehension and then a second time aloud to measure the student's oral reading accuracy. I have done it both ways and found that each works well. An advantage to having the student read each passage only once is that it is much quicker, saving a substantial amount of instructional time for both teacher and student. When giving a student an IRI passage to read, I always remind the student to pay attention to the content of the passage because I will be asking questions about the passage when the student has finished reading it.

Scoring the IRI Reading Passages for Oral Reading Accuracy

As the student reads the passages aloud to you, mark all the student's oral reading miscues on your photocopy of the passage using the following marking system:

Substitutions	*went* Mary wanted a new bike.
Omissions	Mary wanted a (new) bike.
Insertions	*blue* Mary wanted a new ˄ bike.
Teacher assists	*TA* Mary wanted a new bike.
Repetitions	Mary wanted a new bike. ←
Self-corrections	*went (sc)* Mary wanted a new bike.

Scoring systems vary somewhat from one published IRI to another. For example, some IRIs count a **repetition** as an error. Other IRIs count repetitions as correct, while still others give repetitions half-credit. Some IRIs recommend marking off only for those miscues that change the meaning of the passage (**meaning-change miscues**), believing that miscues that don't change the meaning of the passage (**meaning-preserving miscues**) demonstrate that the student is processing the content of the text correctly. Figure 10.5 is an example of the scoring guide from an informal reading inventory passage.

The following system is a good representation of an IRI scoring guide. *Count off for:*

- Substitutions
- Insertions
- Omissions
- Teacher assists
- Skipping an entire line of text, counts as one error.

Do not count off for:

- Repetitions
- Self-corrections
- Dialect variations
- Proper names

After the student has finished reading the passage aloud to you, count the total number of miscues. Compare the total number of miscues to the scoring guide provided below the passage. All commercially published IRIs have a scoring guide based on the number of words in the passage and the criteria listed earlier for determining independent, instructional, and frustration reading levels. If the number of oral reading miscues and the scoring guide suggest that the student is reading at the independent or instructional level, repeat the process with the next-level passage. Continue having the student read passages until he or she scores at frustration level. The highest level at which the student scores on the passages is considered his or her instructional level, the level at which reading instruction should be provided.

It is my experience that most students will read two or three passages aloud before hitting the frustration level. Remember, it is advisable to stop students' reading in mid-passage if it becomes evident that a passage is clearly too hard.

Scoring the IRI Passages for Reading Comprehension

Using comprehension questions. Most commercially published IRIs include six to eight comprehension questions after each reading passage. These may be particularly helpful for newer teachers. You may choose to ask the comprehension questions and keep track of the number of questions answered correctly. You can also keep track of the number of literal-level and inferential-level questions answered correctly to get a sense of how well the student is able to comprehend information that is explicit in the text and how well he or she can make inferences and "read between the lines." Compare the number of comprehension questions answered correctly to the scoring guide for the passage to determine if the student's reading comprehension level is independent, instructional, or frustration level for the passage. Continue providing passages as long as the student scores at the independent or instructional level. The highest level at

Figure 10.5 Sample Marked IRI Page

	ERROR TYPES						ERROR ANALYSIS			
	mis-pronun.	sub-stitute	inser-tions	tchr. assist	omis-sions	Error Totals	Self-Correct.	(M) Meaning	(S) Syntax	(V) Visual
The Pig and the Snake										
One day Mr. Pig was walking to ∧ his town. He saw a big hole in the			1					1	1	
rope snake ss road. A big snake was in the		1							1	‖
hole. "Help me," said the snake,										
"and I will be your (ss) friend." "No, no,"							1			1
said Mr. Pig. "If I help you get										
of bit (ss) out you will bite me. You are			1				1		1	1
a snake!" The snake cried and										
cried. So Mr. Pig pulled the										
snake out of the hole.										
Then the snake said, "Now I am										
bit (ss) going to bite you, Mr. Pig."							1			1
"How can you bite me after										
I helped you out of the hole?"										
said Mr. Pig. The snake said,//										
"You knew I was a snake										
when you pulled me out!"										
TOTALS		1	2				3	1	3	5

Summary of Reading Behaviors (Strengths and Needs)

Note. From *Reading Inventory for the Classroom,* 4th ed., by E. S. Flynt and R. B. Cooter, p. 68, copyright 2001 by Merrill/Prentice Hall. Upper Saddle River, NJ:Merrill/ Prentice Hall. Reprinted by permission.

which the student scores at the instructional level on the reading passages is considered his or her comprehension instructional level, the level at which reading instruction should be provided.

Using retelling. After years of giving IRIs, I increasingly found the comprehension questions provided with the commercially published IRIs to be tedious and sometimes biased and poorly worded. I eventually abandoned the comprehension questions in favor of **retellings** to estimate a student's reading comprehension level. I ask the student to retell the passage in his or her own words. If the passage is narrative, I record information the student provides about the story's setting, main characters, events, and theme. If the passage is expository, I notice if the student's retelling includes the main ideas and supporting details.

In either case, when a student omits important information in the retelling, I ask follow-up questions about the missing information to probe the student's level of comprehension. When scoring a retelling, I make notes using the following guidelines:

* Does the student reflect the story structure of narrative text (setting, characters, events)?
* Does the student use the main idea and detail structure of expository text?
* Are the retellings sequential?
* Are the retellings accurate?

Because a retelling does not use a detailed scoring guide, you refer to your notes to decide whether the student recalled approximately 90% of the passage content (independent-level reading comprehension), 75% (instructional-level reading comprehension), or 50% or less (frustration level). Continue providing reading passages at successively higher levels as long as the student scores at the independent or instructional level.

Scoring the IRI Passages for Listening Comprehension

After the student has reached frustration level on the reading passages, I often choose to read subsequent passages aloud to my student to get a measure of his or her ability to understand text, independent of the ability to read words. As I read each passage aloud, I remind my student to listen carefully "because I will ask comprehension questions after each passage." I either ask the comprehension questions provided by the IRI or I have the student do a retelling. I keep track of the number of comprehension questions answered correctly or the completeness of the retelling so that I can estimate whether the student can comprehend the passage at the independent, instructional, or frustration levels through listening. I continue providing listening comprehension passages as long as the student scores at the independent or instructional level. I stop when the student reaches frustration level. The highest level at which the student scores at the instructional level on the listening comprehension passages is considered his or her listening comprehension instructional level, the level at which he or she should reasonably be expected to comprehend text while reading. This information suggests the student's comprehension level when the demands of word identification are factored out. A large discrepancy between a student's listening comprehension level and his or her sight word recognition and oral reading fluency levels suggests whether instructional emphasis should be placed on word identification or background knowledge and vocabulary building.

Analyzing the Student's Oral Reading Miscues to Determine
Reading Strengths and Weaknesses

After I have finished listening to the student read, it is very instructive to go back to the copies of the reading passages on which I have marked the student's oral reading miscues and examine them for patterns. These patterns can provide insights about whether the student has strengths or weaknesses in aspects of word identification, comprehension, or both. I analyze the student's oral reading miscue patterns for *graphic similarity* (do most of the student's miscues have similar letters to the printed words?), *semantic acceptability* (are most of the student's miscues consistent with the meaning of the passage?), and **self-corrections.** Patterns in the student's miscues can suggest where he or she is focusing attention while reading. A pattern of graphically similar miscues suggests that the student is paying attention to the print. A pattern of miscues with mostly different letters suggests that the student is not paying sufficient attention to the print. A pattern of semantically acceptable (meaning-preserving) miscues suggests that the student is paying attention to meaning, while a predominance of miscues that change the meaning of the passage suggests that the student is not paying sufficient attention to the meaning of the passage. A pattern of many self-corrections suggests that the student is focusing attention on both print and meaning. This is good.

Knowing whether a student is focusing predominantly on print, meaning, or both should greatly influence the instructional guidance you provide. When a student is making too many meaning-change miscues, I provide prompts such as "Does that make sense?" When a student is making too many miscues that don't resemble the printed words on the page, I provide prompts such as "Does that look right?"

Summarizing the Student's IRI Performance

After completing the IRI, review the student's sight word recognition, oral reading fluency, reading comprehension, and listening comprehension level data, along with analyses of the student's oral reading miscues, to develop an overview of the student's reading level and reading strengths and weaknesses. This information is critical to planning reading experiences and activities that will meet the student's instructional needs.

As I described in the chapter vignette, I develop a bar graph to represent each student's instructional levels for sight word recognition, oral reading fluency, reading comprehension, and listening comprehension. I date each bar graph so that I can show each student's level of growth in each of the four reading areas to teachers, parents, and administrators. It is important to remember that an IRI, like any other assessment, represents a single source of data and that data from multiple assessments and classroom performance indicators should always be considered together when making important instructional decisions, such as placement in an intervention program. Figure 10.6 lists five well-known reading inventories.

Running Records

Running records were developed by Clay (2002) as part of the **Reading Recovery** program. Teachers can use running records to serve two essential assessment purposes. First, teachers can determine a student's reading level by calculating the percentage of words the student reads correctly. Second, teachers can use running records to identify a student's reading strengths and areas needing additional instructional support by analyzing patterns in the words the student misread. Running records are popular with teachers because they are quick to administer and can be used on the spot with any text the student is reading.

Figure 10.6 Popular Informal Reading Inventories

Analytical Reading Inventory, 7th Ed. Columbus, OH: Merrill Education, 2003.

Basic Reading Inventory, 8th Ed. (BRI-8). Dubuque, IA: Kendall/Hunt Publishing Company, 2002.

Critical Reading Inventory: Assessing Students' Reading and Thinking. Merrill Education, Columbus, OH: 2004.

Flynt & Cooter. *Reading Inventory for the Classroom.* Columbus, OH: Merrill Education, 2004.

Qualitative Reading Inventory III. New York: Longman, 2001.

Administering and Scoring a Running Record

To take a running record, the teacher must work one-on-one with a student. It can happen during or at the end of a guided reading lesson, during independent reading, at recess, or at any time that makes sense. Sitting side by side, the child reads an unfamiliar book (or one that she's only read once) while the teacher records the child's errors or miscues, using codes for inserted words, skipped words, sounding-out behaviors, repeated words or phrases, words read incorrectly, and self-corrections. A running record can be documented more formally on a running record sheet designed by Marie Clay or less formally on any kind of paper. Sometimes teachers find it easier to take running records if they have a photocopy or transcript of the text the child is reading, but you need to know how to take a running record without a transcript so that you can spontaneously assess a child's reading at any moment.

After the child has read, the teacher calculates an accuracy rate (words correctly read divided by total words) and a self-correction ratio (self-corrections divided by self-corrections plus errors) (Clay, 2002).

Percentage Oral Reading Accuracy

$$\frac{\text{total words correct}}{\text{total words}} \times 100$$

Self-Correction Rate

$$\frac{\text{errors} + \text{self-corrections}}{\text{self-corrections}} = \text{self-correction rate}$$

An accuracy rate of 95% or higher indicates that the text was easy for the child or at the child's independent reading level. An accuracy rate of 90% to 94% indicates that the text was "just right" or at the child's instructional level. An accuracy rate of 89% or lower indicates that the text was hard or at the child's frustration level. At this level, meaning tends to break down.

The **self-correction ratio** is revealing because, if a child corrects one out of every two or three errors (a ratio of 1:2 or 1:3), this suggests she is self-monitoring; that is, she is monitoring her own reading to ensure that it makes sense. If the self-correction ratio is only one self-correction for every five errors, this suggests that she isn't paying much attention to whether what she reads sounds right or makes sense. Worse, if she doesn't correct any errors, then it is possible she doesn't expect reading to make sense or doesn't realize that the purpose of reading is to construct meaning.

Figure 10.7 is a sample of a running record.

Figure 10.7 Running Record

Running Record Sheet

Child's Name: Emmorie Hughes   Grade: 1   Date: October 17

Teacher: Sylvia Read   Text Level: P

Reading Accuracy %: 87   Self-Correction Rate: 1:3

Reading Level: ____ Independent (95-100%)   ____ Instructional (90-94%)   _X_ Frustration (below 90%)

page #	Title: I Can't Said the Ant						E	SC	E M S V	SC M S V
1	√	√	talking ^sc √ / taking	√			1			v
	√	√	√	a / such	loud / a	crash / clatter	3		ms ms ms	
	√	raced / rushed	√	√	√		1		msv	
	So ^sc / To	√	√	√	√	√	1			msv
	Then / There	√	√	√			1		ms	
	√	√	√	pot / pouring	√		1		s	
	- ^sc / was	√	crashed ^sc / cracked	√				2		msv sv
	√	- / a	√	√			1		ms	

Analysis of Errors and Self-Corrections: Emmorie makes very good use of context and sentence structure. Analysis of her oral reading errors suggests that she has good command of consonants and initial consonant blends. She seems to recognize word beginnings accurately, but then substitute other letter-sounds in the middle and endings of words. I would suggest helping Emmorie achieve better balance her oral reading by paying more attention to print cues rather than context as she does now. This text is currently above her instructional level, so I would suggest trying her out on a level M text to see if she reads more successfully.

Using Running Records to Analyze Student Reading Behaviors

Running records are valuable because they can be used to analyze students' reading behaviors. Good teachers look for a pattern in the data. For example, if a child has a tendency to skip easy words, the teacher can coach the reader to slow down and match each spoken word to each word on the page. If the child is skipping words that are difficult to decode, the teacher can coach the child in decoding strategies for difficult words. If the child's decoding strategies tend to break down after he pronounces the first sound in a word, the teacher knows that instruction needs to be focused on strategies for looking all the way through to the end of the word. If the child self-corrects most of his reading errors, the teacher can be fairly assured that he is monitoring for meaning or syntax (the order in which words occur in phrases and sentences) while he reads.

Errors can be further analyzed by deciding if the error was based on meaning clues, syntax clues, or visual clues. For example, if the child says "bike" but the text says "bicycle," the error is consistent with the meaning of the text. Similarly, if child reads "little" when the text says "small," meaning is preserved. In this case, the child needs to be coached to remember to use visual clues as well as meaning clues—to cross-check using at least two sources of information.

Sometimes readers make errors that fit syntactically within the sentence. For example, a child might read "a" for "the" in the sentence "I saw the kid running up the street." If the text says, "The balloon went up in the air," but the child reads "The balloon won't up in the air," you know that the child isn't letting her sense of natural language patterns influence her reading. The coaching for this kind of error should focus on asking the child to reread and notice whether the sentence *sounds* right.

Children use visual (the letters in a word) clues to read, but sometimes incompletely. For example, the text says "The children watched the starfish in the tide pool," but the child reads "The children *wished* the starfish in the tide pool." This shows that the child has paid attention to the visual clues, particularly the beginning and ending of the word *watched,* but has neglected to attend to the middle of the word. Furthermore, this error shows that the child hasn't used meaning or syntax unless he is anticipating the sentence to continue on with something like "The children wished the starfish in the tide pool weren't hiding." Teaching students to attempt a word by pronouncing the first three or four sounds all together usually results in more success.

Children sometimes decode quite literally, reading a word such as *handled* as *hand-leed*. Certainly the child has used visual clues to identify the word, but hasn't been able to access the correct pronunciation because the word isn't in her speaking vocabulary or because she isn't monitoring for meaning.

Using Leveled Texts to Complete Running Records

You need to use a set of leveled texts for running records to have optimal usefulness over the long run. For example, a child might be able to read texts at level G (Fountas and Pinnell, 1996) with 90% to 94% accuracy in the fall, but be able to read texts at level M with 90% to 94% accuracy in the spring. This kind of data is important to record to show the child's progress in reading increasingly difficult texts. Also, certain text levels are associated with certain grade levels. Note that the levels overlap at the beginning and end of grade levels, because the books are arranged on a continuum that levels books in approximate groups; the grade levels listed in Table 10.6 are also approximate and not meant to be used rigidly. Table 10.6 provides an approximate correspondence between the alphabetic leveling system and traditional grade levels. Table 10.6 also provides brief descriptions of text and illustration characteristics associated with each alphabetic level.

Table 10.6 Grade Level and Alphabetic Level Correspondences

Level	Approximate Grade Level	Description
A	K–1	Direct correspondence between text and pictures, consistent format, and ample space between words
B	K–1	One to four lines of text per page; direct correspondence between text and pictures, consistent format, ample space between words
C	K–1	Two to five lines of text per page; simple syntax and natural language, direct correspondence between text and pictures though more of the story is conveyed through the text
D	K–1	Two to six lines of text per page; supportive illustrations, but more of the story is conveyed by the text, words have endings like *ing*, *ed*, and *s*
E	1–2	Three to eight lines of text per page and placement of text on the page varies; text conveys the story, but illustrations support text; longer words and more subtle ideas
F	1–2	Three to eight lines of text per page; print is smaller, literary language is used, story lines are more involved, dialogue is used
G	1–2	Four to eight lines of text per page, longer sentences, literary language, greater variety of vocabulary
H	1–2	Four to eight lines of text per page, longer stories with less repetition
I	1–2	Texts are longer, illustrations provide less support, information books appear at this level, specialized vocabulary is used
J	1–2	Stories are longer and some books are beginning chapter books; nonfiction, folktales, and realistic stories are found at this level
K	2–3	Easy chapter books with illustrations on every page or every other page; illustrations enhance interpretation; literary picture books are found at this level
L	2–3	Longer chapter books with fewer illustrations; stories have more complex plots, more characters, and more description and detail; text is smaller and word spacing is closer
M	2–4	Books are long with small print, close spacing of words, and more words on a page; more background knowledge is required to fully comprehend
N, O	2–4	Texts are much more complex

Figure 10.8 Guidelines for Taking a Running Record

- The sample text should contain at least 100 words (except in lowest levels of texts).
- The text should be unfamiliar or one that the child has read only once before.
- Use check marks for each correct word and record each attempt in full.
- Use the results of a running record to guide text selection for students' individual and group reading lessons.
- Do not use running records to label the child (Colin is a level G reader).
- Words correct divided by total words equals reading accuracy.
- 95% accuracy and above is an easy text at the child's independent reading level.
- 90% to 94% accuracy is a "just right" text at the child's instructional reading level.
- 89% accuracy or less is a hard text at the child's frustration reading level.
- Self-corrections do not count as errors.
- If a line or sentence is skipped, each word counts as an error.
- Repeated errors are counted each time; for example, if the child says "get" instead of "grow" repeatedly (Clay, 2002).
- Errors with proper names are counted only the first time (Clay, 2002).
- If the child gets confused in the text, it is okay to say, "Try that again," and point to the place where the child should begin reading again. This counts as one error. Code this TTA for "try that again."
- If the child asks you for the word, it is okay to tell her the word. This counts as one error. Code this as A for ask and T for told.
- Nonquantifiable behaviors should be noted (e.g., word-by-word reading, stopped to comment on ideas in the text, checked picture, often appealed for help with eyes, read in monotone, etc.).
- One teacher reading another teacher's running record should be able to see exactly what the child did and said.
- Finish the running record with a short statement about where you think the child is as a reader (e.g., "Tina read with confidence and seems ready to move on to more difficult texts" or "Ahmad uses initial sounds when decoding unknown words. He needs to be taught uncover strategy to force his attention to the whole word").

Figure 10.8 provides guidelines for taking a running record, and Figure 10.9 is a tip using benchmark books for assessment.

Phonemic Awareness Tests

As described in chapter 3, phonemic awareness is the knowledge that spoken words are comprised of individual speech sounds that can be manipulated to generate other spoken words. Phonemic awareness and alphabet letter knowledge are the two greatest predictors of eventual success in learning to read (Snow, Burns, & Griffin, 1998).

Teachers can measure a child's level of phonemic awareness through a series of simple sound segmenting, matching, rhyming, and blending tasks (Adams, 1990; Griffith & Olson, 1992; Yopp, 1988, 1995). For example, beginning reading students should be able to count how many words are in a spoken sentence, distinguish rhyming from nonrhyming pairs of words (e.g., *cat-mat*, *map-can*); blend speech sounds (e.g., b-a-t) into words; and isolate sounds in the beginning, middle, and end

Figure 10.9   Assessment Tip: Benchmark Books for Assessment

Some schools create their own assessment kits for taking running records by providing teachers with a common set of benchmark books that represent each guided reading level. Transcripts of the books, including total word counts, make taking running records and figuring out students' accuracy much easier. All students are unfamiliar with the texts.

Publishers also produce kits that serve the same purpose. One widely used assessment instrument is the DRA or Developmental Reading Assessment (Beaver, 2001). It includes leveled books, standardized procedures, observation forms, and records of oral reading that give teachers a flexible tool for ongoing assessment in the classroom as well as periodic assessments for accountability purposes.

of words (e.g., s̲at, d̲o̲g, bot̲h̲). The following **individually administered tests** can give you an indication of your students' levels of phonemic awareness.

Segmenting Words in a Sentence Test

Begin by pronouncing an example sentence or two, point out how many words are in the sentence, and then see if the student can count the words in other similar spoken sentences. For example, say:

> *Listen while I say a sentence.* I like to eat apples. *There are five words in that sentence. Let's count the words on our fingers while I say it again:* I . . . like . . . to . . . eat . . . apples.

> *Now, I am going to say some more sentences and see how well you can count the words.*

> ❀ *I am happy.*
> ❀ *My bike is red.*
> ❀ *The toy is on the floor.*
> ❀ *My dog has brown fur.*
> ❀ *My mom is tall.*

Syllable Counting Test

Cunningham (2000) suggests using the less intimidating term *beats* rather than *syllables*. Again, begin with several examples. Say:

> *Listen to this word* happy. *It has two beats, /hap/ /py/. (Clap while pronouncing the beats.) Now, let's clap it together, /hap/ /py/.*

Repeat the process with a few other example words that are one to three syllables in length (tree, funny, telephone). When you feel that the student understands the task, pronounce the words in the following list.

1. baseball	6. exercise	11. rainbow	16. kangaroo
2. horse	7. run	12. hamburger	17. television
3. butterfly	8. Alexander	13. elephant	18. ballerina
4. mother	9. worry	14. pancake	19. mouse
5. fall	10. doll	15. dance	20. exciting

The following tests were constructed based on a procedure described by Griffith and Olson (1992) and represent aspects of phonemic awareness at the word level. It is recommended that students only do one test per sitting. It is important that these tests be administered in a relaxed, playful manner. You may want to pronounce some of the words in sentences if needed.

Rhyming Test

Use the two example pairs of words to explain the concept of rhyming to the student. Then pronounce each pair of words and ask the student if they rhyme. An average kindergarten student will be correct about 15 times out of the 20.

Example pairs: dog-log   mat-bed

1. *bag-tag*	11. *night-fight*
2. *tug-mom*	12. *put-rap*
3. *seat-beat*	13. *dime-time*
4. *dim-rim*	14. *bet-man*
5. *men-ball*	15. *pot-hot*
6. *tap-him*	16. *walk-miss*
7. *boat-float*	17. *pull-full*
8. *mud-sip*	18. *big-pat*
9. *same-tame*	19. *hope-Sam*
10. *sell-tell*	20. *fun-bun*

Blending Speech Sounds Test

Use the two example words to explain the concept of blending sounds to the student. Then tell the student that you will pronounce some more words sound by sound to see if he can determine the word. An average kindergarten student will be able to get 20 correct.

Example words: i-t   m-an   r-o-pe

1. *i-s*	11. *c-a-t*	21. *h-o-t*
2. *s-ee*	12. *m-an*	22. *h-as*
3. *h-ay*	13. *sh-i-p*	23. *m-e-n*
4. *g-o*	14. *b-e-t*	24. *h-it*
5. *u-p*	15. *s-oa-p*	25. *c-o-mb*
6. *h-i*	16. *f-un*	26. *s-p-oo-n*
7. *E-d*	17. *t-a-me*	27. *r-a-ke-s*
8. *o-dd*	18. *s-eem*	28. *f-l-oa-t*
9. *y-ou*	19. *r-i-pe*	29. *s-t-o-p*
10. *a-t*	20. *h-um*	30. *b-r-ea-k*

Segmenting Speech Sounds Test

Use the example three-phoneme words to demonstrate how spoken words can be broken apart into their individual sounds (phonemes). This is the opposite of the previous exercise. The teacher will say each of the 22 words and then invite the student to give the individual phonemes. Average kindergarten score is 12 correct.

Example words: *pat (p-a-t)*   *be (b-e)*   *rope (r-o-p)*

1. *my (m-y)* _____   *12.* *sky (s-k-ie)* _____
2. *hay (h-ay)* _____   *13.* *drop (d-r-o-p)* _____
3. *bet (b-e-t)* _____   *14.* *flew (f-l-ew)* _____
4. *boat (b-oa-t)* _____   *15.* *lamb (l-a-m)* _____
5. *fix (f-i-x)* _____   *16.* *weep (w-ee-p)* _____
6. *mud (m-u-d)* _____   *17.* *skit (s-k-i-t)* _____
7. *sap (s-a-p)* _____   *18.* *row (r-ow)* _____
8. *peel (p-ee-l)* _____   *19.* *this (th-i-s)* _____
9. *rim (r-i-m)* _____   *20.* *frame (f-r-a-me)* _____
10. *stake (s-t-a-ke)* _____   *21.* *left (l-e-f-t)* _____
11. *bent (b-e-n-t)* _____   *22.* *pie (p-ie)* _____

Conferencing with Readers

You can learn a great deal about students' reading skills and strategies and how well they are comprehending their texts through individual reading conferences. Information from conferences should be used to make instructional decisions about individuals, small groups, or the whole class. Conferences usually happen in the context of Reading Workshop or independent reading when all students are engaged in reading and you can meet with students. Often teachers check in with students to see where they are in the classroom, whether they're on the floor or at a table or desk. They meet with students on a regular basis to:

❧ Ask them questions about their reading
❧ Listen to them read aloud
❧ Help them to make plans about what to read next

Conferences can last anywhere from 2 to 20 minutes depending on the needs of the student. Struggling students will need longer and more frequent conferences than proficient readers.

Using Conferences to Assess Students' Use of Strategies

When you ask students to read aloud, you can observe their reading skills and strategies. For example, do they:

❧ Reread when they think they've made an error or when the text doesn't make sense?
❧ Cover up parts of words they're decoding?
❧ Use picture clues to figure out unknown words?
❧ Track the print with their finger?
❧ Match spoken words with written words (one-to-one correspondence)?
❧ Move their eyes only?
❧ Leave off the endings of words?
❧ Guess words based only on the initial sound of the word?
❧ Guess words based on only the beginning and ending sounds in the word?
❧ Make comments on the reading?
❧ Mumble over difficult words?

❀ Read in a monotone?

❀ Read word by word?

From your observations, you can then decide what strategy or skill students need to be taught. Following a conference you should pick only one thing that you want to ask them to try or that you want to model for them. It is important to have the child try out the strategy right then so that the conference becomes a way to affect future reading habits.

You may decide that a small group of students have similar needs or that the whole class needs to hear about what was learned in the conference too. You can ask the child to help you to teach the strategy to the class. Then the child can feel like an expert, and it helps students to see that they can learn from the mistakes they make. Table 10.7 lists some common reading problem behaviors and accompanying teacher instructional prompts to help students to recognize and correct the behaviors.

Table 10.7   Common Reading Problem Behaviors and Teacher Prompts

Student Reading Problem Behavior	Teacher Instructional Prompt
One-to-one matching is off	Did you run out of words? Try that again. Make sure you point to each word you say.
Guesses word based on beginning sound only	Make sure you read all the way through the word. Uncover the word slowly with your finger. Do you know a word that ends with those letters?
Doesn't self-correct an error	Did that sound right? Did that make sense? Try that again. Which word was hard? You said _____. Does that look right?
Child self-corrects an error	Great! You noticed that it didn't sound right/look right/make sense! You're so smart! Good readers notice when it doesn't make sense and they go back and fix it like you did.
Has chosen a book that is too difficult	Does this book feel comfortable to you? Would you say this book is easy, just right, or hard to read? Read a page from _____ (a book you judge to be more appropriate). How does it feel to read this book compared to the other book? Is this book confusing for you? It's okay not to read it. You want to read books that make sense. Let's try the _____ basket.
Reads word by word	Say that again so that it sounds like you're talking. Listen to how I read it. Now you try. Read that page again and say the words more quickly.
Reader is inactive and wants you to say the word	Wait. Slowly count to five in your head before you provide the word. What could you do to figure out that word? Try rereading that sentence. Start here.
Reader doesn't think about the text	Oh my! What do you think about that? What would you do if you were _____? I wonder what will happen next. What do you think? Tell me what happened on this page. At the end of each page, I want you to tell yourself what happened.

Using Retelling Conferences to Assess Student Comprehension

Retellings, having students tell you about what they have just read, are very effective for figuring out what a student understands from his or her reading. Teachers usually have students retell during individual conferences. When you ask students questions about their books, it is good to have the book in hand, scanning the cover, the back cover, and the page the child is on for information. It helps if you have read the text, but, realistically, if the students are choosing from a large classroom or school library, you may not have read it. But by listening carefully to students you'll be able to tell whether they're understanding the book. If they understand what's going on in the text, they will sound engaged and will usually retell smoothly, with detail and pleasure.

Begin having the student retell with a general prompt, such as "Tell me what this is about." This is called unaided recall. When the student seems to have finished, ask, "What else can you remember?" Do this several times until it seems that she has exhausted her memory. Then you can begin to ask specific questions based on the text's structure. If it is a narrative story, your questions can be based on a simple story grammar. For example, probe the student's knowledge of the story's setting, characters, problem, events, and solution. If the text is informational, your questions can be specific to the content of the text ("Tell me what you learned about how dolphins navigate in the water?") as well as to the nature of nonfiction text structure. Table 10.8 provides teacher prompts for probing students' comprehension of narrative and expository texts.

Using Conferences to Set Reading Goals

Conferences can also be used to set goals with students. Goals can be sent home to parents on a monthly basis and reviewed during parent–teacher conferences. They can also become the focus for future conferences with the student. For example, if the teacher and student have decided that the student should be working on retelling while reading, the student can focus on this and use strategies that the teacher has demonstrated, such as turning pages in the book while retelling or using sticky notes to mark important parts of a text.

Elementary Reading Attitude Survey

It is often said that, along with teaching students *how* to read, we must teach them to *want* to read. As described earlier in this chapter, a student's attitude toward learning will affect his or her persistence toward learning activities. Lipson and Wixom (2003) said that attitude is a "central factor affecting reading and writing performance" (p. 44). Measuring students' attitudes toward reading and reading instruction can alert teachers to those students who will need extra support to discover the rewards of literacy. An attitude inventory can also be given at various times throughout the school year to measure growth or lack thereof in students' attitudes toward reading.

McKenna and Kear (1990) developed a very popular attitude survey based on the comic strip character in *Garfield*. McKenna and Kear approached *Garfield* creator Jim Davis with the idea of drawing four images of Garfield depicting very happy, happy, unhappy, and very unhappy and using these images as indicators on the Elementary Reading Attitude Survey (ERAS). (Davis and his publisher United Features agreed to supply the four images and to permit them to be copied and used by educators.)

Table 10.8   Retelling Prompts for Narrative and Expository Texts

Retelling Prompts for Narrative Texts

Story Grammar Element	Teacher Prompt
Setting	Where did this story take place?
	When did this story happen?
Characters	Who were the characters in this story?
	Who was the main character in the story?
	Describe _____ in the story.
Problem	What is the problem in the story?
	What were the characters trying to do?
Events	What were the most important things that happened in the story?
	What did _____ do in the story?
Solution	How was the problem solved?
	What did _____ do to solve the problem?
Theme	What was this author trying to tell us?
	What did _____ learn at the end of the story?

Retelling Prompts for Expository Texts

What are some of the main ideas in the text?

What are some of the details that tell about the main ideas?

Tell me something interesting you've learned.

What do you think other people will learn from this book?

Are there any confusing parts? Show me.

What was the most important idea in this book?

How did the author organize this book?

Administering the ERAS

The ERAS consists of 20 questions that measure students' attitudes toward both recreational reading (i.e., How do you feel about reading for fun at home?) and academic reading (How do you feel about reading your school books?). Above each question are the four Garfield images. The teacher administers the ERAS to an entire class in about 20 minutes by reading each question aloud twice to the students as they follow along on their printed copies. The students then mark the Garfield image (very happy to very unhappy) that most closely reflects their attitude toward the question. The very happy image receives 4 points, the happy image 3 points, the unhappy image 2 points, and the very unhappy image receives 1 point. The teacher then scores the student responses, creating class scores for recreational reading, academic reading, and total reading. The ERAS was piloted nationally with 18,000 students to establish its reliability and validity.

The ERAS can be used for three purposes: (1) to gather initial attitudinal data about individual students, (2) to create an initial class attitude profile, and (3) to monitor the attitudinal impact of instructional programs. McKenna and Kear suggest administering the ERAS during the first few weeks of school to identify differences in students' attitudes toward recreational and academic reading and also between students' attitudes and reading abilities. This information can be used to plan instruction to enhance students' attitudes where needed and to monitor the effects of instruction on students' attitudes.

I have occasionally modified the ERAS to also measure students' attitudes toward content and instruction in other subject areas. You can do this by photocopying one page of the ERAS questions and images; use white-out to cover the questions, and then compose and type in new questions. For example, before teaching a science unit on the water cycle, you can create a modified ERAS using the Garfield images, but with 5 to 10 questions such as these:

1. *How much do you like learning about science in school?*
2. *How much do you like reading books about science?*
3. *How much do you like doing science projects in school?*
4. *How much do you like learning about rain and snow?*
5. *How much do you like learning about oceans, lakes, and rivers?*

It is always gratifying to see growth in students' attitudes toward reading, reading instruction, and instruction in other content areas. The ERAS questions, images, and technical information can be copied from *Reading Teacher,* 43, (9) (May 1990), pages 626–639.

LOCATING OTHER READING ASSESSMENTS

The assessments described are just a sampling of what is available to teachers for the purposes of screening students for reading problems, diagnosing reading strengths and needs, monitoring progress, and measuring outcomes. The Southwest Educational Development Laboratory (SEDL) has a Web site that lists many norm- and criterion-referenced reading assessments in both English and Spanish. It is a wonderful resource for teachers and others who are looking for reading assessments. The SEDL Web site may be found at:*www.sedl.org/reading/rad/list.html*.

 ### DEVELOPING AN ANNUAL ASSESSMENT PLAN

Effective business leaders rely on data regarding their business expenses and sales revenues to monitor their business growth and make important business decisions. Business leaders who don't rely on data for decision making seldom remain business leaders. Educators in general have a long way to go to develop a culture of relying on assessment data to make educational decisions. I strongly recommend five steps that will help educators to become data-driven decision makers. These steps involve developing and using an annual assessment plan that will direct the implementation and effective use of the assessment–instruction cycle.

1. Meet together as a grade-level team before the beginning of each school year to develop an annual assessment plan. Together as a team you can carefully select and schedule (see Table 10.9) screening, diagnostic, progress monitoring, and outcome measuring assessments to produce a comprehensive assessment plan that will be useful in planning effective instruction.

2. Administer quick screening assessments to all students during the first 2 weeks of school. Record each student's screening assessment data and make a list of those students identified by the screening assessment who will likely need additional instructional support.

Table 10.9 Sample Annual Assessment Plan for Second Grade

Measure	Sep.	Oct.	Nov.	Dec.	Jan.	Feb.	Mar.	Apr.	May
Screening assessment									
DIBELS									
Nonsense Word Fluency	X								
Oral Reading Fluency	X								
Diagnostic assessment									
Qualitative Reading Inventory III		X				X			
Progress monitoring assessment									
DIBELS									
Nonsense Word Fluency	X	X	X	X	X	X	X	X	X
Oral Reading Fluency	X	X	X	X	X	X	X	X	X
Outcome measuring assessment									
California Achievement Test									X
Attitude assessment									
Elementary Reading Attitude Survey	X				X				X

3. Administer diagnostic assessments to those students identified by the screening assessment as needing extra instructional support. Discuss the results of the diagnostic assessments with teaching teammates and plan a series of instructional supports or interventions that will meet these students' instructional needs.

4. Administer progress monitoring assessments on a regular basis. Continue to meet as a teaching team at least monthly in data-analysis team meetings to review the progress monitoring assessment data. Discuss the areas of reading where the students demonstrate strong progress and especially those areas where assessment data suggest more instructional emphasis is needed. Based on this data review, select instructional strategies and materials that will best meet students' instructional needs.

5. Entire school faculties should meet on a quarterly basis to share instructional strengths, needs, and progress across grade levels as identified by assessment data. For example, first-grade teachers can share data about the strengths and needs of their students early in the school year. This information will help kindergarten teachers to know where they should place additional instructional emphases.

Education will become a true profession only when educators use valid and reliable assessment data to make professional decisions about instructional strategies and materials.

 *RECORDING AND ORGANIZING ASSESSMENT DATA*

Effective teachers of beginning reading monitor student progress carefully and extensively (Pressley et al., 2001). The information you collect from assessments needs to be organized in such a way that you can easily find and use it to make decisions or to inform others about a student's progress. Sometimes it is helpful to have a chart of your entire class that gives you the big picture (see Figure 10.10). For example, I like to have my students' results on the QRI and running records of benchmark guided reading books listed on a class chart so that I can see at a glance where everyone is. This helps me to form my initial guided reading groups and decide what kinds of books the children should be checking out from the class library to take home for reading homework. I add to this chart as the year progresses to keep getting a sense of where everyone is, who's making progress, who's on a plateau, and who needs to be moved to another guided reading group.

Many teachers and school districts have developed individual student assessment summaries that list data from all the measures given during the year on a single page for each student. Such summaries allow teachers to see each student's performance level and rate of growth at a glance. These summaries are also very valuable for parent conferences. A sample assessment summary is provided in Figure 10.11.

Figure 10.10   Class Assessment Summary Chart

	QRI Word List **Sept.**	QRI Instructional Level **Sept.**	Guided Reading Level **Sept.**	QRI Word List **Jan.**	QRI Instructional Level **Jan.**	Guided Reading Level **Jan.**	QRI Word List **April**	QRI Instructional Level **April**	Guided Reading Level **April**
Adam									
C.C.									
Daniel									
Davon									
Evan									
Faye									
Forest									
Guillermo									
Jennifer									
Kaden									
Kelly									
Lauren									
Lupe									
Martin									
Oscar									
Randi									
Sam									
Wendy									
Yvette									

Figure 10.11   John's Assessment Summary Form

	Fall, date _____	**Winter,** date _____	**Spring,** date _____
Student Name _____			
Alphabet Letter Names	_____ /52	_____ /52	_____ /52
Alphabet Letter Sounds	_____ /26	_____ /26	_____ /26
Phonemic Awareness			
Recognizes rhyming sounds	_____ /20	_____ /20	_____ /20
Blends speech sounds	_____ /30	_____ /30	_____ /30
Segments speech sounds	_____ /22	_____ /22	_____ /22
Print Conventions			
Tracks left to right, top to bottom	yes no	yes no	yes no
Distinguishes between letters and words	yes no	yes no	yes no
Sight Vocabulary	_____ /220	_____ /220	_____ /220
Spelling Patterns			
Consonants			
Identifies CVC words	_____ /_____	_____ /_____	_____ /_____
Identifies words with consonant blends	_____ /_____	_____ /_____	_____ /_____
Identifies words with consonant digraphs	_____ /_____	_____ /_____	_____ /_____
Vowels			
Identifies words with final silent *e*	_____ /_____	_____ /_____	_____ /_____
Identifies words with vowel digraphs	_____ /_____	_____ /_____	_____ /_____
Identifies words with *r*-controlled vowels	_____ /_____	_____ /_____	_____ /_____
Identifies diphthongs	_____ /_____	_____ /_____	_____ /_____
Passage Reading			
95% to 100% accuracy	level _____	level _____	level _____
90%+ comprehension	level _____	level _____	level _____
Reading Rate	CWPM _____	CWPM _____	CWPM _____

COMMUNICATING ASSESSMENT INFORMATION

Addresses IRA Standard 3.4

Communicate results of assessments to specific individuals (students, parents, caregivers, colleagues, administrators, policymakers, policy officials, community, etc.).

In this age of accountability, teachers and school administrators are talking about assessment and developing their own and others' understanding of it more deeply. It is important that you understand the purpose of assessment tools. For example, standardized tests that are norm referenced are intended to compare students with a national sample of students. On the other hand, standardized tests that are criterion referenced are intended to show how well students have mastered a discrete set of objectives. Informal reading inventories and running records are designed to show how well students read particular books and passages that have been leveled according to difficulty. Teachers need to keep the differences among these assessments in mind when communicating about them to students, parents, and colleagues.

TO STUDENTS

A good assessment is helpful to both the learner and the teacher. When we measure students' growth, we need to help them to see how they can learn from the experience. Some children get a little nervous when they see that we are writing down what they say, but if we explain what we're doing and show them the running record or assessment form we're using, this usually alleviates anxieties about the experience. It's very important to summarize your assessment with the student, focusing on the students' strengths first and then discussing an area or goal for improvement.

TO PARENTS

In our current educational climate, test scores are being posted in newspapers and on the Internet. You need to communicate with parents directly and carefully about their child's progress so that they have a context in which to understand their child's test scores. Many parents want to know their child's level of achievement compared to other children in the same class or grade, and this can be useful information, but they also need to understand how their child has progressed as a reader or writer over time.

Running records, informal reading inventories, and DIBELS subtests are ideal for showing growth over time. You should be able to explain to parents what kind of texts a child was able to read proficiently at the beginning of the year and the kind she is reading proficiently at periodic intervals throughout the school year. For example, if a second grader begins the year reading level H texts with 90% to 95% accuracy and ends the year reading level L texts with 90% to 95% accuracy, you can assure parents that their child's progress is on target. It is very helpful to have available examples of the levels or the benchmark books themselves for parents to see and read. This gives them a concrete idea of how their child has grown as a reader. Some teachers find it helpful to report this kind of information to parents every month in a progress report.

School administrators and teachers should select common assessment instruments for the entire school and district whenever possible to eliminate parent and student confusion. When parents get different kinds of reports from teachers at different grade levels (or even different teachers at the same grade level), they can have difficulty understanding how their child is doing. Since we want parents to be involved in their children's education as much as possible, we should make our assessment and evaluation system as consistent and clear as we can.

Student-Led Conferences

Many schools are using student-led conferences to inform parents of student progress. In cooperation with the teacher, students set learning goals and share them with their parents at conference time. Because they have been included in the process of assessment and evaluation, they have a better understanding of how they're doing—what calls for praise and celebration and what needs improvement. When teachers involve students in this way, they are able to discuss their learning knowledgeably.

To Colleagues

One reason children are assessed at the end of the school year is to provide the next year's teachers with some information about their new students. Standardized tests can be useful to teachers for planning their instruction, precisely because they are standardized—the scoring is done by computer and the reporting is the same for each child. Informal assessments can be just as useful if teachers all use the same one. For example, if everyone uses the QRI (Qualitative Reading Inventory) to assess their students' reading ability at the end of the year, teachers will have a common understanding of what kind of information they can get from the QRI results. Even running records can be standardized when all teachers use the same set of leveled texts— benchmark books for each guided reading level. If a first-grade teacher's running record shows that Maria can read level H books at an instructional level in the spring, the second-grade teacher can assume that Maria will be able to read level H books in the fall (though some summer regression should be expected for many children).

Struggling students often see a resource teacher for extra reading instruction. The resource teacher may have his own assessment that he administers periodically. It is important for the classroom teacher to understand the nature of this assessment so that she can benefit from the information revealed by it. Many resource teachers use curriculum-based assessments, which are a means of deciding what lessons a student needs and with which lesson the child should begin. The resource teacher's curriculum may or may not be the same as the one the classroom teacher uses, but the assessment should still provide useful insight into the child's reading level.

Addresses IRA Standard 3.3

Use assessment information to plan, evaluate, and revise effective instruction that meets the needs of all students, including those at different developmental stages and those from different cultural and linguistic backgrounds.

 CONCLUSIONS

All classroom teachers should be fully committed to the goal of helping every student to read at or above grade level by the end of each school year. Because many students begin the school year already reading below grade level or don't make adequate progress to meet this goal, classroom teachers must be equipped to determine the source of students' reading problems. Some students have difficulty recognizing common spelling patterns and experience decoding problems. Other students may do fine with decoding, but lack the background knowledge and vocabulary to comprehend the meaning of the words they decode. Teachers must be able to screen students to determine which are at risk of developing reading problems and to diagnose the source of these problems. Given the variety of student reading problems in a typical class, teachers must be able to make in-class instructional modifications to try to meet students' instructional needs. Ongoing progress monitoring will tell teachers which students are benefiting from classroom reading instruction and are making adequate progress and which will need additional instructional interventions.

Teachers need not undertake this responsibility alone. Grade-level teaching teams can collaboratively review student assessment data and plan instruction to meet students' needs. School-level resource personnel can also be valuable resources for assisting with assessment and suggesting instructional strategies and interventions. Finally, school administrators can take the lead in seeking district-level and community resources and expertise to address reading instruction needs on a school level. As educators work and plan together with vision and persistence, real differences will be realized in student reading achievement.

 SUGGESTED ACTIVITIES TO EXTEND YOUR LEARNING

1. In an in-class group discussion, brainstorm with your classmates accounts of children you know who may be facing environmental, physiological, emotional, language, and instructional factors that may interfere with their learning (e.g., a child you know from a dysfunctional family that gets very little academic support at home or a child from another country struggling to learn English). What steps could be taken to help such children to overcome these factors?

2. Interview a teacher or a school district curriculum leader. Find out what standardized tests are given, for what purposes, and how they were chosen. Also find out what informal classroom assessments are given and how the data may be used to plan instruction. How well do the formal and informal assessments described provide a comprehensive look at students' education needs and progress?

3. Go on to several assessment Web sites. Explore and see what assessments are available for reading screening, diagnosis, progress monitoring, and outcome measuring. What assessment materials may be downloaded. Suggested Web sites are these:

   Analysis of Assessment Instruments (*idea.uoregon.edu/assessment/index.html*)
   DIBELS (*dibels.uoregon.edu/*)
   PALS (*pals.virginia.edu/*)
   SEDL (*www.sedl.org/reading/rad/list.html*)
   Texas Primary Reading Inventory (*www.tpri.org/*)

 *REFERENCES*

Adams, M. (1990). *Beginning to read: Thinking and learning about print.* Cambridge, MA: MIT Press.

Applegate, M., Quinn, K., & Applegate, A. (2004). *Critical reading inventory: Assessing students' reading and thinking.* Upper Saddle River, NJ: Merrill/Prentice Hall.

Beaver, J. (2001). *Developmental reading assessment.* New York: Pearson Learning.

Block, C. (2003). *Literacy difficulties: Diagnosis and instruction for reading specialists and classroom teachers.* Boston: Allyn and Bacon.

Clay, M. (2002). *An observation survey of early literacy achievement.* Portsmouth, NH: Heinemann.

Cunningham, P. (2000). *Phonics they use: Words for reading and writing.* New York: HarperCollins.

Flynt, E., & Cooter, R. (2004). *Reading inventory for the classroom* Upper Saddle River, NJ: Merrill/Prentice Hall.

Fountas, I., & Pinnell, G. (1996). *Guided reading: Good first teaching for all children.* Portsmouth, NH: Heinemann.

Good, R., & Kaminski, R. (2002). *Dynamic indicators of basic early literacy skills* (6th ed.). Eugene, OR: Institute for the Development of Educational Achievement.

Good, R., Simmons, D., & Kame'enui, E. (2001). The importance and decision-making utility of a continuum of fluency-based indicators of foundational reading skills for third-grade high-stakes outcomes. *Scientific Studies of Reading, 5*(3), 257–288.

Griffith, P., & Olson, M. (1992). Phonemic awareness helps beginning readers break the code. *Reading Teacher 45*(7), 516–523.

Johns, J. (2002). Basic Reading Inventory (8th ed.). Dubuque, IA: Kendall/Hunt.

Kame'enui, E. (2002). Analysis of reading assessment instruments for K–3. Available at: idea.uoregon.edu/assessment/index.hmtl.

Kaminski, R., & Good, R. (1996). Toward a technology for assessing basic early literacy skills. *School Psychology Review, 25,* 215–227.

Krashen, S. D. (1992). *Fundamentals of language education.* Beverly Hills, CA: Laredo.

Leslie, L., & Caldwell, J. (2001). Qualitative Reading Inventory III. New York: Longman.

Lipson, M., & Wixom, K. (2003). *Assessment & instruction of reading and writing difficulty: An interactive approach* (3rd ed.). Boston: Allyn and Bacon.

McKenna, M., & Kear, D. (1990). Measuring attitude toward reading: A new tool for teachers. *Reading Teacher, 43*(9), 626–639.

Pressley, M. (2002). *Reading instruction that works: The case for balanced teaching* (2nd ed.). New York: Guilford Press.

Reutzel, D., & Cooter, R. (2003). *Strategies for reading assessment and instruction: Helping every child to succeed.* Upper Saddle River, NJ: Merrill/Prentice Hall.

Richek, M., Caldwell, J., Jennings, J., & Lerner, J. (2002). *Reading problems: Assessment and teaching strategies* (4th ed.). Boston: Allyn and Bacon.

Snow, C. E., Burns, M. S., & Griffin, P. (1998). *Preventing reading difficulties in young children.* Washington, DC: National Academy Press.

Woods, M. L., & Moe A. (2003). Analytical Reading Inventory (7th ed.). Upper Saddle River, NJ: Merrill/Prentice Hall.

Interventions for Struggling Readers

11

Sylvia Read

Portrait of an ESL Struggling Reader: Lupe Learns to Read

Lupe's family is from Mexico, though she was born in the United States. Her father speaks no English and her mother speaks a limited amount of English. Lupe is a limited English speaker as well. Spanish is the primary language in her home.

When Lupe started second grade, she was reading books at a C level in the guided reading (Fountas and Pinnell, 1996) framework. I was concerned, but ready to provide her with all the instruction and extra help that I could get my hands on. She had gone to the resource teacher at the beginning of the year, but only as an at-risk student, not as a documented special education student. When the resource teacher's caseload grew too high, the resource teacher and I decided that we would work on finding other ways to meet her needs. The resource teacher coordinated our America Reads tutors and made sure that they met with Lupe almost daily.

I met with Lupe daily in a small guided reading group in which we read and reread little books that were at her instructional reading level. She was also given time to read these same books independently while I met with other groups. Once a week, she read with a partner out of our old Heath reading series, which provides lots of practice with familiar stories like Frog and Toad by Arnold Lobel.

Lupe also participated in writing workshop daily. At the beginning of the year, she liked to use her alphabet card to write simple sentences such as "I like apple." By the end of year she was writing simple stories like, "The girl went to the pet store and bought a bird. The bird is red and yellow and green. She bought food for the bird and a cage. She likes the bird a lot. Her mom does not. She says the bird is messy and loud."

The principal of our school also organized an after-school reading program for students at risk. Classroom teachers were paid to work with students in small guided reading groups three days a week after school. After the tutoring hour was over, the students went to the Boys and Girls Club until they were picked up.

By the end of the year, Lupe was reading books at the K and L level. She really liked to read Park's Junie B. Jones and Osborne's Magic Tree House books. She continued to return to old favorites like Eastman's Are You My Mother? and Bridwell's Clifford books. Her ability and enjoyment of reading were evident when she *chose to read or play Sight Word Bingo for free time. Her fluency was improving rapidly and she could retell what she had read with some detail. I felt good about sending her on to third grade with reading skills on a par with many other students in her grade.*

Contrary to claims by some commercial publishers, there are no magic bullet reading programs that will cure every struggling reader (Pressley, 2002). Our best bet to ensure that all students learn to read at or above grade level is to (a) determine the causes of students' reading problems through careful observation and assessment, (b) provide focused instructional interventions that are carefully designed to address these reading problems, (c) continually monitor the effects of the interventions, and (d) make ongoing instructional adjustments as needed (Reutzel & Cooter, 2003).

Teachers often think of instructional interventions as occurring on several levels: (a) instructional modifications implemented by the classroom teacher within the existing reading instruction framework, (b) instructional interventions provided by a special education or other resource teacher, and (c) school-level interventions, such as before-school, after-school, and parent involvement programs. When students are identified as struggling with reading, teachers should first try to modify existing classroom reading instruction to provide additional instructional support. If modifying classroom instruction fails to produce the desired gains in reading achievement, the classroom teacher should consult with school resource personnel to consider placement in a resource program such as Title 1 or Special Education. Additionally, teachers and the principal should work together to develop additional school-level intervention programs to provide additional instructional support for struggling readers. Specifically, this chapter will provide information about the following topics:

- Classroom-based instructional interventions

  More instructional time

  Focused small-group instructional interventions

  One-on-one instructional support
- Resource program instructional interventions

  Title 1 (Chapter 1)

  Special education

  Speech and language programs

  Reading recovery
- School-level instructional interventions

 ## CLASSROOM-BASED INSTRUCTIONAL INTERVENTIONS

MORE INSTRUCTIONAL TIME

Shortly after signing my first teaching contract, I met with my new grade-level teaching team to begin setting up our second-grade curriculum. It was agreed that we would allocate 45 minutes for reading instruction and another 30 minutes for writing. All our students, whether the best or poorest readers in second grade, received the same number of instructional minutes in reading. The National Reading Panel (2000)

Addresses IRA Standard 2.2

Use a wide range of instruction practices, approaches, and methods, including technology-based practices, for learners at differing stages of development and from differing linguistic and cultural backgrounds.

has made it clear that students who struggle learning to read need more instructional time than those who learn to read easily. Teachers may provide extra instructional time through longer instructional groups or extra instructional groups for struggling readers. For example, top reading groups may only meet two or three times per week with the teacher for instruction, while struggling reader groups need to meet with the teacher every day. Top reading groups may discuss what they've read and plan their reading for the next day or two, while struggling readers may receive daily intensive reading skills instruction. Additional instructional time may also be provided through individual tutoring and through before- and after-school instructional programs, which will be discussed in subsequent sections of this chapter.

Focused Small-Group Instructional Interventions

When your assessments show that you have groups of students with similar kinds of reading problems, it makes sense to meet with these children in small groups where you can address their particular needs. The groups need to be flexible; that is, a particular child's group membership will change over time according to his or her current progress and development. A child wouldn't remain in a skills group all year, but rather would move into other kinds of groups as specific skills are mastered.

Using Environmental Print

Using these small, flexible, skills-based groups as an organizational tool, you then need to choose interventions that meet the needs of the students. For example, you might have a group of kindergarten children who don't have a firm grasp on the concept of a word. In a small group, you could examine various kinds of environmental print (fast-food bags, cereal boxes, toy packaging, etc.) and use them to create books. In my first-grade classroom, I had a photo album of street signs, store signs, billboards, and wrappers that my students could read. It is even more powerful to create such a book with the participation of the small group of students who really need to understand the concept of a word and that print carries a message.

The Language Experience Approach

Another powerful strategy to use in small groups is the language experience approach (Nelson & Linek, 1999; see chapter 3). Using small blank books, students draw pictures or glue in magazine pictures and then dictate text that goes with the illustration. The teacher writes the text in conventional print, and the book then becomes the student's personalized reading material. This strategy is excellent for teaching children that print carries meaning and, with repeated practice reading the text aloud, the student learns one-to-one matching of print and voice, the role of punctuation in reading, sound–letter relationships, and the pleasure of creating and reading one's own language. This strategy works particularly well with English language learners, *though it is important to preserve the student's syntax and grammar when taking dictation* so that the student is not confused when trying to read the text.

Magnetic Letters or Letter Manipulatives

Small-group instruction is an ideal time to work with magnetic letters or other letter manipulatives. Using metal cookie sheets (test them to be sure that magnets will stick to them!), students can make words and manipulate the letters to transform the words according to the teacher's directions. For example, when you are working with a small group that needs to better understand how to use rimes and onsets as a decoding strategy, you can direct the students to make the word *light* on their cookie sheet and then tell them, "Remove one letter and change it to an 'n' to make the word 'night.'" You can keep changing the initial letter or letters until many *ight* words have been spelled and read using the magnetic letters. The 37 most common rimes are listed next. Onsets are the consonant or consonants that come before the rime. Together, these and various onsets and rimes make about 500 primary-level words (Adams, 1990).

37 Most Common Rimes

ack	ain	ake	ale	all	ame	an	ank	ap	ash	at	ate
aw	ay	eat	ell	est	ice	ick	ide	ight	ill	in	ine
ing	ink	ip	ir	ock	oke	op	or	ore	uck	ug	ump
unk											

Elkonin Boxes

When a group of students lacks sufficient phonemic awareness, it is helpful to work with an Elkonin box. This is simply a grid of boxes used to help students to separate the sounds in words and count them. For example, the word *cake* has three sounds: /k/ /a/ /k/. Using a series of boxes, the student puts a small counter into each box to represent each sound (see Figure 11.1).

When working with a small group, each child can have a blank grid that has been laminated for durability and a set of math counters. The teacher tells the students a word and helps them to say the word slowly, stretching out the sounds, and each child puts a math counter into a box for each sound they hear.

Align Instruction to Meet Student Needs

There are numerous strategies to use in small group-instruction, but the main point to remember is that the strategy you choose must match the needs of the students. Guided reading groups (described more fully in chapter 7) are an excellent way to organize for small-group instruction, and many of the strategies described throughout this book can be used to explicitly teach students the reading skills they are lacking.

ONE-ON-ONE INSTRUCTIONAL SUPPORT

When students are struggling, they need more attention than they can get from the classroom teacher alone. It can be very beneficial to pull in adult classroom volunteers or older students who can listen to children read and, under your guidance and supervision, provide support while students word-solve and make meaning during their

Figure 11.1 An Elkonin Box

reading. If you have a teacher's aide or paraprofessional, it is important to make sure this person understands your instructional goals for the struggling students the aide will work with and how you want the instruction carried out. Effective teachers of early literacy ensure that this kind of coordination happens with both classroom aides and resource teachers (Pressley et al., 2001).

Using Parent Volunteers

I have made it an important instructional goal that each struggling reader will receive 10 to 15 minutes of individual reading time with me or another adult each school day. Parent volunteers have been very important in helping me to reach this goal. During Back-to-School-Night at the beginning of the school year, I give each parent a note asking how much time they would be willing to volunteer in the classroom each week or month. I list the parents who indicate that they can volunteer an hour in my classroom each week and set up a schedule so that, when possible, I have an hour of parent volunteer time each morning.

Because struggling readers are often poor decoders (Pressley, 2001), my parent volunteers listen to my students read three kinds of texts to build fluency and automatic word recognition: decodable texts, familiar guided reading books, and children's literature books the children choose.

Training Parent Volunteers

I meet with my parent volunteers to train them how to use decodable texts to provide intensive opportunities to practice reading the spelling patterns we are studying in class (see chapter 5). For example, students who still need to work with decodable texts read books from the *Reading for All Learners Program* (Hofmeister, 1996), which has helpful prompts for volunteers and teachers at the bottom of each page. My parent volunteers also listen to my students read fluency-building passages from the *Great Leaps* reading program (Mercer & Campbell, 1996).

I also provide my parents with the guided reading books for one-on-one reading. These books are at each student's instructional level so that, through repeated readings, the students gain the confidence and facility they need to feel like and actually become successful readers.

I also show the parent volunteers how to read and discuss children's literature books that the children choose to build background knowledge and vocabulary and to provide positive experiences reading together for pleasure. My students always feel it is a privilege to read one-on-one with our parent volunteers.

Decodable Texts

Accomplished pianists continue to practice musical scales so that the fingering patterns remain automatic. Beginning readers, particularly those who are struggling, can benefit from similar practice opportunities provided by reading decodable texts that contain a high percentage of decodable words.

Decodable texts are often disparaged by advocates of meaning-centered reading instruction. Such texts are said to promote poor attitudes toward reading, discourage students' use of contextual and semantic information, and lead students away from comprehension, the real purpose of reading. Such accusations would be true if decodable texts alone comprised the entire reading program.

Creating Reading Materials for a Nonreader

Similar to the language experience approach (explained more fully in chapter 3), you can write a piece of text about the child. Begin with an introductory paragraph that includes the child's name and other important information about him or her.

> Travis is eight years old. He lives in Jonesboro. His mom is a nurse. His brother's name is Joey.

Travis and the tutor practice reading this material until he knows it fairly well and then you write a second page with his input.

> Travis likes to catch bugs. He likes ladybugs a lot. He also likes to catch praying mantises. They are sometimes brown and sometimes green. He keeps them in his bug box. He got his bug box for his birthday from his grandpa.

Travis and his tutor practice this reading material over the course of several days until he can read it fairly fluently and accurately. You can keep creating pages of the book for the child to use with the tutor. You can write about things he enjoys, school rules, playground routines, lunchtime activities, and so on.

Each sentence in the story should be written on a sentence strip and then cut apart and reassembled by the child. The child should eventually be able to reassemble the whole paragraph or page using the cut-apart sentences. The child should also write a sentence every day. It could be a sentence from the story or a new one. He or she should try to write it without looking at the text, but with help from the tutor to listen for sounds and write them down. Also, each day a word should be added to a portable word wall or dictionary card, which can be used in the future to help the child with writing sentences.

After the child has experienced success with this teacher-created text, the tutor can move on to using easy books that appeal to the child. Instead of writing every sentence on sentence strips, missed words can be written on index cards. On subsequent days, the missed words are practiced. When the child can correctly read the word on the index card on three separate days (indicated with a check mark or smiley), the card can be retired.

None of this volunteer work with needy students is meant to replace expert instruction from the classroom teacher. This is supplementary help to extend the work initiated by the teacher. For another example, see Cunningham and Allington (2002).

Decodable texts do have a place as one part of a much larger, more comprehensive reading program. Decodable texts provide a temporary boost for students who need additional review and practice to attain automaticity. Focused repeated opportunities to practice and apply reading skills help the light bulb to come on for many struggling students. Decodable texts should not be used lock-step with an entire class or used any longer than necessary, but should be considered as another tool in your instructional toolbox that will meet the needs of certain readers. I use several simple steps when reading decodable texts with my struggling readers.

Focusing the reader.   When reading one on one with a struggling reader, I like to point to the words with my finger as the student reads them. This helps the student stay focused and also keeps the pace from dragging. When the student misses a word and continues to read on without self-correcting, I tap lightly several times on the page below the missed word. When I do this, one of two things happens. Often the student will return to the word, study it, and then read it correctly and continue on. However, sometimes the student will return to the word, study it, and still be unable to read it.

Table 11.1 Onsets and Rimes

Word	Onset	Rime
cat	c	at
blink	bl	ink
chop	ch	op

When a student is unable to decode a missed word, there are several options for helping the student.

Prompting the student.   The first option is to prompt the student into the blending process. I do this by slowly modeling the blending process myself. As I pronounce the first couple of sounds of the word, I hang back and allow my student to take over the blending process and finish the word.

Blending word parts.   Another option is to help the student put together the word parts by blending the onsets and rimes. Onsets are word beginnings, usually the consonant(s) that come before the vowel. Rimes are the vowel and consonants that come after it. Pig Latin is built on the principle of onsets and rimes (at-*cay*, ink-bl*ay*). For example, Table 11.1 shows three words divided into their onsets and rimes.

   To help my students blend word parts, I use my fingers to cover up the onset and focus on decoding the rime first. Then I uncover the onset and help my student to blend that part with the rime we have just studied. For example, imagine that my student cannot decode the word *stick*. I cover up the *st* and help my student to decode *ick*. I ask, "What does this part of the word (*ick*) sound like?" If my student cannot pronounce /ick/, I say, "What sound does *i* make?" I provide my student with the /i/ sound if necessary. Then I ask, "What will *i* say with *ck* added on?" When my student can pronounce /ick/, I uncover the *st* and ask, "What does *ick* say with *st* added on the front?" If my student needs extra support, I might add only the *t* to produce *tick* and then *st* to produce *stick*. For longer words (e.g., str et ch er), use your fingers to focus on each spelling pattern individually. Have the student figure out each spelling pattern and then blend them left-to-right to pronounce the word. This blending of word parts process helps students focus on blending the common word beginnings (onsets) and word endings (rimes).

   Learning this building process is very important for students that struggle with word identification. We have found, happily, that after going through this process repeatedly with students they begin applying it themselves, a big step toward independent word identification.

Blending individual sounds.   The third option when a student cannot decode a word is to use the word to reteach the blending procedure. Say to the student, "Let's say this word the 'slow way' together sound-by-sound: /s/ /t/ /i/ /ck/." Point to the letters as you pronounce their sounds. "Now let's say it together the 'fast way.' Now you say it fast" (student says the word *stick*). With longer words, go through this blending process with parts of the word and then combine. After the student has correctly read the missed word, have him or her reread the entire sentence.

Irregular words.   Irregularly spelled words such as *love, said,* and *is* do not follow the common spelling patterns and cannot be sounded out. Experienced reading teachers quickly distinguish between regular and irregularly spelled words. When words follow the spelling patterns (regular), I help my student decode the words using the procedures described above. However, when a word contains an irregular spelling, I simply tell my student that the word does not follow the pattern or rules, and I provide its pronunciation. For example, I might say something like this to my student:

> *This is the word* is. *It doesn't follow the rules. It looks like it should say /is/.
> But the* s *makes a /z/ sound in this word, so you say* is. *Can you read the
> word* is *in the sentences?*

Many teachers like to put irregularly spelled words on an outlaw words word wall and review the words with the class daily. I have found that my students generally learn to recognize irregularly spelled words just through sheer repetition when they are given ample opportunity to encounter such words repeatedly in decodable texts *and* in the context of meaningful texts.

Repeated Reading

Repeated reading (Chomsky, 1978; Samuels, 1979) allows students to become familiar with printed words and spelling patterns through repeated exposures to the same text. Similar to good music instruction, repeated reading has students read a passage over and over until they can read it fluently and then move on to another passage.

Samuels (1979) suggests that you begin by selecting an interesting passage of about 150 words at the student's instructional level. Read the passage aloud to the student and discuss content and vocabulary as needed. Then have the student read the passage aloud to you. Use a stopwatch to measure how many seconds it takes the student to read the passage. Tell the student how long the reading took and discuss any errors. If the reading takes longer than 1 minute, add the additional seconds to 60 (1 minute and 12 seconds is recorded as 72 seconds). Have the student practice reading the passage alone silently two or three times and then out loud to you with the stopwatch. Show the student his or her time after each reading of the passage. Repeat this process several times until the student's performance has peaked. My experience is that performance usually peaks after three or four readings of the same passage.

Repeated reading can be very motivational as students monitor their performance and want to improve. You may want to construct a chart to record and graph each student's repeated reading times (see Figure 11.2). The following formula will let you calculate each student's reading rate in words per minute.

> *(60 total number of words in the passage) divided by the elapsed time
> (in seconds) equals words per minute.*

You can also get a score that combines both rate and accuracy by subtracting the number of words misread and multiplying 60 by the number of correct words. This is similar to the DIBELS Oral Reading Fluency subtest (CWPM: correct words per minute). CWPM has been shown to be a very good indicator of general reading ability.

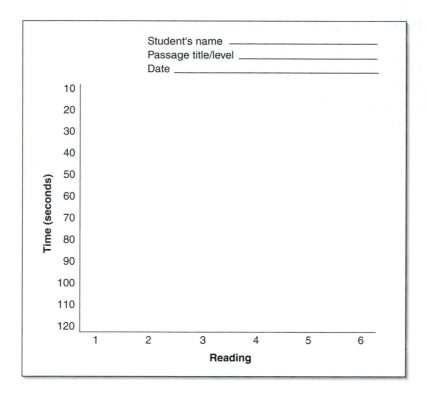

Figure 11.2
Repeated Readings
Line Graph

EFFECTIVE ENGLISH-AS-A-SECOND-LANGUAGE (ESL) INSTRUCTION

Effective ESL instruction uses grade-level curriculum in the content areas as the basis for teaching both language and key curriculum objectives. ESL students need to be exposed to grade-appropriate content area objectives. So content-based ESL instruction integrates content from multiple subject areas into thematic units.

Sheltered instruction (Echevarria, Vogt, & Short, 2004) is a research-based model for teaching English language learners through content area learning. Students are taught the specialized patterns of language use that are unique to academic subjects, while also learning functional language skills. Through sheltered instruction lessons, ESL students learn to read and understand expository prose, write persuasively, argue different points of view, take notes from lectures or text, make hypotheses and predictions, and analyze and synthesize information.

The sheltered instruction lesson should have:

❀ Clearly defined content objectives that are supported by the delivery of the lesson
❀ Clearly defined language objectives that are supported by the delivery of the lesson
❀ Age-appropriate content concepts
❀ Supplementary materials to make the lesson clear and meaningful
❀ Meaningful activities that integrate lesson concepts
❀ Students engaged 90% to 100% of the time
❀ Appropriate pacing

During sheltered instruction lessons, teachers must:

- Make explicit links to students' background knowledge
- Emphasize key vocabulary
- Modulate rate of speech and syntax
- Explain academic tasks clearly
- Use a variety of techniques to make content concepts clear
- Provide opportunities for students to use strategies
- Use scaffolding techniques
- Use a variety of question types, particularly those that involve higher-order thinking
- Provide lots of opportunities for interaction between and among the teacher and students
- Use pairs, triads, and small groups to support the language and content objectives
- Provide sufficient wait time for student response
- Provide, when able, opportunities for students to clarify key concepts in their first language (L1)
- Provide hands-on materials or manipulatives
- Use activities that integrate reading, writing, speaking, and listening
- Review key vocabulary
- Review key content concepts
- Provide feedback to students
- Conduct assessments of learning throughout the lesson

TESOL STANDARDS

The professional organization Teachers of English to Speakers of Other Languages, has an excellent and extensive Web site containing the ESL Standards for Pre-K–12 students: *www.tesol.edu.* They also publish professional journals and books to support teachers of English language learners.

 ## RESOURCE PROGRAM INSTRUCTIONAL INTERVENTIONS

When in-class instructional interventions do not provide the needed levels of improved reading achievement, you should consult with your school's resource personnel to consider placing your struggling students in a resource reading program. There are several kinds of resource programs, each designed to meet the needs of a specific group of struggling readers. Again, because the classroom teacher bears the primary responsibility for reading instruction, placement in a resource reading program should be considered only when in-class interventions have been thoroughly tried and found insufficient. The following sections briefly describe common resource programs for struggling readers.

TITLE 1 (CHAPTER 1)

Title 1 (sometimes called Chapter 1) is a federally funded program that provides additional reading teachers to schools in low-income communities. Students who qualify for placement in Title 1 reading programs are those who are reading below grade level, but who are not thought to have a reading disability. Teachers often refer to Title 1 students as slower learners who simply need extra support. Traditionally, Title 1 reading teachers have provided 30 minutes of daily reading instruction in **pull-out programs:** students leave their homeroom and receive Title 1 instruction in small groups in a resource room. While the extra small-group Title 1 reading instruction was intended to supplement classroom reading instruction, it often had unintended consequences, such as (a) students' missing important instruction in other subjects during the time they were pulled out, (b) Title 1 reading instruction being unrelated to classroom instruction, so struggling readers were being asked to learn two reading programs rather than one, and (c) the stigma attached to leaving the classroom for extra help. More recently, Title 1 reading teachers have been encouraged to provide in-class additional instruction that is coordinated with the classroom reading program.

SPECIAL EDUCATION

Special education (SPED) is also a federally funded program that provides teachers to serve students who have been identified through extensive testing as having a reading or learning disability. While Title 1 students are generally considered to be lower-ability students who are performing at their capacity, Special education students are considered to be normally bright students whose low classroom performance is due to some sort of disability. Once a student has been identified and placed in special education, the SPED teacher uses data from thorough diagnostic assessment to pinpoint the student's reading problems and then develop an individualized education program (IEP) that becomes a legal contract between the school and the student's family. Special education reading instruction typically focuses on providing very specific and sequenced direct instruction.

Speech and Language Programs

Speech and language pathologists provide instruction for students with language difficulties. Often students' language problems are developmental and deal with articulation problems. However, speech and language teachers also serve students with low language skills or with language differences, such as ESL students and students whose dialect differences may impede learning.

Reading Recovery

Reading Recovery (Clay, 1993) is a one-on-one pull-out program developed in Auckland, New Zealand, by Marie Clay for students in the bottom 20% of first-grade classes. Reading Recovery teachers provide 30 minutes of daily instruction that includes five components. First, the Reading Recovery teacher and the student reread a familiar leveled book together. This is generally a book that was used the day before for instruction and practiced at home with family that evening. Second, the Reading Recovery teachers takes a running record of the student reading the familiar book and places the running record in a three-ring binder to document the student's reading growth and needs. The third component of the Reading Recovery lesson is a short phonics lesson, often using magnetic letters to explore and form word families to reinforce spelling patterns. The fourth component is a brief dictation activity: the teacher helps the student to compose and then write a brief meaningful sentence. The teacher also writes the sentence on a cardstock sentence strip that is read by the student and cut into individual words for further practice at home. The final component of the Reading Recovery lesson is for the teacher to introduce a new leveled reader to the student. The teacher helps the student to read through the book and then sends it home for further reading with the family and to be used as the familiar book for the next day's lesson.

SCHOOL-LEVEL INSTRUCTIONAL INTERVENTIONS

Schools that provide effective reading instruction are characterized by strong instructional leadership that brings classroom teachers, resource personnel, and family and community resources together to review school-level reading instruction needs; brainstorm available resources; and together develop school-level programs that complement and supplement classroom and resource reading instruction.

One school envisioned and implemented an early morning volunteer tutoring program for struggling readers. Classroom teachers recommended struggling students to participate in the program, which involved community volunteers who arrived at school 1 hour before the beginning of the school day to tutor students in the school library using lessons materials provided by the students' classroom teachers. Because the school was on the late bus schedule, this time was convenient for everyone. Between 20 and 30 community volunteers arrived each morning and tutored 1 to 3 students each.

Another school noticed that many students congregated on the school playground before school during the 30 to 40 minutes between their being dropped off by their parents and the beginning of the school day. The school's media coordinator, realizing that the media center was vacant during this time, proposed an early morning teacher read-aloud time when faculty members took turns, usually not more than once per month, inviting these students into the media center to listen to teacher read-alouds, rather than waste time on the playground. Students learned that it was a special privilege to be in the media center before school and that any rowdiness would see them back to the playground.

Another elementary principal coordinated the morning schedules of resource teachers and adult volunteers so that this group of adults could arrive together as an instructional support team in classrooms serving struggling readers. This allowed for a daily full hour of very focused small-group reading and writing instruction for the students who needed it the most.

The point is that each school has unique instructional needs and available resources. With the right vision and commitment, enterprising educators can develop school-level programs that provide the additional focused reading instruction needed to help all students to succeed.

CONCLUSIONS

The most effective classroom intervention for struggling readers is a knowledgeable, committed teacher, one who uses assessment data and personal experience to recognize a student's reading strengths and needs and can plan instruction to build on these strengths and meet these needs. Teachers who analyze student achievement data and plan instruction together in grade-level teams and who consult administrators and use resource personnel will have the best chance of making informed and effective decisions. Teachers who are committed to seeing that all their students become successful readers will increase and modify instruction as needed. Experienced teachers always keep their focus on students.

SUGGESTED ACTIVITIES TO EXTEND YOUR LEARNING

1. Identify a struggling reader in your family or neighborhood. Offer to tutor him or her twice per week for about 40 minutes for 8 to 10 weeks. Focus on (1) assessment, (2) meaningful reading, (3) word study, and (4) spelling in each lesson. Use some of the assessment techniques described in chapter 10 to identify specific areas of need. Use some of the instructional techniques described in this chapter to strengthen the student's reading in these specific areas. Keep a tutoring journal of the assessment and instructional techniques you tried, which were most effective, and the student's progress.

2. Interview a classroom teacher and if possible a special education teacher and a Title 1 teacher about the struggling readers they teach, the assessment and instructional methods they use, and their observations about how best to help struggling readers.

REFERENCES

Adams, M. (1990). *Beginning to read: Thinking and learning about print.* Cambridge, MA: MIT Press.

Chomsky, C. (1978). When you still can't read in third grade: After decoding, what? In S. Samuels (Ed.), *What research has to say about reading instruction* (pp. 13–30). Newark, DE: International Reading Association.

Clay, M. (1993). *Reading recovery: A guidebook for teachers in training.* Portsmouth, NH: Heinemann.

Cunningham, P., & Allington, R. (2002). *Classrooms that work: They can all read and write* (3rd ed.). New York: Addison-Wesley Longman.

Echevarria, J., Vogt, M., & Short, D. (2004). *Making content comprehensible for English learners: The SIOP model* (2nd ed.). Boston: Pearson.

Fountas, I., & Pinnell, G. (1996). *Guided reading: Good first teaching for all children.* Portsmouth, NH: Heinemann.

Hofmeister, A. (1996). *Reading for all learners.* Logan, UT: Utah State University.

Mercer, C. D., & Campbell, K. U. (1996). *Great Leaps K–2 reading program.* Gainesville FL: Diarmuid.

National Reading Panel. National Institute of Child Health and Human Development. (2000). *Report of the National Reading Panel: Teaching children to read. An evidence-based assessment of the scientific research literature on reading and its implications for reading instruction.* Washington, DC: National Institutes of Health.

Nelson, O., & Linek, W. (1999). *Practical classroom applications of language experience: Looking back, looking forward.* Boston: Allyn and Bacon.

Pressley, M. (2002). *Reading instruction that works: The case for balanced teaching* (2nd ed.). New York: Guilford Press.

Pressley, M., Wharton-McDonald, R., Allington, R., Block, C., Morrow, L., Tracey, D., et al. (2001). A study of effective first-grade literacy instruction. *Scientific studies of reading, 5*(1), 35–58.

Reutzel, D., & Cooter, R. (2003). *Strategies for reading assessment and instruction: Helping every child to succeed.* (2nd Ed.) Upper Saddle River, NJ: Merrill/Prentice Hall.

Samuels, S. (1979). The method of repeated readings. *Reading Teacher, 32,* 403–408.

Children's Literature References

Bridwell, N. (1985). *Clifford the big red dog.* New York: Scholastic.

Eastman, P. D. (1960). *Are you my mother?* New York: Random House.

Lobel, A. (1970). *Frog and Toad are friends.* New York: Scholastic.

Osborne, M. P. (1993). *Magic tree house: The knight at dawn.* New York: Random House.

Park, B. (1999). *Junie B. Jones and the mushy gushy valentine.* New York: Random House.

Putting It All Together

John A. Smith and Sylvia Read

A DAY IN JOHN'S FIRST-GRADE CLASSROOM: IMPLEMENTING A FIVE-PART LITERACY INSTRUCTION FRAMEWORK

Some years ago I took a leave of absence and exchanged places with a local public school teacher to return to the classroom for a year to teach first grade. My purpose for undertaking this exhilarating and exhausting experience was to develop and provide a balanced and comprehensive reading and writing curriculum. The morning schedule and activities that I describe in this chapter are very typical of our daily activities in the fall of that year.

I was assigned to one of four portable classrooms in back of the building. I was a bit let down at being assigned to a portable until I realized that I would have something that few teachers in the school would have: a thermostat. School began at 9:15 and dismissed at 3:30. Thirty-five percent of the school's students were eligible to receive free or reduced lunch. I did not have a paid classroom aide, but was fortunate to have several dedicated parent volunteers who helped in my classroom throughout the school year.

Like Sylvia's, my curricular emphases, decisions, and actions were based on a set of personal beliefs about literacy teaching and learning:

❀ To be fully effective, literacy instruction must include the following instructional components: teacher read-aloud, independent reading, word study, guided reading, and writing.
❀ A flexible literacy instruction framework provides both needed consistency and coverage.
❀ Literacy instruction requires a 2½- to 3-hour instructional block of time.
❀ Struggling readers need more instruction and more instructional time.
❀ Assessment is an integral and necessary component of instruction.
❀ I set myself a goal that all my first-grade students would leave my class at the end of the year reading on or above grade level.

Daily Schedule

9:00	Students arrive
9:15	Class business
9:30	Teacher read-aloud from a picture book and class singing
10:00	Word study
10:20	Reading time: instruction groups and independent reading

11:20	Recess
11:30	Writing workshop
12:30	Lunch
1:15	Reading aloud from a chapter book
1:35	Math
2:15	Science or social studies unit
3:00	Students with Music or PE teacher (my prep time)
3:30	School day ends

8:00–9:00 A.M.   BEFORE SCHOOL

Even though school doesn't officially start for another 75 minutes, some of my students begin trickling in, anxious to tell me of their latest family events and to see what we'd be doing that day. Most of these early arrivers visit for a few moments and then head outside to the playground to begin burning off a fraction of their limitless energy.

A few of them are some of my lower readers. I have identified about a half-dozen of my 23 students as needing extra support in reading and have made it a priority that each gets one-on-one reading time each school day with me, a parent volunteer, or a university practicum student. I take advantage of this before-school teaching opportunity with a warm invitation of "Hey, let's read together for a few minutes." I pull an extra chair next to my desk and the two of us sit side by side as I listen to one of the students read aloud from a self-selected SSR book, a preprimer, or a page of decodable phonics practice sentences. As the student reads, I help with word identification when appropriate, discuss the content, and make brief notes in a three-ring binder that contains anecdotal records for each student.

When I'm not reading with a student during this morning time, I usually review my plans for the day, make instructional materials, or head to the copy machine to run off another hundred pages of the half-and-half paper my students use each day during writers' workshop. I really enjoy this early morning time that allows me to pay special attention to some of my students and get a running start on the day.

9:00–9:15 A.M.   STUDENTS ARRIVE

The first bell rings, the classroom door flies open, and most of my 23 students begin hanging coats and backpacks on the hooks on the back wall. Some students bring me zipper-locking freezer bags containing the take-home books they have been reading with their parents. Later during the day these bags will be checked in, refilled with new take-home books, and returned to the students. During this 15 minutes, students may converse quietly with friends, peruse my classroom library, play "center" games such as Concentration, read alone or with a partner at a self-selected classroom location, or work on a project at their desks. A few students continue to trickle in right up to the official beginning of the school day.

9:15–9:25 A.M.   CLASS BUSINESS

The final bell rings, students head for their seats, and the school day officially begins. Most of the time, the students' desks are arranged in a horseshoe configuration with the open end of the horseshoe toward the chalkboard at the front of the room (see Figure 12.1). A large shag rug lies on the floor in the middle of the horseshoe. We reg-

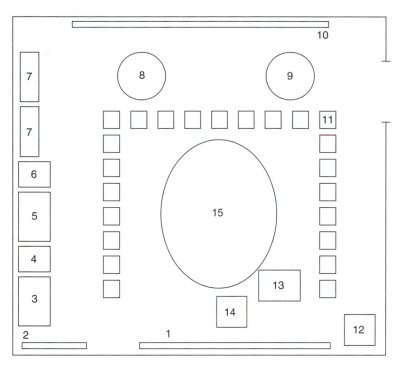

Figure 12.1 John's First-Grade Classroom

1. Chalkboard
2. Flag and pledge chart
3. Thrift shop sofa
4. Reading conference chair
5. Teacher desk
6. File cabinet
7. Bookshelves
8. Listening center table
9. Small-group table
10. Word wall
11. Student desks
12. TV/VCR
13. Thriftshop teacher, reader, author chair
14. Overhead projector for mini-lessons
15. Shag rug for whole-class activities

ularly alternate between activities at the desks and on the rug. This helps keep a feeling of freshness to all that we do. In the back of the classroom are two round tables that serve as a listening center, a place for small-group instruction, and other miscellaneous activities.

I collect the last of the zipper-locking freezer bags, take roll and lunch count, and spend a few minutes welcoming everyone, doing a brief monologue about something silly that happened to me or my family, and providing a preview of the day's highlights. Often, I provide this morning message in written form on the chalkboard. The students really enjoy reading along and trying to predict upcoming words as I write. Today's morning message, "This afternoon, we'll start a new art project and go to the library," also provides an opportunity to examine a meaningful written text for familiar spelling patterns and word parts. Brady comes to the chalkboard and underlines the *th* digraph in *this* and *the*. Sally and Trent each underline an r-controlled vowel in *afternoon* and *start*. Jill also underlines the *st* consonant blend in *start*. Tim, our future linebacker, proudly announces that the word *pro* is part of the word *project*. I too examine the sentence and point out that there are two more r-controlled vowels waiting to be found.

The daily Pledge of Allegiance provides a wonderful opportunity to strengthen students' familiarity with print conventions. I consult my roll book and announce that today's pledge pointer is Abbey. Abbey importantly strides to the front right corner of the room where the American flag hangs above the words to the pledge printed on a piece of chart paper. When she is ready to begin, I call out, "Everybody up, hands on hearts." The class stands and reads the pledge aloud, following along as Abbey uses a yardstick to point to the words. For most of my class, this daily opportunity to see left to right, top to bottom and to match the individual printed words to the, by now, memorized text is very effective in strengthening literacy foundation concepts. It also allows us to show off at the school's annual outdoor flag raising ceremony as it became very evident that our class could say the pledge with more confidence and gusto than any other.

This time for class business ends each morning with my instruction, "Make sure you have two or more silent reading books, and nothing else, on top of your desk and then come to the rug. Remember, I want you to *choose books* that *you know the words.*" Although my grammar is inexcusable, students are reminded to choose books at their independent or instructional level so that silent reading becomes an effective time to build automaticity through reading and rereading words with familiar spelling patterns and word parts in context. Some students hurry to the classroom library to get books, others search their backpacks, and many pull books from inside their desks. As my students seat themselves on the rug, I scan the desks to make sure that each student will have several independent reading books ready to read when the time comes.

Because it's early in the year, some students are reading "Sam books" (short decodable text readers they are familiar with), while other students read *Frog and Toad* or other "I Can Read" books. A few read from preprimers, while some read class-made books from language experience lessons. As the months go by, my students read more challenging texts, including some easy and some harder chapter books.

9:25–10:00 A.M.   TEACHER READ-ALOUD AND SINGING

The next 35 minutes will be devoted to three activities: a brief sharing time, an interactive teacher read-aloud, and singing. My sharing time is typical of most others. My 23 students each have one designated day each week for sharing, although I frequently allow some students to share on other days on an "emergency" basis. Having sharing time on the rug, with the students seated close together, provides a nice, more intimate atmosphere for sharing. Each student takes a minute to tell about a family event or show and describe an interesting object. I generally ask each student a question or two, thus providing added opportunities for the students to use and develop their language, and encourage their classmates to do the same.

As sharing time concludes, I read aloud a picture book. This morning's teacher read-aloud is the story "Cookies" from Arnold Lobel's Newbery Honor book *Frog and Toad Together.*

I first introduce the theme of the story by telling my students of a Saturday afternoon last week when I was watching a football game on TV when I should have been mowing the lawn. I describe how I knew I shouldn't watch the ballgame that afternoon when the lawn needed to be mowed and how I needed *will power* to put down the chips, get up off the couch, and start the lawn mower. After elaborating on the term will power, I ask my students if any of them could tell us about a time when they needed will power to do something they knew they should do. After several accounts of cleaning rooms, changing diapers, and other mostly household chores, I invite my students to listen carefully to the story to see how Frog and Toad needed will power to do something they needed to do.

I read "Cookies" mostly straight through, not wanting to interrupt my students' attention to the characters and events. Occasionally I stop briefly to ask a question or when I sense that some clarification would be helpful. As the story concludes and I close the book, I love to ask, "Well, what did you think?" My students' invariably respond with, "I liked the part when _____. I liked the part when _____. I liked the part when _____." After all the major story parts have been mentioned, I try to raise the discussion to a more personal and thoughtful level by asking, "How did you feel when Frog let the birds eat all the cookies? Is there a lesson in this story?" After the discussion, I tell my students, "Later today we will begin learning to read 'Cookies.'"

A favorite part of each school day is when my 12-string guitar comes out of its case for a usually raucous, always spirited sing-along. We sing lots of children's songs, grown-up songs that are appropriate for children, and songs that we write together as a class. Most days we begin with a song of my choice, usually a new song that we are learning or reviewing. Then I have the day's "song chooser" student select an additional song from the growing Songs We Know list posted on the wall. Someday we'll sing three songs if there's time.

Today I choose to introduce a bouncy new song, "My Old Man Is a Sailor," that I remember from a now long lost Smothers Brothers children's album. The lyrics are as follows:

My old man is a sailor, what do you think of that?

He wears a sailor's collar, he wears a sailor's hat.

He wears a sailor's raincoat, he wears a sailor's shoes,

And ev'ry Saturday evening he reads the Sunday news.

And someday, if I can,

*I'm gonna be a sailor, the same as my old man.**

I begin by singing the song to them and explaining that the phrase "my old man" is another way of saying "my father." After the students have heard me sing the song, I display the lyrics prewritten on a piece of chart paper. I write all my song lyrics on chart paper and tape a coat hanger to the back of each chart at the top. The coat hangers make the charts easy to hang up and display and also easy to store on a chart rack.

With the song lyrics chart in view, I read the words to my students, pointing to the words as I say and discuss them. Now that the words have been both musically and visually introduced, I lead the class in singing the song several times until they begin to sing it confidently.

On this particular song lyrics chart, I had replaced the word *sailor* with a blank line each time it appears in the lyrics.

My old man's a _____, what do you think of that?

He wears a _____'s collar, he wears a _____'s hat.

For a follow-up activity, we brainstorm a list of familiar occupations on the chalkboard. The list grows to include banker, farmer, and basketball player. For fun, I add two suggestions of my own: refrigerator repairman and elementary school principal. I tell my students that we will sing the song several more times, but now substituting in the new occupations we have listed. Singing the song with the two-syllable occupations (banker, farmer) was easy. Basketball player wasn't too bad. But the two tongue twisters I suggested made for some pretty silly and laughable singing. Now whenever we sing "My Old Man's a Sailor," we always begin by generating a new list of occupations to include in the song (my students' favorite occupation to include in

*First verse of "My Old Man Is a Sailor," Words and Music by Oscar Brand, TRO-Copyright 1963 (Renewed) Hollis Music, Inc. New York, NY. Used by permission.

the song seems to be ballerina). After "My Old Man's a Sailor," one or two students get a turn to serve as song chooser.

The emotional and literacy benefits of singing time are tremendous. First, singing creates a sense of community better than almost any other classroom activity. The songs are generally upbeat and often silly and help to get each school day started on a very positive note (please forgive the pun). My students' eyes sparkle as they sing and bounce to the catchy rhythms.

We also get a lot of instructional mileage from singing. Each day, one of my students gets to be the song pointer. Like the pledge pointer, the song pointer points to the words on the song lyric chart with a yardstick as we sing. By springtime, all my students can do this accurately and confidently. We often examine the printed lyrics for familiar spelling patterns and word parts. The powerful motivating influence of music makes daily singing time into a highly effective component of my literacy instruction.

10:00–10:20 A.M.   WORD STUDY

After our teacher read-aloud and singing time, I begin a word study lesson. I had begun introducing my students to the vowel teams spelling pattern (*ai, ay, ea, ee, oa*, and *ow*). Last week I introduced the A Teams (*ai* and *ay*). Today I plan to introduce the E Teams (*ea* and *ee*). I begin by displaying a chart of *long a* and *long e* vowel team word families (see Table 12.1). I quickly review the A Teams and then introduce the *ea* and *ee* spelling patterns.

I explain to the students that the *ea* and *ee* spelling patterns both have two vowels and both make the *long e* sound. I refer my students to the *ea* word families in the third column of the chart. Beginning with my usual question, "Whose turn is it to read first?" I read down the column of *ea* words, showing how the initial consonants and consonant blends combine with *ea* and a final consonant(s) to create the words.

Then we read the column of *ea* words together several times aloud as a class; alternating among first-grade voices, daddy bear voices, and baby bear voices for variety. I teasingly point out that "fifth-grade students are so smart they can start at the bottom of a list and read the words going up to the top." My students protest that they can too and take great delight in proving it to me. As the class begins to read the words confidently we move to "show-off" reading. I ask several of my students to choose three friends, stand, and read the words aloud to the class.

I conclude the lesson by giving each student a blank index card and inviting them to search for and write *ea* words on the index cards during their independent

Table 12.1   Vowel Team Spelling Patterns

A Teams		E Teams	
ai	**ay**	**ea**	**ee**
paid	day	leaf	feed
rain	say	team	jeep
wait	play	heat	sweep
trail	stay	cream	screen
paint	away	treat	freeze
chain	today	teach	cheese

reading and reading at home. Tomorrow they will bring the cards with the *ea* words that they found and we'll create a class *ea* word hunt chart with their words. I expect that some of the *ea* words they'll find will not fit the pattern (*bread, spread, breath*). Such exceptions provide a good opportunity to further clarify and reinforce the concept as my students discriminate whether the vowels in each word make a *long e* sound. The final component of the day's decoding lesson (finding the spelling patterns in connected text) will take place during the next classroom activity, shared reading.

10:20–11:20 A.M.   READING TIME (READING INSTRUCTION GROUPS AND INDEPENDENT READING)

During reading time my students and I alternate among several activities: independent and partner reading, individual teacher–student reading conferences, LEA lessons, shared reading and guided reading lessons, and word study and oral reading fluency group activities. I like to get my students all reading independently for a while, do an individual reading conference or two, and then begin pulling instructional groups together.

Independent Reading

After our word study lesson, my students and I head back to our desks where our independent reading books are waiting. After the word study activities, independent reading provides a nice calming change for us all. My students select from among the books on their desks and begin reading silently to themselves. So that independent reading time is not wasted, I enforce several rules: (1) you have to choose books that you can read, (2) no talking, and (3) no going back to the bookshelf for more books.

I really enjoy these moments when everybody in the classroom is fully engaged, reading a self-selected text at their independent or instructional level. I enjoy watching their lips move as they subvocalize the words. The key to successful independent reading is to make sure that the time is used effectively.

Each day during independent reading I scan my roll book and designate three or four of my students as "special readers" who get the privilege of choosing a special place in the classroom to read. Popular independent reading places include the rug, the old overstuffed couch in the corner, under my desk, in the author's chair, in the closet with the door open, and on or under the tables in the back of the classroom. I also scan my students' book selections occasionally to make sure that they aren't showing off, pretending to read *War and Peace* or some other book above their independent or instructional reading level.

Reading Conferences

Once my students are settled into reading, I call a student to bring his or her independent reading book to my desk for a reading conference. My reading conferences quickly cover three aspects of the student's reading: reading attitude and interests, oral reading fluency, and comprehension. I begin by asking each student what book he or she has chosen and why and jotting down the date of the conference, title of the book, and its level. Then we discuss the student's reading interests such as favorite genre and how he or she learns about and selects books. Then I ask the student to read a paragraph aloud to me as I make notes in my assessment binder about words or spelling patterns the student struggled with, reading rate, and expression. Finally I ask the student to tell me what the book is about, occasionally probing the student's knowledge

Addresses IRA Standard 2.1

Use instructional grouping options (individual, small-group, whole-class, and computer-based) as appropriate for accomplishing given purposes.

Addresses IRA Standard 2.2

Use a wide range of instruction practices, approaches, and methods, including technology-based practices, for learners at differing stages of development and from differing linguistic and cultural backgrounds.

Addresses IRA Standard 2.3

Use a wide range of curriculum materials in effective reading instruction for learners at different stages of reading and writing development and from different cultural and linguistic backgrounds.

of setting, characters, and events (or main ideas and details for expository texts) and asking for opinions about the book. To complete the reading conference, I often give recommendations of other books of potential interest, a brief spontaneous mini-lesson on an appropriate strategy, or an assignment such as rereading a passage to practice fluency or to deepen understanding. These notes are very helpful in identifying students with similar needs, tracking students' progress, and determining instructional topics.

Reading Group Lessons

After one or two reading conferences, I call my shared reading group to the rug in front of the chalkboard and remind them that I had promised them we would learn to read Arnold Lobel's story "Cookies", our teacher read-aloud earlier this morning. I project an overhead transparency of the first page of "Cookies" directly onto the chalkboard. At this point I select my student Erica to serve as the pointer. Erica grabs a pencil, sits in the chair next to the overhead projector, and points to the first word on the transparency.

Again I ask my students, "Whose turn is it to read first?" I read the first page aloud to them, with Erica pointing to the words as I read. Then I invite my students to read the page aloud with me. Erica and I lead the group in several choral readings of the page.

For the show-off part of today's shared reading lesson, I announce that the show-off readers will get a free drink of water after they read aloud. This generates much excitement and my students enthusiastically volunteer for show-off reading. I call on several of the students in my shared reading group, including those with Velcro latches on their shoes; those with stripes on their shirts; those wearing yellow; those whose names start with A, B, or C; and, finally, all those who haven't been show-off readers yet.

The next part of my shared reading group lesson, finding and underlining spelling patterns in the shared reading sentences, is very important. This whole-to-parts step explicitly links the daily decoding lessons to the students' reading of connected text. I begin this portion of the shared reading group lesson by asking the familiar question, "Who can find some of our spelling patterns on the first page of 'Cookies'?" By this time of the school year, my students are very familiar with the a number of spelling patterns they have learned, and immediately hands go up as students scrutinize the sentences. Responding in our standard procedure, Liz says, "Sentence one, the word *Toad* has a vowel team with *oa*." Using a marking pen, I underline the *oa* in *Toad* and then ask, "Who else can find a spelling pattern?" Becca similarly points out, "In sentence two, the word *ate* is a tickle word." Again I underline the identified spelling pattern. Bryce adds, "In sentence one, the word *some* is a tickle word." I use this opportunity to teach why the word *some* looks like but is not a tickle word, making a *short u* sound rather than the *long o* it would make if it followed the pattern. We add some to our list of outlaws, words that don't follow the rules. In the next few minutes we discover together that *baked, even, taste*, and *made* are tickle words; *Frog, smell*, and *cried* contain blends; and *these, they*, and *that* contain digraphs. We also add *one* and *said* to our list of outlaws. The chalkboard is thoroughly marked up, and my students can plainly see that most of what they read is simply combinations of the spelling patterns.

We continue this process for a few more minutes until this first page is pretty thoroughly marked. We conclude the pattern-finding portion of the shared reading lesson with one more choral reading of the page, returning from the parts to the whole. Tomorrow we will reread this page and add one or two more pages. Probably next week, when my shared reading group students can all read "Cookies" reasonably well, we'll turn it into a reader's theater. I underline Frog's dialogue in red on the overhead transparency and Toad's dialogue in blue. The nondialogue narrator parts won't be underlined. I assign one or two students to each part (Frog, Toad, or Narrator) and have them practice a bit, and then they reread the story as a readers' theater. This is a great way to build my students' oral reading fluency while having fun with children's literature.

After the shared reading group lesson, this group of students returns to their seats to continue their independent reading, reading with a partner, practicing their reader's theater part, or finishing a writing activity. I then call one of my two guided reading groups to meet with me for a 10- to 15-minute lesson.

Parent Volunteers

Most mornings during reading time, one of my five parent volunteers arrives in our classroom. During our Back-To-School Night in September I had distributed a sign-up sheet for volunteers, asking who might be able to volunteer weekly, monthly, or on call as needed. Five parents indicated they could volunteer 1 hour each week, so I set up a schedule for each of them to come in on a different day of the week.

In early October I identified six of my students who were not keeping up with their classmates in reading, who needed extra instructional support. I decided that the best use of my parent volunteers was to provide the extra reading instruction for my six struggling readers in the area of basic decoding skills. I met with the parent volunteers and showed them a simple procedure for reading together one on one with a student.

1. Take the student to the sofa in the corner of the classroom and preview the text I had selected (sometimes an *I Can Read* book, sometimes a decodable text, or both).

2. Point to the words in a sweeping motion while the student reads aloud.

3. When the student misreads a word, tap on it to refocus the student on the word.

4. If the student still cannot identify the word, the parent can either (a) prompt the student by pronouncing the beginning of the word and allowing the student to finish it, (b) help the student blend the letter–sounds left to right, or (c) "break and make" the word by covering the onset, decoding the rime, and then putting the two parts of the word back together.

5. Finally, the parent volunteer makes notes for me about the one-on-one reading session, recording the title and page numbers of text read together and any words or spelling patterns that the student struggled with.

My goal was for each struggling reader to get 15 minutes of one-on-one reading time with either myself or a parent volunteer each day. I prepared a reading schedule and a list of appropriate reading texts, and the system worked very smoothly. The parent volunteers would come into my classroom, go to my desk to see which student was next to be read with and which reading text to use, take the student to the couch and read together, and then call the next student over, and so on. I also instructed the parent volunteers to read with my middle and top students on occasion, because all my students loved reading to my volunteers. I am absolutely convinced that these parent volunteers made a huge contribution to the reading success of my struggling readers.

11:20–11:30 A.M.   **WE'RE TIRED. IT'S TIME FOR RECESS**

11:30 A.M.–12:30 P.M.   **WRITING WORKSHOP**

Mini-Lesson

After 10 to 15 minutes of running around outside, my students return to the classroom and find sitting places back on the shag rug in the center of the classroom, ready to begin our writing workshop with a daily 10- to 15-minute mini-lesson (Atwell, 1998; Avery, 2002). Today's mini-lesson will focus on dialogue. I stand in front of the classroom next to an overhead projector, getting ready to write on a transparency a version of my students' writing paper that is being projected onto the chalkboard. For the past four or five days our mini-lessons have been demonstrations of including dialogue in our stories. Today I plan to add two or three sentences to our ongoing class story. The students watch on the chalkboard and read along as I write:

> *Cassie asked, "Where is my pencil?"*
>
> *"It's on the floor," said Juan.*

We read the sentences again together and then discuss how the quotation marks help us to know who's speaking and what's being said. Then I continue on with the class story, adding the following sentence:

> *Joanne said, "Hey, that's my pencil, not Cassie's."*

We read the sentence together and note how the quotation marks help us know what the people in a story are saying. As the day's mini-lesson concludes, my students return to their seats with my reminder, "Remember to put talking in your stories. I want to know what the people in your stories are saying to each other."

Silent Writing

When everyone is seated at their desks, we begin 10 minutes of silent writing. The purpose of silent writing is to give the students uninterrupted time immediately after the mini-lesson so that they may apply the information from the mini-lesson to their writing while it is still fresh in their minds. Everybody writes, including me. We don't talk and walk around the classroom during silent writing.

My students write on what I call half-and-half paper: the top half of the paper is a blank box, and the bottom half is ruled for writing. This paper allows them to write or to organize their ideas through drawing when needed. At the beginning of the school year my students drew extensively, with very little writing. I would go from desk to desk, saying, "Tell me about your picture," and then add a caption below my students' drawings. Soon my students wanted to write their own captions and I helped them to get started. Over the weeks and months, they draw less and write more until, by the end of the year, many of my students have totally discontinued the drawing and use the top half of the paper for their revisions. I keep a large supply of half-and-half writing paper in a small basket at the back of the classroom, and my students know to always keep four to five extra sheets of this paper in their writing folders.

Free Writing Time and Conferences

The 25 to 30 minutes after silent writing are spent in what we call free writing time. During this time, my students may choose to remain at their seats and continue with their writing, write with a partner, illustrate a book they have written, or have a writing conference with me.

Consistently throughout the year, about half the students each day choose to remain at their seats, continuing their writing. I spend this time moving from seat to seat, dragging a first-grade chair with me and conferencing with these students. My conferences always began with my invitation, "Would you please read it to me?" I sit beside the student's desk and follow along as the student reads to me. Much of the writing at this point is invented spelling, which I encourage with a continual reminder of "Just write the sounds that you hear." When a student has written an invented word that I cannot read, I write the correct spelling in very small letters above the word(s) on the student's paper. The purpose for this is to help me to remember what is written when it comes time for typing and printing the story for publication. I do not tell my students that they must correct their spelling at this point, and my notations do not seem to bother or inhibit their expressiveness. In fact, they quickly learn just to ignore it.

We discuss the content of the story first during the conferences. I usually ask what the student plans to add next, or else I ask for more details. For example, Doug is writing about a sleepover at his Grandma's house. I tell him that I'm very curious about Grandma and would like to know more about what Grandma looks like and what she does and says. Occasionally I will also provide a spontaneous individual mini-lesson on some aspect of punctuation (usually use of periods and capital letters) or spelling. This free writing time is often the most challenging part of my day, because I often have three to five students waving to me, indicating that they are ready for a conference. I generally reply with another standard response, "Keep writing. I'll be there as quickly as I can."

Authors' Chair

When I note, during a conference, that a student has four to five pages of new writing, I suggest that he or she go to the chalkboard and sign up for the authors' chair. Usually this amounts to three or four students each day. Authors' chair is the final portion of writers' workshop and provides a daily 10- to 15-minute opportunity for my students to give and receive feedback about each others' writing. The students who have signed up take turns sitting in the large, overstuffed thrift-store chair and reading their pages of new writing to their classmates who are seated on the rug. After each authors' chair student has read, the classmates provide their responses to two standard questions: "What did you like about his or her writing?" and "What would you like to know more about?" The ensuing comments are both reinforcing and informative as my student writers learn how to make their writing interesting to their peers.

Publishing

When I explained to my students that we would soon begin making books out of their writing, we decided as a class that you can't make a book out of one page, or two pages, or even five or six pages. I suggested that I needed at least eight or nine half-pages of writing to make a book. My students accepted this as a matter of course. I showed them how to number their draft pages and staple them together so that they wouldn't waste time each day shuffling and reordering pages.

When one student has written enough for a book, he or she brings it to me to be published. We review the story together and then with a parent volunteer or a college practicum student, or I type the student's story onto a computer (correcting spelling and punctuation like a real editor), electronically paste the sentences into a word processor book template, and then print the book pages for the student to illustrate. When the illustrations are completed, the student's biographical author information page is added at the end, the cover and back pages are laminated, and the book is spiral bound. The finished book is then presented to its proud author to be celebrated in class and taken home to be cherished and praised by family members. I place photocopies of the books in a section of our classroom library for students to read during independent reading time. I save the original handwritten half page manuscripts in each student's portfolio folder to be reviewed and shared at parent conference time.

Our daily writing workshop lasts about 1 hour. Because my students are so highly motivated by having their writing published, they love writing, and the writing workshop time goes by quickly. In fact, the students are very disappointed if we have to miss writing workshop due to a school assembly or some other interruption. After writing workshop, we are very ready for lunch.

AFTERNOON

Altogether, we spend about three hours each morning engaged in reading and writing activities. After lunch, I read aloud a chapter from a novel each day while my students relax on the rug. Math comes next for about 40 minutes, followed by activities from either a science or social studies unit. These activities often involve informational children's book read-alouds and content area writing. Our school day concludes with my students going to either PE or the music specialist.

 ### CONCLUSIONS

Perhaps the largest challenge teachers face is how to provide instruction that is appropriate to a classroom of students who are reading and writing at a wide variety of ability levels. I was able to accommodate differences in students' abilities in several ways. For example, teacher read-alouds provided vocabulary and background knowledge learning and positive emotional associations with books for students at all levels.

I've found that all students benefit from words study lessons as spelling patterns are made explicit and become tools for decoding other unfamiliar words. It's one thing for a beginning reader to be able to distinguish between *pin* and *pine,* but it's also important to understand why these words are pronounced differently and to be able to generalize that difference to other words that contain similar spelling patterns.

During independent reading, all students benefited from the practice and reinforcement of reading self-selected texts at their instructional or independent levels. The level of instructional support I provided in my reading group instruction and the level of texts I asked students to read varied from group to group.

Writers' workshop was wonderful for accommodating students of differing reading and writing ability levels. Students at all levels could write at a comfortable personal pace and receive support and guidance through individual conferences specific to their writing needs. Additionally, all students were highly motivated by writing on self-selected topics and seeing their finished works in print.

Another instructional benefit of using a comprehensive balanced literacy instruction framework is the synergy that occurs among the various instructional components. For example, teacher read-alouds provide students with vocabulary and background knowledge that help them make sense of their reading during shared and guided reading lessons. Word study lessons familiarize students with spelling patterns that they use during independent reading and also during writing workshop. Conversely, writing workshop gives students opportunities to explore letter–sound relationships and spelling patterns they encounter in their reading.

For approximately 3 hours each morning "my students were involved, almost nonstop, with words: hearing, reading and studying words; sharing and playing with words; singing and dramatizing words; and writing and illustrating words" (Smith, 1998, p. 21). Allington (1980) argued that one of the best predictors of improvement in reading ability is the number of words that students process during reading lessons. In other words, authentic literacy activities such as independent reading, partner reading, shared reading, guided reading, and writing facilitate reading achievement whereas filling in blanks on worksheets is of little or no instructional value (Anderson et al., 1985). Although scheduling large blocks of time for literacy instruction in primary grades may be a challenge, it is an investment that we simply must make.

A DAY IN SYLVIA'S SECOND-GRADE CLASSROOM: MEETING YOUNG CHILDREN'S SOCIAL AND ACADEMIC NEEDS

The classroom routines I've established, the instructional procedures I choose to employ, and the mountain of second-to-second teaching decisions I make are all based on a set of my beliefs about teaching and learning. These beliefs are the foundations for everything I do in teaching, from how much instructional time I allocate to the various curriculum subjects to how I interact with individual students during reading and writing conferences. These beliefs enable me to develop a comprehensive and responsive literacy instruction program based on professional knowledge and experience.

My key beliefs about teaching and learning are these:

- Children need boundaries to feel physically and emotionally safe.
- Children need consistency in daily school routines (ideally, at home too).
- Children learn to behave appropriately through modeling, experience, and positive feedback.
- Children need to be able to make choices in order to feel invested in their learning and behavior; however, too many choices are overwhelming.
- The teacher's job is to balance choice and structure, to provide modeling and feedback, and to let children know that they are *seen*, both literally and metaphorically.

Traditionally, early childhood education has emphasized the social needs of children. More and more early childhood has an intense academic focus, even in kindergarten. I believe that we can and must focus on both. However, I also believe academic learning needs to happen in the context of effective social teaching. In my second-grade classroom, the first six weeks of school are just as much about the content of the curriculum as the rest of the year. I don't teach a purely social curriculum at the beginning and wait for the content to come in later. Instead, social skills and community building happen in the context of the entire curriculum. One feature of my classroom that supports both academic and social skills development is its structure. The children live and learn within a predictable structure, and the structure allows me to focus on both their academic and social growth. As Lucy Calkins has recommended:

> I have finally realized that the most creative environments in our society are not the kaleidoscopic environments in which everything is always changing and complex. They are, instead, the predictable and consistent ones: the scholar's library, the researcher's laboratory, the artist's studio. Each of these environments is deliberately kept predictable and simple because the work at hand and the changing interactions around the work are so unpredictable and complex. (Calkins, 2001, p. 12)

The procedures and routines become so familiar to my students that they can tell a substitute teacher or a parent how the classroom operates after having been in my class for only a few weeks. As I explain the structure of a typical day, I also explain how I infuse social skills and language arts into the entire curriculum.

Daily Schedule

9:15	Silent reading
9:30	Morning meeting
10:00	Writing workshop (includes mini-lesson, writing time, and sharing)
10:45	Recess
11:00	Reading (includes teacher read-aloud, whole-class skills lesson, independent reading, and guided reading groups)
12:00	Lunch
12:35	Return from lunch recess, have impromptu class meeting as necessary
12:40	Class meeting
12:50	Math
1:30	Spelling
2:00	Recess
2:15	Integrated curriculum (science, social studies, health education, art, etc.)
2:45	Children go to PE or music
3:15	Pass out praise notes, homework, announcements
3:20	Dismissal bell

9:00–9:15 A.M.   CHILDREN ARRIVE

Before the school day starts, the students have a few jobs to do. They bring in homework, trade their home reading books, sign up for their lunch choice, and select books for silent reading. They put their books at their seats so that they're ready to begin reading when the bell rings. Until then they are free to play quietly with blocks or math manipulatives, talk with friends, build paper airplanes, draw, or read. This free time is important to them. They come to the classroom quickly so that they can enjoy this time. It's important to me that they use this time independently so that I can focus on trading their home reading books, do a quick reading or math assessment, speak to a parent, or confer quietly with a child.

9:15–9:30 A.M.   SILENT READING

We read silently for about 15 minutes. Often one or two children are late arriving, and this allows them to be late (being tardy usually is not the child's fault) without missing instructional time. I read silently too. In some schools, this is a schoolwide time for silent reading, often called DEAR (Drop Everything and Read).

9:30–10:00 A.M.   MORNING MEETING

Morning meeting (Kreite, 2002) follows silent reading and includes greetings, sharing, a group activity, and news and announcements. I begin by signaling the children that silent reading is over by saying, "Okay, let's come to the rug." This lets them know that they should put away their silent reading books and make a circle on the floor. Morning meeting follows a set routine. We begin by figuring out how many students we have in attendance, who is absent, if anyone, and how many people are signed up for the different lunch choices. We do mental math together to figure out the numbers, which the helper of the day then records on the attendance slip. Next, we say the Pledge of Allegiance. The helper of the day is the leader for this activity and signals the class by saying, "Ready, begin." After the pledge, we sit down again and greet each other.

Greeting

The greeting is very important. Each child, every day, is greeted eye to eye by some member of the class. The greeting passes around the circle or across it in various ways depending on the greeting we choose. I teach a repertoire of greetings during the first six weeks of school, and then the children choose from this repertoire for the rest of the year. Greeting each other is a very concrete way for everyone to feel a part of the classroom community.

Sharing

Sharing follows the greeting. Each child has a day of the week when he or she can tell a story or show the class something. I allow only one object or anecdote so that we can keep up a brisk pace. Some children can take too much time and overburden those with shorter attention spans. It's my job to keep things moving along. Sharing is a formal way that each child has to speak in front of a group, an area in language arts that needs to be developed in young children. Emotionally and socially, sharing is a way for every child to be seen and heard by the whole group.

News and Announcements

News and announcements follow the group activity. I write a morning message on a piece of chart paper or a whiteboard easel that gives the students an idea of anything unusual that might be happening that day, and it includes an activity that reinforces academic skills. For example, I might leave out vowel teams in words and as a group, we go back and fill them in. Most often, in second grade, the children read aloud the news and announcements chorally. They almost always have already read it silently as soon as they entered the room that day!

10:00–10:45 A.M.   WRITING WORKSHOP

Mini-Lessons

Sometimes I incorporate a writing mini-lesson into the news, but I also offer writing mini-lessons that are completely separate. Here's what I might say in a typical mini-lesson at the beginning of the school year:

> *I am so excited that it's time to write. I enjoy writing because I get to write about whatever I want. Let's see. . . . What do I want to write about today? I am going to talk aloud the thoughts that are in my head so you can hear them. When you do this, it would help if you did it inside your head so that everyone can concentrate. Here I go. I could write about my trip to New*

York this summer. Or I could write about my dog Rider. He's so funny.
Or maybe I could write about how I feel today. Which one should I do?
I think I will write about how I feel because I like to remember how
I feel on days like this. Okay, here's my paper. I'm going to start by writing
my name up here so if I drop it someone will know who it belongs to. And
I'm going to write the date too, because when I read it later this year I'll
want to know when I wrote it. I'm also going to skip lines when I write.
That way, if I want to change anything I'll have room to draw a line
through it and write it a different way on top. Okay, here I go. (As I write,
I read aloud, but I don't want the children to read aloud because I want to
continue voicing my thoughts.) "I feel very happy today because it is the
first day of school. When I was little, I was always a little bit scared on the
first day of school because everything was so new and I didn't know what
was going to happen. But today I am happy because I am the teacher and
I get to help my students not to be scared like I was when I was their age."
Whew! Writing is hard work, but I think that's all I'm going to write today.
I can write faster than you can because I'm a grown-up, but I wrote about
three sentences and I think you can do that too. Right now your job is to
close your eyes and think about what you want to write about today. It
could be something you did this summer, something important to you,
something fun you like to do, how you feel—anything. When you know
what you want to write about today, I want you to raise your hand. I will
call on you and you will tell your writing idea. I'll give you a piece of paper
and you'll go right to your seat and begin working. Close your eyes now
and start thinking.

This is how my mini-lesson for the whole group ends, but then as I listen to their ideas I get a chance to give them a little feedback. If a student says, "My dog," I'll ask, "What about your dog?" If a student says, "How I feel," I might say, "How do you feel?" I rarely have students tell me that they can't think of anything to write about. If they do, I offer them suggestions based on what others have told me. Often this helps. Sometimes a brief conversation about family sparks an idea. Sometimes nothing helps and it may take a few days before a child writes. After watching others write, hearing others share their writing, and, as a last resort, being told that they must write about not knowing what to write, a reluctant writer will write. Sometimes it's just a rough start and smooth sailing follows. Writing is an idiosyncratic process. Most children find choice motivating; some children need more specific directions, in which case it can be helpful to give a limited range of choices.

Conferences

As the children work on their writing, I circulate around the room, trying to check in with every student. I stop by their seats, kneel down and look them in the eye, and ask them simple questions like "What are you writing about?" Or I say, "Tell me what you're working on." Later, after teaching them how to respond to this question, I'll ask, "How's it going?" which is an opportunity for them to voice a problem they're having with their writing or a chance to celebrate a really good part of their writing by reading a short section aloud to me. Often, at the beginning of the year, children are able to sustain a quiet writing time for only 5 or 10 minutes. Later I push them to sustain this time longer; but in the beginning, when they haven't built up much stamina, I stop the writing time, choose two or three students to share their writing, and we move back to the rug for writing sharing. All these little pieces of the routine require modeling, teaching, practicing, and reminding. I record the student's writing topics and other observations on the Status of the Class form (See Figure 12.2).

Authors' Chair

When a child shares his or her writing, the other children have a very important job. They must listen carefully and respond thoughtfully. This too must be modeled and taught. I model what listening looks like and sounds like and also what it doesn't look like. The audience will respond to the writing in several ways. They will tell the author what they heard in the writing, what they liked, and what parts may have confused them. Sometimes the author wants ideas on where to go next with the writing, and in this case the audience can make suggestions and offer ideas. My job during this time is to model ways to respond to others' writing positively, to ask genuine questions, to politely explain what parts were confusing, and possibly to make gentle suggestions for change. Whether the author takes the suggestions and uses them to revise is entirely up to the author, but I often write a note for the authors who share so that they can remember what was said. I use the Status of the Class form (Figure 12.2) to record who shared.

10:45–11:00 A.M.   RECESS

After sharing, we take a break for recess. Writing and responding to writing are hard work and we all need a break. Some students are so engaged in their writing that they want to continue their writing outside.

11:00 A.M.—12:00 P.M.   READING INSTRUCTION

Mini-Lesson

When we come inside from recess, it is time for reading instruction. I begin our reading time with a mini-lesson. At the beginning of the year, the mini-lessons are almost always review and teaching of phonics and decoding skills or reading aloud from a big book or picture book. After January, mini-lessons tend to be on other skill areas, such as contractions, decoding longer words using chunks, comprehension strategies, and genre instruction. Mini-lessons for reading are short, 10 to 15 minutes, and are aimed at teaching concepts and skills from which the whole class will benefit. After the mini-lesson when I am meeting with small groups or individuals, I can target my instruction more carefully to meet children's individual needs.

Independent Reading

At the beginning of the year, when children need to learn how to operate independently, I don't meet with small groups. They first need to learn how to choose books and read independently. I have tried using centers for reading-related work while I work with small groups, but I have found over the years that teaching the children to interact with books and other print in the room is more effective than setting up centers, which take more adult monitoring than is possible when I am working with small groups. When I have students reading independently, a quick glance around the room tells me quickly who is using their time well.

Figure 12.2   Sylvia's Status of the Class Form

Status of the Class

Date _____

	Writing	Shared	Reading
Alexa	Continue my pets	Tues	Junie B. Jones fluent
Alexis	My cousin's dog	Thurs	smiles when reading the funny parts
Colter	Franklin Basin – snow	Tues	sometimes he skips words he doesn't know
Courtney	Trip to Colorado	Wed	self-corrected when/then
Dakota	Camping w/ family	Tues	self-corrected when she skipped words
Dalton	Ride motorcycles at grandma's	Fri	Up in the Tree - easy
Daniel	Big or little bike book – revising	Wed	very fluent – even with words in parentheses
Emily C.	Bear Lake	Mon	good expression – self-corrected skipped word
Emily P.	Ch. 2 – Yellowstone	Wed	changes word endings – amazing – amazed
Jessica	My cats	Wed	Up in the Tree – easy
Jonathon	continue – Trip to Wolf Creek	Mon	substitutes on little words
Jordyn	Camping		absent
Landon	Trip to Disneyland	Wed	self-corrected when he skipped "old"
Lorena	copying words from dictionary card	Fri	good one-to-one correspondance
Mark	Pets	Thurs	figured out "agreed"; good comp; Fox All Wet
Paisley	Mom and dad running a marathon	Thurs	fluent; good expression
Preston	snowboard skills	Fri	self-corrected Fox All Wet; figured out "serious"
Sarah	Moving to a new house	`Mon	figured out "fingers"
Talan	Bionicles description	Tues	good expression
Tirzah	poetry	Mon	very fluent
Tommie	Going to San Diego		fluent and expressive
Travis	Praying mantis	Fri	working on firming up one-to-one correspondence
Trevor	Kickball	Fri	good expression on question sentence
Tylor	Skate park	Mon	good expression

After a few weeks of whole-class independent reading during which I model, we role-play, they practice, and I remind, I'm ready to start meeting with small groups. Although I spend a week or so meeting with small groups, I keep my eye on the whole group. Charney (2002) calls this "paradoxical groups" because she "pretends" to teach the small groups while actually teaching the whole class. It is crucial to set up my classroom so that I can see everything from the position I take while working with small groups. The children need to know that they can be seen. What they are doing while I am working with a small group is important work: they are consolidating their reading skills by reading independently. But if they sense that I am not paying attention to them, they may feel that what they're doing isn't really important and their attention will falter. Busy work and mindless forms of seatwork are inappropriate; they waste the children's time and mine.

Even when I am teaching the whole class this way, and yet working with small groups, the tasks I set for the small groups teach them how to be productive and self-directed as well. I usually start by having them read books that are somewhat easy. Reading easy books is good for building confidence, fluency, and comprehension. When decoding is not a huge burden, the children's minds are free to make the experience enjoyable, read with speed and expression, and pay attention to the meaning of the text. Also, we have established an important routine of reading easy books first, which will continue even as we move into reading books that are at their instructional level.

Guided Reading Groups

When the students have internalized what independent work feels like, I am ready to begin having guided reading groups in which the students are encountering new words, harder phonics concepts, and longer sentences and stories. My attention will need to be mostly on the children in my small group, catching those teachable moments when they're stuck on a word and I can help with strategies to figure them out. If I'm worried about what the rest of the class is doing, I won't be able to give my fullest and best attention to the learners in my small group. I don't ever stop paying attention to the rest of the class. By fully teaching and practicing independent work habits, I have a much better chance of keeping the classroom running smoothly and allowing everyone, myself included, to feel productive and relaxed. It may seem strange to think that the students and I should be relaxed, but if I'm tense, I convey this to my students. If they're worried about other students bothering them, they're tense and they convey that to me. A tense atmosphere is not a productive one. I aim for a peaceful classroom with a quiet hum of activity.

Guided reading groups are small, preferably two to six children (see Table 12.2). If I have too many small groups, it is impossible to meet with all of them every day. I meet with my struggling readers every day without fail. Those who are reading on or above grade level meet with me one to three times per week. Later in the year, when almost all the students are reading on grade level, I switch to a reading workshop format in which everyone is reading independently the entire time. I continue to meet with my struggling readers every day, but in our small group every child may be reading a different book. It has to be this way after a while, because one child may still be reading at level J while the rest of his or her group has moved on to level L, M, or N. It is critically important to keep children reading at their instructional and independent levels. I try to individualize my instruction as much as possible. I keep track of what reading groups are doing on a simple planning chart. Keep in mind that these

Table 12.2   Example of Guided Reading Groups

Reading groups	Jeff, Donna, Luis, Celia, Fawn (Level J books)	Lupe, Dalton, Travis (Level G books)	Shaylee, Ryan, Evan, Macie, Landon, Lincoln (Level K books)	Bethany, Jordan, Doug, Tristan, Autumn (Level K books)	Tirzah, Jonathan, Daniel, Lakeesha, Jake, Megan (Level N + books)
Monday	Read *Curious George and the Ice Cream*	Reread *Mushroom for Dinner*, introduce and read *Grandpa's Lemonade*		Read *Commander Toad and the Space Pirates*	Begin Literature Circle with *More Stories Julian Tells*
Tuesday		Reread *Grandpa's Lemonade*, introduce and read *The Lion and the Mouse*		Continue reading *Commander Toad and the Space Pirates*; response to book with drawing and a sentence about favorite part	Read *More Stories Julian Tells* independently
Wednesday	Read *Danny and the Dinosaur*	Reread *The Lion and the Mouse* introduce and read *Joey*	Read *Dancing with the Manatees*		Read *More Stories Julian Tells* independently
Thursday		Reread *Joey*, introduce and read *Monarch Butterflies*	Read information about manatees from Seaworld Web site		Discuss *More Stories Julian Tells*
Friday	Partner reading using basal anthology	Partner reading using basal anthology	Readers theater of *The Hidden One: A Native American Legend* from *www.aaronshep.com*	Readers theater of *The Hidden One: A Native American Legend* from *www.aaronshep.com*	Prepare choral reading of "Sarah Cynthia Sylvia Stout," a poem by Shel Silverstein

groups are flexible. If Celia makes faster progress than the others in her group, I move her into a group where the books will challenge her appropriately. On the Status of the Class form (Figure 12.2), I record notes about student's reading behaviors.

12:00–12:40 P.M.   LUNCH AND LUNCH RECESS

12:40–12:50 P.M.   CLASS MEETING

After lunch, there are often recess problems that need to be discussed. If necessary, we have a quick class meeting to deal with these problems. It is also a time to take care of things that need to happen at the beginning of the year, such as establishing class rules, discussing such issues as how to include others in play or free time activities, or perhaps water fountain protocol. Students often need to be heard more than they need to have the problem solved, but nevertheless we work together to come up with possible solutions. We try it, and if it fails, we think of a different solution. It is important that the solution be theirs, that they feel ownership of it. Lots of social skills learning is embedded throughout the day, but morning meeting and class meetings are when these social skills become the content of the instruction. Even young children can learn to present problems without demeaning others, give their own opinions respectfully using "I" phrases, listen while others give their opinions, make eye contact with others, wait to speak instead of interrupting, say positive things about others' ideas, accept multiple solutions, and choose one solution to implement. Language skills are a big part of social skills; clear descriptive speaking and active listening are crucial skills that are being learned and practiced during class meetings. Class meetings are a nice transition into the afternoon. When children feel heard, they are ready to move on and think about complex academic subjects again after a possibly difficult time on the playground.

12:50–1:30 P.M.   MATH TIME

I often start our math time with a question. I might say to the class, "I know there are 25 of you here today, but I'm wondering how many pockets you all have." Quickly, students want to guess or estimate. When a student estimates, I ask how they decided on the answer. Hearing students' thought processes to solve a riddle like this is fascinating to me. It is good for them to have to communicate their thinking. We might not try to find the exact answer on the first day, but the next day I might ask them how we could figure it out exactly. They offer their ideas and we try a few of them. The point of starting with these questions is to get them to think about math as not just computation, but also as problem solving.

I use a combination of resources when deciding how to teach the second-grade math curriculum. My school district has an adopted text, which I follow most of the time. I also use replacement units published by Math Solutions, which features books written by Marilyn Burns and others. These units have whole-class lessons and math centers that encourage children to think deeply about math and games and activities that allow children to use math. I also use worksheets, card games, and dice games to practice math facts.

My students are given lots of opportunities to voice their strategies for thinking about math. They volunteer to demonstrate their strategies for the whole class, and they write about them in math journals. Writing is an important part of math. I may ask them to write how to play a game I've taught them or to explain how they solved a problem. I provide a sentence frame for students who need one. For example, I might write on the board, "There are _____ cubes in the bucket. I figured it out by _____."

During math, students often work in pairs. With younger students I find that groups larger than two can be too cumbersome. One student is apt to sit back or get left out. Even with groups of two, some students don't participate equally; so I clearly teach, model, and have them practice how to take turns, share the responsibilities, and help each other to think (as opposed to telling each other answers). Work habits and social skills are taught all day in every subject area and every moment of the day.

We also have a daily, but brief, computation practice that is scored and returned to the students each day. I take pains to emphasize that they are not competing with each other, but rather with themselves by trying to beat their previous day's score. When I implemented this 5-minute routine (including passing out and collecting papers), my students computation score on the state math test went from 89% to 95%.

1:30–2:00 P.M.   SPELLING

Partner work is important in spelling too. Because the students all have a unique set of words based on their current spelling ability, it would be nearly impossible for me to test all of them (though a first-grade teacher I know tests the kids in groups of six, giving each child his or her words individually). My solution is for the students to have spelling buddies. The main function of the buddies is to give each other practice tests and then to test each other. Every year some children help each other on spelling tests, which in some ways doesn't matter. Even without help, getting all the words right on a "test" doesn't guarantee that a word is memorized. My goal is to have the children understand the importance of spelling in context, so this is what I stress. However, I also discuss with children the importance of honesty and how taking a little test like this loses all its meaning when they have received help from their partners. I make a point of praising children who have made honest mistakes on their test. I say things like, "Great! I'm so glad you were honest when you took this test! You'll have a chance to work on learning this word again next week, and it will be so much easier for you because you've already been learning it this week!" We do study some words in common occasionally. For example, in the spring, we all study contractions and homonyms (e.g., two, to, too).

2:00–2:15 P.M.   AFTERNOON RECESS

2:15–2:45 P.M.   SOCIAL STUDIES, SCIENCE, HEALTH

We spend the last part of the day studying other curriculum areas (social studies, science, health) and extending our learning in these areas through reading, writing, discussion, and activities. In general, I want to foster a deep understanding of a few topics, rather than superficial knowledge of many. I don't have my students make lots of arts and crafts or do any activity that takes up more time than it is worth. I aim for an optimal ratio of learning and time. Keeping a learning log that records ideas generated through read-aloud and discussion is a better use of the children's time than making a caterpillar out of an egg carton. Finding countries on a globe or world map is more valuable than making a papier-mâchée globe. A school day is very short and the curriculum is demanding. I want to make the most of the time we have together.

2:45–3:15 P.M.   PREPARATION TIME

During this time, my students are with the PE or the music teacher. I use this time to plan lessons for the next day, prepare instructional materials, and write a few praise notes for my students.

3:15–3:20 P.M.   PRAISE NOTES

After my preparation time, we gather again on the rug where I ceremonially pass out praise notes. Praise notes are short specific statements about something a child has done that day and why it was important. I try to write one praise note for every child each week. I often write them while conducting reading and writing conferences, while observing a moment of exploration of math material, or during recess. I write them about both social skills and academic skills. I might write, "You used periods in your writing today. That's important because it helps you read it more easily." Or I might write, "You asked Jane to jump rope with you at recess. That's important because you are showing her you care."

My students save these praise notes, count them, and display them on family refrigerators. The parents think they're valuable. This isn't empty general praise—it's specific and it teaches. When I give a child a praise note, I do it publicly (except in special cases) because I want everyone to hear and learn from what one child has done. It reinforces and reminds them of all the things I teach throughout the day. Some weeks I ask students to write praise notes for themselves, and some weeks I ask them to write them for each other. After all the modeling I have done, they have internalized the purpose and tone of praise notes. Often they write about different things than I do because they are able to observe some of the more private moments of the day or small things that escape my notice. But the praise notes I write are especially important to the kids. If I am busy and neglect to write them one day, I am sure to hear about it at the end of the day.

Praise notes fit into my philosophy of teaching and learning because they foster intrinsic motivation and reinforce positive behaviors. Unless I have a student who has a behavioral disorder that requires a behavioral modification program using external reinforcers like points to earn rewards, I do not use stickers, stars, or points. I find it much more powerful to teach students to be productive, well-behaved members of our classroom community throughout the day through modeling, practicing, reminding, and praising.

In addition to interweaving social skills teaching throughout the day, reading, writing, listening, and speaking are vehicles through which we learn across the curriculum. Language arts skills are the tools that make all learning happen. While we focus on the language arts specifically during particular parts of the day, it is important for children to experience reading, writing, listening, and speaking as a way to learn anything and everything. As they use the language arts to learn, through a synergistic effect, their reading, writing, listening, and speaking skills grow stronger and more sophisticated.

 ## CONCLUSIONS

The two classrooms described in this chapter worked well for us. We offer them as examples of teachers orchestrating time, materials, activities, and assessments to meet students' needs. We weren't teaching published programs. Rather we were flexibly selecting and implementing specific activities within a general reading and writing instruction framework. Our intent is not that you try to mimic what we have done. It is our hope that you will take the general principles and specific activities described in this book and create your own flexible and comprehensive instructional programs for teaching young readers and writers.

 ## SUGGESTED ACTIVITY TO EXTEND YOUR LEARNING

1. Interview a primary-grade classroom teacher about his or her classroom organization. What are the most important reading curriculum elements included each day? How much time is allotted to these elements each day? What reading and writing instruction materials and programs are used? How are the physical space and furniture in the classroom arranged to maximize classroom routines

and learning. What records (class rolls, assessment data, observational notes, student work samples) are kept and used to track and plan student learning? How are other classroom teachers and resource personnel involved in your instructional decision making? How are parent and other volunteers used in the classroom?

 ## REFERENCES

Allington, R. (1980). Poor readers don't get to read much in reading groups. *Language Arts, 57*(8), 872–881.

Anderson, R. C., Hiebert, E. H., Scott, J. A., & Wilkinson, I. A. G. (1985). *Becoming a Nation of readers: The report of the Commission on Reading.* Champaign-Urbana, II: Center for the Study of Reading.

Atwell, N. (1998). *In the middle: New understandings about writing, reading, and learning.* Portsmouth, NH: Heinemann.

Avery, C. (1993). *And with a light touch: Learning about reading, writing, and teaching first graders.* Portsmouth: NH: Heinemann.

Calkins, L. (2001). *The art of teaching reading.* New York: Longman.

Charney, R. (2002). *Teaching children to care: Classroom management for ethical and academic growth, K-8.* Greenfield, MA: Northeast Foundation for Children.

Kreite, R. (2002). *The morning meeting book (Expanded ed.)* Greenfield, MA: Northeast Foundation for Children.

Smith, J. (1998). Mr. Smith goes to first grade. *Educational Leadership, 55*(6), 19–22.

Children's Reference

Lobel, A. (1979). Cookies. *In Frog and Toad Together*. New York: HarperTrophy.

Word Parts We Use Chart

Word Parts We Use

Beginner Words	can, bed, sit, hog, rub
Blend Words	s<u>n</u>ip, fa<u>st</u>, <u>br</u>and
Digraph Words	mu<u>ch</u>, <u>sh</u>ed, wi<u>th</u>, <u>wh</u>en
Tickle Words	same, fine, rope, tube
Vowel Team Words	m<u>ai</u>d, pl<u>ay</u>; gr<u>ee</u>n, t<u>ea</u>m; c<u>oa</u>ch, b<u>ow</u>l
R-controlled Vowel Words	c<u>ar</u>d, h<u>er</u>, b<u>ir</u>d, f<u>or</u>, t<u>ur</u>n
Diphthong Words	b<u>oy</u>, p<u>oi</u>nt; l<u>ou</u>d, c<u>ow</u>; ch<u>ew</u>; str<u>aw</u>

Spelling Patterns and Chunks List

 SHORT VOWEL CVC WORDS

a: cab, jab, lab, tab, add, bad, dad, fad, had, lad, mad, pad, rad, sad, bag, rag, tag, wag, am, dam, ham, jam, Pam, ram, Sam, an, ban, can, Dan, fan, Jan, man, pan, ran, tan, van, cap, gap, lap, map, nap, rap, sap, tap, zap, gas, pass, at, bat, cat, fat, hat, mat, pat, rat, sat, ax, Max, tax, wax, Jazz

e: Ed, bed, fed, led, red, Ted, wed, beg, bell, fell, sell, tell, well, yell, hem, Ben, den, hen, men, pen, ten, yes, bet, get, jet, let, met, net, pet, set, vet, wet, yet

i: bib, fib, rib, bid, did, hid, kid, lid, rid, if, big, dig, fig, gig, jig, wig, Bill, dill, fill, gill, hill, ill, Jill, kill, mill, pill, quill, till, will, dim, him, Jim, rim, Tim, in, bin, fin, pin, sin, tin, win, dip, hip, lip, nip, quip, rip, sip, tip, zip, hiss, kiss, miss, it, bit, fit, hit, kit, knit, lit, mitt, pit, quit, sit, wit, fix, mix, six, fizz, Liz

o: Bob, cob, job, rob, rod, cog, dog, fog, hog, jog, log, doll, Tom, on, bop, cop, hop, mop, pop, top, dot, got, hot, lot, not, pot, rot, ox, box, fox, pox

u: cub, rub, tub, bud, dud, mud, bug, dug, hug, rug, tug, gum, hum, yum, bun, fun, gun, run, sun, cup, pup, us, bus, fuss, but, cut, hut, nut, rut, buzz, fuzz

 SHORT VOWEL WORDS WITH CONSONANT BLENDS

a: blab, crab, drab, grab, slab, back, pack, black, snack, act, fact, clad, glad, Brad, raft, flag, brag, drag, snag, camp, clam, clamp, damp, lamp, slam, ramp, scram, stamp, swam, tram, clan, bran, plan, span, and, band, brand, grand, land, hand, sand, stand, ant, pant, plant, clap, flap, scrap, slap, snap, strap, trap, wrap, ask, class, grass, cast, fast, last, past, flat, that, brat, scat, spat, swat

e: Fred, sled, sped, left, held, elf, self, smell, spell, belt, felt, melt, help, stem, fence, end, bend, blend, lend, mend, send, spend, tend, trend, bent, cent, dent, sent, spent, tent, vent, went, step, crept, kept, slept, swept, wept, desk, dress, best, crest, nest, pest, rest, test, vest, west, zest, next, text i: crib, kick, sick, stick, skid, slid, squid, sniff, gift, lift, twig, milk, silk, drill, frill, grill, skill, spill, still, film, slim, swim, trim, grim, limp, grin, skin, spin, prince, wind, hint, lint, mint, tint, glint, print, splint, sprint, squint, blip, clip, drip, flip, grip, skip, slip, snip, trip, lisp, crisp, bliss, fist, list, mist, wrist, twist, flit, grit, skit, slit, spit, split, twit

o: blob, slob, snob, block, clock, lock, rock, sock, soft, clog, frog, slog, smog, pond, crop, drop, flop, plop, slop, stop, cost, lost, slot, spot

u: scrub, stub, spud, stuff, plug, slug, drug, snug, bump, jump, pump, spun, stun, dunk, junk, skunk, bunt, hunt, punt, plus, bust, dust, just, must, rust, trust

SHORT VOWEL WORDS WITH CONSONANT DIGRAPHS

ch: bench, bunch, catch, chap, chat, check, chest, chick, chill, chin, chip, chop, chunk, crutch, ditch, fetch, flinch, hatch, hitch, itch, latch, lunch, match, much, munch, patch, pitch, punch, rich, switch, such, trench, which, witch

sh: bash, brush, bush, cash, crash, fresh, hush, mash, mush, rash, rush, shed, shelf, dish, fish, shin, ship, gosh, Josh, shock, shop, shot, shred, shut, splash, swish, trash, wish

th: bath, Beth, math, moth, path, than, that, them, then, thin, thrill, thud, with

wh: what, when, whim, whip, whop

LONG VOWEL SILENT E WORDS

a: face, lace, race, fade, made, wade, safe, cage, page, bake, cake, fake, Jake, lake, make, quake, rake, sake, take, wake, bale, dale, gale, male, pale, sale, tale, came, fame, game, lame, name, same, tame, cane, Jane, mane, pane, ape, cape, tape, base, case, ate, date, gate, hate, Kate, late, mate, rate, cave, Dave, gave, pave, save, wave, daze, faze, gaze, haze, maze

e: pete, Gene, Steve, these, scene

i: dice, ice, mice, nice, rice, vice, hide, ride, side, tide, wide, knife, life, wife, bike, dike, hike, like, file, pile, dime, lime, time, dine, fine, line, mine, nine, pine, vine, wine, pipe, ripe, wipe, fire, hire, tire, wire, wise, bite, kite, quite, site, dive, five, hive, live, size

o: lobe, robe, code, rode, Coke, joke, poke, woke, yoke, hole, mole, pole, role, sole, dome, home, bone, cone, tone, zone, dope, hope, rope, hose, nose, rose, note, vote

u: Sue, cube, tube, dude, rude, huge, Duke, mule, rule, dune, June, tune, cute, mute, fuse

LONG VOWEL SILENT E WORDS WITH BLENDS AND DIGRAPHS

a: brace, place, space, trace, blade, grade, shade, trade, stage, flake, brake, shake, snake, stake, stale, whale, shame, chase, crave, grave, shave, slave, blaze, craze, glaze, graze

i: bribe, scribe, tribe, price, slice, spice, thrice, twice, bride, glide, pride, slide, stride, strife, spike, strike, smile, while, chime, crime, grime, prime, slime, shine, spine, swine, twine, whine, gripe, snipe, stripe, swipe, sprite, white, write, drive, strive, thrive, prize

o: globe, probe, broke, choke, smoke, spoke, stroke, stole, whole, slope, chose, those, drove, stove, froze

u: blue, clue, glue, true, Bruce, prune, chute, flute

VOWEL TEAM WORDS (VOWEL DIGRAPHS)

ai: aid, maid, paid, raid, fail, hail, jail, mail, nail, pail, rail, sail, tail, aim, gain, lain, main, pain, rain, vain, bait, wait

ay: bay, day, hay, jay, lay, may, pay, ray, say, way

ea: pea, sea, tea, peace, easy, read, bead, lead, leaf, beak, leak, peak, weak, deal, heal, meal, real, seal, veal, beam, seam, team, bean, dean, lean, mean, heap, leap, eat, beat, heat, meat, neat, seat, tease, peace, leave, weave

ee: bee, fee, knee, see, free, tree, three, deed, feed, need, reed, seed, weed, greed, beef, peek, seek, week, feel, heel, kneel, peel, seem, queen, seen, teen, beep, deep, jeep, keep, peep, seep, weep, beet, feet, meet

oa: load, road, toad, loaf, soak, coal, foal, goal, foam, roam, loan, moan, soap, boat, coat, goat, moat, oat

ow: mow, low, row, sow, tow, bow

VOWEL TEAM WORDS WITH BLENDS AND DIGRAPHS

ai: snail, trail, claim, plain, slain, brain, chain, drain, grain, train, Spain, sprain, stain, strain, faint, paint, saint

ay: clay, play, slay, gray, pray, tray, stay, spray, stray, sway

ea: flea, each, peach, beach, bleach, reach, preach, teach, plead, bleak, creak, freak, sneak, speak, squeak, streak, tweak, squeal, steal, cream, dream, gleam, scream, steam, stream, clean, cheap, beast, east, feast, least, yeast, cleat, please, cheat, pleat, treat, wheat, greasy, weave, leave

ee: free, three, tree, bleed, breed, freed, greed, speed, tweed, cheek, creek, Greek, sleek, steel, wheel, green, screen, creep, sheep, screech, speech sleep, steep, sweep, cheese, fleet, greet, sheet, sleet, sweet, tweet, street, breeze, freeze, sneeze, squeeze, sleeve, sneeze, wheeze

oa: broach, coach, poach, roach, cloak, croak, groan, boast, coast, roast, toast, float, gloat, throat

ow: blow, crow, flow, grow, show, snow, bowl, own, grown

R-CONTROLLED VOWEL WORDS

ar: bar, car, far, jar, tar, star, card, hard, yard, large, dark, bark, Mark, park, spark, shark, arm, charm, farm, barn, yarn, harp, art, cart, chart, part, smart, start

or: or, for, nor, porch, bore, core, chore, more, score, shore, snore, sore, store, tore, wore, storm, born, corn, horn, morn, horse, sort, sport

er: her, clerk, jerk, germ, term, fern, stern, verse, Bert, nerve, serve, swerve

ir: fir, sir, bird, girl, firm, dirt, flirt, shirt, skirt, birth, third, first, thirst, squirt

ur: fur, church, urge, surf, turkey, curl, burn, turn, curse, nurse, purse, hurt, curve

VOWEL DIPHTHONG WORDS

oy: boy, joy, toy

oi: choice, voice, boil, coil, foil, oil, soil, spoil, toil, coin, join, joint, point, noise, poison, moist

ou: couch, ouch, loud, proud, bounce, bound, ground, mound, pound, round, sound, count, house, mouse, out, pout, shout, trout, mouth

ow: bow, cow, how, now, pow, wow, crowd, flower, power, shower, tower, owl, down, town, plow, brow, chow, crowd, growl, clown, brown, crown, drown, frown

aw: claw, flaw, draw, jaw, law, paw, raw, saw, straw, thaw, hawk, crawl, scrawl, shawl, dawn, fawn, lawn, yawn

ew: dew, few, knew, mew, new, blew, brew, chew, crew, drew, flew, grew, threw, screw, stew, view

MISCELLANEOUS CHUNKS

These chunks are irregular spellings

ack: back, black, crack, flack, hack, Jack, lack, Mack, pack, rack, sack, shack, slack, snack, stack, tack, track, whack

*all: all, ball, call, fall, hall, mall, tall, wall

ank:	bank, blank, clank, crank, drank, flank, Frank, plank, prank, sank, shrank, spank, tank, thank, yank
ash:	bash, cash, clash, crash, dash, flash, gash, hash, lash, mash, rash, slash, smash, stash, trash, wash
ell:	bell, cell, dell, dwell, fell, sell, shell, smell, spell, swell, tell, well, yell
est:	best, jest, nest, pest, rest, test, vest, west
ick:	brick, chick, click, Dick, flick, lick, pick, Rick, sick, slick, stick, thick, tick, trick, wick
*ight:	bright, fight, flight, fright, knight, light, might, night, right, sight, slight, tight
*ing:	bring, cling, ding, fling, king, ping, ring, sing, sling, spring, sting, string, swing, thing, wing, wring, zing
*ink:	blink, brink, chink, clink, drink, kink, link, mink, pink, rink, shrink, sink, slink, stink, think, wink
ock:	block, cock, clock, dock, flock, lock, mock, rock, smock, shock, sock
*old:	bold, cold, fold, gold, hold, mold, old, scold, sold, told
*oo (as in *zoo*):	boo, moo, too, zoo, food, mood, goof, proof, roof, moon, noon, soon, spoon, boom, doom, broom, room, zoom, coop, loop, hoop, snoop, stoop, cool, fool, pool, drool, spool, school, loose, moose, choose, boot, root, booth, tooth, smooth, snooze
*oo (as in *good*):	good, hood, wood, stood, hoof, woof, foot, soot, book, cook, hook, look, took, brook, crook, shook, cookie
*ould:	could, should, would
*tion:	action, fraction, motion, nation, potion, station
uck:	buck, chuck, cluck, duck, luck, muck, pluck, snuck, stuck, truck, tuck, yuck
ump:	bump, clump, dump, grump, jump, lump, pump, plump, slump, stump, thump
unk:	bunk, chunk, clunk, drunk, flunk, hunk, junk, punk, plunk, slunk, sunk, spunk, stunk, trunk
y as long e:	baby, berry, daddy, muddy, puppy, penny, marry, cherry, bunny, candy, hurry, study

 *SILENT LETTERS*

wr (silent w)	write, wrap, wrong, wreck, wrench, wrist
kn (silent k)	knee, kneel, knit, knack, knock, knob, knuckle, know, known, knowledge, knight
mb (silent b)	dumb, numb, crumb, thumb, lamb, bomb, climb, comb, plumb, plumber, tomb
gn (silent g)	sign, gnome, gnu

 **CONTRACTIONS**

Words	Contraction
I am	I'm
you are	you're
we are	we're
they are	they're
he is	he's
she is	she's
he has	he's
she has	she's
I have	I've
you have	you've
we have	we've
they have	they've

 **DECODABLE "BIG WORDS"**

WORDS WITH SHORT VOWELS

address	difficult	happen
animal	disappear	helicopter
astonish	disaster	himself
athletic	discuss	hospital
attack	distance	hundred
banana	dragon	imagine
basketball	elegant	insect
breakfast	elephant	instant
bucket	entrance	kitchen
cabin	examine	magic
cactus	expect	magnificent
Canada	experiment	octopus
cement	fabric	opposite
challenge	family	ostrich
chicken	fantastic	plastic
children	finish	present
cricket	grandchildren	president
crosswalk	grandfather	principal
dentist	grandmother	pumpkin
different	grandparents	rotten

second	suggested	until
seven	suspenders	vanish
sixty	themselves	visit
skeleton	thumbtack	volunteer
Spanish	ticklish	yellow
suddenly	tunnel	

WORDS WITH SILENT E

arrive	escape	lemonade
ashamed	excuse	limestone
baseball	exercise	nickname
basement	extremely	ninety
bracelet	driveway	perfume
casserole	duplicate	recognize
celebrate	entire	reptile
clothesline	escape	satellite
complete	excitement	sidewalk
computer	favorite	skateboard
concentrate	fireplace	sometime
cornflakes	grateful	surprise
crocodile	hillside	tadpole
decide	iceberg	telephone
describe	illustrated	toothpaste
embrace	invite	

WORDS WITH VOWEL TEAMS

approach	neatly	seacoast
cleaner	oatmeal	seaweed
coastline	peaceful	straighten
complain	people	teacher
creature	rainbow	teammate
dainty	raincoat	treatment
eager	raindrops	underneath
exclaimed	rainstorm	always
explain	reason	today
feature	remain	crayons
hailstone	rowboat	yellow
increase	sailboat	follow
maintain	sailors	

WORDS WITH R-CONTROLLED VOWELS

afterward	forgotten	permanent
another	forty	person
apartment	furniture	picture
backyard	further	refrigerator
birthday	garbage	shiver
butterfly	hamburger	shortcut
carefully	important	silver
carpenter	interrupt	stubborn
catcher	kindergarten	supermarket
caterpillar	leftover	suppertime
cinder	literature	surprise
conversation	lizard	temperature
correct	manager	thirty
cover	manners	thunder
dangerous	morning	transform
department	mother	treasure
different	never	understand
discover	number	underwater
doctor	operator	watermelon
experiment	orange	wonderful
forest	partner	yesterday
forget	perform	

WORDS WITH DIPHTHONGS

oy
annoy
destroy

ou
about
around
fountain
mountain
outside
playground

thousand
without

oi
oilcan
pointed

aw
awful
strawberry

ew
newborn
newspaper

ow
downtown
eyebrows
flower
powder
powerful
tower

OPEN SYLLABLE WORDS

baby	behind	beside
become	believe	between

beyond
bicycle
department
destroy
direction
donate
female
finally
human
library

local
microscope
moment
nature
notice
polite
pretend
prevent
private
program

protect
remember
remove
respect
responsible
return
rewriting
secret
silent

MISCELLANEOUS PARTS

tion

addition
attention
collection
constellations
construction
conversation
creation
decoration
description
destruction
direction
edition
expedition
fashion
illustration
imagination
information
instruction
invention
mention
motion
nation
questions
production

relationship
section
selection

y as e

activity
anymore
anything
battery
carefully
chimney
curly
everything
family
Freddy
hardly
Henry
majesty
mommy
probably
quickly
seventy
twenty
unhappy

le

adorable
ankle
apple
bubble
circle
comfortable
crackle
giggle
handlebar
horrible
impossible
incredible
invisible
mumble
people
puddle
puzzle
rattle
remarkable
terrible
tremble
turtle
vegetable

Final Silent E Flashcards

made	hide
robe	cube
Jane	pine
note	tube

same	mane
cape	cane
ride	bite
rode	dude

Vowel Team Flashcards

rod	road
got	goat
pan	pain
net	neat

mad	maid
bat	bait
red	read
men	mean

Spelling Pattern Bingo

		FREE		

cab	den	bit	Bob	mud
hat	red	fin	mop	rug
van	ten		got	fun
zap	jet	rip	hot	gum
mad	fed	wig	jog	nut

chat	bake	price	rain	cream
fright	bring	flash	how	toy
jaw	shed		whale	choke
heat	slight	swing	mash	down
boil	claw	lawn	treat	point

Spelling Test Page

Name _____   Name _____   Name _____

1. _____   1. _____   1. _____

2. _____   2. _____   2. _____

3. _____   3. _____   3. _____

4. _____   4. _____   4. _____

5. _____   5. _____   5. _____

6. _____   6. _____   6. _____

7. _____   7. _____   7. _____

8. _____   8. _____   8. _____

Story Maps

Story Map	
Characters	
Setting	
Problem	
Solution	
Main Events	1. 2. 3.

Simplified Story Map	
Setting	
Characters	
Events	
Theme	

Story Map Response Form

Name _____

The book I read is _____

The most important character is _____

because _____

_____

This story takes place in _____

_____

_____

The problem in this story is _____

_____

The problem is solved when _____

_____

_____

A lot of interesting things happen in this story. The first thing that

happens is _____

_____

In the middle of the story, _____

_____

At the end _____

_____

_____

International Reading Association Standards for Reading Professionals

 *OVERVIEW*

Element	Description
	Standard 1: Foundational Knowledge
1.1	Demonstrate knowledge of psychological, sociological, and linguistic foundations of reading and writing processes and instruction.
1.2	Demonstrate knowledge of reading research and histories of reading.
1.3	Demonstrate knowledge of language development and reading acquisition and the variations related to cultural and linguistic diversity.
1.4	Demonstrate knowledge of the major components of reading (phonemic awareness, word identification and phonics, vocabulary and background knowledge, fluency, comprehension strategies, and motivation) and how they are integrated in fluent reading.
	Standard 2: Instructional Strategies and Curriculum Materials
2.1	Use instructional grouping options (individual, small-group, whole-class, and computer-based) as appropriate for accomplishing given purposes.
2.2	Use a wide range of instruction practices, approaches, and methods, including technology-based practices, for learners at differing stages of development and from differing linguistic and cultural backgrounds.
2.3	Use a wide range of curriculum materials in effective reading instruction for learners at different stages of reading and writing development and from different cultural and linguistic backgrounds.
	Standard 3: Assessment, Diagnosis, and Evaluation
3.1	Use a wide range of assessment tools and practices that range from individual and group standardized tests to individual and group informal classroom assessment strategies, including technology-based assessment tools.

(continued)

3.2	Place students along a developmental continuum and identify students' proficiencies and difficulties.
3.3	Use assessment information to plan, evaluate, and revise effective instruction that meets the needs of all students, including those at different developmental stages and those from different cultural and linguistic backgrounds.
3.4	Communicate results of assessments to specific individuals (students, parents, caregivers, colleagues, administrators, policymakers, policy officials, community, etc.).

Standard 4: Creating a Literate Environment

4.1	Use students' interests, reading abilities, and backgrounds as foundations for the reading and writing program.
4.2	Use a large supply of books, technology-based information, and non-print materials representing multiple levels, broad interests, and cultural and linguistic backgrounds.
4.3	Model reading and writing enthusiastically as valued lifelong activities.
4.4	Motivate learners to be lifelong readers.

Standard 5: Professional Development

5.1	Display positive dispositions related to reading and the teaching of reading.
5.2	Continue to pursue the development of professional knowledge and dispositions.

Note. Adapted from Professional Standards and Ethics Committee, International Reading Association. (2003). *Standards for reading professionals—revised 2003.* Newark, DE: International Reading Association. Reprinted with permission. *Available from www.reading.org/advocacy/standards/standards03_revised/*

Glossary

Accretion   the process of adding information to one's existing schema.

Alphabetic principle   the understanding that the sounds in spoken words are represented by alphabet letters in printed words.

At-risk students   students who, for any number of reasons, are struggling to learn to read and are at risk of reading failure.

Automaticity   the point where readers can identify printed words effortlessly, quickly, and accurately so that attention can be allocated to comprehension.

Balanced reading instruction   an instructional philosophy popular in the late 1990s that focused on combining phonics and comprehension instruction.

Basal reading programs   basic reading programs used by many schools. Basal reading programs, sometimes called core reading programs, include a teacher's manual, student reading books, and accompanying instructional materials.

Benchmark   a standard or performance level that students should be able to achieve. For example, third-grade students should be able to read a third-grade or level P book.

Big books   enlarged-format picturebooks that enable teachers to highlight print concepts for small and large groups of students.

Blending sounds   the process of blending the speech sounds represented by printed letters to pronounce words (c . . . a . . . t: cat).

Choral reading   a pair, small group, or whole class of students reading a text aloud in unison, often together with a teacher, generally as a form of instructional support.

Chunk   teachers often refer to common word endings or rimes such as *all, ock, ight*, and *ing* as chunks.

Comprehension strategies   procedures that students intentionally apply to improve reading comprehension, such as predicting, clarifying, questioning, and summarizing.

Comprehensive reading instruction framework   an expanded version of balanced reading instruction that focuses on teaching and combining *all* major aspects of reading and writing.

Consonant blend   two consonant letters side by side wherein you hear both consonant sounds: *sp*ot, *tr*ip, *blend*.

Consonant digraph   the *ch, sh, th*, and *wh* consonant pairs wherein you do not hear either consonant sound, but rather a different sound.

Constructivism   a theory of learning that proposes that students construct their own understanding of the world by interacting with it and reflecting on their experiences.

Context   the meaningful aspect of text that students combine with phonics and sentence structure to identify words.

Core curriculum   a current term for a basal reading program that provides instructional materials and strategies for teaching all essential elements of reading and writing.

Criterion-referenced tests   standardized tests that compare students to a criterion or benchmark level of performance. This test will report what percentage of students from a class or school has mastered specific instructional concepts. The emphasis is on informing instruction.

Critical comprehension   the highest level of comprehension where, like a film or literary critic, students go beyond understanding a text to evaluating the quality of a text.

Cross-checking   the process of confirming word identification accuracy by making sure that printed words look right (phonics), sound right (sentence structure), and make sense (context).

Cueing systems   sources of information, including letter–sound relationships (phonics), meaning (context), and sentence structure (syntax), that readers use to identify printed words.

Decodable texts   texts with a very high percentage of decodable words (*Dan can fan Nan in the tan van*) that provide focused opportunities for students to practice reading spelling patterns.

Decoding   using letter–sound, contextual, and syntactic information to identify printed words.

Diagnosing   the process of looking very closely at various aspects of a student's reading, such as phonemic awareness, sight word recognition level, oral reading accuracy, and reading comprehension to identify specific reading strengths and needs.

Diphthong   the *oy, oi, ou, ow, ew*, and *aw* vowel pairs wherein you do not hear either vowel sound, but rather a different vowel sound, sometimes called a vowel variant.

Direct instruction   teaching reading skills to students very explicitly, clearly, and sequentially, as opposed to letting students infer or guess.

Divergent responses   when we expect students to have differing responses to questions or problems, we expect divergent responses. The opposite is convergent responses, for which there is one right answer.

Evaluative questions   did the author convince you that Sally was a trustworthy person? How did the author convince you? Was this a good story? Evaluative questions ask students to evaluate the effectiveness of a piece of writing.

Explicit and systematic   instruction that features clear, direct teacher explanation and modeling of a cumulative sequence of instructional concepts.

Expository text   information text, often about science and social studies topics, as opposed to narrative text (stories).

Expressivist tradition   in writing instruction, this tradition emphasizes having students find their personal voices and develop their identities through writing.

Final silent *e*   the common spelling pattern wherein the silent *e* on the end of a word often makes the preceding vowel "say" its long vowel sound, as in *same, tide, bone,* and *tune*.

Fluency   reading with sufficient speed, accuracy, and expression so that readers can devote most of their attention to comprehension of the text.

Frustration level   the reading difficulty level at which a student is unable to identify more than 90% of printed words in a text or understand more than 50% of a text's meaning and thus is likely to become frustrated.

Gradual release of responsibility   a teaching model wherein a teacher (1) models or demonstrates a reading skill to students, (2) performs the skill with students together, and (3) invites students to perform the skill for the teacher. A synonymous term is "reading to, with, and by students."

Graphophonic cues   a technical term for letter (graph)–sound (phonic) information that readers use to identify printed words.

Guided reading   a reading group instruction strategy by which the teacher introduces an instructional-level text and then listens to and teaches group members individually as they each read at their own pace.

Independent reading   students reading texts at their instructional or independent level, often as the teacher instructs other students in small groups.

Independent reading level   when a student can read a text with 95% accuracy or better, the text is at the student's independent reading level.

Individually administered test   any test administered to students one on one, as opposed to group-administered tests.

Inferencing   the process of drawing conclusions as we read, given the evidence in the text and what we know about the world. For example, if the text says that the main character sees smoke in the distance, we may infer that there is a fire.

Inferential comprehension   the level of comprehension where readers must draw on their background knowledge to fill in gaps and make sense of text (reading between the lines).

Inferential questions   why was Sally's jacket torn and dirty? Inferential questions require the reader to draw conclusions based on evidence in the text and background knowledge. Maybe Sally's jacket was torn and dirty because the text says that she had been playing in an abandoned building, and usually abandoned buildings are dirty places.

Inflected   when a word has an ending attached to it, such as it*s*, wash*es*, and brush*ed*.

informal reading inventory (IRI)   a reading test that uses a series of graded word lists and passages to identify a student's reading level and reading strengths and needs.

Instructional reading level   when a student can read a text with 90% to 94% accuracy, the text is at the student's instructional reading level.

Instructional support   instructional techniques such as providing students with vocabulary and background knowledge, prereading texts aloud to or in unison with students, and helping students to identify printed words. Teachers should vary the amount of instructional support they provide based on students' needs.

Interactive read-aloud   a very effective way to teach comprehension when the teacher engages the students by previewing the book, asking for predictions and connections to prior knowledge, stopping at purposeful moments to emphasize specific ideas in the text, asking guiding questions, and using oral or written responses to bring closure to the selection.

Interactive writing   similar to language experience approach, except the teacher shares the pen with the students. The teacher invites students to come to the chart paper and write words or parts of words that the teacher has chosen.

Interventions   additional reading instruction programs provided to students who do not make adequate progress with the classroom core reading program.

Invented spelling   beginning writers spelling words the way they sound (*wen* for *when*; *wuns* for *once*), rather than conventionally. Invented spelling is a transitional stage on the road to conventional spelling.

Language-experience approach (LEA)   a reading instruction strategy for beginning readers through which students express their ideas about a topic to their teacher, who writes the students' words on chart paper and then teaches the students to read their own words.

Learning disability   a learning problem that hinders a student from learning to read at an expected level.

Leveled books   short picture books that increase in gradual levels of difficulty according to characteristics such as word and sentence length, familiarity of words and concepts, print and illustration placement, and font size.

Listening comprehension   the ability to comprehend text that is read aloud, rather than provided in print form. Listening comprehension is often seen as a measure of a student's background knowledge and vocabulary.

Literacy learning   the learning of both reading and writing.

Literal comprehension   the basic level of comprehension where readers recognize information that is clearly provided in the text (it's there in black and white).

Literal questions   what color jacket was Sally wearing in the story? Literal questions can be answered simply by reading and finding the answer right there in the text: "Sally's red jacket was torn and dirty."

Literature circle   a teaching model wherein a small group of students reads a text on their own and then gets together to discuss their responses, connections, questions, and favorite parts.

Low SES students   low socioeconomic students or students from low-income families.

Manipulating sounds   students changing speech sounds to create words (*pan-pat-sat-mat-man-fan*).

Manipulatives   physical letters such as letter flashcards and plastic magnetic letters that students can handle and manipulate during instructional activities.

Mapping   a common teaching strategy for building students' background knowledge by writing a topic (such as mammals) in the middle of a chalkboard and then writing students' brainstormed examples (bears, cows, dogs, mice, horses) around the topic word.

Masking activity   a word identification teaching strategy: a teacher covers parts of words using index cards with cutout slots to help students decode words part by part.

Mastery teaching   a direct instruction teaching approach in which students must completely master a concept, such as CVC words, before they may move on to learn a subsequent concept, such as consonant blends.

Meaning-change miscues   reading errors that change the meaning of a sentence or passage. For example, "Bob slept in his *horse*," instead of the intended word *house*.

Meaning-preserving miscues   reading errors that do not change the meaning of a sentence or passage. For example, "Bob slept in his *home*," instead of the intended word *house*.

Meaningful texts   texts that are written to convey meaning, as opposed to decodable texts that are written to provide decoding practice.

Metacognition   the higher-order thinking that we do when we actively monitor and control our thought processes while learning. In short, we think about our thinking.

Mini-lesson   a 5- to 10-minute reading or writing lesson that highlights a single instructional concept.

Miscues   a more current term for oral reading errors, including students' substituting, inserting, and omitting words while reading.

Narrative text   stories, as opposed to information texts.

Nonsense words   made-up printed words such as *shap* and *bime* that are often used in reading tests to assess a student's ability to decode.

Norm-referenced tests   standardized tests used to compare groups of students to other groups of students, for example, comparing schools to other schools within a district or districts to other districts within a state. The emphasis is on comparing groups.

Onset   the consonant(s) at the beginning of a syllable or one-syllable word (*c*/an, *st*/op, *ch*/ip, *str*/eet).

Oral language   teachers often use this term to refer to a student's vocabulary size and ability to express oneself with words. Oral language is one of the foundations of printed language.

Outcome measuring   assessment that shows how well students are doing at the end of a school year.

Phoneme   a speech sound. The word /sat/ has three phonemes: /s/ /a/ /t/. The word /chop/ has four letters, but only three phonemes: /ch/ /o/ /p/.

Phonemic awareness   students' understanding that spoken words are composed of individual speech sound, (/p/ /a/ /n/), that can be segmented, blended, and manipulated to form other spoken words. Phonemic awareness is the conceptual foundation for readers blending the sounds of printed letters to read printed words.

Predictable text   beginning reading texts with very explicit repetitious sentence patterns that support students' use of sentence structure and context to identify printed words. Examples of predictable texts include "Brown bear, brown bear what do you see? I see a red bird looking at me" and "Would you, could you in a box, would you could you with a fox."

Pre-primer reading books   reading instruction books at the beginning first-grade level.

Primer reading books   reading instruction books at the middle of first-grade level.

Print conventions   characteristics of print, including left to right, top to bottom, and punctuation.

Progress monitoring   assessments that are given frequently throughout a school year to show how quickly students are progressing in reading.

Pull-out programs   Title 1, special education, speech and language, and other intervention or resource programs that are provided by a resource teacher in a resource room outside the student's own classroom. Pull-out programs are sometimes criticized for being disconnected from students' classroom reading instruction.

R-controlled vowels   a spelling pattern in which the letter *r* follows a vowel and changes its pronunciation, as in *car*, *her*, *sir*, *for*, and *fur*.

Reader-response theory   a theory of reading developed by Louise Rosenblatt. It suggests that the meaning of the text resides not in the text alone, but rather is a product of the interaction among the reader, the reader's experiences, and the text.

Reading Recovery   a popular reading intervention program designed for struggling first-grade students to help them to catch up to grade level. Reading Recovery features daily one-on-one tutoring in word study, meaningful reading, writing, and running record assessments.

Reciprocal teaching   a lesson format for teaching four comprehension strategies; the teacher models *predicting* passage content, *clarifying* unfamiliar words, asking *questions* about, and *summarizing* a passage, followed by students applying the same four strategies.

Reliability   the *consistency* characteristic of tests. You can be sure that data from reliable tests are accurate and consistent.

Repeated reading   an instructional strategy for building students' oral reading fluency by having them read and reread a passage multiple times, often to a stopwatch, and charting the amount of improvement each time.

Repetition   when a student reading aloud stops and rereads one or more words. Some informal reading inventories count repetitions as errors. Others do not.

Resource teachers   Title 1, special education, speech and language, and other teachers who provide special services to struggling students.

Retelling   a student's oral summarizing of a passage. Often used as a measure of reading comprehension.

Rime   the vowel and consonant (s) that form the ending part of a syllable or one-syllable word (c/*an*, t/*ime*, b/*oat*, c/*ar*). Good readers learn to mix and match printed onsets and rimes to identify words.

Round-robin reading   the traditional reading group practice of having students taking turns reading aloud one at a time in order.

Running record   a quick reading assessment: a teacher listens to a student read a passage aloud, notes the number of words missed; and calculates an oral reading accuracy percentage for the purpose of placing students in instructional level texts. Teachers can also use running records to analyze patterns in students' oral reading errors to determine reading strengths and needs.

Say something   a structure for increasing the amount of discussion that occurs during a read aloud. Students choose a partner first; then, when the teacher stops the reading, the partners face each other and "say something" about the text.

Scaffolded writing   a child decides what sentence she wants to write and then the teacher draws lines to represent each word in the sentence. The child writes each word to the best of her ability on the lines provided.

Schema theory   this theory purports that all humans have rules or scripts for organizing their understanding of the world. New information is understood best when children can connect it to their existing schema for an idea.

Scope and sequence   a *list* of reading skills to be taught in a reading program and the *sequence* in which they are to be taught.

Screening   an assessment usually given early in the school year to identify students who are likely to have problems learning to read so that instructional interventions may be provided.

Segmenting sounds   the ability or process of hearing a spoken word and breaking it into its individual sounds (cat: c . . . a . . . t). Segmenting is the opposite of blending.

Self-correction   when a reader misreads a word, recognizes the error, and goes back and corrects the error without teacher direction. Generally viewed as a positive indication that students are monitoring the meaningfulness of their reading.

Self-correction ratio   the number of self-corrections a student makes compared to the total number of oral reading errors.

Shared reading   a reading instruction strategy for early readers in which a teacher introduces a text to students, often through a picture walk; reads the text aloud to the students; reads the text aloud in unison with the students; has the students read the text aloud to the teacher; and then provides follow-up reading skills instruction.

Sight vocabulary   often refers to two kinds of words: (1) very common words (*a, the, and*) that readers quickly memorize from seeing them so often and (2) irregularly spelled words (*of, does, one*) that must be memorized because they can't be sounded out.

Spelling patterns   common printed letter combinations such as *consonant blends* and *final silent e* that students learn to recognize and use to identify printed words.

SSR   sustained silent reading. A popular term for students reading silently on their own, often while the teacher provides instruction to other students in small groups.

Story grammar   elements such as setting, characters, events, and theme that are common to almost all stories.

Structural analysis   using word parts such as prefixes, suffixes, contractions, and compound words to identify words.

Subtext strategy   a way to teach inferencing with students that involves them imagining what characters might be saying in the illustrations of books and creating speech or thought bubbles containing their words.

Syntax   the structure of sentences (subject–predicate, adjective–noun, etc.) that readers combine with letter–sounds (phonics) and meaning (context) to identify words.

Teacher modeling   teachers demonstrating to students how to apply a reading skill or strategy.

Validity   the *appropriateness* characteristic of tests. The DIBELS Initial Sound Fluency subtest is valid for measuring aspects of phonemic awareness, but it is not a valid test for measuring reading comprehension. Teachers should only use tests to measure aspects of reading that they were designed to measure.

Vowel team   a spelling pattern, sometimes referred to as a vowel digraph, in which two vowels appear side by side and the first vowels "says" its long sound and the second vowel is silent, as in p*ai*d, s*ay*, st*ea*m, f*ee*d, b*oa*t, and m*ow*. Vowel teams are not to be confused with vowel diphthongs in which two vowels make a different sound, as in p*oi*nt and ch*ew*.

Webbing   see *mapping*.

Word bank   a collection of word cards that a student has learned, often stored in a zipper-locking bag or recipe box. Word banks are used for reviewing words students have learned and also during writing as a spelling reference.

Word families   words that share a common spelling pattern, such as the *an* family: *an, ban, can, Dan, fan, man, pan, ran, tan,* and *van*. Word families provide instructional examples for teaching spelling patterns.

Word identification   another instructional term for using letter–sound, contextual, and syntactic information to identify printed words. Word identification is more comprehensive than phonics, which focuses only on using letter sounds to help to pronounce words.

Word structure   see *structural analysis*.

Word study group   a small group of students pulled together for extra instructional sessions in a word study concept.

Zone of proximal development   term coined by Vygotsky for the difference between what a child can do with help and what he or she can do without guidance.

Index